second edition

PUBLIC PERSONNEL MANAGEMENT
Contexts and Strategies

DONALD E. KLINGNER
Florida International University

JOHN NALBANDIAN
University of Kansas

Prentice-Hall, Inc. Englewood Cliffs, New Jersey 07632

Library of Congress Cataloging in Publication Data

Klingner, Donald E.
  Public personnel management.

  Includes index.
    1. Civil service—Personnel management. 2. Personnel management. 3. Public administration. I. Nalbandian,
John. II. Title.
JF1601.K56 1985   350.1   84–8287
ISBN 0–13–737990–0

Editorial/production supervision and
  interior design: Marjorie Borden
Manufacturing buyer: Ron Chapman/Barbara Kelly Kittle

Printed in the United States of America

10 9 8 7 6 5 4 3 2 1

ISBN 0-13-737990-0   01

Prentice-Hall International, Inc., *London*
Prentice-Hall of Australia Pty. Limited, *Sydney*
Editora Prentice-Hall do Brasil, Ltda., *Rio de Janeiro*
Prentice-Hall Canada Inc., *Toronto*
Prentice-Hall of India Private Limited, *New Delhi*
Prentice-Hall of Japan, Inc., *Tokyo*
Prentice-Hall of Southeast Asia Pte. Ltd., *Singapore*
Whitehall Books Limited, *Wellington, New Zealand*

Contents

CHAPTER 6   RECRUITMENT   83

CHAPTER 7   SELECTION AND PROMOTION   97

Part III   Allocation of Human Resources

CHAPTER 8   HUMAN RESOURCE PLANNING   125

Part VI Control and Adaptation of the Personnel Function

Introduction*

Public personnel management, as a field of public administration, has undergone considerable development in the last fifty years. Personnel professionals now have available a wide range of techniques they can apply toward the efficient acquisition, allocation, and development of human resources.

The elaboration of these techniques signifies the acceptance of a rational, problem-solving approach to dealing with an organization's human resources. However, the advance of rational personnel management has occurred at a cost: By emphasizing the "one best way" to complete a task, personnel professionals have ignored the diversity that actually exists. Specifically, they have tended to overlook the impact that different organizational objectives and environments have on the effectiveness of personnel management techniques. As a result, many consequences of personnel techniques which affect employees, the organization, or society are defined as falling outside the study and practice of personnel management.

Ideas and concepts drawn from the literature of organization theory and administrative behavior furnish the opportunity to develop a dynamic

*The approach to public personnel management described in this introduction is drawn from several sources: Donald E. Klingner and John Nalbandian, "Personnel Management by Whose Objectives?," *Public Administration Review,* Vol. 38, No. 4 (July–August 1978), 366–72; Donald E. Klingner, *Public Personnel Management: Contexts and Strategies* (Englewood Cliffs, N.J.: Prentice-Hall, 1980); and Donald E. Klingner and John Nalbandian, "Public Personnel Management: A Values Perspective," a paper presented at the National Conference of the American Society for Public Administration, Denver, Colo., 1984.

and realistic view of personnel management. We approach the problem of developing a new theoretical framework in five segments:

1. What is the current approach to personnel management?
2. What are its consequences?
3. What other approach is available?
4. What benefits for academicians, personnel professionals, and employees are associated with the new approach?
5. How does this approach relate to the outline of this book?

The Present Approach to Public Personnel Management

During the past half century, the study of public administration has shifted focus from a discussion of management principles within an organization to analyses of relationships among environmental pressures, organizational structure and technology, and managerial processes. An awareness of the impact of external events on policy outcomes has complicated but enriched our understanding of the tasks and characteristics of "good management." Management is now viewed not just as the art of planning, organizing, staffing, directing, and controlling, but also as the rational process of matching the organization's diverse social and technical systems with environmental resources and constraints, in order to achieve objectives.

However, personnel management has lagged behind in this developmental process. The focus of inquiry is still directed toward discovering the "one best way" to perform a function rather than on examining contexts, functions, techniques, and consequences within a contingency-based arrangement. Several factors contribute to the lag in development of public personnel theory.

First, much of public personnel administration is dictated by laws, rules, and regulations historically aimed at eliminating political discretion in the management of human resources. Political reformers assumed that the removal of patronage from public employment would both increase governmental efficiency and protect the rights of individual employees and applicants.

Second, professors of public administration have often viewed public personnel management as a barren area for theoretical study. Historically, it seems that academicians have accepted the view that personnel management consists of the routine application of a practitioner's "bag of tricks." While organizational researchers deal extensively with questions of resource allocation and maintenance, they seem to downgrade the role of personnel professionals in designing or evaluating systems for the allocation and development of human resources. The academicians' orientation may be a holdover from the "administrative techniques" theory prevalent 40 to 60 years ago, in which a distinction was drawn between policy-level decisions and routine administration. In this school of thought, when attention is focused on personnel administration, it tends to be toward the development of routinized solutions to personnel management problems.

This orientation on the part of the academician relates to the aforementioned statutory and procedural nature of public personnel management. The development of theory in any field requires attention to a number of fluctuating variables. Simply stated, the theorist attempts to relate the fluctuation in one set of variables to effects in another set. Historically, the normative emphasis in public personnel administration has been to reduce these kinds of variation in pursuit of a merit system. Thus the conditions allowing for the development of theoretical thought in the public personnel field largely have been absent.

The field's legal heritage and the tendency of academicians to view public personnel management as a collection of low-level techniques have created a dilemma for personnel managers. This dilemma is the third factor impeding development of public personnel theory; for despite the shift of administrative theory away from absolutist, "one best way" thinking, personnel managers are still implicitly encouraged to believe that this type of solution is both possible and desirable. This discourages them from openly discussing, at least with academicians, the role conflicts and policy questions that arise from their professional responsibilities. It therefore remains plausible for academicians to view the field as a collective of administrative techniques practiced by those who are too timid—or lack the intelligence—to do more interesting work.

Consequences of the Present Approach

The factors contributing to the lagging development of public personnel theory have several practical consequences for academicians, personnel managers, and employees. First, current texts commonly present a sequential discussion of functions pioneered by Glenn Stahl in the 1930s and drawn from Luther Gulick's acronym (*POSDCORB*) for the responsibilities of management. This discussion commonly includes the history of civil service law and the structure of personnel systems, human resource planning, recruitment, testing, selection and promotion, performance evaluation, training, pay and benefits, collective bargaining, and disciplinary action and grievances. There is little logic to this sequence, aside from the chronological impact of these techniques on individual employees. There is no answer to the academician's fundamental question, "How do the pieces fit together?"

Second, personnel managers are implicitly encouraged to ignore the value dimension of their decisions and to support the illusion that personnel management is the value-free application of management-oriented techniques. Yet this implied assumption stands in remarkable contrast to the highly political atmosphere within which personnel managers actually operate. Rather than there being one best way of personnel management, there exists a variety of personnel policy choices which have different outcomes for employees and client groups competing for a scarce resource—public jobs.

For example, an agency may be forced to reduce personnel expenditures because of budget cuts brought about by a revenue shortfall or a change in legislative priorities. Should these personnel reductions occur by not filling positions as they become vacant, by laying off employees, or by renegotiating collective bargaining agreements so as to cut pay and benefits? What are the implications of these different options with respect to affirmative action compliance, organizational productivity, or employee rights? Existing methods of teaching personnel management encourage personnel managers to view these conflicts as outside the purview of "traditional" personnel management, and more properly the concern of elected officials, affirmative action compliance officers, or labor negotiators.

As this example illustrates, personnel management involves value-laden alternatives that will have dramatic impact on the way human resources are acquired and developed. Yet administrators are given few guidelines for testing the appropriateness of a given solution under organizational conditions. Current personnel management theory provides no adequate answer to the personnel manager's question, "What action should I take now?"

Third, the implicit focus of personnel management theory on techniques gives scant attention to their cumulative impact on employees. Despite extensive contributions to the knowledge of administrative behavior from research in the applied behavioral sciences, there has been little transfer of this knowledge to personnel management practice. A personnel manager's disregard for the cumulative impact of personnel management decisions on employee aspirations and attitudes can have these organizational consequences:

> *Job design:* Jobs designed to meet present organizational needs may not provide for the development of employee career aspirations. The message often conveyed is, *"We* want you now; *you* take care of your future."
>
> *Promotion:* A cynical attitude toward authority relationships within the organization can develop when criteria for promotion are not well developed, when they are inequitably applied, or when promotional opportunities are not widely advertised.
>
> *Productivity:* Employees will be unable or unwilling to change behavior in accordance with feedback from supervisors if they do not know what is expected of them, are not given feedback concerning their performance, are not trained to do the job properly, or are not rewarded for doing it well.

Approaches to personnel management that do not deal with the cumulative impact of personnel practices on employees do not equip supervisors or personnel managers to adequately answer the employee's question, "What can I hope for in this job?"

What Other Approach is Available?

The alternative is to view public personnel management not as a collection of techniques, but as the interaction of four dominant values— administrative efficiency, individual rights, political responsiveness, and social equity—that have shaped the development and application of these techniques. The essential points of this model, which are the basis for the first four chapters of the book, are noted briefly below.

This approach builds upon the models developed by other scholars who have presented the field in terms of the historical progression of events which symbolize the effect of a succession of alternative objectives or values. For example, the Pendleton Act (1883), which created the federal civil service, arose out of a reaction against patronage (political responsiveness) and a desire for greater administrative efficiency and protection of individual rights of employees and applicants. The civil rights movement of the 1960s generated increased use of personnel systems to achieve social equity. The increased strength of public sector unions in the 1970s, coupled with federal court cases supporting the constitutional protections of public employees, emphasized the importance of individual rights and the role of unions in representing employees.

Public personnel management is a turbulent field that comprises the interaction of shifting values and core functions. The core functions are those which public agencies must perform in order to permit public employees to work competently under satisfying working conditions: to *procure* employees, to *allocate* work and rewards among them, to *develop* their skills, and to develop and maintain (*sanction*) the terms of the employment relationship. Therefore, it is important that students not only understand the core functions, but that they also appreciate how conflicts among shifting values can influence the appropriateness and desirability of alternative techniques in a particular situation.

For example, budget cuts may require personnel managers to choose from alternative techniques for reducing personnel costs: a hiring freeze or slowdown, a reduction-in-force, contracting out, the elimination of part-time and temporary positions, or renegotiation of collective bargaining agreements to reduce employees' pay or benefits. Traditionally, personnel managers have had little guidance in choosing from these alternatives other than the maxim, "It depends on the situation." A values perspective enables them to assess the impact of alternative solutions on conflicting values, and to select the solution that best fits. Specifically, the severity of the required reduction (the extent to which *political responsiveness* is the dominant value) will determine whether a drastic solution such as a reduction-in-force is the only answer, or whether other alternatives are appropriate. If concern for *individual rights* is strong, and a reduction-in-force is required, layoffs will likely be on the basis of seniority. If *social equity* is important, RIF provisions will be modified to avoid proportionately greater layoffs among underutilized groups (minorities or women). Strong concern for both these values will prompt efforts to renegotiate pay and benefits downward, so as to avoid layoffs that would hurt either value.

If an agency is adding employees, the value dimension of public personnel management will be especially evident in the conflict among competing definitions of merit. Proponents of *political responsiveness* will want the positions to be filled politically, outside of the civil service system. Managers will want greatest emphasis placed on setting high standards, so that applicants selected for the positions will be able to perform them with a minimum of orientation and training. Affirmative action advocates will prefer recruitment methods or selection criteria that allow greatest opportunity for minorities and women to be selected. Current employees will want recruitment for the new positions to be restricted to the present workforce. The relative priority of these values, in the context of the situation, will determine how the positions are classified (exempt or civil service), what qualifications are established for them, and how they are filled.

Benefits of the Proposed Approach

By viewing public personnel management as a turbulent field, and by examining specific situations from the perspective of conflict among four values, this approach enables us to provide answers to the three previously proposed questions:

1. Academician: "How do the pieces fit together?"
2. Practitioner: "What action should I take now?"
3. Employee: "What can I hope for in this job?"

The approach developed in this book enables academicians to view the choice among personnel techniques from a theoretical perspective. That is, by viewing public personnel management as a turbulent field, and by examining specific situations from the normative perspective of conflict among four values, they can predict or explain the effectiveness of particular solutions in particular contexts. By defining the field so as to emphasize the interplay of conflicting values on a body of techniques, they can generate the theory and research necessary to the development of public personnel management as a field of study.

By allowing and encouraging practitioners to focus on the alternative outcomes of policy choices involving personnel techniques, this approach will make it easier for them to assess the appropriateness of a given technique under organizational conditions. Rather than supporting the illusion that personnel management is the value-free application of management-oriented techniques, this approach will encourage personnel managers to examine the range of public policy choices that have different outcomes for the employee and client groups competing for scarce organizational resources. In addition, as it encourages a wider-ranging scope for the field of public personnel administration, this approach will begin to provide a more realistic picture of professionalism in human resources management. Traditionally, the term "personnel professional" has meant the isolation of personnel administration from politics—yet this definition is outdated. The real world experience of human resource management is deeply intertwined with politics. Professionalism in human resource management will gain contemporary meaning as it begins to more systematically explore the interplay between values and techniques.

By focusing on values such as individual rights and social equity, this approach makes it easier for individual employees to identify those personnel functions that are most directly related to their own employment opportunities. By focusing on the conflicts among these values, this approach allows employees to use the outcome of these conflicts as a means of assessing their relative power within the organization. Because employees, acting individually, clearly carry the least weight in the decision-making process, it implicitly establishes collective bargaining as the mechanism by which the *sanctions* process can result in the establishment of organizational procedures that favor employee interests.

A value-analytical framework which views personnel management decisions not as the implementation of general principles such as merit or equity, but as choices whose efficacy is determined by their responsiveness to four conflicting values, provides a suitable frame of reference for academicians, practitioners, and employees.

How Does This Approach Relate to This Book?

This book is a discussion of personnel concepts and techniques, organized in terms of the four conflicting values (social equity, political responsiveness, administrative efficiency, and employee rights). Chapters 1 to 4 are an introduction to the field, its history, the dominant values that have shaped it, and the relationship between those values and personnel techniques. Chapters 5 to 20 discuss personnel techniques, clustering them according to the function that most strongly influences the activity (see table).

Organization of This Book

VALUE	FUNCTION	ACTIVITIES	CHAPTER
Social equity	Procurement	Affirmative action	5
		Recruitment	6
		Selection and promotion	7
Political responsiveness	Allocation	Human resource planning	8
		Job analysis and classification	9
		Job evaluation and pay	10
Administrative efficiency	Development	Productivity	11
		Performance appraisal	12
		Training and development	13
		Motivation	14
		Safety	15
Individual rights	Sanctions	Labor-management relations	16
		Discipline and grievances	17
		Employee rights	18

The last two chapters focus on coordination of these values through the human resource management evaluation process, and on the outcome of value conflicts in terms of the future of the field.

Each chapter consists of an introduction, a set of learning objectives, and presentation of concepts and techniques. Examples are provided that underscore the relationship between values and techniques, and the application of these relationships to specific situations involving various levels of government (federal, state and local). To facilitate learning, each chapter also includes suggested references, key terms, discussion questions, and an exercise or case study designed for classroom use.

It is our hope that academicians, practitioners, and employees will find this book useful in clarifying and expanding their view of the field. If so, it will in some measure repay our debt to those who have enhanced our own understanding.

Acknowledgments

Many people have contributed to the development of this book. The initial impetus to write the first edition came from H. George Frederickson, then the primary author's colleague at Indiana University and now president of Eastern Washington University.

The book's most distinctive feature is its application of organization theory to public personnel management. Many of our colleagues have aided in the development of this approach. Foremost among them is Gilbert B. Siegel, who served as our mentor at the University of Southern California over a decade ago.

A number of other authors have emphasized the importance of value conflicts in public personnel management, and so led us to the development of the model used in this book. Chief among them are Lawrence C. Howard, Charles Levine, Lloyd Nigro, David H. Rosenbloom, and Jay Shafritz.

We would like to thank the many colleagues who reviewed the first edition of this book and earlier drafts of the second. Among them are Walter Broadnax, Richard W. Gable, Barbara Romzek, David H. Rosenbloom, Joyce Ross, and Gilbert B. Siegel.

Without the assistance of Stan Wakefield, Assistant Vice President and Executive Editor at Prentice-Hall, none of this would have been possible. We would also like to thank his assistant Audrey Marshall and our production editor Marjorie Borden for their contributions to the quality of the finished product.

We would like to express our appreciation to those organizations whose use of this book for training or member service has contributed to its success. They include the International Personnel Management Association, the International City Management Association, and the Open Learning Fire Science Program.

Naturally, all errors of omission and commission are the responsibility of the authors. We would appreciate any comments you have concerning this book.

Lastly, we wish to thank the many students who used previous versions of this book in graduate and undergraduate courses. Their need for a more meaningful approach to public personnel management, and their continued skepticism of our earlier attempts to unify theory and practice, has been the toughest test of the materials presented here. It is to them, and to their need to close the gap between myth and reality in public personnel management, that this book is dedicated.

Donald E. Klingner
John Nalbandian

I want to acknowledge my immense debt to Don Klingner, who so graciously and generously invited me to join him in rewriting an already successful text. While this kind of offer is uncommon in the academic enterprise, it is quite in keeping with Don's character and the spirit of our collaboration over the years. Our professional relationship works well, cemented by personal friendship.

Together we owe an intellectual debt to our predecessors, teachers, and contemporary critics. Individually, Don sustains our collaboration with his patience, his willingness to listen, and his unbelievable drive and capacity for work.

John Nalbandian

1

The Practice of Public Personnel Management

Audrey Van Ness, a program analyst in an area office of the U.S. Department of Housing and Urban Development (HUD), began working for the federal government ten years ago as a clerk typist. Prior to that she spent 18 years as a housewife. Audrey now serves as a liaison between the headquarters staff in Washington, the regional office of HUD in Kansas City, and her own area office. Her coordinating duties bring her in contact with auditing and management information functions within the area office.

Pat Schafer works for a state department of Social and Rehabilitation Services (SRS) in the Midwest. Her job is classified as a Social Service Administrator III; her working title is Administrator of the Preventive Health and Specialized Services Section in the Division of Medical Programs. Basically, Pat is in charge of part of the health insurance program for low-income people—Medicaid—in her state. In essence she negotiates rates and methods of reimbursement, and coverage of medical services. In addition, she oversees a contract with a private-sector computer service outfit that assists in SRS' processing of some 300,000 Medicaid claims per month in this state.

Steve Coon has worked as a police officer in a city of 50,000 residents for 11 years. He is one of 80 officers and 20 civilians in a police department that employs about 20 percent of this city's employees. Steve entered law enforcement without any prior experience at a time when civil disturbances shook this city, which then doubled its force from 20 to 40 officers. Turnover within the department is minimal, and Steve, now 40, expects to remain at his current rank until retirement. He is a member of the Fraternal Order of Police, and his local association bargains with the city over wages and working conditions under a meet-and-confer labor law.

Beth Cigler teaches in a rural school just outside of a medium-sized city. She and a colleague teach 31 children in two classes that combine grades 1, 2, and 3 and 4, 5, and 6. For 13 years Beth has taught at this school, which has gradually declined in student enrollment and staff, yet with parent support and insistence has managed to keep its doors open. Prior to her present experience, she taught fourth grade in another Midwestern state. She is a member of the local branch of the National Education Association, a professional association of school teachers, which hesitates in some quarters to call itself a union.

These are four of the 15 million people who work for federal, state, and local governments, and school districts in this country.

By the end of this chapter you will be able to:

1. Describe the size and range of activities that federal, state, and local governments provide
2. Identify the amount of money governments spend on salaries and fringe benefits
3. List the kinds of activities comprising the field of public personnel administration
4. Describe a merit system and its underlying principles
5. Describe the challenges a career civil service system poses for the principle of citizen responsiveness in a democratic society

THE SIZE AND SCOPE OF PUBLIC EMPLOYMENT

While in the public's view federal employees often symbolize government bureaucracy, in reality they constitute only about 17 percent of all public employees. The number of people state and local governments employ has generally risen over the past decade with some 80,000 units of local government accounting for nearly two-thirds of all civilian public employment.[1] Moreover, over half of these local government employees are school teachers, school administrators, or other school system personnel.

Figure 1–1 reveals these trends in public employment.

Figure 1–2 shows the distribution of public employment in federal, state, and local government.

With some 100 million people working in the United States, public employees account for nearly one out of every six wage earners.

What kind of work do these people perform? Table 1–1 shows the public service functions federal employees perform compared to state and local employees.

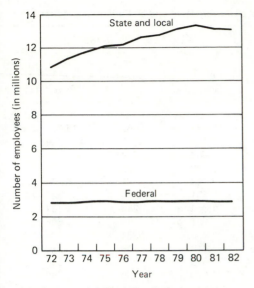

FIGURE 1–1. Public Employment: October 1972–October 1982 (Source: U.S. Bureau of the Census, *Public Employment in 1982.* Series GE82-No. 1. U.S. Government Printing Office, Washington, D.C., 1983.)

Table 1–1 shows that while the overwhelming number of public employees work at the state and local level, those employed in national defense and international relations, the postal service, and in space research and technology work exclusively at the federal level. Most state and local employees, in contrast, and few federal workers are employed in the fields of education, highways, health and hospitals, and police work. This kind of

FIGURE 1–2. Number of Public Employees by Level of Government in October 1982 (Source: U.S. Bureau of the Census. *Public Employment in 1982.* Series GE82-No. 1. U.S. Government Printing Office, Washington, D.C., 1983.)

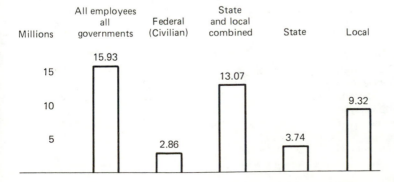

TABLE 1–1.   Public Employment by Level of Government and by Function: October 1982

Function	OCTOBER 1982		
	All Governments	Federal Government (Civilian)*	State and Local Governments
Employees (thousands)			
Full-time and part-time	15,933	2,862	13,071
National Defense and International Relations	1,026	1,026	—
Postal Service	664	664	—
Space Research and Technology	23	23	—
Education	6,749	17	6,733
Highways	531	4	527
Health and Hospitals	1,664	256	1,407
Police Protection	721	56	665
Natural Resources	458	264	195
Financial Administration	418	106	312
General Control	610	60	550
All Other	3,070	388	2,682

*Comprises all Federal civilian employees, including those outside the United States.

Source: Bureau of the Census. *Public Employment in 1982.* Series GE82-No. 1. U.S. Government Printing Office, Washington, D.C., 1983.

division of labor is hardly surprising in a political system like ours, where the Constitution, legislation, judicial opinion, and public sentiment reflect a long-standing but occasionally fluctuating predisposition to keep governmental control as close to the taxpayer as feasible.

TABLE 1–2.   Employment of State and Local Government by Function: October 1982

Function	ALL EMPLOYEES (FULL-TIME AND PART-TIME IN THOUSANDS)		
	Total	State Government	Local Government
All Functions	13,071	3,747	9,324
Education Services:			
Higher Education	1,881	1,496	385
Instructional Employees	650	455	195
Other Employees	1,231	1,041	190
Elementary and Secondary Schools	4,756	23	4,732
Instructional Employees	3,090	15	3,076
Other Employees	1,665	9	1,656
Local Libraries	95	—	95
Other Education	96	96	—

TABLE 1-2. *(Continued)*

Function	Total	ALL EMPLOYEES (FULL-TIME AND PART-TIME IN THOUSANDS)	
		State Government	Local Government
Social Services and Income Maintenance:			
Public Welfare	393	174	219
Hospitals	1,157	570	587
Health	250	117	133
Social Insurance Administration	103	103	—
Transportation:			
Highways	527	244	283
Air Transportation	23	2	21
Water Transportation	14	6	8
Public Safety:			
Police Protection	665	76	589
Police Officers Only	493	50	444
Fire Protection	310	—	310
Firefighters Only	285	—	285
Correction	285	185	100
Environment and Housing:			
Natural Resources	195	158	36
Parks and Recreation*	243	28	214
Housing and Community Development	92	—	92
Sewerage	103	(Z)	102
Sanitation Other than Sewerage	116	(Z)	116
Governmental Administration			
Financial Administration	312	121	191
General Control	550	119	431
Local Utilities	396	18	378
Water Supply	135	(Z)	135
Electric Power	74	4	71
Gas Supply	13	—	13
Transit	174	14	160
State Liquor Stores	15	15	—
All Other and Unallocable	494	193	301

Note: Statistics for local governments are estimates subject to sampling variation. Because of rounding, detail may not add to totals.

—Represents zero.

Z Less than one-half the unit of measurement shown.

*In previous years the State employees working in parks were counted in the "Natural resources" category and the State employees working in recreation were counted in the "All other and unallocable" category.

Source: Bureau of the Census. *Public Employment in 1982*. Series GE82-No. 1. U.S. Government Printing Office, Washington, D.C., 1983.

Table 1–2 shows in more detail the functions state and local public employees perform.

A division of labor can also be seen among many of the services that state and local governments provide. Within the field of public education, higher education falls within the domain of the states while elementary education belongs within the purview of local governments. Police and fire protection also remain the responsibility of local governments, as does the provision of utilities.

Tables 1–1 and 1–2 show clearly that the most frequent contact between citizens and government is likely to occur at the local level—education, police, fire, sanitation, libraries, and utilities. It is important to keep in mind, however, that while one governmental level may actually employ the people who provide a particular service, it may not be responsible for funding the service and it may not necessarily control the kind of service provided. For example, in the field of elementary education, local school boards may rely on state taxes in addition to local property taxes, and they will operate within statewide curricular boundaries. If teachers are certified, the state, not individual school districts, will do this as well. As another example, state and local government employees and private construction firms may build and maintain highways, but a large amount of the money for this service often comes from federal sources.

In summary, the information in these tables shows that public employees provide a considerably diverse set of public services. To accomplish this, they bring a tremendous variety of backgrounds, skills, and knowledge to the public service as well.

THE COST OF PUBLIC EMPLOYMENT

These services, of course, cost money, the bulk of which goes for salaries and wages. Governments generally provide services rather than goods, and traditionally service delivery requires a heavy investment in labor.

Table 1–3 shows the amount of tax money spent at various levels of government on current operations in fiscal year 1980–1981. The current operating budget for a governmental unit includes money allocated for compensation, supplies, materials, and contractual services—in other words, money for day-to-day expenses. It also shows the amount specifically allocated to salaries and wages, which is of interest to us.

Table 1–3 shows that 46 percent of current operations for all levels of government combined are absorbed in salaries and wages. Local government, which includes school districts, reveals an even greater percentage. Salaries and wages account for 56 percent of local government expenditures. This may seem like a considerable investment in personnel, and it is. But the figure is still larger because expenditures for salaries and wages

TABLE 1–3.   Government Expenditures by Level of Government: 1981–1982

| | AMOUNT (MILLIONS OF DOLLARS) | | | | |
| | | | State and Local Governments | | |
Expenditure	All Governments	Federal Government	Total	State	Local
Current Operations	639,524	265,891	373,633	133,152	240,481
Salary and Wages	294,439	104,285*	190,154	56,627	133,527
Percent Salary and Wages	46	39	51	43	56
Percent Salary and Wages Including 25% Fringe Benefits	58	48	64	53	69

*Includes pay and allowances for military personnel amounting to $57,991 million.

Source: Bureau of the Census. *Governmental Finances in 1981–82.* Series GF82-No. 5. U.S. Government Printing Office, Washington, D.C., 1983.

contained in the table exclude fringe benefits, which might range over 40 percent of one's salary. So, for example, assuming that the employer's contribution to Social Security, retirement, unemployment compensation, health insurance, and workman's compensation amounts to a modest 25 percent of a person's wages, the total personnel cost for all governments rises from $294 billion to $368 billion, which is 58 percent of current operating expenses. For local governments, the personnel cost approaches 69 percent.

In summary, well over half the cost of the day-to-day expenses of government goes to support personnel. If for no other reason than this one, the size of a government's work force, its salary levels, the way public employees are hired, assigned work, assessed, and terminated, are likely to come under close scrutiny.

PUBLIC PERSONNEL ACTIVITIES AND TASKS

So far the size, the scope, and the cost of public employment have been explored. With this general outline in mind, we can gradually begin to describe the field of public personnel administration. In an initial step, the following exercise will introduce you to the kinds of activities usually considered the domain of public personnel management.

Imagine that you are an administrator in the Department of Corrections in a state on the Eastern seaboard. There is a renewed emphasis on utilizing the corrections system to rehabilitate prisoners rather than simply confining them. In this hypothetical context of legislative blessing, fiscal largess, and legal flexibility, as secretary of the department you are asked to put together a plan to accomplish this mission.

You have a large budget and several facilities are available. What do you need to do now in order to staff these facilities to accomplish your mission? One of your first steps might be to hire new staff (assume that you do not have to worry about the existing employees). Reasonable enough. But how do you know whom to hire, how many people to employ, and how much to pay them? Most of us never would confront questions like these because organizations of any complexity already have position titles and descriptions, pay grades, and budgets to guide or in some cases constrain deliberations on these kinds of decisions. But someone, sometime had to come to grips with these concerns—although rarely from scratch. But back to the exercise.

In reviewing the general mission, the secretary and planning staff might think of more concrete goals and objectives. Once this is done, they can create various divisions or departments responsible for particular goals or objectives. Then within divisions and departments specific work assignments will describe what is expected of each role. These work roles can also be divided hierarchically so people can determine what kind of authority they will have in this organization.

Once the division of labor is complete, qualifications sought from potential job applicants can be determined. In other words, once you have an idea about what a particular job is supposed to consist of, you can, at least theoretically, determine what knowledge, skills, and abilities it may take to perform the job. After determining the market value of these qualifications you can establish pay rates. All of these tasks so far can be accomplished in large measure without any personal knowledge of who your employees might be. This may not always be a wise idea, but it can be achieved.

Now the department is ready to hire staff to get the new job done. This requires advertising available jobs and recruiting applicants. Once people are recruited some method must be used to select those who will become your employees if they like your terms of employment. How will you determine the skill level of the applicants? Will you give them a written test? Will you try to verify information that applicants have provided about past work records? Will you interview the applicants? How will the interviews be conducted? Who will be involved? What will this whole process cost?

Once these kinds of plans are implemented and staff is hired, they must be oriented to their work, trained, and their performance subsequently assessed. They must find some measure of continuing agreement between their own changing needs and what the department wants and in turn can provide them.

Some of these employees will eventually quit, be fired, or retire. Others will be transferred to different jobs, and some will be promoted as new work develops and generally as a reward for past performance.

Inevitably, some employees will fail to perform up to expectation.

TABLE 1–4. Core Activities of Public Personnel Management

Advertise, recruit, select labor

Divide and assign work; pay employees; promote, transfer, fire, lay off employees

Train, assess, coach, motivate employees

Discipline; negotiate and bargain with labor about working conditions; provide grievance and appeals procedure

Design personnel management system; establish role of personnel department and relationships with the budget staff and line management; maintain information and forecasting systems relevant to other activities

Thus it would be useful to develop ways of bringing them back into line. This will undoubtedly involve a method to discipline employees and in turn to allow them to appeal personnel actions such as an unfavorable performance assessment.

Finally, it will be useful to organize the way you will accomplish these human resource management tasks in order that they not only be accomplished fairly and efficiently but also that they reflect changing conditions both inside and outside the department.

Table 1–4 lists the personnel management activities described in this hypothetical example.

These are the core personnel activities that must be attended to in any complex organization. While they are the focus for much of public personnel administration, it may seem confusing to the new student in this field to realize that the personnel department rarely actually carries them out. The personnel department has two main responsibilities. First, it assists in developing methods to conduct these activities and facilitates their accomplishment. Second, it monitors the way these activities are carried out to make sure they are performed fairly, according to their intent, and within policy and legal constraints. Actually, employees who supervise other employees perform the bulk of personnel work, and the personnel officer is rarely responsible for deciding whom to hire, fire, transfer, promote, and discipline. Similarly, the assignment of work, training, and assessing of employees is done by all supervisors and managers. The personnel department assists and oversees the way others manage the personnel in an agency or government. The role of the personnel officer is more fully described in Chapter 4.

WHAT IS A MERIT SYSTEM?

A public personnel system consists of methods systematically used to perform activities like those listed in Table 1–4 as well as the rules and regulations that constrain the use of those methods. "Merit" is a term frequently encountered in descriptions of public personnel systems. A merit system quite simply is one where personnel actions are taken on the basis of the knowledge, skills, and abilities of current employees and job applicants rather than factors like personality or political affiliation. So, for example, a person would be hired based on knowledge, skills, and abilities required to do the job, and paid according to the value placed on those specific qualifications. Employees would be assessed and disciplined and rewarded according to their job performance. A merit system consists of impersonal rules, procedures, and techniques that grow out of the principles listed in Figure 1–3.

These principles reflect what Hugh Heclo[2] has identified as the civil service ideal. A government personnel system where activities in Table 1–4 are carried out on the basis of merit is characterized by (1) open access to jobs, (2) competitively determined selection and promotion, (3) removal and discipline for failure to perform in the job rather than for any partisan political reason, and (4) political neutrality of civil servants both in partisan political activities and in the performance of their work.

One might wonder why merit systems pay so much attention to protection from political influences. The answer to this question and the evolution of the ideal Hugh Heclo describes are found in the history of public personnel administration, discussed in Chapter 3. A few contemporary examples will preview the kinds of political incidents that rally support for merit systems.

The New York Times reported that U.S. Senator Dale Bumpers was seeking a Congressional investigation of a story that the Interior Department, under guidance from the Republican National Committee, dropped ten scientists from a nonpartisan advisory board. According to news reports, the Interior Department sent to the Republican National Committee a list of 14 scientists being considered for appointment to the nonpartisan advisory committee on offshore oil leasing. The list was contained in a memo entitled "Appointment Clearance Request."[3]

While this incident occurs outside a formal merit system, the objection Senator Bumpers raised was based on what he considered the inappropriate intrusion of partisan politics into what should be a decision based on the knowledge, skills, and abilities of the applicants.

Another incident, this time in Boston, demonstrates the vulnerability of public jobs to political pressure. As reported in *The New York Times*, Mr. Edwin F. Colby was dismissed from his job as deputy chief traffic engineer at the Boston Redevelopment Authority because he refused to make a contribution of time or money to the re-election of Mayor Kevin H. White in 1979. According to Colby, on February 7, 1979, all employees of the agency were called into a meeting, attendance was taken, and the Mayor addressed the group indicating that everyone in City Hall would have to work in the campaign. The city officially attributed Colby's dismissal to budgetary cutbacks and also explained that employees of the Redevelop-

1. Recruitment should be from qualified individuals from appropriate sources in an endeavor to achieve a work force from all segments of society, and selection and advancement should be determined solely on the basis of relative ability, knowledge, and skills, after fair and open competition which assures that all receive equal opportunity.

2. All employees and applicants for employment should receive fair and equitable treatment in all aspects of personnel management without regard to political affiliation, race, color, religion, national origin, sex, marital status, age, or handicapping condition, and with proper regard for their privacy and constitutional rights.

3. Equal pay should be provided for work of equal value with appropriate consideration of both national and local rates paid by employers in the private sector, and appropriate incentives and recognition should be provided for excellence in performance.

4. All employees should maintain high standards of integrity, conduct, and concern for the public interest.

5. The work force should be used efficiently and effectively.

6. Employees should be retained on the basis of the adequacy of their performance, inadequate performance should be corrected, and employees should be separated who cannot or will not improve their performance to meet required standards.

7. Employees should be provided effective education and training in cases in which such education and training would result in better organizational and individual performance.

8. Employees should be:
    a. protected against arbitrary action, personal favoritism, or coercion for partisan political purposes, and
    b. prohibited from using their official authority or influence for the purpose of interfering with or affecting the result of an election or a nomination for election.

9. Employees should be protected against reprisal for the lawful disclosure of information which the employees reasonably believe evidences:
    a. a violation of any law, rule, or regulation, or
    b. mismanagement, a gross waste of funds, an abuse of authority, or a substantial and specific danger to public health or safety.

FIGURE 1–3. Merit Principles (Source: Taken from Civil Service Reform Act of 1978.)

ment Authority were not formally subject to Civil Service protection because the agency was established by the Mayor. Colby's case is making its way through the courts.[4]

The primary defense against political influence over public employment decisions is inclusion of a job or group of jobs into a merit system where by law, if not in reality, political influence is minimized. The claim in Boston is that the Redevelopment Authority was not covered by merit system protections, and thus it would not be unreasonable to expect these employees to make campaign contributions.

THE DILEMMA BETWEEN MERIT SYSTEMS AND POLITICAL RESPONSIVENESS

Every merit system contains rules, procedures, and regulations to minimize political influence in hiring, promotion, and termination. But this protection from politics creates a central dilemma for a government based first and foremost on the principle of responsiveness to the people. Briefly stated, how can civil servants who are not subject to election and who are protected from arbitrary dismissal be held accountable to the desires of the people?

This is more than a theoretical question. Since the storehouse of expertise regarding public problems in large measure resides in this country's career civil servants, they often perform influential roles in proposing legislation, writing regulations to implement already enacted legislation, and in exercising discretion in the implementation of public policy. This observation holds at all levels of government.

One of the more popular answers to this enduring question involves the overlay of another personnel system on top of a merit system. This system often includes positions involving policy making and those that elected officials rely on in confidence and trust. These positions vary in number and kind depending upon the government and agency, and are often referred to as "exempt" positions, exempt from merit system protections. People who occupy these positions serve at the pleasure of an elected official such as a governor or an elected body such as a city council or school board. Individuals selected to occupy these positions might include the secretary of a state agency and his or her special assistant, an administrator of a federal agency, a deputy secretary, assistant secretaries, and special counsels. At the local level they might include a city manager and various department heads, and in large jurisdictions a school superintendent might be a political appointee. In still other personnel systems exempt status may be sought in some subordinate position, simply to provide more decision making flexibility regarding personnel actions to those responsible for policy development and implementation.

Creation of exempt positions represents an attempt to provide elected officials with legitimate political influence over the career civil service. Political appointees usually represent either the philosophy of the elected officials or the programmatic preference of these officials.

When looking at how government officials are selected, transferred, and rewarded, it is important to distinguish between three different levels: elected officials; politically appointed officials; and career civil servants who are also appointed but, ideally, on the basis of merit, not partisan political affiliation nor, in most cases, philosophy.

This book focuses on the career civil service and merit systems. But considerable attention is paid to the kinds of political pressures merit systems are subject to. It should be understood that a merit system itself results from political action. Merit systems evolve through legislation, legislative amendments, executive orders or directives, and with administrative refinements in implementation. Thus, even though a merit system may exist in two different governmental units, there may be considerable differences both in the design of that system and how seriously it is utilized or enforced.

SUMMARY

In this initial chapter, the size, the scope, and the cost of public employment have been described. In addition, the kinds of activities generally included in public personnel administration were identified. The term "merit system" was introduced, and political threats to the concept of this system were described in order to demonstrate that in large part merit systems have evolved as a reaction to negative political influences over personnel activities. This chapter ended with a brief discussion of how the insulation of career civil servants from political influence creates a dilemma for democratic government.

KEY TERMS

merit system
political appointee
political responsiveness
career civil service
partisan politics
core personnel activities
public personnel management

DISCUSSION QUESTIONS

1. Compare and contrast the size, scope of activities, and cost of public employment at the federal, state, and local levels of government. At what level do most personnel activities take place? Why do you think that despite the relatively small number of public employees at the federal level, so much popular and academic attention is focused on the federal civil service?

2. Table 1–4 lists in five groups the core activities of public personnel management. For each group, pick a word or phrase to summarize the activities in that particular group. Draw a diagram that shows what you think are the most important relationships among these groups of activities.

3. Describe a merit system. Why do you think merit systems have become so pervasive in public employment? A considerable number of employees whose jobs are covered by merit system provisions also belong to a union. Even though you have not yet read about labor relations in the public sector, review the principles of merit and speculate on the areas of compatibility as well as conflict between these principles and union membership.

4. Describe the dilemma that a career civil service poses for a democratic government. What is one resolution to this dilemma? Develop one other solution and speculate on the consequences both positive and negative of your proposal.

5. What do you think are the primary responsibilities and perspectives that the elected official, political appointee, and career civil servant bring to governmental service? Speculate on the way these perspectives complement as well as establish barriers for each other.

NOTES

[1]*1982 Census of Governments,* Series GC82(P)-1 (Washington, D.C.: U.S. Bureau of the Census, 1982), p. 1.

[2]Hugh A. Heclo, *A Government of Strangers* (Washington, D.C.: The Brookings Institution, 1977), p. 20.

[3]*New York Times,* March 28, 1983, p. 10.

[4]*New York Times,* March 6, 1983, p. 14.

2

The Study of Public
Personnel Management

The previous chapter drew a broad outline of the practice of public personnel management, and this chapter focuses on the study and analysis of that practice. This book reflects a systems perspective with the following theme: Personnel management within any government or agency results from compromises over conflicting expectations about the purposes and methods of managing people. These expectations grow out of different societal values that are filtered through economic, political, and social conditions and expressed in legislation, executive direction, and judicial interpretations affecting the practice of public personnel management.

By the end of this chapter you will be able to:

1. Identify and define five core personnel functions
2. Identify three basic elements of conflict in public personnel administration
3. Describe with examples the differences between a closed and open system, and describe the relationship between environmental demands and supports in a social system
4. Identify four values that have an impact on the way the core personnel functions are performed
5. Briefly describe several laws that affect the conduct of public personnel administration

SYSTEMIC FUNCTIONS

The common denominator in public personnel systems, regardless of governmental level, is found in the functions a personnel system must perform in order to permit public employees to competently complete their work under satisfying working conditions. These functions are derived from the personnel activities listed in Table 1–4. These activities have already been grouped, and in Table 2–1 the categories are labeled.[1]

Putting aside the *control* and *adaptation* function briefly, Table 2–1 identifies four functions found at the core of any personnel system. All public organizations must have methods to *procure* employees; to *allocate* employees to the work and divide the work among the employees; to *develop* the knowledge, skills, and abilities of the employees; and they must work out some method of establishing and enforcing the terms of the employment relationship—the *sanction* function. The methods of fulfilling these functions may differ according to political jurisdiction and form of government, public service performed, occupations involved, and whether or not a union represents the employees. But these functions remain the core of public personnel management, and a glance through the table of contents will show that this book is organized around them. In addition to these functions, every complex organization will attempt both to *control* the way these functions are fulfilled and to make sure the organization's methods of human resource management *adapt* to changing environmental conditions when necessary.

Methods developed to fulfill these functions will become systematized through rules, procedures, and techniques designed to both facilitate the accomplishment of these tasks and to ensure that they are carried out fairly, according to their intent, and within policy and legal constraints.

TABLE 2–1.   Core Functions of Public Personnel Management

FUNCTION	TASKS
Procurement	Advertise, recruit, select labor
Allocation	Divide and assign work; compensate labor; promote, transfer, separate labor
Development	Train, assess, coach, motivate labor
Sanction	Discipline; negotiate and bargain with labor about the terms of employment and the employment relationship; provide grievance and appeals procedure
Control and Adaptation	Design personnel management system; establish role of personnel department and relationships with fiscal staff and line management; maintain information and forecasting systems relevant to procurement, allocation, development, and sanction functions

The human resource management system that develops out of planning and from trial and error must itself be judged on two abstract criteria. First, the personnel system must be formal and stable enough so those responsible for the procurement, allocation, development, and sanctioning of employees can do so reliably and efficiently. Efficiency, whenever it is demanded, requires stability. Second, this system must adapt to changing conditions both inside and outside the organization. Obviously, this system cannot change and remain stable simultaneously. The art of managing a personnel system—as with any other administrative system—is found in the tension between these two necessities.

SOURCES OF CONFLICT, AND JOBS AS SCARCE RESOURCES

It is commonly assumed that these core personnel functions can be carried out simply and routinely in an agency. This impression may have been given in the Department of Corrections exercise in Chapter 1. In large measure, this assumption hides the real dynamism in the field of public personnel administration, where conflict is inherent for several reasons. First, as indicated earlier, the payroll allocated for public services constitutes a significant portion of any government's expenditures. For this reason alone the number of public sector jobs, and the criteria used to allocate them among the eligible work force, are subject to conflicting demands and perspectives.

The second element of conflict is that public sector jobs are scarce resources for those eligible to occupy them. Quite simply, public employment in the United States has been a source of upward social mobility for over 150 years for those at the lower end of the socioeconomic scale. Moreover, public employment is often the main avenue of fulfillment for citizens interested in public service in areas like national defense, foreign affairs, police and fire services, and education.

Lastly, public employment is frequently a road to power and influence for the citizen who develops professional or technical expertise. The influence of civil servants—hired on the basis of their knowledge, skills, and abilities—on both the formulation and implementation of public policy is commonly acknowledged. Thus, whoever can influence the number and kinds of people hired in the public sector will actually influence public policy priorities both today and tomorrow.

Public employment, then, is a scarce resource in American society, and conflicts will quite naturally occur over the procurement, allocation, development, and sanctioning of public employees at a public policy level whether in a national forum or local school board.

The next chapter will illustrate the historical and contemporary influence of conflicting expectations on the core personnel functions. At this point, it is sufficient to remember that public employment is a scarce resource to many people for many different reasons. In the remainder of this chapter, we will attempt to develop more fully the framework for viewing this interaction between conflicting expectations and core functions.

SYSTEMS THEORY AND EXTERNAL INFLUENCES ON CORE PERSONNEL FUNCTIONS

A system does not exist. It is an idea, a mental tool that can be used to help describe and explain—in short, to help us understand and learn. A system consists of a set of parts or components that relate to each other in some predictable fashion to produce some result. If one can isolate the components and draw a box around them, then out of one end of the box an arrow will indicate the results or output of the system. At the other end of the box one will find an arrow leading into it. This input channel activates the system components and provides them with energy and directions of some sort. Figure 2–1 depicts in a very simplistic fashion this systems idea. A video game, a thermostat, a dishwasher, and a stereo outfit, for example, can all be described as systems.

A natural system is a little more complex than these mechanical systems, with the prototypical examples coming from the field of biology. We describe the human body in terms of several subsystems: respiratory, reproductive, and digestive systems. These components are found in some regularized relationship, but they are much more susceptible to input variation than mechanical systems. The video game will accept only a limited kind of input. It will accept or reject your quarter or token, and will accept nothing else. You can move Pac-Man left, right, up, or down, but those are the only movements you can make. Short of spilling your Coke on it, pulling the plug, or taking a hammer to it, there is very little you can do to prevent the video game from working in its programmed fashion.

The inner workings of your body are much more susceptible to outside influence. Stress or changes in temperature or diet influence the workings of the components with results that will show much more variety than the video game ever will. For example, for some people stress will produce a headache, for others a skin rash; still others might find themselves with

FIGURE 2–1. Elementary Systems Perspective

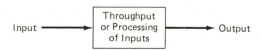

an upset stomach. So the workings of a natural system are much more influenced by the environment that surrounds it.

The systems concept was initially used to describe mechanical and living phenomena, as one can tell by the systems language we often use to describe ourselves and our machines. More recently, social phenomena have come under the analytical scrutiny of the systems theorist. Thus, it should not come as a surprise that in the last 20 years or so organizations have been viewed in systemic terms.

In this book we are trying to look at the management of people in an organization or governmental jurisdiction from a systems standpoint. We have drawn our box around the core functions introduced in this chapter—procurement, allocation, development, and sanction.

Obviously, the components of a social system—those methods, techniques, and procedures used to fulfill the core functions—will find themselves in a much less predictable interaction than will the components of mechanical or natural systems. In fact, in social systems some of the components may not even be readily identifiable. Only by picking out some phenomenon or result one wishes to explain and by tracing the relationships believed to produce it can one be confident whether or not the relevant system components have been included in the box.

In addition to the elusive nature of the components themselves and the variation in their relationships, social systems are much more dependent upon environmental demands and fluctuations than either mechanical or natural systems. Organizations as social systems are subject to many more diverse expectations than other systems.

Despite the loose fit between the original notion of the mechanical or closed system and the social system—a system open to influence from its environment—the idea of a public agency as a social system provides powerful explanations of governmental processes. In focusing on public personnel management, three central open systems ideas are particularly important to understand.

First, public personnel systems include the core component functions of procurement, allocation, development, and sanction. This is true whether referring to federal, state, local employees, school district or special district personnel. These functions and their relationships will be developed throughout the book.

The second systems idea that shapes the discussion in this book is the notion that social systems are particularly vulnerable to uncertainty and demands in their environments, and that what happens inside an organization is highly dependent upon what is happening outside it. For example, one cannot understand the upswing in production of small cars in the United States auto industry without knowing about Japanese competition. Similarly, the competition itself has been fueled by an appreciation of the cost of energy by the American car-buying public. In the public personnel

field, the emphasis on test validation and uniformity in selection procedures is the direct result of judicial interpretation of Title VII of the Civil
Rights Act of 1964. As another example in the personnel field, one can
note that recently the recruitment, training, retention, and discipline of
military personnel have become less problematic than in the 1970s. The
economic recession of the early 1980s, rather than anything the military
has done, has made military life relatively attractive to young men and
women.

As shown in Figure 2–2, system inputs can be described in terms of
demands and supports. Demands are placed on the public agency, and
supports are provided to the agency, but they do not always come from the
same group. For example, the Department on Aging in your state will
receive federal legislative mandates and administrative guidance, regulations, and money as well. The state legislature will also appropriate money
for certain programs. The Area Agencies on Aging, which are local field
units in the aging network mandated in federal legislation, will make demands on the State Department on Aging; advocate groups, other agencies
that have some jurisdiction over services to older adults, and the agency's
own employees all will make demands as well. In order to survive, the state
Department on Aging must selectively satisfy these demands, translating
their satisfaction into new or renewed support for itself. So, for example,
the state agency must meet the federal demands for fiscal accountability
and yet provide its field offices with the kind of flexibility they demand in
the use of funds to meet the needs of older Americans within their jurisdiction. If the state provides the area offices with too much flexibility, this may
gain them support with the state legislature, but it may jeopardize federal
support. The point here is that the dynamics inside an agency must be
designed to produce outcomes that will satisfy a conflicting set of demands
in a way that will generate continuing support for the agency in terms of
good will, budget, and legislation consistent with its sense of purpose.

The _third_ point that emerges from the open systems view is that
organizations must not only adapt to changing demands in order to generate support, but also must remain efficient. A closed system is the most
efficient; an open system is the most adaptable. Organizations as social

FIGURE 2–2.   Systems Design with External Demands and Supports

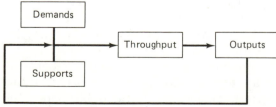

systems must be both open to their environment and impervious to it. For example, after an election involving party turnover in a large jurisdiction, the personnel system will change by permitting the new administration its share of new appointments. It will also, however, resist change by protecting most positions—those covered by merit system protections—from political influence.

Figuratively speaking, in order to accomplish these seemingly conflicting purposes the organization will try to seal off that part of its operations most technically involved in the agency's mission. In human resource management at a state or local level, for example, these would be personnel technicians who review job descriptions and requests for reclassifications, who prepare lists of job applicants eligible to be hired and who do initial testing of applicants, who review performance-appraisal forms to see they are being completed correctly, and who are involved in planning revisions or new aspects of the personnel system. In addition, at a technical level one would find the first-line supervisors and managers who are actually hiring new employees, assigning them work, and reviewing their performance.

Once these kinds of relatively technical operations can be sealed off from fluctuating demands, the operations can assume a degree of uniformity and predictability and can be judged according to how efficiently they are performed.

On the other hand, the agency must constantly survey its environment for new sources of support and demands that have the potential of altering the way the core functions are being performed. This is top management's responsibility in an agency. More than anything else, top management's role is to ensure that what the technical people are doing is legitimately needed by those who can influence allocation of necessary supports or resources. For example, where there is a central personnel agency that serves and oversees personnel administration in several departmental agencies, supports can be forthcoming or be withheld by these departmental or client agencies.

Between these two conceptual layers in an agency is a third one that must serve the role of translator. It must translate the technical core's need for certainty and predictability to top agency personnel who are in touch with the agency's environment. And it must translate the needed changes negotiated at top levels into enough certainty and direction that the technical core can perform its altered work efficiently. This is illustrated in the affirmative action field where the highest levels in an organization or government may negotiate a consent agreement with a federal agency that has found the offending government lax in living up to its Equal Employment Opportunity (EEO) commitment. The affirmative action office, rarely at the summit of an organization hierarchy, will have to translate the meaning and importance of the agreement to lower levels in the organization, where most of the hiring takes place. Moreover, if the affirmative action office is doing an effective mediating job it will not allow an agreement to be reached which those who actually do the hiring either cannot or will not implement.

The tension one can expect between middle management and managers at the technical level is common in all organizations. What is unique in the public agency is the tension between high-level administrators in the middle layer and those at the top layer, because those at the top are usually political appointees who change at least as often as every election and who often bring partisan political views to bear on the agency's priorities.

Some people view public personnel management as a dull field of study and practice because they have confined their view to the technical level, exhibiting a closed systems orientation. That is, they think public personnel administration is classifying positions, filling out performance ratings, administering tests, and keeping paperwork on personnel transactions, all internal organizational activities. On the other hand, some see public personnel administration as nothing but a political process; this is because they have limited their view to public policy debate that would affect the outcome of human resource management in a government or agency. For example, this view would call attention to policy debates over legislation leading to jobs programs, or the impact of unemployment on the availability of health benefits, or the demographic profile of the work force and the implications for the supply and demand of labor. Obviously, public personnel administration is both a technical and political area of study and practice; it simply depends on what you are looking at. With a systems perspective on organizational analysis, this book attempts to incorporate both views.

VALUE INFLUENCES ON PUBLIC PERSONNEL MANAGEMENT

Now that the basic systems framework has been developed we want to begin identifying the general outlines of environmental influences on the core functions. These influences are reflected in values that are filtered through contemporary economic, political, and social conditions resulting in legislation or laws, executive direction, and judicial review and interpretation that affect the core personnel functions.[3] (See Fig. 2–3.)

We can now look generally at some of the values, conditions, outcomes, and consequences interwoven throughout the book.

The values people hold, the deep-seated beliefs that underlie the choices they make, shape public policy directions at all levels of government. As a culture, we all share certain values that are particularly relevant to an understanding of the methods and constraints in public personnel systems. These values follow:

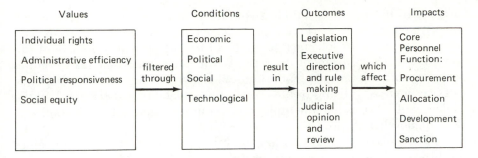

FIGURE 2–3. Impact of Values on Core Personnel Functions

The *rights of the individual* should be protected from capricious and arbitrary governmental decisions. The judicial branch of government is deeply involved in the protection of these rights.

Administrative *efficiency* is sought in the implementation of public policy. "Yankee ingenuity" suggests the innovative character prized in the culture, the impersonal processing of citizen claims; and the importance placed on individual advancement based on one's own merits, reflect the importance of efficiency. The executive branch of government is associated most frequently with efficiency.

As a democratic form of government, the value of *responsiveness* assumes a premier moral quality. Government is assessed in terms of how *effectively* it responds to and *represents* the people. Legislative actions may be judged in terms of operational efficiency, but more importantly an elected body is supposed to be responsive rather than efficient.

Social equity is the last value singled out. Not only are public services and opportunities supposed to be fairly distributed, but people who have been deprived the opportunity to enter the individual competition for society's rewards should be compensated. This value is especially salient with regard to groups of people like veterans and other minorities. Legislatures and the courts are particularly active in pursuit of this value.

These values serve as criteria to judge the wisdom of government actions, and they shape the allocation of scarce resources in the community. Indeed, the history of public personnel administration—especially the procurement and allocation aspects—deeply and permanently reflects these values.

CONDITIONS AND OUTCOMES

These values are filtered through the economic, political, and social environment and they emerge in the form of laws, executive direction, and judicial interpretations. Economic conditions influence the availability of jobs in both the public and private sector as well as the demands for public services. For example, in recessionary times, efficiency becomes accentuated, jobs become scarce, and less voluntary turnover occurs. Public as well as private employers become more selective in their hiring decisions, and the competition for jobs increases, thus focusing societal values most importantly on procurement criteria. At the same time that tax revenues decrease and jobs are cut from the public payroll, the demands for public services increase. Hiring freezes constrain availability and efficiency in the delivery of services like unemployment compensation, job banks, welfare, and mental health programs.

Political conditions also filter the values, accentuating different values at different times. For example, at the national level when political parties change office following an election there is considerable attention focused on the responsiveness value as the new administration assumes control of the bureaucracy. At other times, say for example following a scandal like Watergate or attempts to manipulate merit systems for political motives, a reaction may favor administrative efficiency over politics and focus attention on the rights of employees.

Social conditions also create a value context that influences public personnel administration. At the conclusion of a war it is not unusual for public sentiment to favor special opportunities and access to public jobs for veterans. In the 1960s, with racial tensions high, issues of social equity in the distribution of jobs became paramount. And most recently, the social as well as economic concern for equality between the sexes has placed the issue of wage comparability on the public personnel administration agenda.

Technological changes also have a significant impact on public personnel issues and activities. They create fluctuations in the job market by creating new jobs, making others obsolete, and requiring gradual changes in many others. For example, new employment categories have been created in the computer field, but many jobs in heavy industry are becoming obsolete, and secretarial jobs are broadening into information management. Thus, technological changes not only influence the supply and demand for different types of skills, but they have an impact on human resource planning, recruitment techniques, the emphasis on training in skill-deficient areas, and the relationship between the market value for specific skills and the public sector's ability to compete for scarce labor.

Values, filtered through a contemporary fabric of economic, political, social conditions, and technological change, ultimately find concrete expression in three basic ways: executive direction, legislation, and judicial review and interpretation.

Executive direction takes a variety of forms ranging from decisions about the inclusion or exclusion of positions in a merit system to degree of emphasis on objectivity in performance appraisal. But broadly speaking, direction from the executive arm of government, which is formally charged with the execution of public policy, is much more likely to reflect the values of efficiency and effectiveness than the rights of employees and social equity. Where an executive is elected this distinction begins to blur, but to the extent that the executive function identifies itself with the "administrative" or implementation side of government, it will value efficiency and effectiveness. Thus, the orientation to personnel administration is toward managerial flexibility and the ways the core personnel functions can be best handled to promote these values.

The values of responsiveness and social equity find sympathetic outlets in elected bodies, which of course are sensitive to the will of the people. Thus, major initiatives for jobs programs, elimination of discrimination in personnel practices, and equity in compensation often emanate from legislatures. But it would be much too limiting to suggest that legislative bodies disregard efficiency, effectiveness, and individual rights. In fact, because the major values that ultimately shape public personnel policy and administration often conflict, their resolution requires compromise—political action.

Because public policy must legitimately be reflected in legislation, major contemporary influence can be found in several of the laws described in Table 2–2.

In reviewing these laws it is important to realize that some apply only to the federal government; others are national laws that permit few exclusions. Moreover, state and local laws overlap many of these same areas, and provide more coverage in some cases.

In addition to executive and legislative direction, the judicial system has had its own impact on public personnel management. The direction of this influence recently has been toward social equity and protection of the constitutional rights of employees. In their work, the courts wind up interpreting legislative meaning and reviewing the legitimacy of the law in light of constitutional provisions. The importance of the judicial system on every core personnel function is clearly indicated throughout this book, with numerous references to court cases that the student of public personnel administration will become familiar with. In this introductory chapter one example may suffice to demonstrate this influence.

The issue of sexual harassment is becoming a major and complicated issue in the area of employee rights. It is an issue that seems destined to be defined through a series of *legal* questions. Is sexual harassment considered sex discrimination in accord with the Civil Rights Act of 1964? What is the employer's responsibility if a supervisory employee sexually harasses another employee? Who is financially liable in a sexual harassment case—the employer or the person actually alleged to have committed the act? Does sexual harassment have to result in an adverse personnel action like a poor performance rating before it is legally considered discrimination?

This is only one example of the important role the judicial system plays in public personnel administration. The relationship between the

TABLE 2–2. Major Regulations Affecting Public Personnel Administration[4]

REGULATIONS	FUNCTION	ADMINISTRATION/ENFORCEMENT	PROVISIONS
Veterans Preference Act of 1944	Procurement	U.S. Office of Personnel Management	Gives veterans preference in certification and selection procedures in the federal government. This is usually accomplished by adding 5 or 10 points to a veteran's passing grade on an examination. Similar laws are in effect in state and local governments.
Executive Order 11246	Procurement	Office of Federal Contract Compliance Programs, U.S. Department of Labor	Bans employers, including state and local governments holding federal contracts in excess of $10,000, from employment discrimination on the basis of race, color, religion, sex, or national origin. Covered employers must take affirmative action to achieve equal employment opportunity.
Age Discrimination in Employment Act of 1967	Procurement Allocation	Equal Employment Opportunity Commission	Bans discrimination in public or private employment for people at least 40 but less than 70 years old. Mandatory retirement prior to age 70 is banned unless for bona fide occupational reasons. No upper age limit for most federal employment.
The Vietnam Era Veteran's Readjustment Assistance Act of 1972	Procurement Allocation	Office of Federal Contract Compliance Programs, U.S. Department of Labor	Requires employers, including state and local governments holding federal contracts in excess of $10,000, to take affirmative action to employ and advance disabled veterans and veterans of the Vietnam era.
Rehabilitation Act of 1973	Procurement Allocation	Office of Federal Contract Compliance Programs, U.S. Department of Labor	Requires employers, including state and local governments holding federal contracts in excess of $2,500, to take affirmative action to employ and advance qualified handicapped individuals.
Title VII of the Civil Rights Act of 1964 amended by the Equal Employment Opportunity Act of 1972	Procurement Allocation Development	Equal Employment Opportunity Commission	Bans discrimination in hiring, firing, wages or any terms, conditions, or privileges of employment based on race, color, religion, sex, or national origin. Public and private employers with over 15 employees are affected. Amendments in 1972 require affirmative action to redress past discrimination.

Law	Type	Responsible Agency	Description
Fair Labor Standards Act (Wage-Hour Law) of 1938	Allocation	Wage-Hour Division, U.S. Department of Labor	Through amendments and court decisions this Act now applies to private employers, the federal government, and some state and local employees. It requires payment of a minimum wage with time and a half overtime.
Equal Pay Act of 1963	Allocation	Equal Employment Opportunity Commission	Prohibits wage discrimination based on sex. Covers private sector employers subject to the Wage-Hour Law and state and local employers.
Classification Act of 1966 and Federal Pay Comparability Act of 1970	Allocation	U.S. Office of Personnel Management	Provides for uniform categorization of white collar jobs in the federal civil service based on equal pay for substantially equal work. Federal Pay Comparability Act transferred responsibility for salary adjustments from Congress to the President in accordance with private sector wage comparisons. State and local governments have similar laws and procedures which, along with collective bargaining agreements, aim to produce equitable classification and pay plans.
Occupational Safety and Health Act of 1970	Development Sanction	Occupational Safety and Health Administration, U.S. Department of Labor	Requires private sector employers to provide safe working environment. Employees required to comply with OSHA rules. Federal agencies are subject to special OSHA duties, and state and local governments are indirectly covered.
Privacy Act of 1974	Sanction	Office of Management and the Budget	Regulates the collection, maintenance, use, and dissemination of information about federal employees. Designed to provide safeguards against invasion of employee privacy. Similar laws in effect in many states and local jurisdictions.
Civil Service Reform Act of 1978	Sanction	Federal Labor Relations Board	Establishes for first time the right of federal employees to bargain under the law. The basic scope of bargaining remains the same as under previous Executive Orders, which formerly authorized labor relations. Bargaining not permitted on wages or benefits, and strikes and slowdowns prohibited. Most states now have laws covering collective bargaining. Scope of bargaining generally is larger than in the federal government.

TABLE 2–3.   Core Values and Major Avenues of Outlets

VALUES	OUTLET
Individual rights	Judicial process and opinion
Efficiency	Administrative arm of government
Responsiveness	Legislation
Social equity	Judicial process and opinion; legislation

core values and their primary avenue of expression is summarized in Table 2–3.

SUMMARY

This chapter began with a description of procurement, allocation, development, and sanction as core personnel functions. These functions are subject to strong environmental pressures because jobs are scarce resources and so much tax money goes toward the salary and wages of public employees. Ultimately, these pressures can be traced to four societal values: individual rights, efficiency, responsiveness and effectiveness, and social equity. These values are filtered through a fabric of economic, political, and social conditions, and technological changes. They emerge in executive directions, legislation, and judicial actions focused on the way the core personnel functions are carried out.

KEY TERMS

procurement
allocation
development
sanction
control and adaptation
closed system
open system
system demands
system supports
individual rights
efficiency
responsiveness
effectiveness
social equity

DISCUSSION QUESTIONS

1. Discuss the core personnel functions to make sure you understand them. Pick out one function and identify the values and conditions that have the greatest contemporary impact on it.
2. What are the major differences between viewing public personnel administration as a closed versus an open system?
3. Identify the four values that shape public personnel administration. Show how these values might conflict. What are the consequences of this conflict for public personnel management?
4. How does the judicial system's emphasis on individual rights and due process affect the demand that personnel systems facilitate administrative efficiency?

CASE STUDY*

The Reagan Administration has minced no words in its criticism of affirmative action programs. The President's efforts would focus on special treatment for identifiable victims of discrimination with abandonment of broader-based hiring and promotion quotas. But the real challenge to affirmative action may be found more in contemporary economic conditions rather than political philosophy.

The 1980s followed a decade of affirmative action efforts that brought the number of blacks and Hispanics to 11.7 percent of the Boston police force. In 1981 the city of Boston, confronted with rising expenses, decided to balance its budget by laying off police and firefighters. A federal judge told the city this would have to be done without reducing the percentage of minorities on either force.

This meant that some minority officers would retain their jobs while white counterparts with more seniority would lose theirs. Seniority is the uncompromising cornerstone of unionism, and the Boston police and firefighters, like those in so many cities, are members of a bargaining unit. On the other hand, civil rights activists fear that the hard-won gains of the 1970s may fall easy prey in recessionary times if seniority is adhered to in personnel cutbacks.

The critical question here is whether a nondiscriminatory seniority system, which the courts have traditionally upheld as consistent with the Civil Rights Act of 1964, can be overridden in order to protect workers hired to remedy a past pattern of discrimination in hiring and promotions.

1. The conflict in this case centers on a scarce resource in public personnel management. What is the resource this conflict is all about?
2. What core personnel function in Boston does this conflict most clearly affect?
3. Contrast this case with the hypothetical establishment of the Department of

*Adapted from a story in *Newsweek*, April 25, 1983, pp. 95–96.

Corrections in Chapter 1. Show how one case better illustrates an open systems perspective and the other a closed systems perspective. In terms of understanding how public personnel systems work, what is the difference between taking an open versus a closed systems view?

4. Which of the values introduced in this chapter are expressed in this case?
5. What do you think would be a reasonable resolution to this conflict?

NOTES

[1]The functional categories appear in Gilbert B. Siegel, ed., *Human Resource Management in Public Organizations: A Systems Approach* (Los Angeles: University Publishers, 1973).

[2]Several of the basic ideas used here are introduced in James D. Thompson, *Organizations in Action* (New York: McGraw Hill, 1967).

[3]The seeds of this idea are found in Charles H. Levine and Lloyd G. Nigro, "The Public Personnel System: Can Juridical Administration and Manpower Management Coexist?" *Public Administration Review,* 35 (1975), 98–107.

[4]A very helpful source in compiling this table was *Public Personnel Administration: Policies and Practices in Personnel* (Englewood Cliffs, N.J.: Prentice Hall, Inc., 1973 and regularly updated).

3

Conflict and Compromise in the History of Public Personnel Management

The management of public employees—their procurement, allocation, development, and sanction—is achieved through political compromise. The conflicting demands placed on public personnel systems frequently reflect the value perspectives introduced in Chapter 2. Public personnel systems are expected to be *responsive* to the will of the people as filtered through political leadership, to promote efficiency through the procurement and development of skilled employees, to provide a vehicle for *social equity*, and to protect the *rights* of employees. These values illuminate the history of public personnel management presented in this chapter, and their enduring nature offers an insightful perspective on the following current events. See if you can identify the values found in each example.

> A bill approved with only one dissenting vote in the California State Senate would allow the incoming superintendent of schools a freer hand in hiring and firing top administrators in the State Department of Education. The bill would shift six top positions in the department, according to a December 30, 1982, *Los Angeles Times* report, to "exempt" status. After the new superintendent, Bill Honig, defeated three-term incumbent Wilson Riles in November, he discovered he could fill only two of the 1400 other jobs in the department. The rest were held by civil servants or managers on four-year appointments.

> According to a March 4, 1983 article in *USA Today*, U.S. Senator Rudy Boschwitz called for the resignation of Anne McGill Burford as chief of the Environmental Protection Agency. The Senator called for the President to name a scientist to head the EPA and to restructure the agency in a way that would end political influence on its actions.

John Hope III, acting staff director of the United States Commission on Civil Rights, said that the White House and federal agencies were undermining the commission's ability to monitor enforcement of federal civil rights laws, according to a March 20, 1983 report in the *Kansas City Star*. The article relates the disappointment of commission officials in their attempts to obtain data on the race, sex, and ethnic origin of all high-level presidential appointees.

In the small town of Ottawa, Kansas, ten probationary teachers brought a lawsuit against the Ottawa Board of Education for failure to rehire them. The teachers contend that the board's decision not to rehire them violated a "reduction-in-force" procedure spelled out in a union contract. As reported in the March 25, 1983 *Lawrence Journal World,* the board contends it has the right not to renew the contracts of nontenured teachers, and it followed proper procedures according to state law.

By the end of this chapter you will be able to:

1. Describe the differences between a patronage system and a merit system
2. Describe the reform movement at the end of the nineteenth century as a reaction to government by spoils and as a predecessor to scientific management
3. Explain the connection between administrative neutrality, scientific management, and efficiency in government
4. Explain why the desire for responsive and effective government in the 1930s and 1940s conflicted with the policing role of the public personnel administrator
5. Describe how the Civil Service Reform Act of 1978 represents a response to the value conflicts that preceded it
6. Identify three competing concepts of merit

BRIEF HISTORY OF PUBLIC PERSONNEL MANAGEMENT

This short review is designed to show the heritage of current public personnel systems and to suggest that the values which shaped that history play a forceful role today as well. Others have studied and described this history in detail elsewhere, focusing on economic, political, and social conditions and their influences on civil service systems. This chapter interprets that history as a fabric of conflicting values—individual rights, efficiency, responsiveness and effectiveness, and social equity.

PUBLIC PERSONNEL ADMINISTRATION AND PATRONAGE

Andrew Jackson articulated a philosophy of patronage in public administration with his election as President in 1828. It was Jackson's view that public jobs in the federal sector were quite simple to master and that they belonged to the common people.

Earlier appointments to federal service had been made with apparent care and an eye toward both individual competence and loyalty to the emerging Union. But in large measure the appointments were taken from the landed gentry and upper class of the Eastern seaboard. Jackson's election, which roughly coincided with the development of political parties, signaled not only the power of the frontier and movement west, but also a desire of the common people and political parties for their share of government. They would have it with appointments to public sector jobs in departments like the Postal Service, Customs, and Treasury. In a way Jackson's view represented the initial reform movement in public personnel administration.

If patronage—that is, the availability of government offices and appointment to them largely on the basis of political loyalty—was a means of bringing the people closer to government, it was also a reaction to an earlier government by the upper class. And it would spawn its own reaction, another reform movement with its touchstone being the Pendleton Act of 1883. But before describing this reaction, a brief elaboration of personnel administration by patronage will provide a needed context.

Frederick Mosher[1] dates the patronage period from Jackson's election to passage of the Pendleton Act. While the Act is a watershed in the reaction to patronage at the federal level, as late as 1888, when New York City comprised only Manhattan and a slice of the Bronx, the Tweed political machine in New York controlled some 12,000 jobs and a $6 million payroll.[2] Patronage flourished in the nineteenth and early twentieth century at the federal, state, and local levels. In its excesses, when patronage politics turned into politics for personal gain, the system became known for the "spoils" of electoral victory.

In the large cities in the latter part of that era, party politics prevailed, with parties organizing themselves into political machines in some places. These machines were designed from street-level up, with precinct workers, district committees, assembly districts, and county committees arranged in a sort of political hierarchy whose mission was to nominate candidates and win elections. With electoral victory of candidates who had been nominated in conventions of loyalist delegates came the opportunity and obligation to dispense patronage or public jobs to those who had worked hardest for the party organization. Party loyalty would be verified, a political clearance might be issued, and in return the new jobholder would pay, often monthly, a political assessment to the party. This amount, perhaps 2 percent of one's salary, went to pay party officials and for use in future elections.

The patronage system was not without virtue. While administrative efficiency suffered, it clearly was not a primary value for immigrant citizens who in the latter part of the nineteenth and early twentieth century accounted for over half the population of large urban centers in this country. Effective party machines, partisan political leaders, and local precinct workers brought government to these people not only in the form of jobs, but as assistance in filling out citizenship papers and other government forms, by helping to secure a needed license for a new business, by offering sympathy during a funeral or presenting a gift at a wedding. In return, the "patron" expected only a vote.

But patronage served more than the perpetuation of parties and machines, and it is these other functions that have prevailed to this day. At the federal level Congress and the President have vied for years over control of patronage appointments. Patronage was a currency, a scarce resource. As Paul Van Riper[3] points out, in a constitutional government where power is fractionalized vertically into federal, state, and local units of government and horizontally into executive, legislative, and judicial arms, patronage could be used to solidify political factions and sway votes on difficult public policy issues; and Presidents have successfully done so throughout history. For example, in 1893, President Grover Cleveland permitted influential Senator Daniel W. Voorhees control over patronage of federal offices in his home state of Indiana in return for Voorhees' support for repeal of the Sherman Silver Purchase Act. In 1981, in a more subdued vein but nevertheless presumably as a political investment or dividend, the White House permitted Senators Dole and Kassebaum of Kansas to handpick regional directors of specific federal agencies in the Kansas City area. This is common practice at all levels of government.

In addition to the older party function and as a continuing currency in executive/legislative relations, patronage is also frequently used where available to bring into appointed offices people loyal to either the elected leader or body. These politically appointed officials usually serve at the pleasure of the elected leader and occupy confidential positions or positions in a bureaucracy considered to be of a policy-making nature. In the city management form of local government the manager sits outside the merit system. In large cities some department heads may fall into this category, exempt from merit system rules and protections. The same is true at the state and federal levels where political appointments are used to increase the responsiveness of career bureaucrats protected from dismissal for partisan political purposes, to the direction desired by elected leaders.

Patronage appointments still exist at all levels of government but not nearly in the number or for the political purposes of post-Civil War days. Patronage turned to spoils and exploitation of the public good especially after the Civil War when the nation expanded economically. This was the time of robber barons, rags-to-riches stories, and social Darwinism with economic survival of the fittest. It was the time of enduring technological innovations large and small, like the telegraph, telephone, Pullman sleeping car for the railroads, gasoline motorcar, typewriter, adding machines, cash registers, incandescent light, and the Bessemer process used to transform iron ore into steel.

It was also a time when economic activity overwhelmed the limited role expected of government. The economic excesses of the time, the monopolies, the trusts, corruption, and land-grabs stimulated government's role as a regulator of business, but this role was late in coming. The limited role of government as a protector of individual competition and property was no match for business interests; in fact, government office was easily turned to personal gain.

Political officeholders, both elected and appointed officials, could "sell" franchises, construction contracts, harbor facilities, and public land. They had innumerable opportunities to make money for themselves and to channel moneymaking opportunities to favored friends and away from political enemies. It is no wonder that control over patronage was a hot political issue in many places, for there was much money to be made in these appointments.

It would be naive to assume that the buying and selling of influence in government has disappeared. The ABSCAM scandal, the use of money to influence the awarding of TV cable franchises, the power struggle in Chicago in 1983 between newly elected antimachine Mayor Washington and machine-backed aldermen, and numerous incidents of political campaign contributions being used to gain political influence and favors attest to the continuing value of access to and control over government and personnel appointments.

THE REFORM MOVEMENT AND PENDLETON ACT

Passage of the Pendleton Act of 1883 by Congress in large measure represents a reaction against this exploitation at the federal level. As with any major legislation, the Pendleton Act can trace its passage to political, economic, and social factors, but its legacy is found in the social and moral tone of the Act.

The Pendleton Act was an early attempt to lay the groundwork for a career in a civilian public service. In other words, it tried to provide a basis for a long-lasting commitment to public service and an opportunity to establish a career as a civil servant.

The Act had two specific aims. First, in the procurement function it would promote the efficiency of government by emphasizing job-related qualities of applicants rather than their political affiliation and loyalty. Second, with regard to the sanction function, it sought to protect employees from personnel decisions based on partisan political aims.

In the history of public personnel management, the Pendleton Act deserves special attention for several reasons connected to these purposes:

> It laid the basis for the gradual development of a civilian public service protected from the political turn of electoral events. Continuity in governmental functions would continue even with the changing of elected officials.

The President had the authority to bring groups of federal employees under the protection of the "merit system." Over the years, this has occurred gradually, often with an outgoing President covering under the merit system a group of employees who had been politically appointed just before his departure from office.

The Pendleton Act and the reform movement of the time were essentially negative in tone. Their primary goal was the removal of politics from administration, to protect the rights of employees from political pressure. It was assumed that if politics were removed from the procurement and allocation processes, efficiency would naturally result. Unfortunately, personnel management tools that would eventually provide the positive thrust to the efficiency aim, namely, testing, classification of positions, uniformity of pay schedules, and performance appraisal techniques, had not yet been developed with any degree of sophistication.

As a negative movement, the policing role of public personnel administration was established with the Pendleton Act. Earlier it was suggested that public personnel administration is concerned with facilitating fulfillment of the core functions and, in addition, placing constraints on methods of doing so to ensure the protection of employees from political pressures. This policing role and the present-day juridical concern with the protection of employee rights are legacies of this reform movement.

The Pendleton Act reauthorized the idea of a Civil Service Commission, a bipartisan, independent federal agency to oversee the embryonic development of a permanent civil service. This commission idea is noteworthy on two counts. First, the commission was to operate independently of legislative and executive control. Public personnel administration was symbolically portrayed as a politically neutral administrative function. Second, it was assumed that one agency could effectively perform what have become in its subsequent history conflicting purposes—facilitating human resource management and controlling it to prevent political abuse of the merit system.

Patronage systems in some measure grew out of the belief that previous governmental appointment practices had not adequately represented the rank and file American. The Pendleton Act, the second great reform in the public personnel field, was similarly motivated. The excesses, corruption, and public employment for personal gain convinced reformers that the public service of the late 1800s was unresponsive to the public good. The remedy, however, created a new dilemma for the democratic theorist if not for the person on the street.

EFFICIENCY: ADMINISTRATIVE NEUTRALITY AND SCIENTIFIC MANAGEMENT

How can a civil service whose members are nonpolitically appointed and promised job security be held accountable by the people? The answer was found in the concept of *political neutrality,* which Frank Goodnow[4] developed in some detail at the turn of the century.

Administration is a technical skill and it can be applied neutrally regardless of who is in charge of the political reins. Politics establishes the ends and purposes of public policy, and administrators carry out those purposes. Neutrality is the price the civil servant pays for tenure in office.

The concept of the politically neutral civil servant dovetailed with a movement toward "efficiency" that developed early in the twentieth century. Out of the corruption in government during the late 1800s and early 1900s, and from the contraction of unbounded economic opportunity, emerged a fascination with this concept of efficiency.

Commissions at all levels of government were established to study efficiency in government operations. Efficiency was reflected in two offshoot movements. The first was the idea of administrative neutrality. In the second decade of this century the city manager plan of government was first adopted in a few municipalities and serves as a prototypical illustration of this concept. The city manager was and still is expected to be an expert in administration of local government. The manager would serve at the will of the city council, an elected body, and thus the manager would not be covered by civil service protection. Those who worked below the manager would usually be included in what would be called the classified civil service. The manager was the expert who could translate the civil servant's need for policy direction to the elected officials and, in another turn, could move the civil service in the direction desired by those elected officials who would be held accountable to the public. The manager's preferences would only count to the extent that his or her expertise could influence the council.

While the political neutrality of administration was one expression of the efficiency movement, *scientific management* was another. Scientific management was the application of engineering principles to the analysis and organization of work with particular focus on the scheduling of work processes and on what is now called the *design of jobs*. The principles of scientific job design were:

> *Specialize* the job so a worker would not have to waste time switching from one job to another.
> *Standardize* the job according to the one best way of performing it and link it to other standardized jobs.
> *Simplify* the job so it could be easily learned.

The tools of scientific management were a stopwatch and, later, a movie camera so a worker's every movement could be described, analyzed, and subsequently planned on the basis of efficiency of movement.

More than anything else, scientific management was built on the power of classifying, categorizing, and organizing. And the movement was not limited to the field of employment. Samuel Haber[5] reports than an advocate of scientific management in Chicago was Melville Dewey, who at this time developed the Dewey Decimal System—all knowledge classified into ten categories. The fervor of the movement is captured in an anecdote which claims that Dewey often spelled his name "Melvil Dui" for the sake of efficiency.

Why is this period important in the history of public personnel administration? While the Pendleton Act espoused efficiency as well as the elimination of politics from personnel decisions, the tools needed to develop efficient procurement and allocation methods were not available in 1883. The application of science to administration in the twentieth century began to provide the tools, for example, in the area of position classification.

The principles of position classification, captured in the federal Classification Act of 1923, are quite congruent with the kind of thinking of the day. Position classification, as will be discussed in a later chapter, is no more than the categorization of jobs or positions according to their similarities and differences. It is the Dewey Decimal System in different clothes and context.

The intellectual force of scientific management in the history of public personnel management should not be underestimated. To Frederick Taylor, the father of the movement, scientific management was, indeed, more than a method; it was a revolutionary force in the business world. It promised in his mind to alleviate contemporary labor strife by providing labor and management with a mutually beneficial tool. Management would elicit more from the worker, and the worker, who would be paid a piece rate, would be eager to adopt the scientifically designed new work methods. In Taylor's scheme labor and management work together, and guiding them both is the *planner* who both designs and schedules the work. The planner, of course, is a political neutral in labor-management relations.

It is this neutrality that demands our attention. Scientific management promised not only to enhance efficiency, but also by precluding politics from entering the world of administration it became associated with the moral virtue of reform, very similar to the city manager plan. The dual goals of the Pendleton Act, at least in intellectual terms, could now be realized.

Position classification is often cited as the cornerstone of personnel management. This is so not only because of its centrality among personnel functions, but also because it epitomizes the efficiency-morality link. Classification is purported to be a tool (efficiency) for management in its handling of human resources as it provides a uniform occupational terminology, offers a base for an equitable and logical pay plan, translates labor costs into impersonal positions that can be added, subtracted, averaged, and moved about to create organizational charts; it clarifies career ladders, and it aids in the recruitment, selection, training, and assessment processes through its specification of position duties and needed qualifications.

At the same time it can be used to minimize political or administrative abuse (morality) and protection of individual rights with regard to personnel functions. Pay rates are tied to positions so individual favorites cannot be paid more than others. The work to be performed is specified in a description of duties. Thus, hiring people at a high salary and asking them to assume few if any responsibilities is minimized. Budgets are allocated in terms of positions so ceilings can be established to preclude hiring. Units may be assigned an average position grade, thus insuring that they will not become top heavy.⟩

The force of this link between efficiency and morality has had a tremendous influence on contemporary public personnel systems. Not only are personnel administrators frequently seen as "keepers of the morals," but personnel systems are also often imbued with an inflated virtue so that any attempt to change them is seen as tampering with a moral good.

THE EMERGENCE OF ADMINISTRATIVE EFFECTIVENESS

Even though efficiency has remained an important governmental value, the reaction to public personnel administration as a neutral administrative function was not long in coming. During the Great Depression, President Franklin D. Roosevelt revised the limited purpose of government in the affairs of Americans into a new, dynamic role of major responsibility and initiative that would continue into World War II and thereafter. His response to the economic conditions of the times included the creation of several New Deal agencies like the Agricultural Adjustment Administration, National Recovery Administration, Civilian Conservation Corps, Tennessee Valley Authority, Public Works Administration, and the Federal Emergency Relief Administration.

A new value—*effectiveness*—symbolically captures the intellectual direction in the field of public administration at the time. The value of responsiveness asks, "Are these the needs and problems to be solved?", while the efficiency value asks: "How much will the solution cost compared to the return?" The value of effectiveness poses a different question: "Are we accomplishing what we set out to do?"

Effectiveness and responsiveness as values demanded bureaucratic imagination and flexibility to develop appropriate governmental responses to economic distress. Seeking this flexibility strained the notion of public personnel administration as a neutral, technical administrative function.

When Roosevelt took office some 80 percent of the federal work force was covered under the merit system. However, the allocation of positions to the new agencies was made outside of the merit system. Thus, by 1936, while the total number of federal employees had increased, the number covered under civil service protection dropped to about 60 percent. Roose-

velt took advantage of the personnel flexibility permitted in the establishment of agencies outside the federal merit system. His actions represented
a new kind of patronage, one made to foster programmatic ends in addition to maintenance of party strength and as a currency in execu-
tive/legislative relationships. That is, he worked around the merit system to
bring to government people who would build programs consistent with his
own philosophy and vision of government.

Presidents Roosevelt, Truman, and Eisenhower all established commissions to study the organization of the executive branch of government.
Their mission is reflected in the titles "Committee on Administrative Management" and "Commission on Organization of the Executive Branch of
Government." Note that the term *efficiency*, which was a part of President
Taft's "Commission on Economy and Efficiency" in 1909, and the creation
of a "Division of Efficiency" in the Civil Service Commission in 1912, is
absent from these later commissions.

The theme running through the reports of these commissions was
that public personnel administration is not a neutral administrative function, and it should be restructured clearly as an administrative service in
the executive branch. This would be no different from personnel administration in a firm where the personnel administrator is an arm of
management.

Implications of the findings of these commissions as well as the sentiment in the 1940s that public personnel administration had evolved into a
"triumph of techniques over purpose"[6] were twofold:

> These commissions raised an important question that had been buried under
> the hope that intellectual neutrality would work in practice. Who does the
> public personnel administrator serve? Management, the employee, or per-
> haps the merit system itself? The earlier answer, that both labor and manage-
> ment would benefit by maintenance of the system itself, could no longer
> suffice in a time when governmental program development and implementa-
> tion chafed under the bit of civil service rules and restrictions designed to
> uphold the merit system.
>
> The need for administrative flexibility in the core personnel functions was
> becoming clear. The Civil Service Commission had become in practice a
> centralized control mechanism, policing personnel actions and delegating
> mainly detail work to its personnel counterparts in the agencies. This came at
> a time when public administration and personnel administration began to
> develop as a profession and field of study, and federal agencies in the 1930s
> began to develop their own personnel departments and were ready for the
> decentralization of personnel administration that eventually followed.

Indicative of the sentiment of the time, in 1945 an article entitled
"Let's Go Back to the Spoils System" was published in *Harper's Magazine*.[7]
While responsibilities for personnel functions gradually were decentralized
to various agencies in the federal government, the idea of personnel ad-

ministration as a staff function to administrative executives did not catch on in the federal government until the Civil Service Act of 1978, much later than it had in many state and local governments.

There were two primary reasons for this reluctance at the federal level. First, Congress was hesitant to relinquish power to the President. At the local level, the closest person to an administrative executive was the city manager, who served at the pleasure of the city council. The second reason was fear that the merit system might be undermined for partisan political purposes if the President were given more discretion over the core personnel functions. Manipulation of the merit system during President Nixon's Administration and skepticism regarding the quality of appointments in the Carter and Reagan Administrations lend some credence to this fear.

So far in this review the value of responsiveness has been associated with patronage and with the theoretical dilemma raised with the creation of a civil service whose members are protected from political dismissals. Protection of individual employees from political pressure is seen in the Pendleton Act. The Act's other goal of efficiency is expressed in both scientific management and the concept of administrative neutrality. And both managerial effectiveness and political responsiveness are captured in the work of the various commissions on government organization.

SOCIAL EQUITY

Social equity as a value made contemporary inroads into public personnel policy and administration in the 1960s and 1970s with Equal Employment Opportunity legislation and subsequent judicial interpretation. But the expectation that the civil service would provide a vehicle for social equity probably made its strongest impact after WWI and WWII with various legislative provisions for preferential treatment to veterans in their search for reentry into the civilian work force.

Among these preference provisions are those which permit extra points to be added to tests a veteran might take in application for federal employment. Many states and local governments have similar provisions. The use of the federal service as a vehicle for social equity is indicated by the fact that in 1934 some 25 percent of the federal work force were veterans while veterans comprised only 10 percent of the population as a whole. Between 1946 and 1949 the total percent of veterans in federal jobs changed from 31 to 47 percent. Preferential treatment for veterans is supported by two arguments. First, veterans are compensated as payment for their sacrifices on behalf of other citizens, and second, for the time they lost in military service, which they might otherwise have invested in building a civilian career.

As can be seen, the use of public employment to redress a social inequity is not unusual, and when one adds other public employment programs of the 1930s and the 1960s and 1970s, including the Manpower Development and Training Act (MDTA) of 1962 and the Comprehensive Employment Training and Assistance Act (CETA) of 1973, the power of the equity claim is evident.

An enduring equity influence on public personnel administration at all levels of government promises to be Title VII of the Civil Rights Act of 1964, amended in 1972, along with judicial interpretations of that Act. The Act prohibits unfair discrimination based on race, age, sex, or religion in employment decisions in both the public and private sector.)

Judicial interpretations of Title VII have established that when an employment decision adversely affects a disproportionate number of members of one of the groups protected under the law, the charge of unfair discrimination can be alleged regardless of whether the discrimination was intended or not. Actively developing programs to recruit and select members of protected classes for employment has been called "affirmative action."

The impact of equity claims on public employment decisions has been significant, and it promises to remain so in the following ways:

> The legitimacy of equity claims on public employment opportunities attests to the importance of government as a source of work and as an avenue of social mobility in this country.
>
> Highlighting the value of social equity points up the shortcomings of traditional definitions of merit. On the one hand, while merit systems have purported to be neutral, in fact they limit the realization of social equity claims and thus their impact is rarely neutral. On another hand, an unintended result has been the scrutiny given to employment tests and other tools used to assist in personnel decisions. While testing has been upheld as a component of merit systems since the Pendleton Act itself, assessment of most employment tests, until recent attention showered on them by judicial interpretation of Title VII, has demonstrated little relationship between test scores and subsequent job performance.
>
> The claim to social equity via Title VII has involved the judicial system in public personnel management more than any other time in this country's history. The consequences of this involvement have yet to be fully experienced.

THE CIVIL SERVICE REFORM ACT OF 1978:
A CULMINATION OF VALUES

The last touchstone event in this brief review is the Civil Service Reform Act of 1978. It is still too early to place any legitimate historical perspective on this legislation, but symbolically it addresses many of the conflicts and reflects the values revealed in early parts of this history.

The Act has three basic provisions of particular interest here. It follows the lead of many state and local governments by eliminating the politically independent Civil Service Commission and creating two separate bodies: the Office of Personnel Management (OPM), and the Merit Systems Protection Board (MSPB). It creates a Senior Executive Service (SES) similar to an idea proposed in the second Hoover Commission report some 25 years earlier. This service consists of some 7000 senior members of the permanent civil service who are subject to more flexible assignment and transfer practices than previously permitted by civil service rules. And last, the Act attempts to tie pay to performance for civil servants in the SES and in the managerial ranks immediately below them.

These three features stand out for several reasons:

Symbolically, the creation of OPM and the MSPB divorces the policing role of public personnel administration from its facilitation role.

This division also recognizes the importance of OPM as a staff function in the executive branch of the federal government. No longer is personnel administration formally seen as a neutral administrative function.

The issue of responsiveness of the career civil servant to political direction has been addressed with the SES. Since it now is easier to assign and remove senior executives and to hold out money in a carrot and stick fashion, the act permits more political influence over the federal bureaucracy.

With the pay for performance provisions in the Act, the federal government has taken an important symbolic step to deal with the development core personnel function in public personnel management. Except for the fluctuating emphasis on training in recent years, and periodic changes in assessment methods, the history of public personnel management at all levels of government has focused primarily on procurement, allocation, and sanction functions of human resource management, with lesser emphasis on development.

What can be learned from this historical review? First, public personnel administration is a field of multiple values that can easily conflict. These values have shaped the way the core personnel functions have been conducted over time, and they will continue to shape the practice of public personnel management in the future.

Second, each value has its own advocates, and the legitimacy of each value endures in the fabric of this society. Thus, while there may be a temporary lull in the influence of one value in favor of others, over time each value will be expressed in administrative reorganizations of the personnel function, legislation, judicial opinions, and professional norms that affect public personnel management.

And last, while the concept of merit has traditionally been viewed as value free, each value identified in this history carries its own special definition of merit. The next section of this chapter describes these definitions.

COMPETING CONCEPTS OF MERIT

The traditional concept of merit, which is commonly used today, stems from the belief that when personnel decisions are based on knowledge, skills, and abilities of job applicants and employees, an efficient public service free from illegitimate partisan political influence will result. This definition of merit is assumed to have self-evident virtue, a premise easily traced to its embodiment of morality and efficiency.

But what are the consequences of taking this definition of merit for granted? If responsiveness of a bureaucracy to political direction is sought, it will not be found with procurement decisions based on the traditional concept of merit. For example, inquiring into the religion of a job applicant will not reveal the person's knowledge, skills, or abilities to perform a job, but it may be a relevant, though possibly illegal, query if the hiring social service agency makes abortion referrals. Political responsiveness refers not only to partisan loyalty, but as in this example it can refer to a philosophical, programmatic, or even personal attitude as well. Most recently, many of President Reagan's choices for federal appointments have been based primarily on political philosophy rather than knowledge, skills, and abilities to perform the administrative jobs being filled. The important point to remember with regard to responsiveness is that the people elect the President along with some policy expectations, and in order to implement a philosophy the elected official must be given the discretion to secure a politically sympathetic and trusted staff.

Pursuit of social equity through the civil service may also compromise the traditional definition of merit. The quickest implementation of social equity would require classification of individuals into or out of the group to be compensated. This may occur through preferential treatment, quotas, or good-faith efforts, where two otherwise traditionally meritorious candidates for a job are finalists, with the decision going to the member of the class deserving compensation.

SUMMARY

In this chapter the history of public personnel administration was briefly reviewed and interpreted in light of four general values: protection of individual rights, efficiency, political responsiveness and effectiveness, and social equity. We have illustrated how external forces influence the way the core personnel functions, especially how the procurement and allocation functions are performed. The conflicting nature of these values was described as well as the distinct criteria of merit associated with each. As a concluding thought it might be useful to isolate some of the value conflicts with which public personnel systems must live.

The idea that a public personnel system could facilitate line management's handling of personnel decisions to promote efficiency as well as police those transactions to protect individual rights was assumed with a traditional definition of merit. While intellectually the two goals may seem compatible, in practice they conflict because of the flexibility line management prefers in its handling of personnel. Protecting the merit system places limitations on that flexibility. In other words, the traditional concept of merit carries within it the seeds of conflict.

Political responsiveness as a value can conflict with merit based on knowledge, skills, and abilities. To minimize this conflict, in most public personnel systems a number of positions, usually of a confidential or policy-making variety, are designated outside the merit system and are available to elected officials as political appointments. Tension in public personnel systems focuses on how many and which positions these will be and also which political focus will influence this special recruitment and selection process. Relationships between top-level career civil servants and politically appointed civil servants often are characterized by this kind of tension.

Social equity as a value often compromises a traditional definition of merit because it credits nonmerit qualities. Veterans preference provides the classic example, but newer examples in the affirmative action area have similar effects.

While there are many current issues to be dealt with in this book, these are some of the recurring ones and, because at their base they reflect value differences, they will influence the current issues as well.

KEY TERMS

efficiency
effectiveness
responsiveness
social equity
individual rights
merit
patronage
Pendleton Act
Civil Service Reform Act of 1978
political neutrality
scientific management

DISCUSSION QUESTION

Describe each of the four values that influence the development of public personnel administration. Which of these values complement each other? How do they conflict? How does each imply its own definition of merit?

EXERCISE

The following conversation takes place among three members of a state government: Brenda Simon, Secretary of the hypothetical Department of Corrections introduced in Chapter 1; her administrative assistant, Mary Rodriguez, and Larry Gordon, from the Governor's office. They are talking about applicants for the recently vacated unclassified position of deputy secretary in the Department of Corrections.

1. Which definitions of merit are being expressed in this conversation? Give examples.
2. Which candidate do you think represents the most "meritorious" choice?

BRENDA: Well, I don't know about you two, but in my book this John Simpson seems to have enough experience to handle the job. I need someone who can take over the internal operations of the agency while we get this new program off the ground. But what really impressed me was his commitment to the policy direction we're headed in.

MARY: You know I admire your judgment, Brenda, but does he really have the skill to pull the job off? We know Don Johnson is doing a fine job now as a division director. He already knows the ropes around here, and I think he's ready for a bigger job. Besides, it's about time we got another minority into this sacred secretarial hut!

BRENDA: Hold on, Mary. You know I support our affirmative action program. I gave you a boost some time ago, I remember.

MARY: Now wait a minute! Let's not dredge up the history on that one. You know very well I was qualified for this job. This is now, and Don's qualified.

BRENDA: Mary, Don may be able to do the job; I'm not as convinced as you, but this Simpson is on target when it comes to supporting the philosophy behind the new program. And the more I think about it the more I need that commitment to make this thing go. There's a lot at stake in making the program a success. Don's pretty hardheaded when it comes to seeing us turn this agency into what he feels is a softhearted bunch of social workers.

LARRY: Look, folks, I hate to complicate things for you, but the Governor's been getting pressure to find a spot for Jim Masington.

MARY: Jim who? I never heard of him.

BRENDA: Well, I have. He worked pretty hard in the Governor's last campaign, didn't he?

MARY: Oh no! I can see it coming.

LARRY: Don't get excited. Just give the guy some consideration. Brenda, you know the Governor went out on a limb to give you the chance to experiment with this new program, and he may need a favor here.

MARY: I just don't like the politics in all this.

BRENDA: Look, Larry, I want to help, but I need someone who is committed to this program.

MARY: And I think we'd better get someone who can manage the internal operations of this agency.

LARRY: Well, I think you just ought to look at Masington's application. You know that's all the Governor is asking.

BRENDA: Thanks, Larry, I want to think about this. Mary, let's get together on this tomorrow afternoon.

MARY: Politics!

Would this conversation have taken place if the Corrections Department were hiring a new typist? Not likely. In this conversation a classic confrontation occurs between the need for someone who is technically competent to perform as a manager and someone who is committed to a programmatic philosophy. It is hoped they will find someone who meets both criteria. Masington's application adds a partisan facet to the responsiveness criterion. Obviously, what is a "meritorious" selection according to one person may differ from another's choice. It is important to know what criteria are being used, for they determine the rules of the game.

NOTES

[1]Frederick C. Mosher, *Democracy and the Public Service,* 2nd ed. (New York: Oxford University Press, 1982).

[2]William L. Riordon, *Plunkitt of Tammany Hall* (New York: Dutton, 1963), p. xii.

[3]Paul P. Van Riper, *History of the United States Civil Service* (Evanston, Ill.: Row, Peterson and Company, 1958). Van Riper's work has influenced several ideas in this historical review.

[4]Frank J. Goodnow, *Politics and Administration: A Study in Government* (New York: Macmillan, 1900).

[5]Samuel Haber, *Efficiency and Uplift: Scientific Management in the Progressive Era, 1890–1920* (Chicago: University of Chicago Press, 1964), p. 73.

[6]Wallace S. Sayre, "The Triumph of Techniques over Purpose," *Public Administration Review,* 8 (1948), 134–37.

[7]John Fischer, "Let's Go Back to the Spoils System," *Harper's,* 191 (October 1945), 362–68.

4

Role and Dynamics
of Public
Personnel Management

PERSONNEL ADMINISTRATION AND MEDIATING
RESPONSES

The systems framework has led to a description of public personnel management in terms of its core functions, namely, procurement, allocation, development, and sanction of human resources. Frequently these functions are subject to conflicting demands emanating from an environment comprised of not only legislative, judicial, and other executive or administrative bodies or interests, but also special-interest groups such as employees inside the agency, veterans and civil rights organizations, professional associations, and women's groups outside the agency.

The values identified in Chapter 2 are represented in this environment. When filtered through contemporary political, economic, and social conditions, they emerge in the form of specific demands like a legislated wage ceiling, a judicial mandate regarding hiring practices, administrative requirements for more flexibility in personnel procedures, or a professional association's lobbying for certification as an employment prerequisite. But because maintenance of stability is important for those whose work is technically encompassed within the core functions, their work is sealed off from this bombardment of demands, which must more or less formally find their way to the core. In other words, bridges are erected to connect the core with these environmental demands. In so doing they mediate potentially drastic and sudden impacts of the environment on the core functions. These metaphorical bridges take the form of contemporary, dynamic human resource activities. The action in public personnel management is found in these activities because theoretically they represent the clash between the need of the personnel core to change in order to maintain its legitimacy and, at the same time, to remain stable enough to retain a sense of identity and to operate efficiently.

By the end of this chapter you will be able to:

1. Identify the purpose and describe four mediating activities
2. Describe the specific connection between each set of value-mediating, activity-core personnel functions
3. Describe three new areas of emphasis in modern public personnel management
4. Differentiate between the traditional role of the personnel officer and a more contemporary role
5. Describe how rules designed to protect the merit system can encourage violation of it
6. Describe two decisions the public personnel administrator must face in order to become more professional

MEDIATING ACTIVITIES IN PUBLIC PERSONNEL MANAGEMENT

The mediating function, that is, the regulating and softening of environmental demands on core personnel functions, is located in those activities connected with affirmative action, human resource planning and cutback management, productivity, and labor relations and the rights of employees.

Affirmative action includes those activities an organization undertakes in response to social equity pressures like Title VII of the Civil Rights Act of 1964 and subsequent judicial interpretations and administrative directives. An example would involve the redesign of professional jobs in an agency to separate out the nonprofessional duties that can be performed without professional certification but which may provide entry-level access to members of a protected class. Another example might be the development of hiring goals in conjunction with the union local to increase the number of minorities working in an agency. Similarly, agreements to incorporate affirmative action goals in personnel cutback processes could be included within the span of this bridge.

Human resource planning and cutback management involves activities designed both to buffer and to deal with external threats to existing expenditure levels and programs. For example, until recently few local governments had developed detailed reduction-in-force procedures to guide them in layoffs. With cuts in federal funds to local governments straining taxing capacity, which services to cut, how many employees to let go, and how to accomplish the reduction both fairly, legally, and in a way that would preserve essential services and employee morale can be found on this bridge.

Activities connected to demands for productivity improvements include reassessments of staffing levels, alternative job designs, altering reward systems to increase their motivating potential, reappraising the potential utility of performance evaluation plans, and paying more attention to work goals through concrete specification of desired employee performances.

On the labor relations bridge are activities that will affect the terms under which employees will work. For example, the negotiation of work-security provisions or a grievance procedure, or establishment of a labor-management work committee to sort out differences before they turn into grievances would be included. In addition to labor relations, the constitutional rights of employees, protection from sexual harassment, and reduction of vulnerability to financial liability of public employees all would be included in this mediating area.

VALUES, MEDIATING ACTIVITIES, AND CORE FUNCTIONS

In the history described in Chapter 3, each value was connected implicitly to a core personnel function. Table 4–1 visually captures these associations.

The mediating activities intervene between the relationship of the abstract values and the core personnel functions found in Table 4–1. The four contemporary mediating activities—affirmative action, human resource planning, productivity, and labor relations—all reflect both historical and ongoing concerns over the criteria to be used in procurement decisions, the responsiveness of public bureaucracies to legitimate political direction, the concern with efficiency of the public service, and the entire issue of the rights of employees. However, a more specific scheme is portrayed in Table 4–2.

The relationships are drawn more rigidly than intended. In actuality, each value influences each mediating activity and core function. In turn, each mediating activity affects the way all the core functions are fulfilled. For example, collective bargaining is a process that can produce an agreement to require a person to be a member of a union in order to be hired

TABLE 4–1. Relationship between Values and Core Personnel Functions

VALUE	CORE FUNCTION
Social Equity	Procurement
Responsiveness and Effectiveness	Allocation
Efficiency	Development
Individual Rights	Sanction

TABLE 4–2.   Intervention of Mediating Activities Between Values and Core Functions

VALUE	MEDIATING FUNCTION	CORE PERSONNEL FUNCTION
Social Equity	Affirmative Action	Procurement
Responsiveness and Effectiveness	Human Resource Planning and Cutback Management	Allocation
Efficiency	Productivity	Development
Individual Rights	Labor Relations and the Rights of Employees	Sanction

(procurement), specify promotion and layoff policies (allocation), provide for specific training opportunities for its members (development), and establish a grievance procedure (sanction). A similar case can be made for affirmative action. Despite these fluid relationships, we have tried to match mediating activities with the core function where the greatest impact is felt. The most significant aspect of collective bargaining is the definition it provides for the employee-employer relationship, for the formulation of terms of employment. Thus, the connection is made to the sanction function.

Similarly, the current emphasis on productivity captures the influence of efficiency on the development function. Attention focuses on the motivation of employees to produce, and how activities in the development function relate to employee motivation. The responsiveness value impacts the allocation function through discussions and deliberations regarding program priorities, staffing, and salary ceilings. Finally, the social equity value impacts most forcefully on activities relating to hiring within the procurement function, and these activities are mediated in the affirmative action field. Each major part of the rest of this book is organized around a core personnel function and begins with a chapter on the appropriate mediating activity.

The identification of mediating activities raises interesting questions about the boundaries of public personnel management in any particular personnel system. In the first place, it broadens the traditional boundaries of the field from technical to political concerns, and in so doing it illustrates the limited role that traditional personnel departments have assumed in human resource management. None of the mediating activities necessarily falls within the scope of a traditional public personnel department, yet each can dramatically shape the way an agency or government fulfills its core personnel functions.

Study of the mediating activities highlights the political as well as technical nature of public personnel management. The political nature of mediating activities is graphically illustrated where they impinge upon one another. For example, the legislative decision to reduce service levels might produce an agency decision to make cutbacks in personnel based on employee work records. This logic might run into a seniority system in one of the areas of service reduction. An accommodation to the seniority system might then activate an affirmative action response that layoffs based on seniority will unduly affect minorities who, under a recent affirmative action push, are formally low in seniority. In fact, this hypothetical example parallels the real Boston police case presented at the end of Chapter 2.

Trying to negotiate a reasonable solution to these issues in the cutback situation will raise the stakes of human resource management decisions considerably and will push the deliberations outside the personnel department's boundaries. For instance, in the hypothetical case above, the committee to review the reduction-in-force procedure might be comprised of members throughout the state civil service system as well as members of the personnel division.

This draws attention to a second area where personnel administration becomes political. Dynamics in each of the mediating activities will bring responsible organizational members in contact with the external environment that affects that particular core area. As an example, during budget deliberations the heads of state agencies and civil servants with programmatic responsibilities will discuss with legislators the implications of anticipated budgetary decisions on agency productivity, its ability to hire top talent, and its ability to respond to client needs. These examples suggest that in addition to social systems responding to changing conditions they also actively protect their core by attempting to influence their environment in order to continue to work in a way that will produce valued outcomes.

While an important consequence of highlighting mediating activities is an increased awareness that personnel management usually goes beyond what occurs in personnel departments, it also raises the critical issue of the role and power of the personnel department and administrator, the subject of the next section.

ROLE OF THE PUBLIC PERSONNEL
ADMINISTRATOR

Mediating activities now in existence will strongly influence human resource management in the future. In stepping back from them to gain some perspective, one can discern three emphases shaping the direction of public personnel systems. First, the dynamics in the mediating areas of affirmative action and the rights of employees indicate that public personnel management is becoming more juridical in nature. Redress to the courts in the face of personnel procedures that have been proven to be unfair to minorities (however unintentional) has thrust the courts into many areas of human resource management. Court opinions have mandated hiring quotas, have made theoretical concepts like reliability and validity common vocabulary in testing units, have struck down partisan patronage dismissals, and, with recent emphasis on the constitutional rights of employees, have invigorated public personnel administration's all-too-comfortable reliance on due process in personnel management.

It is not only the courts themselves that have reinforced the emphasis on due process and individual rights, but also collective bargaining in the public sector can be expected to increase in importance, thus creating a more formal avenue for employees to assert their rights and to define their relationship to management.

The combination of juridical and collective employee inroads into the areas of employee rights and freedoms raises fundamental questions of whether merit systems are becoming obsolete and whether public personnel systems rather than attempting neutrally to serve both management and employee should identify management as its primary client.

The second area of emphasis relates to the increased attention paid to productivity, and it is found in the knowledge gained from the behavioral sciences. These include fields like psychology, social psychology, sociology, anthropology, and political science. With labor costs comprising a large portion of government budgets, public agencies slowly but increasingly are turning to the behavioral sciences for ways of attracting the best employees and creating conditions that reward good performance and deal with poor performance.

Progress has been made in designing motivating potential into jobs rather than relying on traditional principles of specialization, standardization, and simplification to divide labor. Compensation plans are being developed with fringe options from which employees can choose. While money for activities like supervisory training, management development, team building, and organizational development is still in short supply, more and more verbal recognition is being given to the importance of developing and rewarding competent managerial performance. Moreover, contemporary experiments with quality circles—employee problem solving groups—implicitly recognize the importance of work groups in addition to the individual employee in the behavioral dynamics of the work place.

The third area of emphasis has to do with the importance of human resource planning and the fiscal implications of personnel decisions. This emphasis boils down to a much greater awareness of the relationship between fiscal and personnel decision making. Personnel issues like turnover, absenteeism, use of sick leave, and even employee morale are being subjected to "costing" formulas that may increase the salience of human resource management to those sensitive to cost accounting.

On the other hand, in an era of fiscal prudence, the personnel implications of fiscal decisions can become equally relevant. For example, what is the cost in morale and managerial credibility when a personnel system institutes a pay for performance-appraisal system and, following an initial round of evaluations, discovers that too much money is required to reward superior performance? This happened when Congress balked at and reduced money for bonuses managers in the National Aeronautics and Space Administration (NASA) were scheduled to receive in accordance with implementation of the Civil Service Reform Act of 1978.

As another example, in an investigation of a scandal involving city building inspectors failing to perform their work in Kansas City, Missouri, it was revealed that the salary the city could afford to pay its inspectors was not competitive with salaries in the private-sector market. Thus a question is raised about the quality of worker attracted to this particular job.

These, then, are the three areas we believe the field of public personnel management is headed toward: labor relations and the rights of employees, the applied behavioral sciences, and the interplay between personnel and fiscal decision making. Present-day public personnel systems in general seem ill-prepared for this future.

Current emphases are revealed in the way contemporary personnel departments are organized. Figure 4–1 illustrates the way a larger public personnel department might be organized into sections to handle recruitment and testing, classification and pay, retirement and benefits, promotions and reassignments, grievances and appeals, and training. Also included might be a labor relations and affirmative action section. It would not be unusual, however, to find these last two sections, especially the affirmative action office, not coming under the formal authority of the personnel department.

In very large departments, a central personnel agency or section might be comprised of units like these to coordinate and control the work of personnel offices in the field or in other agencies to which personnel administration has been decentralized. In smaller departments, these ac-

FIGURE 4–1. Typical Personnel Department in Large Jurisdiction

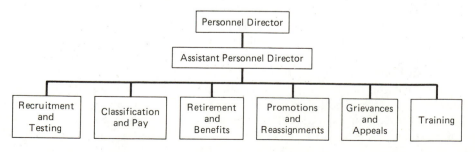

tivities might be combined into the duties of just a few people. And in some of the smallest government units personnel activities would simply consist of paperwork handled as part of someone's regular duties.

In the area of recruitment and testing, the personnel office might be responsible for developing schedules of tests for jobs that are frequently available, like secretary, clerk, and maintenance worker. They would advertise vacant or new positions, conduct an initial review of job applications, and administer tests. Some personnel officers might conduct an initial interview with applicants and evaluate test results. The personnel department would compile a list of those eligible for employment, maintain the list to ensure it is up-to-date as job applicants secure other employment, and it would provide a list of eligibles to managers in units where vacancies actually exist. The manager would conduct interviews and select one of the applicants. The personnel office would then process the paperwork required to employ and pay the person. The training officer might at some point conduct an orientation for new employees.

The classification and compensation branches are responsible for maintaining the system of positions that have been categorized into a plan according to some criteria like degree of difficulty and responsibility. The pay system is usually tied to the classification system with jobs involving similar degrees of difficulty and responsibility being compensated equally. Periodic checks are conducted to compare the actual work a person is performing with the duties outlined in a job description relevant to the position. This division would also review line managers' requests for the reclassification of a position. Yearly updates of the pay plan would be performed in anticipation and implementation of pay raises.

A retirement and benefits section would be responsible for maintaining records like eligibility and use of sick leave and vacation time, enrollment and maintenance in various health insurance programs, and life insurance purchases. Personnel in this section might also be involved in studies and negotiation of health benefit packages. Eligibility and processing of retirements, including calculation of authorized retirement benefits, would also be handled in this section.

The personnel department must also keep track of and process all personnel promotions, transfers, and dismissals. It will also have a section that establishes and staffs an employee grievance and appeals procedure. People who work in this section would be responsible for advising supervisors throughout the organization of the appropriate paperwork necessary in the event of an appeal, and they would make arrangements for implementation of the grievance process.

A training officer might be responsible for orienting new employees to the organization and their benefits. This individual might also keep track and distribute notices of training opportunities, and this section might also be responsible for conducting training, for example, to familiarize supervisors with the technical aspects of a newly developed performance appraisal system.

More progressive personnel departments might be called upon for analyses, like use of sick leave, and distribution of ratings on employee performance appraisals. They might be asked to develop new methods of evaluating employees and experiment with innovations in selection techniques such as the use of assessment centers, or to work with the systems analysts to computerize personnel and pay records. They might also develop an employee counseling or assistance program, and be available as behavioral science consultants to departmental managers contemplating changes that will affect the human dynamics in their operation. Moreover, they might be asked to establish the cost of turnover, monitor frequency of grievances in various departments, and "cost-out" a proposed pay raise.

What conclusions can be drawn from this variety of activities? Two stand out. First, traditional public personnel management falls into the procurement, allocation, and sanction areas with much less emphasis on analytical work or the developmental function. In addition, both employees and line management are seen as clients, and they are perceived as being served through the merit system. The traditional public personnel department is a closed system whose work primarily consists of record keeping and the processing of personnel transactions, especially in smaller government agencies or units of government. The mediating activities identified earlier fall outside the boundaries of the personnel department just described.

Second, the most important conclusion is that the functions of procurement, allocation, and sanction, conducted as if in a closed system, represent the classical merger of efficiency and morality. This cornerstone of public personnel administration emerged from linkage of the reform movement with the era of efficiency that occurred between the end of the Civil War and the beginning of the New Deal.

Public personnel administration will move slowly into the mediating activities because of this heritage, which cautions that politics and public personnel administration do not mix. The problem with this traditional caution is that most public personnel systems have moved beyond the threat of serious and consistent partisan political abuse. But in doing so a new kind of threat has emerged, a threat implied several years ago in Wallace Sayre's article describing public personnel administration in the 1940s as "the triumph of technique over purpose."

BENDING THE RULES IN FAVOR OF MERIT

In the search to protect the merit system from political abuse, rules and regulations have been promulgated with the effect of reducing managerial discretion and flexibility in the handling of personnel. For example, to prevent the arbitrary and rapid promotion of an employee who is a managerial or political favorite, a certain minimum time in grade may be required prior to a promotion. This restriction penalizes the truly exceptional employee whose knowledge, skills, and abilities might warrant much quicker than average promotions.

The demand for managerial flexibility in the handling of personnel came to light particularly during the Roosevelt Administration, when administrative effectiveness was reinforced as a value in public administration. The limits placed on managerial discretion to protect the merit system create situations where it becomes rational to bend the rules to accomplish the results intended in the original vision of reform—entrance and advancement in a public service career according to ability.

Personnel rules can be bent in many ways to secure results oftentimes congruent with merit system principles but hindered by merit system practices. For instance, job descriptions can be written with a specific applicant in mind, a position can be reclassified upward to retain a valuable employee when a promotion is not possible, and a person can be hired in a succession of temporary appointments when there is a hiring freeze on permanent positions.

However, the curious observation to be made about the bending of the rules is that once discovered, new rules are added to prevent future occurrences. The rigidity of the merit system, which stimulated the rule-bending in the first place, is easily reinforced when a new rule is added to prevent future abuses.

PROFESSIONALISM IN PUBLIC PERSONNEL ADMINISTRATION

Many personnel administrators find themselves in the difficult position of defending a system that encourages its own abuse. The abuse comes not so much from partisan political sources any longer, but because public personnel systems themselves can hinder objectives they seek, namely, effectiveness and efficiency. The abuse also comes from the lack of a consistent professional orientation of the public personnel administrator. Take for example a large personnel system where, in addition to a central personnel division, each agency has its own personnel section. The agency's line managers will expect their personnel section to bend the rules when necessary, and if they don't they are likely to be seen as disloyal. The central personnel division expects the agency's personnel section to uphold the merit system, and when the section tries to be flexible it is seen as playing politics. Finally, the employees expect the personnel section to represent their interests, and when the section tries to be neutral, it is accused of representing management. Thus, professionalism in public personnel administration rests on at least two fundamental decisions.

First, the question of whom the public personnel officer serves must be settled. The view that the personnel officer can serve the interests of both management and labor is more of an intellectual than practical expectation. Serving two masters whose interests frequently clash puts the personnel officer in a compromising position in which there are few rewards from either management or labor.

The decline of civil service commissions in favor of personnel departments within the executive branch of government, a trend endorsed in the National Civil Service League's Model Personnel Law of 1970, symbolizes a movement toward resolution of this question in favor of management. But a more important element in this decision will be the role of labor unions. The more that labor unions protect employee rights, the less relevant the policing purpose of the merit system becomes, and the more vivid the managerial role of personnel departments will appear.

Second, professionalism centers on expertise that clients value. Considering management as the primary client of public personnel systems of the future, this expertise will be found in the mastery of the knowledge associated with the mediating activities identified earlier. To reiterate, personnel administration of the future, in addition to its technical role, will emphasize activities that formally extend it beyond its present technical core: labor relations, the rights of employees and due process in personnel management; reliance on the applied behavioral sciences to achieve productivity and improve the quality of public employees' working life. Finally, it will emphasize the relationship between fiscal and personnel administration, including human resource planning.

SUMMARY

Intervening between environmental demands for changes in the way the core personnel functions operate and the need at the technical level of personnel management for stability are four mediating activities—affirmative action, human resource planning and cutback management, productivity, and labor relations. These activities function as a bridge where environmental demands for change in the personnel system and the internal expectations for stability are negotiated.

The future role of the public personnel administrator is found in acceptance of an open systems perspective as well as mastery of these activities, which rarely fall naturally within any organizational division's formal scope of responsibility. These activities suggest that contemporary knowledge, skills, and abilities of personnel officers will involve labor relations and the legal aspects of human resource management, the applied behavioral sciences, and the relationship between personnel management and fiscal planning.

In addition to developing a mastery over these mediating activities a successful forward movement in the field of public personnel management requires an unequivocal answer to the question "Who does the personnel officer serve?"

KEY TERMS

mediating function
four mediating activities
juridical nature of public personnel management
applied behavioral sciences
human resource planning
managerial flexibility in personnel management

DISCUSSION QUESTIONS

1. Identify the intervening role of the mediating activities in a public personnel system. What does it mean to describe a mediating activity as a "metaphorical bridge"? A bridge between what?
2. Draw and describe a diagram that includes the following parts: mediating activities; economic, social, political conditions and technological changes; four core values; four core personnel functions; legislative, executive, and judicial outputs.
3. How would you differentiate between the traditional role of the personnel officer and a more modern role? What are the new areas of knowledge, skills, and abilities a contemporary personnel office must develop? How do these new areas relate to the mediating activities?
4. Describe how the rules designed to protect the merit system can encourage its own abuse. How does the link between efficiency and morality make it difficult to change a public personnel system?
5. If you were on an International Personnel Management Association Committee on "Professionalism in Public Personnel Administration," what issues would you ask the committee to address?

EXERCISE

Review these job specifications and answer the questions that follow.

PERSONNEL OFFICER I

00-05-1-001

Definition of Work

This is technical and administrative personnel management work in a small or moderate-sized institution within an agency, or in an assigned phase of a larger personnel program.

Work involves planning, organizing, and directing a personnel program in a smaller institution within a central agency such as Social and Rehabilitation Services and the Department of Corrections; or administering a specialized phase such as training, recruiting, or classification in a large personnel program; or assisting in administering the total personnel program in a large state agency. Work may include responsibility for employee benefits, safety, labor relations, and transactions. Work usually includes providing guidance and advice to organizational officials in developing and adopting internal personnel policies, procedures, and practices, and maintaining effective liaison with central personnel officials. Supervision may be exercised over clerical and other employees. Work is performed independently under administrative supervision and is reviewed through records, reports, and conferences for adherence to Civil Service and internal policies and regulations.

Examples of Work Performed

Plans, organizes, and directs a personnel program; performs work associated with classifications, labor relations, workmen's compensation, benefits, affirmative action, transactions, and recruitment; directs the preparation of transaction or position description forms.

Directs a limited training program in a large agency; designs and maintains an orientation program for employees; develops and maintains supervisory and other functional training programs in such areas as personnel, payroll, and budget; exercises functional supervision over technical and professional employees involved in training programs.

Directs a comprehensive recruitment program; supervises clerical and other employees in interviewing, screening, and selecting applicants, as well as contacting vocational schools, placement agencies, universities, and other sources to secure the services of qualified personnel to fill agency vacancies.

Interviews job applicants; reviews their qualifications for employment; informs applicants of Civil Service examination and certification procedures and provides them with information on agency personnel needs; refers promising applicants to agency supervisors.

Assists in a classification program; maintains a position inventory and current position descriptions; classifies or reclassifies positions to lower-level classes; prepares organizational charts; counsels employees and departmental employees concerning procedures in classification.

Supervises a small group of clerical employees engaged in nontechnical personnel activities.

Interprets Civil Service laws, rules, and procedures to departmental officers and employees, and interprets departmental and employee needs to the Central Personnel Division.

Performs related work as required.

Required Abilities, Skills, Knowledge

Knowledge of public personnel administration theory and practice including position classification, salary administration, employee performance evaluation, employment and placement methods, management-employee relations, affirmative action-equal employment opportunity, recruitment, employee benefits, and staff training and development.

Knowledge of supervisory methods and techniques.

Knowledge of English usage and written communication format.

Ability to communicate information concisely and accurately.

Ability to read, interpret, and apply written information to daily work.

Ability to interact with employees, supervisors, management officials, representatives from other state agencies, and the general public in order to establish and maintain effective working relationships with them.

Ability to carry out work with only general administrative guidelines and policy direction.

Ability to use arithmetic (addition, subtraction, multiplication, division, percentages).

Education and Experience

Graduation from an accredited four-year college or university with 20 semester hours of coursework in personnel, public, or business administration, counseling or guidance or psychology. Technical or professional experience in personnel work may be substituted for the required college study on a year-for-year basis.

1. Whom does this personnel officer serve?
2. What do you think are the primary duties and responsibilities? How do these relate to the core personnel functions?
3. What connection do you see between the job specifications and the mediating activities?
4. Would you conclude that this job is more oriented toward a traditional or modern personnel role?
5. How would you rewrite the specifications to make them more contemporary? Can one person be responsible for all that you have written into your new job specifications?

5

Affirmative Action

Affirmative action represents one of the "cutting edges" of public personnel management. It is a mediating variable that affects the way the agency recruits, hires, and promotes employees. It is also a societal value that proposes an organizational decision rule—employees should be hired, assigned, and promoted so that their percentage is proportionate to the percentage of their counterparts in the available labor market.

Affirmative action supports using public jobs to enforce public policy outcomes. Specifically, it favors achieving the value of social equity by recruiting, hiring, and promoting people from different societal groups, in proportion to their percentage of the population. This objective conflicts with other selection criteria and values, among them seniority, administrative efficiency, and political responsiveness. For example, it challenges the traditional emphasis of collective bargaining on seniority as the basis for promotion or retention, particularly during periods of limited agency growth or cutback management. Second, in questioning the job-relatedness of traditional selection criteria, it challenges managers' predictable bias toward objective testing, education, and experience as indicators of applicant quality. Lastly, by increasing the pressure on elected officials to fill appointive jobs with proportional representation of women and minorities, it indirectly attacks the "old boy" network that has traditionally been the mechanism by which top administrative positions have been filled.

Affirmative action is one of the most critical public personnel activities because of its crucial role in the procurement process, and its conflict with other values that have traditionally affected this process. In recent years, however, societal values have altered to reflect increasing concern with political responsiveness and administrative efficiency. This trend has placed increased pressure on the value of social equity and the affirmative action process by which it is accomplished.

Despite this apparently declining importance, affirmative action will have a significant effect on public employment, although probably not the same effect as was initially intended. It has brought the courts into the public employment arena more strongly than ever. And the judicial impact on public employment has penetrated all the core personnel functions. The *Uniform Guidelines* have asserted that equal employment opportunity provisions extend to all employment decisions, including allocative functions like training opportunities; development functions like performance appraisal; and into the sanction arena with a renewed emphasis on procedural due process.

The lasting impact of affirmative action may be found in the penetration of judicial values into public personnel management. These values include most clearly the rights of individuals and due process in decision-making. We hope that a major outcome of this impact will be the continued progress toward more objective and performance-related job analyses, pay plans, job descriptions, and performance appraisal techniques; and toward more emphasis on procedural due process in employment decisions.

By the end of this chapter you will be able to:

1. Understand why confusion exists between equal employment opportunity and affirmative action, and distinguish between them
2. Discuss legislation and executive orders that require affirmative action compliance by public employers
3. Describe the process of voluntary and involuntary affirmative action compliance
4. Describe the impact of the judicial system in interpreting and enforcing affirmative action laws
5. Understand how to prepare an affirmative action plan for a public agency

EQUAL EMPLOYMENT OPPORTUNITY AND AFFIRMATIVE ACTION

Most people, including many public officials, consider equal employment opportunity (EEO) and affirmative action (AA) to be the same thing. They are not. EEO law provides for equality of treatment; AA law provides for preferential treatment of certain groups. Thus, EEO most closely reflects the value of individual rights, while affirmative action is intended to ensure another value—social equity.

Given that EEO and AA are often referred to in the same breath and are almost invariably the responsibility of the same public agencies, it is understandable how confusion between them has arisen and been perpetuated. Yet the distinction between them can be made clearer by remembering that they are based on two different laws—EEO on Title VII of the 1964 Civil Rights Act, and AA on the 1972 Equal Employment Opportunity Act.[1]

With a few exceptions, Title VII prohibits employers, labor organizations, and employment agencies from making employee or applicant personnel decisions based on race, color, religion, sex, or national origin. Although it originally applied only to private employers, the concept of EEO was extended to local and state governments by 1972 amendments to the 1964 Civil Rights Act. These revisions also increased the authority of the designated compliance agency (The U.S. Equal Employment Opportunity Commission, or EEOC).

By contrast, affirmative action not only prohibits discrimination, but *requires* employers, unions, and employment agencies to take positive steps to reduce underrepresentation through the preparation and implementation of affirmative action plans (AAPs). The two most critical laws enforcing the value of social equity, through the achievement of proportional representation, are Executive Order 11246 and the 1972 Equal Employment Opportunity Act (which really concerns AA rather than EEO).

Executive Order 11246 (signed by President Johnson in 1965) prohibited such discrimination by most employers providing goods or services to the federal government. Furthermore, it required those with 50 or more employees, and government contracts of $50,000 or more annually, to prepare a written plan identifying any underutilization of women and minorities, and establishing goals and timetables to correct it. This executive order has had great impact, since all subcontractors of covered contractors must also comply—regardless of the size of their contracts or the number of their employees. By 1981, this executive order applied to more than 29,000 companies, including all major corporations and universities— 41 million workers in all.[2] A subunit of the U.S. Department of Labor (The Office of Federal Contract Compliance Programs) prepares regulations and enforces this order. Under the 1972 Equal Employment Opportunity Act, state and local governments were also required to file affirmative action plans, and to take the same types of remedial action required of federal contractors.

Given the different objectives of EEO and AA, it's easy to see how enforcement strategies might conflict. Take the use of quotas for minority hiring or promotion. Under AA, an affirmative action plan might establish a goal of hiring more minorities or women until their percentage of employees in the organization equalled their percentage of representation in the population. Under EEO, however, concern for the protection of each applicant's or employee's rights would prevent the establishment of a hiring quota ("three of the next 10 employees hired must be black," for example)—unless such a quota were established by a court order or a consent decree. Also, under cutback management conditions, it has often proved difficult to achieve either goals (because of the importance of seniority as a promotion criterion) *or* quotas (because of freezes on hiring or promotions).

OTHER LEGISLATION AND EXECUTIVE ORDERS

Although Title VII, EO 11246, and the 1972 Equal Employment Opportunity Act illustrate most clearly the meaning of EEO and AA—and the differences between them—other laws, executive orders, and court cases are also important.

1. *The Equal Pay Act of 1963* is an amendment to the Fair Labor Standards Act of 1938. It prohibits employers from discriminating against employees with regard to pay on the basis of sex. The law requires "equal pay for equal work" and defines equal work as that "the performance of which demands equal skill, effort and responsibility."[3]

2. *The Age Discrimination in Employment Act* prohibits employers from discriminating in employment on the basis of age. It specifically protects employees aged 40 to 70. Its coverage was extended to state and local government employees by amendments to the Fair Labor Standards Act in 1974.[4]

3. *Title VI of the Vocational Rehabilitation Act of 1973.* Section 503 of this Act requires all employers with federal government contracts over $2500 to take affirmative action to hire and advance in employment qualified handicapped individuals, that is, those who with reasonable accommodation can perform the essential functions of the job.[5]

4. *The Vietnam Era Veteran's Readjustment Assistance Act of 1974* requires federal government contractors, including state and local agencies which receive federal grant funds, to employ and advance in employment disabled veterans and veterans of the Vietnam era.[6] For federal agencies, this law augments the *Veteran Preference Act of 1944,* as amended, which provides employment preference for disabled veterans and their dependents.

AFFIRMATIVE ACTION COMPLIANCE: VOLUNTARY AND INVOLUNTARY

Once an EEO/AA law is passed by the legislature, it must be executed by the executive branch of government, and enforced by the judiciary. This is true for both the federal laws itemized above and the fair employment laws passed by individual states. At the federal level, a number of different agencies are responsible for affirmative action compliance: the U.S. Equal Employment Opportunity Commission (EEOC), the Department of Labor (Wage and Hour Division, and the Office of Federal Contract Compliance

Programs), and the Department of the Treasury (Office of Revenue Sharing). These laws, the employers and practices they cover, and compliance agencies are shown in Table 5–1.

Table 5–1 identifies the source of external environmental impact, particularly with regard to an agency's or government's procurement function, and it shows that the EEOC has primary responsibility for compliance of federal agencies with affirmative action laws. It is assisted by the Department of Labor, which enforces the Equal Pay Act and the Age Discrimination in Employment Act.

The 1972 Equal Employment Opportunity Act also requires that *state and local* governments develop their own affirmative action plans. Indeed, pressure for passage of the 1964 Civil Rights Act originally came from those states that had passed state "fair employment practice" laws prior to the enactment of federal legislation. Typically, states have created an equal employment opportunity office within their personnel department or department of administration. This office assists and monitors state agencies in assessing utilization of minorities and women, developing affirmative action plans, and implementing specific programs necessary to achieve them. The EEOC has oversight responsibility for state affirmative action programs.

Most urban counties and larger cities also have an affirmative action compliance office attached to either their personnel department or department of administration. The role of this office, and compliance procedures relative to the EEOC, are the same as for state agencies. Both states and substate governments that receive grants or contract funds from the federal government are also responsible for complying with the guidelines of the Department of Labor, Office of Contract Compliance Programs. At times, the compliance process is rendered difficult by differences of opinion among compliance agencies over the appropriateness of a particular agency's personnel policies and procedures.

In practice, both the EEOC and the DOL may delegate their own administrative oversight functions, with congressional approval, to other federal agencies that are more directly responsible for assisting and monitoring state and local agencies in that functional area. For example, the U.S. Department of Education is responsible for monitoring the affirmative action plans of local school districts, while the Department of Health and Human Services is responsible for monitoring the plans submitted by federally assisted hospitals and clinics.

Since 1978, all federal affirmative action compliance agencies have used identical regulatory standards to determine whether underemployment exists and whether selection criteria are valid. These are the *Uniform Guidelines on Employee Selection Procedures*, issued jointly on August 25, 1978, by the EEOC, the DOL, the Department of Justice, and the U.S. Civil Service Commission (now the Office of Personnel Management).

TABLE 5-1. Public Agency AA/EEO Laws and Compliance Agencies

LAW	PRACTICE COVERED	AGENCIES COVERED	COMPLIANCE AGENCIES
Age Discrimination in Employment Act of 1967, as amended (1978)	Age discrimination against employees aged 40–70	All public agencies	Department of Labor (DOL)
Civil Rights Act of 1964 1. Title VI 2. Title VII (as amended, 1972)	Employment discrimination (all practices, particularly testing, selection, promotion, and training)	All agencies receiving federal funds; all public agencies, state and local governments, and educational institutions	EEOC; if conciliation fails, EEOC may file charges in federal court on behalf of plaintiffs
Equal Employment Opportunity Act (1972)	All employment practices which discriminate on the basis of nonmerit factors	All public agencies	EEOC
Vocational Rehabilitation Act of 1973, Section 503	Discrimination against the physically handicapped	All public agencies	Department of Labor
Equal Pay Act of 1963	Equal pay for equal work regardless of sex	Those with employees covered by the Fair Labor Standards Act, including (since 1972) all elementary and secondary teachers and administrators	Wage and Hour Division, Department of Labor, under provisions of the Fair Labor Standards Act
E.O. 11246 E.O. 11375	Nonmerit discrimination (all practices covered by Title VII); affirmative action programs required	Federal contractors and subcontractors	Office of Federal Contract Compliance Programs (DOL); other federal agencies have delegated responsibility for ensuring compliance of their own contractors
1976 amendments to the Revenue Sharing Act of 1972	All employment practices which discriminate on the basis of nonmerit factors	All recipients of federal revenue-sharing	Department of the Treasury (Office of Revenue Sharing)

⟨Voluntary affirmative action compliance occurs when a public agency complies with affirmative action laws (and pursuant regulations issued by compliance agencies) through the preparation of an affirmative action plan which (1) identifies underutilization, (2) establishes full utilization as a goal, (3) develops concrete plans for achieving full utilization, and (4) makes reasonable progress toward full utilization.

Involuntary affirmative action compliance occurs when a public agency alters its personnel practices as the result of investigation by a compliance agency resulting in a negotiated settlement, when the employer settles out of court with a compliance agency by means of a consent decree, or by court order.⟩Understanding these three types of involuntary compliance requires some background knowledge of the process by which compliance agencies investigate employers.

An applicant or employee who believes he or she has been denied rights under an affirmative action law may file a complaint with the appropriate compliance agency (that is, with the agency responsible for execution of the particular law). Generally, the history of affirmative action compliance has been characterized by a steadily increasing number of complaints, with considerable delays in their investigation. For example, the number of complaints filed with the EEOC increased from about 5000 in 1976 to 70,000 in 1976.

Filing a complaint results in a formal investigation, which may result in the complaint being rejected or the compliance agency filing a formal complaint against the employer. Frequently (in over half the EEOC's cases), complaints have been resolved "administratively" (with a finding in favor of neither the applicant nor the agency). This occurs when an applicant moves or changes jobs, which is quite likely since the average waiting time to investigate a complaint is over 30 months.

⟨Once a complaint is formally filed by the compliance agency, the employer may acknowledge this complaint's validity by agreeing to the changes in its employment practice specified by the compliance agency, plus whatever specific remedies are prescribed to "make whole" the injury to the employee or applicant. This acknowledgment is termed a *conciliation agreement*. It is entered into by the employer primarily to avoid costly litigation and court interference in cases where a court decision would likely go against the employer.

A *consent decree* is a second type of involuntary affirmative action compliance. It is an agreement between an employer and a compliance agency negotiated with the approval of a court, and subject to court enforcement. Unlike the conciliation agreement, it is usually entered into by an employer in litigation who "smells" defeat. In such cases, the employer may consider it advantageous not to admit guilt, and to agree to terms which may be more advantageous than those resulting from a guilty verdict. However, some consent decrees have resulted in the payment of substantial damages—such as the 1973 settlement between American Telephone & Telegraph and the EEOC, which cost AT&T about $15 million.[7]

The most damaging form of involuntary compliance is a *court order*. In situations where a compliance agency has taken an employer to court over alleged affirmative action violations, and neither a conciliation agreement nor a consent decree can be agreed upon, a guilty verdict against the employer will result in court-ordered remedies. These can include mandatory hiring quotas, changes in personnel policies, and financial compensation for the victims of discrimination. Because of the cost and unfavorable publicity associated with lengthy litigation resulting in a guilty verdict, public officials will generally do their best to avoid this outcome.

Involuntary compliance carries the threat of the ultimate financial penalty—loss of federal aid to the noncomplying public agency. Amendments were added in 1976 to the Revenue Sharing Act of 1972, making suspension of federal funds a mandatory administrative procedure in cases where investigation reveals that discrimination has occurred and conciliation efforts fail. These amendments require the federal Office of Revenue Sharing (ORS) to investigate complaints within 90 days, and empower the Secretary of the Treasury to suspend all federal funds to the agency within 30 days from the date of the ORS's ruling.[8]

COURT CASES

The judicial system is responsible for enforcing compliance with those administrative action laws. Equally important, court cases (or case law, as they are sometimes called) serve to resolve conflicts between laws and administrative regulations. Such conflicts occur because laws and regulations result from interest group pressure, and interest groups frequently have competing goals. This is true even within a single field such as affirmative action.

For example, the Age Discrimination in Employment Act makes it illegal to discriminate against those aged 40 to 70. This age limit was previously 40 to 65, until it was raised in 1976. Yet because of previous patterns of employment discrimination, it can safely be concluded that most employees protected by this law are white males. One effect of this law, though certainly not intended, has been to delay the advancement of minorities and women into managerial positions. Thus, the new law has made it more difficult for employers to comply with the affirmative action requirements of statutes such as the 1972 Equal Employment Opportunity Act.

Affirmative action is also confusing in that enabling legislation is frequently quite vague as to the ways in which the law is to be executed. In most cases Congress or a state legislature will simply create an administrative agency and delegate to it the authority to develop rules and regulations to execute the intent of the law, within limits determined either by the size of its budget or the outcome of subsequent budget hearings.

The federal court system has acted in this fashion to resolve a number of issues arising out of affirmative action law. Chief among these have been the following: (1) how is discrimination determined? (2) under what circumstances is discrimination legal? and (3) what remedies are appropriate?

The most easily understood definition of discrimination is *prima facie* discrimination, which occurs when an employer does not hire any representatives of a particular group despite their availability in the labor market. Such blatant discrimination, commonplace before the passage of the 1964 Civil Rights Act, occurs only rarely today. The more widely utilized definition is the so-called "bottom line," which holds that discrimination can be considered to have occurred against a person if (a) he or she is a member of a particular group protected by law, and (b) the percentage of employees from that group hired by that employer is significantly less than their percentage in the available labor market. It should be noted here that whether the employer intended to discriminate is irrelevant as long as the effect of discrimination against an individual or group can be demonstrated. While this definition may seem complex, in practice it simply requires that a compliance agency compare census data with the employer's affirmative action compliance reports. If women, for example, constitute 50 percent of the labor market and only 20 percent of an agency's employees, it is evident that females are being discriminated against. While such incidental factors as the size of the agency or the nature of the local labor market may alter such calculations somewhat, most cases of discrimination are evident enough to be detected "interocularly" rather than "statistically." That is, they hit you between the eyes! This "bottom line" definition of discrimination was first enunciated in the *Uniform Guidelines,* issued by the federal government. Under this definition, parts of a selection process that have an adverse impact may continue to be used as long as the total process results in no adverse impact (discrimination) against a particular group. While the general concept of proportional representation meets with court approval, the "bottom line" definition of discrimination was voided by the U.S. Supreme Court in *Connecticut v. Teal,* June 21, 1982. As a result of this case, it is to be expected that employers will have to validate each portion of a battery of selection criteria.

Discrimination by itself is not illegal. The illegality of discrimination, under affirmative action law, occurs only to the extent that it is based on factors unrelated to job performance. What's the difference? Let's take an example and see. The authors of this text are both over 35, short, and neither has had any experience as a basketball player. Would it be discriminatory to deny either of us the opportunity to try out for the Los Angeles Lakers? Of course it would—others would be given the chance to make the team and we would not. Would this discrimination be legal? Yes, it would be, on grounds that rejection was legitimately job-related. As any avid fan could tell you, the chances of a person over 35, and without any basketball experience making a professional team are so slight as to be nonexistent. Federal courts have used the same logic in resolving similar affirmative action complaints that have arisen. Once a plaintiff has demonstrated that discrimination has occurred against him or her, it is up to the employer to demonstrate that the discrimination was job-related. This principle, which will be further clarified in Chapter 7, was enunciated in the landmark case of *Griggs v. Duke Power Company.*

Once discrimination has occurred, and it is found to be based on factors unrelated to the job, what remedies are available to "make whole" the injury done to the employee or applicant? Generally, the interest of the court has been to restore to the employee or applicant the employment rights he or she would have had if the original discrimination had not occurred. This can include back pay, priority consideration for promotion, plus punitive damages if the discrimination occurred deliberately rather than inadvertently. For example, the court awarded retroactive seniority from the date of their employment applications to black applicants denied jobs as long-distance truck drivers.[9] Conversely, other cases cloud the issue of intent and effect. *Burdines v. Texas Department of Community Affairs* concludes that the employer is not liable for discrimination unless the employee or applicant can demonstrate discriminatory intent. Likewise, *International Brotherhood of Teamsters v. United States* affirmed that bona fide seniority systems (those not created or maintained for purposes of racial discrimination) were immune from being overturned, provided that any discriminatory effect occurred prior to the effective date of Title VII.[10]

Finally, it is clear that federal courts are sensitive to charges of "reverse discrimination" against white males. In *Bakke v. The Regents of the University of California,* the Court declared it illegal to reserve a quota of slots for admission to medical school for minority students who were less qualified than other white applicants who were rejected. Race could be considered as one factor affecting an admissions decision, but not the only factor.[11] But in *United Steelworkers of America v. Weber,* the Supreme Court held that Title VII does not prohibit private, voluntary race-conscious affirmative action plans provided that (1) the plan is temporary, (2) it is undertaken to eliminate manifest racial imbalance, (3) the imbalance is in traditionally segregated job categories, and (4) the plan does not require the discharge of white workers or create an absolute bar to their advancement. In effect, *Bakke* was a split decision supporting individual rights; *Weber* a split decision supporting social equity. It remains to be seen how future court decisions will reconcile these values, which often conflict.

In sum, the key to voluntary affirmative action compliance lies in viewing it as a remedy for deficiencies in personnel practice—not as a vehicle for pursuing objectives that go beyond those remedies. Recently, the EEOC itself learned a painful lesson on this difference. The Supreme Court, ruling on a class action suit brought by a white male attorney on behalf of all white males who had sought professional positions in the agency since 1974, held that the EEOC's affirmative action plan was too aggressive, that minority and female representation exceeded labor force expectations, and therefore disadvantaged white males.[12]

HOW TO PREPARE AN AFFIRMATIVE ACTION PLAN

The resolution of questions such as those discussed above has injected the courts into the public employee procurement function as never before. Moreover, in order to meet the minimum standards for compliance with the 1972 Equal Employment Opportunity Act (as public employers) or of Executive Order 11246 (as contractors of the federal government), affected employers must prepare an affirmative action plan and have it ready to submit to the appropriate compliance agency, either the EEOC or the OFCCP, when asked to do so. Fortunately, preparation of the plan itself is not difficult, though it may later be difficult to justify some of the agency's previous employment practices, or to win administrative support for the implementation of alternatives. An affirmative action plan involves three stages: (1) conduct a utilization analysis, (2) establish affirmative action goals, and (3) develop programs for attaining them.

A utilization analysis is simply a comparison of the numbers and percentages of employees in an agency against their numbers and percentages in the local geographic area, and/or the "relevant labor market." First, let's deal with the question of which groups we are talking about. The *Uniform Guidelines* lists five distinct "classes" of employees, with each class being divided into male and female:

1. American Indian or Alaskan Native
2. Asian or Pacific Islander
3. Black, not of Hispanic origin
4. Hispanic
5. White, not of Hispanic origin

The affirmative action office may collect this information through personnel records, taking a "head count," or a combination of these techniques. It helps to be aware, however, of the importance of classifying individuals correctly. For instance, the personnel manager of a Georgia aerospace firm was fired some years ago when it was discovered that his efforts to improve the hiring of minorities had resulted in the addition of several Indian engineers to the staff. Unfortunately, they did not qualify as minorities because they were from the subcontinent of India, rather than people "having origins in any of the original peoples of North America, and who maintain cultural identification through community recognition or tribal affiliation."[13]

Next, the personnel manager or affirmative action compliance officer should compare the agency's utilization of particular groups with their availability in the appropriate labor market. Availability is a difficult concept. It includes the following candidates: those currently employed in the occupation, those qualified but currently employed in another occupation; those trained in the occupation; those experienced but currently employed, etc. These data can be obtained from a variety of sources: the Bureau of the Census (U.S. Department of Commerce), the Bureau of Labor Statistics and the Women's Bureau (U.S. Department of Labor), the EEOC, and the respective employment services in each state.

Availability is also influenced by the geographic boundaries of the appropriate labor market. For example, a local government recruiting for a maintenance worker may consider only a local labor pool, and therefore simply post a job vacancy announcement and advertise in the local paper. In this case, the "defined labor market" would consist of that geographic and occupational area reached by these methods. This would differ from the usual practice in recruiting a public agency director. In this case, the geographic area would be regional or national, and advertisements would be placed in nationwide professional journals (for example, *Public Administration Times*). If there is a great difference between the availability of minority group members in a particular geographic area or occupation, the chances are great that proponents of affirmative action for that group will suggest that the recruitment pool be widened (either geographically or occupationally) so as to offer that group's members a greater opportunity for consideration.

The comparison of current versus ideal (proportional) utilization is best accomplished through the use of an Availability Analysis Work Sheet. An example is shown in Figure 5–1.

The second stage in preparing an affirmative action plan is to set a goal. Usually this is expressed as the representation of all groups in proportion to their representation in the available labor market. In other words, proportional representation. If the difference between the proportion of a particular group in the agency and in the labor market is great, you can conclude that discrimination has occurred and make proportional representation your goal. If the difference between these proportions is slight, and if the agency employs less than 50 employees, you may wish to use an appropriate statistical technique to determine the likelihood that the group is actually being discriminated against. The appropriate statistic is the *standard error of a proportion*, and instructions for its use can be found in the statistical appendix to this chapter.

The third stage of an affirmative action plan is the development of a

Labor Market		Occupation						Adjusted Availability
		(1) Major Occupation		(2) Other Intermediate Occupation		(3) Detailed Occupation		(4)
		No.	%	No.	%	No.	%	%
Defined Labor Market	TOTAL (Both Sexes)		100		100		100	
	Total Male Black Hispanic Asian American American Indian Other							
	Total Female Black Hispanic Asian American American Indian Other							
Next Larger Labor Market	TOTAL (Both Sexes)		100		100		100	
	Total Male Black Hispanic Asian American American Indian Other							
	Total Female Black Hispanic Asian American American Indian Other							

FIGURE 5–1. Availability Analysis Work Sheet

plan that describes how the agency intends to correct underutilization in specific program areas. Plans should specify the activity, time frame, responsible unit, and measurable objectives. Here are some examples:

1. Action: Identify four target positions that can be filled by upward mobility
   Responsible Official: Division Directors
   Target Date: February 24, 198___
2. Action: Prepare position descriptions and reclassifications for these positions (if necessary)
   Responsible Official: Personnel Department
   Target Date: April 18, 198___
3. Action: Prepare and distribute job vacancy announcements
   Responsible Official: Personnel Department
   Target Date: May 17, 198___

4. Action: Fill positions through selection and/or promotion
        Responsible Official: Personnel Director, Department Directors
        Target Date: July 1, 198___

AFFIRMATIVE ACTION AND THE PUBLIC MANAGER

In addition to its specific impact on the public personnel manager, affirmative action has a more general impact on all public managers and supervisors in that it affects the rules by which the procurement function is carried out. Thus, conflicts between social equity and merit, or even among alternative definitions of social equity, result in the application of confusing and contradictory decision rules regulating the procurement function.

During periods of agency growth, such as the 1960s and 1970s, managers could overcome these conflicts by hiring more people from all groups—as long as the "pie" was getting larger, everyone could get a bigger piece. Consequently, it was relatively easy for agencies to overcome barriers to compliance. For example:

> Agencies unable to recruit sufficient minorities or women were advised to target recruitment efforts toward those community organizations, schools, or media oriented toward these groups.
>
> Agencies unable to find sufficient minorities or women, even after targeted recruitment efforts, were encouraged to consider lowering the job qualifications to increase the size of the applicant pool.
>
> Agencies unable to promote sufficient minorities to more responsible positions were advised to consider remedial training, revision of qualifications for the promotional position, or promotional quotas enforced by being incorporated into the organization's reward system for managers.

However, during the 1980s, when allocation issues are paramount, affirmative action has come under increasing pressure. Its fundamental value conflicts remain, and it is no longer possible for everyone's employment opportunities to remain constant, much less increase, due to pressures for cuts in government spending. This means that values other than social equity can be expected to have much more influence over the procurement function than they otherwise might. For example, as economic and political conditions encourage emphasis on the value of administrative efficiency, concerns with productivity rise and procurement decisions influenced by factors not associated with productivity can be expected to recede. In addition, economic uncertainty increases the demand for public employment because people who value job security perceive the public sector to be less subject to layoffs than is the private sector. This means that different interest groups will increase their demands for public jobs to be allocated on the basis of whatever criterion benefits their members most. Thus, the political conditions that fostered concern for social equity in the 1960s and 1970s have given way to economic issues in the 1980s. As these conditions change, the value emphasis that affects public employment pressures can be expected to change as well.

One effect this has on public managers is that they tend to perceive affirmative action as increasingly onerous. Not only does it deprive them of flexibility and discretion in the procurement process, but also it is not likely to result in the selection of the best-qualified employees when knowledge, skill, and ability are the desired selection criteria. This means that managers will seek to evade responsibility for compliance by continuing to comply with the "letter of the law," but not with its spirit. That is, they will pick the person they want for the job, and then seek to reconstruct a selection or promotion logic that will "document" the legitimacy of the selection or promotion for affirmative action compliance purposes.

This tendency may be increased by the perception of many public managers that the Reagan Administration is less interested in affirmative action than have been previous administrations.[14] While this perception is based partly on statements by Reagan Administration officials criticizing the use of quotas or "red tape" in hiring, it is also fostered by the feeling that the Reagan Administration is not actively encouraging the goal of affirmative action.

This shift in values away from social equity and toward administrative efficiency places the personnel department in a difficult position because this department is responsible both to line managers for providing high quality applicants, and to outside affirmative action compliance agencies for full utilization of different disadvantaged groups. Understandably, cutback management heightens this role conflict by increasing pressure for productivity while maintaining pressure for social equity. Typically, personnel directors will respond by arranging a compromise, attempting to persuade compliance agencies of their "good faith efforts" while resisting the imposition of quotas rather than general affirmative action goals, and they will try to persuade supervisors to seriously consider giving employment preference to qualified women and minorities, other things being equal. It is not an easy task.

However, the perception by many administration officials that affirmative action is opposed by top executives is not entirely accurate. In most instances, executives would rather have clarity concerning decision rules than anything else, even if those rules placed other objectives ahead of what they perceived to be organizational efficiency or effectiveness. Because the meaning and the validity of affirmative action laws are based on case law, even a sudden change in the policy of a particular administration can do little to change compliance policies in the short run—though budget cuts or hiring freezes can have a tremendous effect on the agency's enforcement capacity. For example, if an employee files a complaint of discrimination with the EEOC, it will take that agency up to three years to conclude its investigation. If, on the basis of that investigation, the EEOC concludes that a violation of either affirmative action law or regulations has occurred, it must then take the agency to court if the agency will not voluntarily agree to sign a conciliation agreement. It can take several more years for the case to work its way through federal district and appellate court dockets, and to the Supreme Court if necessary. It is therefore safe to conclude that the same delays would occur in the dismantling of affirmative action policy, as had occurred in its construction.

In addition, the record of the Reagan Administration is by no means one of total opposition to affirmative action. For example, the U.S. Office of Personnel Management agreed in 1981 to a court supervised plan that would phase out the PACE examination—the primary written test for entry-level federal managerial jobs—and replace it with selection devices that are valid and that do not result in a disproportionate number of failures among black and Hispanic applicants.

Nor can it be concluded that the opposition of a particular presidential administration will bring about the demise of affirmative action. Political indifference and economic uncertainty create a difficult climate for affirmative action, but women and minorities are much more educated concerning their rights under existing affirmative action laws, and they are much more willing to take allegations of discrimination to court than they might have been 30 years ago.

AFFIRMATIVE ACTION AND PERSONNEL MANAGEMENT

Affirmative action is important to our understanding of public human resource management in three ways. First, it focuses upon the values and objectives of public employment by asking the question: "What should the general criteria be for allocating public jobs?" Second, affirmative action translates this value question into rules which the organization can then use to make individual decisions on recruitment, selection, and placement. Lastly, affirmative action is the response of individuals and groups inside the agency to the agency's application of decision rules, particularly with respect to the individual's perception of the equity and predictability of those rules.

For example, many police departments are operating under consent decrees that require that they take affirmative action to hire more minorities and women. That is, they are required to alter their recruitment, selection, or promotional policies and practices until the percentages of minorities and women approach their percentage of the population. The legal ideal is proportional representation, which supposedly demonstrates that all people have an equal opportunity to be considered for the position, regardless of race, religion, sex, age, or handicap. Yet other definitions of equity also affect selection. Most municipal civil service system rules give preference to veterans (that is, they add five or ten points to the passing score of veterans). This gives white males an advantage over equally qualified minorities and women in that a larger proportion of veterans are white males than is their proportion in the population. Or selection may be limited to those who can pass a strenuous physical examination, even though physical prowess may be a small part of the job. This test could bar older or handicapped candidates from consideration.

In each of these cases, conflict exists over what constitutes equity in public employment. More important, at least from the organization's viewpoint, is that conflict exists over the decision rules that govern selection. Is employment preference to be given to those from underrepresented groups, or to veterans, or to older or handicapped people? What happens when the organization is faced with a conflict between these values? Whom does it hire?

This conflict affects various people differently. Those applicants who are members of a particular group (say, veterans) are likely to favor the selection criterion that results in the greatest employment opportunity for their group.

SUMMARY

Affirmative action is a mediating function that has had a profound effect on public agency procurement (recruitment, selection, promotion and reassignment). It is based on the value of social equity, which is embodied in many federal laws and enforced by many affirmative action compliance agencies.

For the public personnel manager, affirmative action means preparing an affirmative action plan that determines underutilization and provides for various programs to correct it. For the public manager in general, affirmative action exacerbates existing conflicts over two questions: What criteria control procurement? How are conflicts among these criteria resolved?

Despite the current eclipse of social equity due to the renewed emphasis on other values (primarily administrative efficiency and political responsiveness), affirmative action will continue to have a profound impact on public administration because of its control over the procurement process and the increasing role of the judicial system in regulating employment decisions and ensuring procedural due process.

KEY TERMS

equal employment opportunity
affirmative action
Title VII
U.S. Equal Employment Opportunity Commission (EEOC)
Office of Federal Contract Compliance Programs (OFCCP)
Office of Revenue Sharing (ORS)
unfair discrimination
job-related
conciliation agreement
appropriate labor market
"bottom line"
adverse impact
Uniform Guidelines
affirmative action plan
utilization analysis
underutilization
proportional representation
case law

DISCUSSION QUESTIONS

1. What are the definitions of equal employment opportunity and affirmative action, and what is the distinction between them?
2. What federal agencies are responsible for affirmative action compliance? How do they coordinate their activities?
3. How has case law affected the interpretation of affirmative action legislation and executive orders? Identify five significant cases and discuss their importance.
4. What are the three important steps in the preparation of an agency affirmative action plan, and how is each of them carried out?
5. How has affirmative action affected public managers in general?
6. How has affirmative action affected public personnel management? What is its impact likely to be in the future?

EXERCISE: AFFIRMATIVE ACTION PLANNING

The City of South Fork has 1000 employees. Table 5–2 shows employee distribution by race, sex, and job type.

Compare this actual utilization with the percentage of each affected class in the South Fork labor market (see Table 5–3).

TABLE 5–2.   Utilization Analysis of City of South Fork

AFFECTED CLASS	MANAGERIAL POSITIONS	OTHERS	TOTAL
White male	175	325	500
White female	20	280	300
Black male	4	96	100
Black female	1	9	10
Hispanic male	0	80	80
Hispanic female	0	10	10
Native American male	0	0	0
Native American female	0	0	0
Total	200	800	1000

Next, answer the following questions about the utilization or under-utilization of different groups.

1.   What is the percentage of different affected groups employed in the city government of South Fork?
2.   Utilizing either estimates or the statistical significance of a proportion (see the statistical appendix to this chapter for instructions on how to use this statistic), determine which of the affected groups is underutilized in city government.
3.   Regardless of the extent to which affected groups are underutilized, are females generally utilized or underutilized in managerial positions in South Fork's city government? Use either estimates or the statistical significance of a proportion to determine your answer.
4.   What specific solutions would you recommend to correct underutilization problems? Consider each of the following: job design, recruitment, selection, promotion, and training.

TABLE 5–3.   Analysis of South Fork Labor Market

AFFECTED CLASS	NUMBER OF EMPLOYEES	PERCENTAGE
White male	15,000	30
White female	15,000	30
Black male	4,000	8
Black female	4,000	8
Hispanic male	6,000	12
Hispanic female	5,000	10
Native American male	500	1
Native American female	500	1
Total	50,000	100

5. What problems might you encounter in seeking to implement these solutions in a contemporary American city? How would you seek to overcome them? How successful do you think your efforts would be?

NOTES

[1]*The Civil Rights Act of 1964*, P.L. 88-352, 78 Stat. 241, 28USC ss. 1147 [1976]; *The Equal Employment Opportunity Act of 1972*, P.L. 93-380, 88 Stat.514, 2-0 USC 1228 [1976].

[2]E. Richard Larsen, *Sue Your Boss* (New York: Farrar, Straus, and Giroux, 1981), p. 130.

[3]*The Equal Pay Act of 1963*, P.L. 88-38, 77 Stat. 56, 29 USC ss. 206 [1976].

[4]*The Age Discrimination in Employment Act of 1967*, P.L. 90-202, 81 Stat. 602, 29 USC ss. 621-634 [1976].

[5]Vincent Ochoa, "Sections 503 and 504: New Employment Rights for Individuals with Handicaps," *Amicus*, Vol. 2, No. 5 (September 1977), 38–44.

[6]The Vietnam Era Veteran's Readjustment Assistance Act of 1974, S. 402, P.L. 93-508, 38 USC s. 2012.

[7]Equal Employment Opportunity Commission, *Eliminating Discrimination in Employment: A Compelling National Priority* (July 1979), pp. III–(5-11).

[8]Larsen, pp. 105–26.

[9]*Franks v. Bowman Transportation Company*, 424 U.S. 747, 47 L.Ed.2d 444, 96 S.Ct. 1251 [1976].

[10]*International Brotherhood of Teamsters v. United States*, 97 S.Ct. 1843 [1977].

[11]Cheryl M. Fields, "In the Wake of Bakke," *The Chronicle of Higher Education*, Vol. 16, No. 18 (July 10, 1978), 1 ff.

[12]*Equal Employment Opportunity Compliance Manual* (Englewood Cliffs, N.J.: Prentice-Hall, Inc., November 19, 1982), pp. 5–6.

[13]U.S. EEOC, instructions to Form EEO-4.

[14]Robert S. Greenberger, "Firms Prod Managers to Keep Eye on Goal of Equal Employment, *Wall Street Journal* (May 17, 1982), 20–21.

STATISTICAL APPENDIX

The *standard error of a proportion* is a computation of the likelihood that the proportion or percentage of employees from a particular group in an organization is representative of their proportion in the available labor market. For example, 20 percent of an employer's work force may be black. If 25 percent of the applicants in the available labor market are black, what is the likelihood that the company is discriminating against blacks in its employment practices?

To find the standard error of a proportion,

1. compute the following formula:

$$\sigma \text{ prop} = \sqrt{\frac{pq}{N}}$$

when: p = the proportion of a particular group in the available labor market
$q = 1 - p$
N = the number of employees in the company

2. find the significance of σ prop in z score units by the following formula:

$$z = \frac{p_s - p_t}{\sigma \text{ prop}}$$

when: p_s = the proportion of a particular group in the company
p_t = the proportion of a particular group in the general labor market
σ prop = the standard error of the proportion

Example

Thirty percent of the employees in an employer's available labor market are black. Twenty percent of the 200 employees in the company are black. Are blacks being discriminated against (underutilized) by the employer?

$$\sigma \text{ prop} = \sqrt{\frac{pq}{N}}$$

when: $p = 0.3$
$q = 0.7$
$N = 200$

$$\sigma \text{ prop} = \sqrt{\frac{(0.3)(0.7)}{200}}$$

$$\sigma \text{ prop} = \sqrt{\frac{0.21}{200}}$$

$$\sigma \text{ prop} = 0.032$$

$$z = \frac{p_s - p_t}{\sigma \text{ prop}}$$

when: $p_s = 0.2$
$p_t = 0.3$
σ prop $= 0.032$

$$z = \frac{0.2 - 0.3}{0.032}$$

$$z = 3.125$$

Analysis of a table of z scores, found in most statistics texts, shows that there is less than a one-tenth of one percent probability that a z score as large as this would be obtained by chance if the employer were not discriminating. Therefore, statistically significant evidence exists that the employer is discriminating against blacks. The significance of differences in percentages of groups increases as the number of employees in the sample increases.

6

Recruitment

In an era of cutbacks in government agencies, it may seem strange to include a chapter on recruitment. Yet this topic is important, even under today's conditions, for recruitment programs within public agencies are influenced not only by economic factors and program priorities, but also by existing affirmative action laws and court decisions. There are still some occupations for which public agencies are actively recruiting, and in filling these it is necessary to understand affirmative action law and its impact on the recruitment process.

By the end of this chapter you will be able to:

1. Discuss the objectives of public agency recruitment
2. Differentiate between recruitment of career bureaucrats and political executives
3. Evaluate the impact of economic conditions, affirmative action laws, and court decisions on the recruitment process
4. Describe recruitment techniques used by public agencies to attract applicants to shortage-category occupations
5. Develop a recruitment plan for a public agency

OBJECTIVES OF RECRUITMENT

Public agency recruitment has several major objectives corresponding to the opposing values introduced in Chapters 2 and 3. First, advocates of social equity view recruitment as the initial step in placing more employees from various affected groups in government jobs. Second, advocates of administrative efficiency view recruitment as the process by which qualified employees are attracted to government jobs. Lastly, advocates of political responsiveness view recruitment of political executives as the means by which elected officials can gain and keep control over career bureaucrats in government agencies.

As would be expected, each of these advocates tend to view the recruitment process differently. Affirmative action proponents see recruitment as an advertising or marketing device to increase the "pool" of available applicants. The existence of this pool can then be used to increase pressure on government agencies to hire more minorities, women, handicapped people, and so on, for it contradicts the common response of managers: "We'd love to hire more . . . , but we can't find any who are qualified!" In addition, being eligible for government positions can serve as an incentive to underutilized groups to maintain or increase their efforts toward further education or professional experience, which would in turn increase their marketability.

Public personnel managers are primarily involved with the recruitment of employees who occupy civil service positions in local, state, or federal agencies. These are the "bureaucrats"—police officers, secretaries, teachers, and administrators—who comprise most of the government's employees. Personnel managers work closely with line managers to attract qualified applicants to available positions. Hence, their objective is a managerial one, namely, achieving predictable or increased productivity while keeping recruitment costs low. Public personnel managers view recruitment as the process that gives them access to potential employees. Naturally they favor maintaining as large a pool of eligible applicants as possible. However, this desire is curbed by the cost of recruitment, for overly large applicant pools will increase the cost of selection without necessarily attracting more highly qualified applicants. Moreover, an unduly large applicant pool will increase applicant pressure for selection, thereby raising false hopes among applicants and creating a public relations problem for the agency.

Therefore, particularly during uncertain economic conditions, public agencies tend to favor limited recruitment efforts "targeted" toward those particular occupations forecasted as being needed by the agency. On the other hand, agencies do not wish to unduly discourage potential applicants, for changing economic or political conditions may spark a need for more active recruitment efforts.

Existing employees generally have little interest in the recruitment process unless the agency is recruiting from outside for applicants to fill promotional vacancies for which they consider themselves qualified. Naturally they would prefer selection from within the agency under these circumstances.

Outside organizations (such as universities seeking to place graduates, or civil rights organizations reflecting the social equity mission of the public service) prefer recruitment strategies that provide their clientele with maximum opportunity to apply for public jobs, and a fair chance of being selected for them. Because people must apply for public jobs before they have a chance of being selected for them, some of the same environmental conditions and values affect recruitment as well as selection.

RECRUITMENT OF POLITICAL APPOINTEES

The two previous objectives of recruitment involve recruitment as a tool of social equity, or recruitment as a technique for maximizing managerial efficiency. A third objective, which was briefly mentioned in the previous section, will be discussed here, namely, recruitment as a strategy for ensuring political responsiveness.

The public often views government agencies as run by career bureaucrats: people who issue statements, hold press conferences, and are the subject of media coverage. Yet few of these individuals are career government employees. Almost all agency heads at the local, state, or federal level are political appointees. That is, their positions are not classified, they are not appointed as the result of a competitive examination, and they serve at the pleasure of the elected officials who appointed them. At the federal level, the following positions are political appointments: all Cabinet Secretaries, Assistant Secretaries, and Under-Assistant Secretaries; all heads of commissions and independent agencies; all judges; most congressional employees. At the state level, political appointments comprise most judges, legislative employees, and heads of administrative agencies. At the local level, all department heads, the city clerk, and city manager serve at the pleasure of an elected council, commission, or mayor (depending on the particular structure of local government). If one is unfamiliar with a particular organization, the difference between appointed and career officials can usually be determined by asking which positions are "classified" and which are "exempt." Classified positions are filled through the civil service system and are thus career appointments; exempt positions are outside the civil service system, and are thus filled by political appointment.

Political appointees view public employment from different perspectives than do career administrators. The political appointee owes primary allegiance *upward*—to the elected official who appointed him or her. Political appointees have been named to their posts because of political or psychological loyalty to the elected official. They usually are not familiar with the structure or functions of the government agency they run, although the appointment may have been based on a solid background of related experience in the private sector. Political appointees are likely to perceive career bureaucrats as politically unresponsive, in that their loyalties are to programs or policies that have been part of previous administrations. Hence, appointed officials may view civil service protections as "red tape" that keeps "unproductive civil servants" in their jobs. Naturally career bureaucrats see continuity in public policy as dependent upon them, and they can easily come to view political appointees as "unprofessional."

These differences in the perceptions and objectives of career bureaucrats and political appointees highlight one of the continuing tensions within public employment—the conflict between the values of managerial efficiency and political responsiveness. Even more interesting, they occur within a personnel activity—recruitment—where the fundamental value affecting the process is social equity, as defined by affirmative action laws and enforced by administrative agencies and judicial pronouncements.

EXTERNAL INFLUENCES ON RECRUITMENT

Three environmental influences have a major effect on public agency recruitment policies and practices: economic conditions, political factors, and affirmative action laws and court decisions.

Economic conditions are important because, as will be discussed in the chapter on human resource planning, they affect the supply of applicants for public jobs, which are viewed as being more stable, and therefore less subject to layoff, than are jobs in the private sector. An economic recession will normally increase the number of available applicants for public employment. It will at the same time decrease the number of people resigning jobs in public agencies in order to enter the private sector. The budget process "drives" human resource planning for public agencies, in that forecasts of human resource needs are developed within limits set by revenue projections. A recessionary economy will reduce projected revenues, particularly for governments that rely heavily upon progressive and elastic taxes (such as income taxes), or upon tourism. Lower revenue projections will cause lower recruitment efforts since the demand for new employees will be reduced.

Political factors influence recruitment because changes in program priorities affect the relative supply and demand for various occupations. In the 1960s, President Kennedy's pledge to "put a man on the moon by 1970" created thousands of jobs for aerospace workers, but just as quickly, cutbacks in the manned space flight program in the early 1970s put these same people out of work.

The sheer size of government employment, particularly in a city like Washington, D.C., where a large percentage of employees work for the federal government, means that public agencies' needs will have a great impact on the labor market. Increased demand for a particular "shortage

Economic Growth:

1. Scarcity of qualified applicants
2. High demand for internal promotions and external recruitment
3. Open and continuous recruitment

Economic Decline:

1. Surplus of qualified applicants
2. Low demand for internal promotions and external recruitment
3. Recruitment managed or targeted toward shortage-category occupations

FIGURE 6–1.　Economic Conditions and Recruitment

category" occupation will drive up salaries for those jobs. If pay scales are not flexible enough to accommodate higher wages for people in these positions, the result is likely to be higher turnover or recruitment of applicants with lesser qualifications. At the same time, a depressed economy enables government agencies to increase their hiring standards and lower turnover rates, thereby leading to increases in efficiency.

Lastly, affirmative action laws and court decisions have had a fundamental effect on recruitment. Title VII of the 1964 Civil Rights Act, for example, prohibits discrimination in any "employment practice," including recruitment. The Age Discrimination in Employment Act (1967) specifically protects individuals aged 40 to 70; and Section 503 of the Vocational Rehabilitation Act of 1973 extends similar protection to the handicapped.

These laws have required that public agencies be much more explicit about how they advertise job vacancies. In brief, they must recruit so as to give all possible applicants an equal opportunity to be informed about, and to apply for, available vacancies. If particular groups are underrepresented in the agency, recruitment efforts must be targeted toward individuals from those groups.

One court decision has made recruitment easier for local governments. In *McCarthy v. Philadelphia Civil Service Commission* (1976), the Supreme Court upheld a Philadelphia law requiring city employees to live within the city limits.[1] The Supreme Court ruled that the residence requirement was neither arbitrary nor irrational, and that it did not interfere with the constitutional right of public employees to travel. Obviously several different arguments are enhanced by this decision. First, since minorities tend to live within cities rather than suburbs, it may be viewed as a strategy for increasing the employment opportunities of minorities. Second, since city employees who live within the city may be assumed to be more concerned about their fellow residents than those who live outside the city, the legality of residence requirements has a possible effect on employee productivity. Third, since residents of the city vote in municipal elections and nonresidents do not, this decision could support local political machines who maintain power by exchanging votes for jobs. Lastly, residence requirements are economically justified because they give the city a chance to recoup its funds by encouraging employees to spend there.

CENTRALIZED RECRUITMENT TECHNIQUES

Public agency recruitment techniques may be either centralized or decentralized. If the agency has several thousand employees, and if different departments recruit large numbers of clerical or technical employees for the same types of positions, centralized recruitment will frequently be used because it is more cost efficient. If recruitment is centralized, the central personnel agency will be responsible for requesting from agency personnel managers periodic estimates of the number and type of new employees needed in the future (the next quarter or fiscal year). The staffing needs of all agencies are entered into a computer, after being classified by occupational code and salary level, and a summary listing of all projected new hiring needs is produced.

In reality, producing an accurate projection of new hiring needs is rarely this simple. To begin with, it is not always possible for agencies to predict with accuracy their needs a year ahead of time. A political crisis, or a budget cut, can drastically affect their recruitment needs, and hence the quality of the estimate. Central personnel agency recruiters also realize that agency personnel managers will tend to overestimate the number of employees they require, just because from their point of view it is better to have too many applicants than too few. Naturally this conflicts with the need of the central personnel agency to reduce selection costs by reducing the number of applicants to the minimum number needed to ensure that all available positions are filled with qualified applicants. In addition, specialized positions require a greater ratio of applicants to projected vacancies, because a higher percentage of applicants is likely to be rejected by the selecting agency as not meeting the specialized requirements of the position, although they might all meet the general entry requirements for the field.

Based on all these considerations, the central personnel agency will issue a job announcement, which formally notifies applicants that a vacancy exists. To meet affirmative action laws and regulations, each job announcement must include the following information:

1. Job title, classification, and salary range
2. Duty location (geographic and organizational unit)
3. Description of job duties
4. Minimum qualifications
5. Starting date

6. Application procedures
7. Closing date for receipt of applications

The extent of recruitment efforts once a job vacancy is announced will depend upon several considerations: the geographic area of consideration, the length of time during which applications are accepted, and the necessity for targeted recruitment efforts. Typically, professional and managerial positions have a larger geographic job market than do clerical or technical positions. While recruitment for the latter may be local (conducted either through newspaper advertisements or phone calls to the local office of the state employment service), recruitment for the former may be regional or national (involving recruiting agencies or advertisements in national professional newsletters). Generally, job vacancies are "open" longer if the position is managerial than if it is clerical. This is because the creation of a larger geographic job market means that applicants take longer to learn about the vacancy and to submit their applications; and because agencies are generally able (and required) to predict managerial vacancies further in advance than clerical or technical ones.

If the agency underutilizes women or minorities, it will be interested in targeting recruitment efforts toward individuals from these groups. Community organizations, churches, shopping centers, minority newspapers, state employment services, and minority recruitment centers are all possible avenues for targeted recruitment. Given the hesitancy of many minorities and women to apply for jobs in public agencies in which they have historically had little opportunity for employment, it is to be expected that recruitment would also occur over a longer period of time if it were targeted toward these individuals.

DECENTRALIZED RECRUITMENT TECHNIQUES

Decentralized recruitment is most likely to occur in agencies that are relatively smaller, for which recruitment needs are limited, and in which each agency basically employs different types of workers. It is almost always used for professional, scientific, or administrative positions peculiar to a particular agency. For example, smaller towns may not have enough vacancies to utilize the services of a central personnel department. Or the department heads may have successfully argued that their particular employees are unique to their own department, and that it is therefore more appropriate to handle recruitment and selection on a departmental level. Departments of police, public works, and sanitation are likely to make this argument at the municipal level. Particularly during a recession, where demand for public jobs is great but the number of available openings is few, many agencies will find it more effective to utilize decentralized recruitment because no cost savings can be gained through the increased efficiency which is possible with centralized recruitment.

If recruitment is decentralized, individual public agencies will go through essentially the same steps as are required for centralized recruitment, except that dealings with the central personnel agency are omitted. Agency personnel managers will work directly with the supervisors in their agencies to make periodic estimates of new hiring needs. Then agency recruiters will meet with agency affirmative action specialists to determine whether recruitment efforts should be targeted toward specific minority groups. After evaluating both the need for new employees and the affirmative action goals of the agency, the agency personnel director will determine what recruitment efforts are required. The job announcement process is exactly the same as occurs through a central personnel agency, except that applicants are requested to send their applications to the individual agency.

While individual agencies are likely to favor decentralized recruitment because it gives them more control over the process, it has the disadvantage of reducing the control that the chief executive has over expenditures or affirmative action compliance. In a centralized personnel system, for example, the chief executive will be able to stop new hiring simply by forbidding the central personnel agency from recruiting any new applicants, and from sending the names of any applicants already on the register (list of eligibles) to individual agencies. In a decentralized system where the chief executive has no direct control over the recruitment process, it is more likely that individual agency directors will insist on their right to recruit people to meet program needs, and to manage their own budgets more autonomously.

In addition, decentralized recruitment is more likely to result in reliance upon word-of-mouth recruitment techniques, particularly in smaller agencies. If underutilization of women or minorities is a problem, word-of-mouth recruitment will probably make it worse, in that existing employees will be those most likely to discuss the job vacancy with their white, male friends. Group pressure will make it unlikely that they will seek out qualified applicants who might be regarded by their coworkers as "different." In this situation, it is particularly important that formal job announcement and application procedures be scrupulously observed, and that recruitment efforts targeted toward the appropriate groups be enacted.

Some agencies utilize a combination of centralized and decentralized recruitment. For example, a central personnel agency may authorize individual agencies to recruit and test applicants independently, subject to audit by the central personnel agency once they have been hired. This compromise will provide for a greater degree of centralized control than is possible with a decentralized system, while at the same time providing agencies with timelier and more flexible recruitment than may be available from a central personnel agency.

"NAME REQUESTS"—POLITICS AND CIVIL SERVICE COMBINED

The use of "name requests" is a practice common in the federal government and in some state and local agencies. The practice attempts to combine the objectives of political responsiveness and managerial efficiency in the recruitment process. Under this system, agency personnel managers and supervisors actively recruit individuals whom they wish to hire in their agency. Or elected officials request career bureaucrats to see if a certain person is qualified to be hired for a civil service position in the agency. Following this lead, the agency personnel manager will then advise the "preferred" applicant to apply for eligibility to the central personnel agency. As soon as the individual receives his or her eligible notice of rating, the agency sends a certification request to the central personnel agency asking that this applicant be certified to them if he or she is within reach on the register. Particularly for higher-level administrative or professional vacancies, up to 90 percent of those hired through outside recruitment may be found through the name-request system rather than through "open" requests (agency requests for certification which ask only for the most qualified applicants, without specifying a particular applicant by name).

Some commentators dislike the name-request system because it leads to cronyism in hiring and may work against the social equity or administrative efficiency objectives of the agency. In addition, this system may restrict employee rights. It is often charged that agencies, by tailoring the job specification to match the exact qualifications of the "name request" whom they wish to hire, unfairly exclude other qualified applicants who are already on the register. However, defenders of the practice point out that it allows the agency to interview and preselect qualified applicants, thereby reducing the paperwork the central personnel agency must normally complete for all eligible applicants, regardless of their level of interest in the job or the agency's interest in hiring them. In the last analysis, they contend the agency's manager and personnel department are the most qualified to make the selection decision. After all, they are the ones who will have to meet agency objectives through the newly hired employee; and they are the ones who will suffer the consequences if the employee is unqualified for the position.

From our perspective, it is easy to see the name-request system as an attempt to combine both managerial efficiency and political responsiveness. If it works well, managers get employees who meet at least the minimum civil service standards for efficiency, plus political officials have cemented a friendship or furthered their own program objectives. Of course, it may not work well, for one of these values may be achieved at the expense of the other. In addition, the basic objection to the practice comes from advocates of social equity and individual employee rights, who justifiably claim that the "name-request" system restricts access to public jobs.

PUBLIC AGENCY RECRUITING IN THE 1980s

Given uncertain economic conditions, stable or declining revenue forecasts, and continued pressure for affirmative action compliance, what are public agencies currently doing about recruitment?

Some are not recruiting. Since personnel costs (pay and benefits) normally constitute about 70 percent of the typical public agency's budget, a hiring freeze is one of the easiest methods of reacting to a revenue shortfall. Others, however, have adopted modified hiring freezes, which make it necessary to justify the creation of new positions or to fill existing ones. If nothing else, these hiring slowdowns place an increasing burden on the line manager, or agency personnel officer, to justify the need for hiring a new employee.

Despite these general trends, two classes of public agency continue to recruit actively in most areas of the United States—health care facilities and law-enforcement agencies. This recruitment is due to the fact that these are unusual labor markets. Even under current economic and political conditions, job vacancies exist and salaries must remain competitive to prevent job-hopping. Agencies in these areas utilize the techniques one would expect in a situation where the demand for applicants exceeds the supply. They conduct massive recruitment, advertising, and public relations campaigns; they pay current employees bonuses for referring to the personnel office applicants who are later hired by and remain with the agency; they conduct recruitment efforts targeted toward economically depressed areas. For example, police departments in the growth states of Texas and Florida have conducted extensive recruitment in more economically depressed northern cities, in hopes of inducing laid-off or apprehensive law-enforcement officers to migrate south. Hospitals conduct the same type of recruitment campaign for nurses.

These examples indicate that the market for many technical and managerial employees is complex, fragmented, and constantly changing. Shortages may appear and disappear quickly. This means that for potential shortage-category occupations, personnel managers must continue to inform potential applicants of the vacancy, maintain their interest in the job, and raise the interest of those candidates who have been identified as prime candidates for positions when and if they become available.[2] This means matching applicants with a job not only on the basis of the skills and abilities required, but also on the relationship between the values of the applicant and the opportunities the job offers for the fulfillment of those values.[3]

In conclusion, it must be remembered that recruitment is not an isolated function. The demand for new employees in an agency is determined by the growth of the agency, which is in turn determined by changes in program priorities set by or for that agency or government. In addition, the need for recruitment is affected by the utilization and turnover rate among existing employees. For example, many state welfare agencies, even those currently operating under budget cuts, have a continual need to hire additional caseworkers. Why is this? Budget cuts have led to increased demands that caseworkers meet higher productivity figures, either because a recessionary economy has increased case loads, or because caseworker positions have been abolished when attrition occurs in order to save salary dollars for the agency. As a result of these increased case loads, caseworkers must spend less time with each individual client. Hence, they can only help those whose needs are minimal, yet they are constantly confronted by those clients whom they soon realize the agency has insufficient resources to help. This leads to conflict between the agency's perception of the caseworkers' role, borne out of budget necessity, and the caseworkers' own perception, based on the value of client service. This role conflict leads, in many cases, to resignation from the agency. This is particularly true if the job description given them during the recruitment process differs from the one they see after working in the position.

The point of this example is that recruitment is the front end of the staffing process. It is affected by the utilization and retention of employees after they are hired. But how employees are recruited also affects their turnover rate.

SUMMARY

Recruitment is an important personnel function because it reflects the impact of three opposing values on public personnel management: social equity, managerial efficiency, and political responsiveness. The varying objectives of advocates of these three values, and the different ways in which they approach the recruitment process, show how these values are put into practice.

Recruitment is related to the environment not only by values but also by economic and political conditions that affect the demand and supply of public agency employees. Program priorities are set externally. Economic conditions determine the supply and quality of available applicants.

It is important that an agency's or a government's recruitment practices take these three values into account. Not only must managerial efficiency and political responsiveness be attended to, but also the recruitment process must be coordinated with the agency's affirmative action objectives.

KEY TERMS

applicant
eligible
targeted recruitment
shortage-category occupation
residence requirement
job vacancy
job announcement
classified position
exempt position
"name request"
centralized recruitment
decentralized recruitment

DISCUSSION QUESTIONS

1. How do each of the following values influence public agency recruitment objectives and methods?
   a. social equity
   b. political responsiveness
   c. employee rights
   d. administrative efficiency
2. How do political, economic and budgetary considerations influence public agency recruitment?
3. What affirmative action laws and court cases have had the greatest impact on recruitment? Why?
4. Compare and contrast the decentralized and centralized recruitment process. What are the characteristics, advantages, and disadvantages of each system?
5. How can recruitment efforts be targeted toward shortage-category occupations, or toward underutilized groups?
6. How does the "name-request" system attempt to balance the values of managerial efficiency and political responsiveness? Why is it opposed by advocates of social equity and employee rights?
7. How can methods of recruitment affect turnover rates?

EXERCISE

You are the director of personnel for a large public hospital in south Florida. Despite the fact that you pay salaries that are competitive with those of other area hospitals, you have a chronic shortage of nurses. In order to determine how best to address the issue, you schedule a meeting with the director of nursing. Together, you assemble the following facts related to the situation:

The hospital employs about 800 nurses in the following areas: obstetrics, pediatrics, critical care, oncology, medical-surgical, and geriatric. From among these fields, the greatest demand is for critical care and oncological nurses.

The average turnover among staff nurses is 40 percent annually. This is much higher than other hospitals in the area. Most turnover occurs among those who have worked for the hospital less than three years.

The clientele of the hospital has been slowly changing from mostly Anglo to primarily black and Hispanic. This change matches the changing composition of the neighborhood within which the hospital is located.

The director of nursing maintains a network of professional colleagues at area colleges and vocational training centers. These provide a steady flow of applicants into the hospital, though primarily for Licensed Practical Nurses (LPNs) and non-nursing positions.

The hospital belongs to the South Florida Nurse Recruiting Association, which conducts cooperative advertising campaigns to recruit nurses in northeastern cities, the Philippines, Jamaica, and Canada.

Many employees leave because they find the administrative structure and procedures of the hospital frustrating and confusing, particularly at the unit level. Some feel that bureaucratic procedures and paperwork are considered more important than quality of patient care.

Many applicants who are interested in working as nurses in the hospital cannot qualify because they have relatively poor command of English. Although many of the hospital's patients are Haitian or Cuban, and therefore speak Creole or Spanish, the state license examination for nurses who wish to practice in the state is given in English.

The hospital's reputation is that of a "zoo"—a diverse array of patients, a workload that continues to expand to meet any increases in staff and financial resources, and high turnover contributing to lack of administrative continuity.

Nurses are treated as employees but are not encouraged to develop close relationships with other employees, or to feel a part of their work unit. Little orientation is provided; what is given is technical and procedural.

On the basis of this information, what suggestions can the two of you (the personnel director and the nursing director) develop to ease the recruitment problem among nurses? Develop a list of suggestions, bearing in mind the following points:

Recruitment is related to utilization and retention of personnel.

Some changes in hospital policy may require approval of the JCHA (Joint Committee on Hospital Accreditation), the State Board of Nursing, or the legislature. As you develop each suggestion, consider whether the hospital has the authority to make the change independently, or whether review and approval by some outside body would be required as well.

NOTES

[1]*McCarthy v. Philadelphia Civil Service Commission,* 96 S. Ct. 1155[1976].

[2]Michael Still, "The Technicalities of Hiring Technicians," *Personnel Management* (December 1978), 44–48.

[3]Gene E. Burton, "How to Prevent Dry Rot in College Recruiting," *The Personnel Administrator* (September 1975), 56–58.

7

Selection and Promotion

In most big cities, the selection and the promotion of police officers are hotly contested political issues. Advocates of increased efficiency insist that objective criteria (such as physical standards and test scores) be used. Elected officials want the flexibility to promote lieutenants and captains on the basis of their values and program priorities. Lastly, proponents of social equity insist that both of these criteria be modified in order to place more minorities or women on the force. Each time the police come under fire for alleged incompetence, brutality, or corruption, value advocates will use this opportunity to argue for a change in selection or promotion criteria and methods. This example illustrates the importance of these activities, and the procurement function in general, to public personnel management.

By the end of this chapter you will be able to:

1. Discuss the objectives of selection and promotion
2. Describe the laws relating to these activities in public agencies
3. Discuss the relationship between these activities and affirmative action, particularly with respect to the "bottom line" definition of discrimination
4. Describe the criteria for validating a selection or promotion criterion, including content, construct, and empirical validation
5. Discuss the advantages of alternative selection and promotion methods
6. Develop a strategy for validating selection and promotion criteria

OBJECTIVES OF SELECTION AND PROMOTION

Inasmuch as recruitment, selection, and promotion are all procurement functions, it could be expected that the same values and objectives would influence selection and promotion as were discussed in Chapter 6 relative to recruitment. This is the case. Promotion differs somewhat from selection, however, in that its objective is also *allocational*; that is, directed toward the distribution of rewards among employees.

Elected legislators and chief executives often view the bureaucracy as unresponsive to their values, program priorities, or personal preferences. Therefore they seek to establish selection and promotion criteria that emphasize compatibility with the elected official's political philosophy and programmatic aims. The way this goal is implemented can take a variety of forms, ranging from a "spoils system" in which most positions are filled through political patronage, to a "merit system" in which almost all employees are career civil servants with political appointees as agency heads.

In contrast, career civil service executives usually seek to insulate "their" agencies from political turmoil by endorsing selection and promotion criteria that emphasize technical qualifications and abilities. For example, they will defend the use of minimum standards of education and experience, written ability tests, objective performance standards, and credentials or degrees. In addition, though, they seek the flexibility in selection procedures that will allow them to use their experience in judging the potential of an employee.

The reason for this value conflict, which will be discussed in greater detail in Chapter 11, is that while both elected officials and career civil servants support "increased government effectiveness," each group tends to bring a different perspective to its work. Elected officials evaluate an agency program according to whether it is *responsive* to the public's needs, or *effective* at accomplishing the objectives of elected officials. Career civil servants also emphasize responsiveness and effectiveness, but in many types of governments (predominantly federal, state, and large cities) the executive civil servant must be responsive to the potentially opposing demands of the chief elected officials and the legislature.

In contrast to the elected official, the career civil servant, guided by technical expertise gained through a combination of longevity and experience, places more emphasis on *efficiency*—whether a program produces the maximum amount of services from allocated resources (regardless of the relationship of these services to interest group needs or legislative intent).

The public policy-making and implementation process is therefore a continuing accommodation between these values. While elected officials have the advantages of being able to achieve oversight through enabling legislation, appropriations, and the appointment of agency heads, career civil servants have the avantages of resisting control through their greater longevity, knowledge of agency programs and personnel, and subject area expertise. Thus, the relationship often results in a good deal of tension, not because each group is trying to obstruct the other, but because each group is genuinely interested in implementing the values that underlie its perspective.

This conflict notwithstanding, the dominant value influencing the public agency procurement process in recent years is social equity, because it represents the most current challenge to traditional procurement values. It can be assumed that affirmative action advocates would seek to modify selection and promotion criteria to favorably affect employment opportunities for particular groups, based on the justification that these groups had either been underutilized historically, or were deserving of preference because of their societal contributions. Naturally they would seek to appease proponents of political responsiveness and administrative efficiency by conceding that prospective employees meet minimum criteria established in light of these values. The frustration in trying to reconcile the values of political responsiveness and administrative efficiency has been a defining characteristic of public versus private personnel administration for some time. While utilization of public personnel systems to promote social equity in this country is not uncommon, in recent decades it has become the source of frustration, conflict, and hostility because it has centered on the issue of race in hard economic times.

The most effective way to deal with an equity claim is through the establishment of employment quotas. But this solution is rarely available, except as a court-ordered remedy for demonstrated discrimination. Hiring quotas based on nonmerit factors conflict most directly with the value of administrative efficiency.

Thus, a negotiated compromise must be reached between the values of social equity and efficiency. The compromise must be general enough to be acceptable to proponents of both values, yet specific enough to provide useful guidance to those who actually write the rules and guidelines that govern hiring practices in a local government agency. This compromise is worked out through the metaphorical bridge of affirmative action, where societal value conflicts and technical needs of personnel systems are mediated. Language such as the following is usually included in an affirmative action plan: "With two job candidates of equal qualifications, preference will be given to the minority applicant."

A major thesis of this book is that value conflicts that cannot be resolved at a societal level will result in unsuccessful attempts to reach consensus on operational rules for the application of those values to agency decisions. Advocates of opposing values will seek to impose decision rules on the situation that implictly (or explicitly) favors their value. This will be opposed by proponents of other values, who favor opposing decision rules. Given this situation, it could be expected that the laws favor special interests and could be contradictory (they are), and that this would result in the frustration of managerial efforts to develop clear selection and promotion criteria (they have).

SELECTION AND THE LAW

Generally speaking, the same constitutional provisions, laws, and executive orders apply to selection and promotion as were discussed in relation to affirmative action in Chapter 5.

1. The Fourteenth Amendment guarantees the equal protection of the law to all citizens.
2. Title VII of the 1964 Civil Rights Act, as applied to public agencies by the 1972 Equal Employment Opportunity Act, prohibits employment-related discrimination on the basis of nonmerit factors.
3. The Age Discrimination in Employment Act of 1967 (as amended in 1976) prohibits discrimination against people aged 40 to 70.
4. The Veteran Preference Act of 1944 provides for employment preference for veterans applying for federal jobs; and the Vietnam Veteran Readjustment Act of 1974 provides specific protection for Vietnam-era veterans.
5. Title VI of the Vocational Rehabilitation Act of 1973 prohibits employment discrimination against those with physical handicaps.

SELECTION, PROMOTION, AND AFFIRMATIVE ACTION

Affirmative action laws have affected selection and promotion in a number of areas. Chief among these are the definition of discrimination, the defensibility of discrimination on the basis of job-related criteria, and the appropriateness of remedies to discrimination. The last topic was discussed in Chapter 5; the first two will be discussed here.

Chapter 5 presented the concept of proportional representation as an organizational strategy reflecting the decision rule of granting preference, among equally qualified persons, to those belonging to the most underutilized group. Thus, one method of detecting discrimination (also known as underutilization or adverse impact) is by comparing the percentage of individuals from different groups in the organization with their percentage in the general population, or in the relevant labor market. Significant differences between the two percentages can be "eyeballed," or demonstrated statistically (significant difference of a proportion).

A second method of detecting discrimination is the 80 percent rule. This rule, presented in the 1978 *Uniform Guidelines*, states that discrimination has occurred against a particular group if the selection rate for that

TABLE 7–1. The 80 Percent Rule

ETHNIC GROUP	NUMBER OF APPLICANTS	NUMBER OF SELECTIONS
White Male	20	5
White Female	20	8
Black Male	15	5
Black Female	10	4
Hispanic Male	15	3
Hispanic Female	20	0
TOTAL:	100	25

group is less than 80 percent of the selection rate for the group with the highest selection rate. If this sounds confusing, look at an example to see how it works in practice.

An imaginary government agency has 25 job vacancies during one year. One hundred people apply for these jobs. The number of applicants and selections from each group are shown in Table 7–1.

Now, compute the percentage of selections to applicants from each group by dividing the number of applicants into the number of selections. According to this formula, these groups had the following selection percentages: white males: 25 percent, white females: 40 percent, black males: 33 percent, black females: 40 percent, Hispanic males: 20 percent, and Hispanic females: 0 percent. Next—and this is where it gets tricky—find the group with the highest selection rate, and divide that selection rate into the selection rate for each of the other groups. Where the result of this computation is less that 80 percent, discrimination has occurred against that particular group relative to the group with the highest selection rate. Table 7–2 shows how it looks in tabular form.

From Table 7–2, it can be seen that 25 percent of white males were selected, as opposed to 40 percent of white females and black females. Is the difference in selection rates large enough to demonstrate that adverse impact has occurred? Yes, it is. Dividing the selection rate for white females or black females (40 percent) into the selection rate for white males (25 percent) yields a result of 62.5 percent (or, to state it another way, 25 is 62.5 percent of 40). Since this result is less than 80 percent, discrimination (adverse impact) is held to have occurred against white males. Check to be sure you understand this method of computation by computing whether discrimination has occurred against other groups in Table 7–2.

The 80 percent rule is the key to the EEOC's "bottom line" definition of adverse impact. That is, adverse impact is deemed to have occurred if the total effect of a selection process results in a selection rate for any

TABLE 7–2. The 80 Percent Rule, continued

ETHNIC GROUP	NO. OF APPLIC- ATIONS	NO. OF SELECTIONS	% SELEC- TIONS	% SELECTIONS COMPARED TO HIGHEST	DISCRIM- INATION?
W Male	20	5	25	62.5	yes
W Female	20	8	40	(highest)	—
B Male	15	5	33	82.5	no
B Female	10	4	40	(highest)	—
H Male	15	3	20	50.0	yes
H Female	20	0	0	0	yes

particular group of less than 80 percent of the selection rate for the group with the highest selection rate. Until recently, it was held that this did not make it illegal for individual portions of a selection process to have a discriminatory impact, as long as the end result (cumulative effect of the process) was not discriminatory. For example, the selection process for firefighters might involve an application form, a background investigation, a written test, a physical examination, and a performance test. Under the "bottom line" doctrine, the local government would not have to show the job-relatedness of any of these requirements as long as their cumulative impact resulted in a passing rate for any particular group of at least 80 percent of the passing rate for the group with the highest pass rate.

This reasoning was rejected by the Supreme Court in *Connecticut* v. *Teal* (1982). In this case, the High Court was called upon to decide the validity of a test used by the state to select employees as supervisors. Whites passed this test at a rate of 80 percent; blacks passed at a rate of 54 percent. Although the total appointment rate for blacks was highly favorable—of the 48 black applicants who passed the test, 23 percent were promoted, as compared with 13.5 percent of the 259 white applicants who had passed it—the Supreme Court ruled that a high *utilization* of blacks did not excuse the discriminatory treatment of those blacks who did not pass the test, unless the test itself could be shown to be job-related.[1]

It is no overstatement to assert that *Connecticut* v. *Teal* is one of the most significant affirmative action cases to be heard in the past ten years. Clearly, it prevents both employers and the EEOC from relying on the "bottom line" definition of adverse impact. It requires the elimination of the use of parts of an examination process as a barrier; and it reemphasizes the need for establishing the job-relatedness of tests through validation as set forth in the *Uniform Guidelines*. Yet it is ironic that pressure for test validation—which should come from administrators interested in better employee performance—has instead come from affirmative action advocates concerned about the detrimental effect of invalid, culturally-biased tests on social equity.

TEST VALIDATION

The impact on selection processes stemming from affirmative action, then, concentrates on what constitutes acceptable qualifications and how job qualifications are determined. This emphasis is seen in the area called *test validation*—the determination of the extent to which a selection device is related to a job. Even though validity is stimulated through a social equity concern, it is theoretically consistent with the value of administrative efficiency as well. What is curious, however, is the infrequency with which selection devices in the public or private sector were validated prior to the 1964 Civil Rights Act and pursuant court cases such as the one described earlier in this chapter. In other words, pursuit of the social equity value has pushed merit systems into a trap of their own making. While merit systems purport to promote efficiency, until recently most utilized selection devices that could claim only a modest degree of job relatedness. In addition, they also were discriminatory against women and/or minority group members.

But affirmative action law, and subsequent case studies, established the relationship between test validation and employer defenses of discrimination as lawful. After a plaintiff has demonstrated adverse impact to the satisfaction of a compliance agency or federal court (using either *prima facie* discrimination, the underutilization rule, or the 80 percent rule), it is then the responsibility of the defendant (the employer) to demonstrate the validity of the selection requirement. In other words, validation of a selection or promotion criterion is not legally required unless adverse impact has resulted from its use. This fundamental doctrine and the concept of validity as justification for discrimination were first clarified by another Supreme Court case—*Griggs* v. *Duke Power Company.*

Prior to the passage of the 1964 Civil Rights Act, it was alleged that the Duke Power Company had routinely discriminated against blacks by denying them employment in all classes of jobs except as laborers. After 1964, it was argued, the company continued to discriminate against blacks, but instead of using blatantly discriminatory practices, it instituted a new requirement: Employees wishing to transfer to nonlaborer positions would first have to pass a mathematical and verbal aptitude test. Somewhat coincidentally, blacks passed this test at a much lower rate than did whites. When questioned about its use, company officials claimed that the test was legal under Title VII; it was a professionally developed employment test that could therefore be legally used to separate qualified from unqualified employees. Even though its impact on blacks was admittedly discriminatory, this discrimination was neither intended nor illegal under Title VII. In other words, it was not unfair discrimination.

When the Supreme Court ruled on this case in 1970, it established several fundamental provisions that have remained viable to this day in affirmative action law. Initially, it defined a test as any selection or promotion device used to award or deny an applicant a position, regardless of whether it is a written test, an education or experience requirement, or a background investigation.

Once the plaintiff has demonstrated adverse impact, it is the responsibility of the defendant (the employer) to demonstrate that this discrimination is legal, that is, that it is job-related. The *Uniform Guidelines* established three validation strategies as acceptable: empirical, construct, and content validation.

Empirical validation, also known as *criterion validation,* requires that a test score be significantly correlated, in a statistical sense, with important elements of job performance. For example, let's assume that we have developed a written test that we wish to use to examine applicants for the position of personnel director. Over the past several years we have given this test to several hundred applicants, hired them regardless of the results, and later evaluated them on the basis of a performance evaluation test (which actually measures desired work performance). When we compare the written test results with the performance evaluation scores, we get the results shown in Table 7–3.

This test is unquestionably a good predictor of subsequent performance as a personnel manager. If you had to state the relationship between pre-employment test scores and subsequent job performance, you would conclude that the test score, divided by ten, was a very close approximation of the subsequent performance evaluation. Of course, this assumes that a

TABLE 7–3. Empirical Test Validation

APPLICANT NAME	TEST SCORE	PERFORMANCE EVALUATION SCORE
Allen	70 (out of 100)	7 (out of ten)
Smith	45	4
Jones	93	9
Hammell	94	10
Wolfe	88	9
Kendall	62	6
Taylor	55	6
Mendoza	82	8

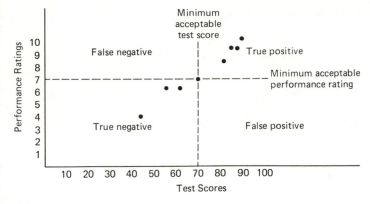

FIGURE 7–1. Test Scores and Job Performance

satisfactory performance can be established and measured by the organization's performance evaluation system, an issue discussed in Chapter 12.

The relationship between these test scores and subsequent job performance scores is plotted in Figure 7–1. The matrix is divided into four quadrants separated by a passing grade of 70 on the test and a minimum performance rating of 7. The goal of any selection device is to place most "hires" into the upper-right quadrant. These are the people who score well on the selection device and then also turn out to do well on the job. Similarly, another goal of a good test is to place applicants in the lower-left quadrant, such that those who do poorly on the test would also be those who would do poorly on the job.

The more scores that fall in these two quadrants, the more valid a test is; in other words, the better job it will do of predicting subsequent work performance. Most tests do not have anything near the predictive quality of our example. This means that people who do poorly on the test might end up doing well on the job (the upper-left quadrant), or that other applicants might score high on the test but not perform well on the job (the lower-right quadrant). Table 7–4 summarizes these relationships. The more valid the test, the easier it is to produce true positives and true negatives; the less valid the test, the greater the occurrence of false positives and false negatives. It is extremely rare that a test will have as much predictive validity as the example in Figure 7–1. However, using regression analysis techniques described in the statistical appendix to this chapter, test specialists can set minimum acceptable test scores that guarantee, at least to the point of high statistical probability, that applicants who score above this level on the test will perform satisfactorily as employees. Also, such techniques can be used to determine whether tests are valid for all races and ethnicities.

Construct validation involves both identifying psychological traits or aptitudes that relate to successful job performance and devising a test that

TABLE 7–4. Test Scores and Job Performance

	TEST SCORE	JOB PERFORMANCE
1. True Positives (hire, do well)	high	high
2. True Negatives (not hire, do poorly)	low	low
3. False Positives (hire, do poorly)	high	low
4. False Negatives (not hire, do well)	low	high

measures these traits. For example, most insurance companies give psychological tests to applicants for sales positions. These tests purport to measure the applicant's congeniality, outgoing nature, liking for people, and other traits supposedly related to the ability to sell. Typically, these tests have been developed by identifying the best salespeople in the organization, giving them a psychological test measuring a variety of traits, and establishing a personality profile of the "ideal salesperson." This profile is then used as a yardstick against which the characteristics of applicants are measured. Those who approximate this yardstick are hired; those who do not are more carefully screened.

Content validation requires that minimum qualifications be logically related to the duties of the position for which they are required. This type of validation requires that the job be analyzed to determine its duties, the particular conditions that make work easy or difficult, realistic performance standards, the skills, knowledge, and abilities required to perform these tasks up to these standards under these conditions, and the minimum qualifications required to ensure that an applicant would have these SKAs (Knowledge, Skills, and Abilities). For example, it is logical to assume that a prison guard, responsible for transporting prisoners by car from one location to another, would be required to have a chauffeur's license before being hired for the position. An example of the application of the relationship between content validation and job analysis is given in the section on results-oriented job descriptions (RODs) in Chapter 9.

Content validation, therefore, links the functions of affirmative action and job analysis. But in addition, it connects them with a third function, productivity. This is because the establishment of a logical relationship between duties and qualifications is not only a defense of *validity*, but is also a justification for discriminating between qualified and unqualified applicants on the basis of their anticipated *performance*. It would follow from this that a content-valid job description (such as a ROD) could be used to assess the validity of a selection or promotion criterion by measuring the performance of an employee hired on the basis of that criterion. As we will see in Chapter 12 on performance evaluation, one appraisal method—the behaviorally anchored rating scale (BARS)—has been developed with this objective.

While each of these validation methods is equally acceptable to the EEOC (and other federal affirmative action compliance agencies), each is considered appropriate for different circumstances. Empirical validation requires that the organization hire many employees in the same type of work during a short time period, and some authors suggest that a group of several hundred employees is necessary.[2] Under the best of conditions, it would also require that the agency hire people who fail the test. After all, going back to Table 7–4, a valid test must not produce false negatives. In sum, empirical validation takes time and money, and it can be impractical for organizations that hire few people in a job class.

Construct and content validation both require relatively thorough job analysis to determine, respectively, the psychological traits or skills required for the position. Yet construct validity can be determined for a variety of jobs in different organizations, as long as those jobs are in the same occupational category (police officer, secretary, and so on). But because it requires the services of research psychologists, construct validation is beyond the abilities of most smaller public agencies. Its validity also depends upon the relationship between traits and performance, a link that is sometimes difficult to establish. This leaves content validation as the method of choice in the overwhelming majority of public positions. Its advantages are strengthened when one realizes that the development of RODs can result not only in content validation, but also in the enhancement of productivity and the clarity of performance expectations between employees and their agencies.

Table 7–5 shows the comparative advantages of alternative validation methods.

As *Griggs* v. *Duke Power Company* concluded, the use of a professionally developed test (aptitude or ability) does not in and of itself qualify the test

TABLE 7–5. **Comparative Advantages of Alternative Selection and Promotion Validation Procedures**

	VALIDATION PROCEDURE		
APPROPRIATE CONTEXT	Criterion	Construct	Content
1. Meets federal guidelines	yes	yes	yes
2. Requires job analysis	some	thorough	thorough
3. Requires large sample	yes	no	no

as legal under Title VII. Although the Tower Amendment to the 1964 Civil Rights Act (Section 703[h]) specifically approves the use of "professionally developed ability tests," provided that such tests are not "designed, intended or used to discriminate because of race, color, religion, sex or national origin,"[3] other court decisions have held that the mere fact that a test is professionally developed does not guarantee that its use is proper in a certain organizational context.[4]

In addition, what would normally be classified as nonmerit factors (for example, race, sex, or religion) may be used to exclude members of a particular group from employment consideration if membership in a certain race, religion, or sex is a legitimate job requirement. For example, chaplains may be required to be of a certain religion. However, the exclusion must be based on *business necessity* rather than mere convenience. For instance, the lack of separate bathroom facilities is not sufficient grounds for excluding women from a work site; it may be costly to build additional facilities, but this is not an insurmountable hardship. It is fair to say that employers who looked for considerable latitude in affirmative action laws through the liberal interpretation of bona fide occupational qualifications (BFOQs) and "business necessity" have been disappointed by the interpretation of these phrases by the federal courts. Clearly, these interpretations have acted so as to restrict the scope of these potential loopholes in favor of applicants and employees.

SELECTION AND PROMOTION METHODS

Before proceeding with a discussion of selection and validation methods, it will be useful to identify various steps and responsibilities in the staffing process:

1. Identify human resource needs
2. Seek budgetary approval to create and/or fill the position
3. Develop valid selection criteria
4. Recruit
5. Test or otherwise screen applicants
6. Prepare list of qualified applicants
7. Interview most highly qualified applicants
8. Select most qualified applicant

Different jurisdictions or agencies will carry out these general steps in different ways. The important point to be made here is that the line manager—the person the potential hire will actually be working for—is most heavily involved in steps 1, 2, 3, 7, and 8. The job of the personnel department is to assist the line manager in finding and hiring the best-qualified applicant (a *staffing* role), and to ensure that the staffing process takes place without the undue influence of politics or favoritism (a *policing* role).

The next step in the selection process is establishing the minimum qualifications for a position through job analysis. This concerns the particular methods used to measure the extent to which applicants or employees possess these qualifications. Nine methods are commonly used: review of biographical data, aptitude tests, ability tests, performance exams, references, performance evaluation (for promotional assessment of current employees only), interviews, assessment centers, and a probationary period.

A review of an applicant's education and experience, through a standardized application form, is fundamental to the selection process. One author estimates that over *one billion* résumés and job applications are completed and reviewed annually. Even if education and experience are not important selection criteria, they do serve other important purposes: They are a tally of the number and the qualifications of applicants for research and record-keeping purposes; they provide a basis for interviewing; and they serve as a component of the personnel record of selected applicants. Research suggests that the data provided through job applications are more valid and reliable than information provided during interviews.[5]

Four types of written tests are commonly used for selection purposes: aptitude, characteristics or traits, ability, and performance. Aptitude tests measure general intelligence or cognitive ability (for example, the federal government's now-discontinued Professional, Administrative Career Entrance (PACE) examination, or the Otis-Lennon). Aptitude tests are both relatively inexpensive to administer and score, and highly reliable. Some commentators are wary of the ease with which responses to psychological tests can be "faked" to match the presumed desired responses to the set of the test scores. However, interitem reliability checks can reduce the likelihood of this occurring. The validity of such tests, however, can range from minimal to moderate, depending on the quality of the job analysis and the resultant construct validation of the aptitude as a predictor. Several factors contribute to low validity. For one thing, as standardized tests, they are not adaptable to the particular objectives, conditions, or circumstances of different positions having the same title and general range of duties. As a consequence of this, some experts consider aptitude tests generally reliable for training purposes but less so for selection.[6] Others, however, consider them particularly useful for screening large groups of employees,[7] particularly if they are carefully validated so that they are not inherently biased against minority group members.[8]

A second type of paper-and-pencil test measures the applicant's personality traits or characteristics. The resultant personality profiles are then compared against profiles of current employees considered successful in the position, or against traits judged as job-related through construct validation. Examples are the Edwards Personality Preference Scale (EPPS), the Minnesota Multiphasic Personality Inventory (MMPI), and the Strong Vocational Aptitude Test.

Ability tests measure the extent to which applicants possess generalized abilities or skills related to job performance through empirical or construct validation. Examples would be verbal or mathematical ability, such as the Scholastic Aptitude Test (SAT) or the Graduate Record Examination (GRE).

The more closely an ability test simulates actual job tasks and context, the more it becomes a performance test. For example, tests of typing ability are given for varied typed content using different typewriters. A performance test would be position-specific in that it would measure an applicant's ability to type a given kind of material on the specific machine used on the job. Research studies generally confirm that ability tests are validly related to subsequent job performance.[9] While ability tests have been attacked as racially or culturally biased, further research will improve their validity.[10]

References are an important selection method. They are usually used to verify educational and employment records or to obtain information about the applicant's skills or personality. Their validity depends upon the opportunity that the individual used as a reference has had to observe the applicant, and upon the relatedness of this relationship to the prospective job. Understandably, references are usually positive, thereby limiting their effectiveness as selection tools. This weakness was accentuated by the passage of the Buckley Amendment (1974), which requires public agencies to acquire waivers from applicants before references can write confidential letters of recommendation.[11]

Previous performance evaluations are often used to assess potential for reassignment or promotion, or even qualifications for a particular promotional vacancy. They are valid to the extent that the ratings are based on job performance, and this performance involves the same skills or abilities as are required in the prospective job. Their reliability is based on the extent of interrater agreement among previous supervisory evaluations.

Interviews are a popular selection or promotion method. Most organizations will not hire an employee without one, because they believe the interview gives them the opportunity to observe an applicant's appearance and interpersonal skills, and to ask questions about subjects not adequately covered in the application form.[12] However, interviews are not recommended as a primary selection method. Not only do they take a good deal of the supervisor's time,[13] but they also require the supervisor to be a trained interviewer.[14] Since interviews are a prime method of rejecting candidates who look good on paper but might not fit into an organization, they are subject to close scrutiny as invalid selection criteria.[15] This will be particularly true with the Supreme Court's 1982 decision (*Connecticut* v.

Teal) invalidating the "bottom line" definition of adverse impact in favor of one focusing on each element of the selection or promotion process.

What, then, are some good guidelines to follow concerning interviews? If they are used to screen out applicants, they must be validated by the same methods as are other selection devices, that is, justified by job analysis and supported by a content validation strategy.[16] Structured interviews, those using a prepared series of questions relating to the position, previous experience, career objectives, etc., are preferable to unstructured ones. Panel interviews (those involving more than one interviewer) are more reliable than individual interviews, though they also increase the cost of this already expensive selection method.[17]

Assessment centers attempt to present several applicants with simulated job situations in order to stress their performance on job-related tasks. They are used in both the public and private sectors; in the public sector their use is most prevalent among law-enforcement organizations. If performance criteria are validated, they can be useful in selection, promotion, and career development. However, many centers seek shortcuts in the selection process as a way of bypassing validation procedures or ethical considerations.[18]

The last selection or promotion method is the probationary appointment. This technique possesses the highest possible validity and reliability factors because it measures actual performance on the job. However, it also carries the highest cost and greatest risk to the organization, since a potentially unqualified employee may occupy a critical position until he or she makes enough serious mistakes to be considered unfit for that position. The use of the probationary period places upon supervisors the responsibility of "weeding out" unsatisfactory or marginal employees before they attain career status (and hence the right to grievance hearings to protest a discharge after they have attained a "property interest" in their jobs), and upon personnel managers the responsibility of developing valid probationary period evaluation systems.

As might be expected, choosing among these nine alternative selection and promotion methods is difficult. These methods have differing degrees of validity, or job-relatedness. Second, they have varying degrees of reliability, or the consistency of scores for one applicant over time. Third, they range from the inexpensive to the costly. Even beyond these three criteria of validity, reliability, and cost are the values that alternative methods can enhance or retard. Those who favor agency efficiency tend to support selection methods that measure quantifiable qualifications cheaply and easily. This would include biodata, tests, and credentials. Those who favor political responsiveness support selection methods which provide information about an applicant's values or personality, or those which maximize flexibility for the hiring official. These are references, interviews,

TABLE 7–6.   Comparison of Selection Methods

METHOD	VALIDITY	RELIABILITY	COST
1. Biodata	moderate	high	low
2. References (letters of recommendation)	low	low	low
3. Aptitude tests	moderate	moderate	low
4. Characteristics or trait tests	moderate	moderate	low
5. Ability tests	moderate	moderate	moderate
6. Performance tests	high	moderate	moderate
7. Interviews	low	low	high
8. Assessment centers	moderate	high	high
9. Probationary appointment	very high	very high	very high

and the probationary period. Likewise, advocates of social equity favor reliance on the probationary period. They fear that tests and minimum education and experience, while easy to measure and effective at reducing the size of the applicant pool, will reject minority applicants who could perform well if hired ("false negatives").

Because each of these selection methods differs in value orientation, cost, validity, and reliability organizations must compare them.[19] Table 7–6 summarizes their comparative advantages. Usually standardized test scores are used to "screen out" persons unable to meet the basic requirements for a position, while interviews, assessment centers, or a probationary period are used to select the most qualified applicant from among those who are basically qualified.[20]

TEST VALIDATION STRATEGIES

Our discussion of test validation procedures indicated that this process is often time-consuming and costly. Given the limited resources of many personnel departments—and the unwillingness of personnel directors to devote resources to validation studies unless a selection or promotion system is questioned—how should public personnel managers treat the entire issue of validation? Our previous discussion in this chapter has indicated that validation is theoretically useful not only for social equity, but also for increased administrative efficiency. That is, a test that is valid will not only be legally defensible under affirmative action laws, but it will also result in the hiring of "true positives" and the rejection of "false negatives."

Yet while it is theoretically sound to validate *all* criteria for employment, personnel professionals may wish, or be forced by circumstances, to adopt the next best approach, summarized as follows:

1. *Identify the classes of positions with the largest number of employees.* Since most public organizations are pyramidal in nature, these are likely to be entry-level positions or first-level supervisory positions. It is easier to conduct empirical validation studies with large groups of employees; and these positions are likely to be those subject to the greatest pressure for access by different groups.
2. *Identify the positions most likely to be the subject of an affirmative action investigation or lawsuit.* Indications of this might be the rate of internal complaints, the experience of other similar organizations, or the presence of a high percentage of minority group members or women in lower-level positions from which the position in question is considered a promotion or a desirable lateral reassignment.

Given these two factors, personnel managers should prepare a schedule according to which selection procedures for all organizational positions will be periodically reevaluated. In presenting a budget request to management, personnel managers should emphasize the comparative costs and consequences of validation procedures versus affirmative action investigations or lawsuits. Remember—it can cost several thousand dollars to validate a test, but a successful lawsuit will cost several times this amount in court costs and attorneys' fees, plus the added expense of compensatory damages to the aggrieved employees or applicants.

The existence of a schedule for test validation will not in and of itself validate tests, but it may convince an EEOC investigator that your organization is making a "good-faith effort" to improve the job-relatedness of selection and/or promotion procedures. In such cases, the personnel managers should consider using the lever of impending administrative or legal sanctions to improve their bargaining power vis-à-vis management for additional funding for validation studies. In addition, the relationship between test validation and productivity would be an additional argument in its favor.

SUMMARY

Selection and promotion are important because they epitomize the conflict among the values of political responsiveness, agency efficiency, and social equity. The predominant impact of social equity on these activities is evidenced by the importance of affirmative action law.

These laws and regulations require that any test (selection or promotion device) be job-related. This can be demonstrated through empirical, construct, or content validation methods, each of which has its own advantages. Most agencies use combinations of selection methods, beginning with biographical data and ending with interviews or probationary appointments, to ensure that applicants possess the skills, knowledge, and abilities required for their jobs. This also helps balance the values enhanced by different selection methods.

Given limited resources, it is sometimes necessary for organizations to validate tests piecemeal. In order to do this most effectively, validation efforts should be targeted toward the tests for those positions most likely to be the focus of affirmative action controversies.

DISCUSSION QUESTIONS

1. Why can it be said that selection and promotion reflect conflict among the values of political responsiveness, agency efficiency, and social equity?
2. What are the laws relating to public agency selection and promotion procedures?
3. What is the "bottom line" definition of adverse impact? What is the 80 percent rule? How do they both relate affirmative action to the selection and promotion process?
4. What are empirical, construct, and content validation methods? What are their comparative advantages and disadvantages?
5. Enumerate the selection and promotion methods used by public agencies. What are their comparative advantages and disadvantages?
6. What strategy should public personnel managers employ for validating selection and promotion criteria?
7. Why has emphasis on test validation come from the courts rather than advocates of administrative efficiency?

KEY TERMS

Title VII of the 1964 Civil Rights Act
Equal Employment Opportunity Act of 1972
Age Discrimination in Employment Act of 1967 (as amended, 1976)
Vietnam Veteran Readjustment Act of 1974
Veteran Preference Act of 1944
Title VI of the Vocational Rehabilitation Act of 1973
proportional representation
underutilization rule
80 percent rule
adverse impact
"bottom line" definition of adverse impact
Griggs v. *Duke Power Company*
Connecticut v. *Teal*
test
job-relatedness
Uniform Guidelines on Employee Selection Procedures

EEOC
empirical validation
construct validation
content validation
"business necessity"
"bona fide occupational qualification" (BFOQ)
validity
reliability
performance test
probationary appointment
assessment center

EXERCISE: PICKING A MINORITY RECRUITMENT DIRECTOR FOR A STATE POLICE DEPARTMENT

You have recently been appointed by the Governor of your state as Personnel Director of the State Police. This organization consists of about 1000 State Police officers and 200 civilian employees. Its primary mission is to promote highway safety through enforcement of traffic laws and assistance to motorists.

In recent years, the State Police organization has come under increasing public criticism. The major grievance is that too much attention is being paid to writing traffic tickets and enforcing the 55 MPH speed limit; a more proper focus would be on organized crime and drug trafficking, which law-enforcement officials privately admit is both growing and impossible to stop through the efforts of local law-enforcement agencies. In addition, many people believe that the State Police discriminates against women and minorities in both employment and enforcement of traffic laws.

Morale is low among younger officers, who see themselves as victims of societal conflicts. Turnover among recruits, those who have completed a three-month training course at the State Police Training Center, averages 25 percent during the first year. Reasons most often given for leaving the organization are working conditions, lack of immediate promotional opportunities, and the feeling that promotion is based on politics or personality rather than performance.

Many observers consider the State Police to be a highly political organization because its top administrative positions are gubernatorial appointments. Some observers believe that, as a result, top management lacks experience in law-enforcement or management, and that this reduces the morale and effectiveness of the organization.

As Director of Personnel for the State Police, your task is to select an assistant who will be solely responsible for developing, administering, and

TABLE 7–7.   Minority Recruitment Director

CANDIDATE	GROUP A	GROUP B	GROUP C	GROUP D	GROUP E
Harold Murphy					
Willie Jones					
Norma Sikorsky					

evaluating a minority-recruitment program for the agency. The three résumés shown are those that you and your screening committee have picked as being the most qualified of several hundred applicants who responded to nationwide advertising for the position. You have scheduled each applicant to report for an interview; you have completed the interview process; and it is now time to rank the three applicants.

Divide into work groups with four or five people in each group (Groups A, B, C, and so on). Within 25 minutes, place all three candidates in rank order, based on their qualifications for the position. Before you do so, be prepared to defend your selection by developing answers to these questions:

1. What job duties are most important to the position? (*example*: planning a recruitment program)
2. What skills, knowledge, and abilities will successful applicants need? (*example*: be able to communicate with people from different backgrounds)
3. What minimum qualifications will successful applicants need? (*examples*: education, experience, credentials or licenses, other qualifications)
4. In what rank order should the candidates be placed, on the basis of your answers to questions 1 through 3? (See Table 7–7.)
5. Why is the applicant you chose the most qualified of the three?
6. What selection criteria were most important in making the choice? (See Table 7–8.)
7. Which value (political responsiveness, agency efficiency, or social equity) is most enhanced by your selection decision and criteria? Is this an appropriate definition of "merit" in this situation?

(Questions continue on p. 120.)

TABLE 7–8.   Selection Criteria

CRITERION	GROUP A	GROUP B	GROUP C	GROUP D	GROUP E
Education					
Experience					
Credentials					
Race/sex					
Politics					
Other (specify)					

Willie Jones
1327 W. Addison St.
Minneapolis, Minn.

Employment History:

1971-present: Assistant Dean of Admissions at Northern Minnesota State Teachers College. Responsible for minority recruitment, minority financial aids, and internship programs for a 25,000 student state university offering a range of undergraduate programs. Since 1971, the percentage of minority students has increased from 3 percent to 13 percent of the student body.

1969-1971: Administrative assistant to the Dean of Admissions, Texas Technical Institute. Responsible for review of applicants for admission, counseling of minority students, and administration of minority financial aid programs.

1964-1969: Major, U.S. Army. Responsible for a variety of combat and staff assignments in the U.S. and overseas. Rifle Platoon Leader responsible for the health, morale, welfare, and safety of 43 men (1964-1965). Company Executive Officer (1965-1966). Battalion Air Operations Officer responsible for scheduling aircraft and helicopters to support personnel and units of the battalion in South Viet Nam (1966-1967). Battalion Advisor 11th Airborne Division, ARVN: one of twenty officers selected to advise in combat 10 ARVN Airborne Battalions in the use of U.S. weapons and tactics.
Awards and Decorations:
Silver Star, Bronze Star Medal with "V" Device for Valor (2 Oak Leaf Clusters), Air Medal, Army Commendation Medal with "V" Device for Valor, and Purple Heart (2 Oak Leaf Clusters).

Education:

B.A. in History, Jackson State University, Mississippi, 1964.

Personal Data:

5' 11"
180 pounds
married, two children
excellent health

Harold Murphy
3732 18th Street
Arlington, Va.

Employment History:

1974–present: Personnel Director for Northern Virginia Community College. Responsible for management of labor relations, staff recruitment and selection, training, and affirmative action compliance. Responsible for representing NVCC in first collective bargaining session with staff union.

1972–1974: Assistant to the Personnel Director, Tennessee Industrial-Technical College, Nashville. Responsible for position classification, grievances and appeals, and labor-management relations for 300 staff employees.

Education:

M.S. in Government (Personnel Management), The George Washington University, Washington, D.C. Wrote master's thesis on "Minority Recruitment Problems and Prospects in Virginia State Government." 3.87 GPA. (1971).

B.A. in Business Administration (Personnel Management), The George Washington University (1968). Senior honors thesis on "Conflicts Between Seniority and Affirmative Action Guidelines in Public Labor Management Relations." Phi Beta Kappa, Pi Sigma Alpha, Woodrow Wilson Fellowship, cum laude.

Professional Activities:

"Managing Labor Relations in State University Systems," American Association of University Personnel Administrators Conference, New Orleans, March 1974.

Personal Information:

married
good health

References:

upon request

Norma Sikorsky
P.O. Box 6597
Salem, Oregon

Employment:

1972–present: Assistant to the Governor of Oregon, responsible for the development of statewide affirmative action plans for state agencies. Supervised three employees with a staff budget of $100,000. Made recommendations on affirmative action to state agency heads. Responsible for extensive coordination and public relations work with state and local minority representatives and groups. Represented the state at numerous affirmative action conferences.

1968–1970: Deputy Assistant Director for Education, State of Oregon. Responsible for advising the Assistant Director on secondary curriculum matters throughout the state. Developed and implemented the first race relations program used in Oregon high schools (1970). Developed and implemented statewide curriculum changes in women's athletic programs.

1960–1966: High school teacher, Clackamas High School, Coos Bay, Oregon. Responsible for teaching social studies, civics, and athletics.

Education:

M.A. in Education, University of Oregon, Eugene (1968)

B.A. in Education, University of Oregon, Eugene (1960)

References:

Governor Tom McCall, Oregon

Simon Merkle, Ed. D.
Director for Education
State Office Building
Salem, Oregon

William Jackson, Director
Equal Employment Opportunity Commission
Salem, Oregon

8. How confident are you that the selection criteria you used are job-related?
9. How would you validate the criteria if asked to do so by a federal court or an affirmative action compliance agency?

STATISTICAL APPENDIX

This appendix presents the statistical terms and techniques used to demonstrate predictive and concurrent validity. For more detailed information, please refer to one of the statistical references at the back of this appendix.

1. To find the mean ($\bar{x}$), add all the individual values of a variable and divide by the number of individual values:

$$\bar{x} = \Sigma \frac{x}{N}$$

where

$\bar{x}$ = the mean of a variable
Σ = sum of
N = number of individual values

2. Measures of dispersion (standard deviation) indicate the tendency of a variable to vary from the mean.
    To find the standard deviation of a variable:

   a. Find the mean
   b. Find the difference between each individual value and the mean
   c. Square each difference
   d. Add these squared values and compute their mean
   e. Find the square root of this number

$$\sigma = \sqrt{\frac{\Sigma(x - \bar{x})^2}{N}}$$

   where

   σ = standard deviation
   x = each value of a variable
   $\bar{x}$ = mean of a variable
   N = number of individual values

3. Regression analysis (Pearson product-moment correlation coefficient) yields a number between -1.0 and $+1.0$, which shows the extent of relationship between two variables. -1.0 is a perfect negative correlation (as one variable increases, the other decreases). A perfect positive correlation is $+1.0$ (both variables increase or decrease together). No relationship between two variables is indicated by 0.
    To find Pearson's r:

   a. Compute the means of both variables (x and y)
   b. Compute the standard deviations of both variables
   c. Multiply each value of x by its associated value of y and add these products
   d. Compute Pearson's r using this formula:

$$r = \frac{\frac{\Sigma xy}{N} - \bar{x}\bar{y}}{\sigma_x \sigma_y}$$

where

r = Pearson's r
Σxy = the sum of the xy products
N = number of paired cases
σ_x = standard deviation of x
σ_y = standard deviation of y
$\bar{x}$ = mean of x
$\bar{y}$ = mean of y

4. A regression line is the best straight line equation for predicting one variable given the other of the pair (that is, predicting x from y or y from x).

    To find the regression line (a general equation of the form $y = a + bx$), use either equation (1) or (2).

    $$b = r\frac{\sigma_y}{\sigma_x} \tag{1}$$

    $$a = y - b(x) \tag{2}$$

    where

    y = the criterion variable (job performance)
    x = the predictor variable (pre-employment test score)
    a = the point at which the regression line crosses the vertical axis
    b = the slope of the regression line

5. Standard Error of the Estimate. Because a straight line does not always adequately describe the relationship between two variables, the accuracy of the best straight line predictor of y from x must be qualified by computing the standard error of the estimate.

    $$\text{SEE} = \sigma_x \sqrt{1 - (r)^2} \quad \text{(for predicting } y \text{ from } x) \tag{3}$$

    $$\text{SEE} = \sigma_y \sqrt{1 - (r)^2} \quad \text{(for predicting } x \text{ from } y) \tag{4}$$

    where

    σ_x = the standard deviation of x
    σ_y = the standard deviation of y
    r = Pearson's r

6. Cutting point. To establish the "cutting point," or minimum acceptable test score from which to predict successful job performance (the criterion), follow these steps:

    a. Compute Pearson's r for x and y
    b. Establish the minimum acceptable performance evaluation score
    c. Find values of a and b for the regression equation between x and y
    d. After setting y at the minimum acceptable performance level, solve the equation for x ($y = a + bx$).
    e. Compute the SEEs for x and y
    f. Multiply SEE (for predicting y) by 1.96, and *subtract* the resulting product from the value of x obtained in step d. There is at least a 95 percent chance that a person scoring below this point would not achieve above the desired performance level on the criterion variable (step b).

Exercise

Given this set of test scores and a second set of on-the-job performance scores,

1. Compute Pearson's r.
2. How significant is this measure?
3. State the regression equation.
4. Find the standard error of the estimate.
5. What is the cutoff score to ensure minimal performance at 7?

x Test Scores	y Performance Scores	x Test Scores	y Performance Scores
90	9	85	9
60	6	75	7
75	8	70	6
80	8	65	5
45	4	85	8

When you have answered these questions, check your answers.

x	$(x - \bar{x})$	y	$(y - \bar{y})$	$(x - \bar{x})^2$	$(y - \bar{y})^2$	(xy)
90	17	9	2	289	4	810
60	−13	6	−1	169	1	360
75	2	8	1	4	1	600
80	7	8	1	49	1	640
45	−28	4	−3	784	9	180
85	12	9	2	144	4	765
75	2	7	0	4	0	525
70	−3	6	−1	9	1	420
65	−8	5	−2	64	4	325
85	12	8	1	144	1	680
730	0	70	0	1660	26	5305

$$\bar{x} = \frac{\Sigma x}{10} = 73 \qquad \bar{y} = \frac{\Sigma y}{10} = 7$$

1. $\sigma_x = \sqrt{\dfrac{\Sigma(x - \bar{y})^2}{N}} = \sqrt{166} = 12.9$

$\sigma_y = \sqrt{\dfrac{\Sigma(y - \bar{y})^2}{N}} = \sqrt{\dfrac{26}{10}} = 1.6$

$$\frac{\dfrac{\Sigma xy}{N} - \bar{x}\bar{y}}{\sigma_x \sigma_y} = \frac{\dfrac{5305}{10} - (73)(7)}{(12.9)(1.6)} = \frac{530.5 - 511}{20.6} = 0.95$$

2. Significant at 0.01 level of probability

3. $b = r\left(\dfrac{\sigma_y}{\sigma_x}\right)$ $a = \bar{y} - b\bar{x}$

   $b = 0.95\left(\dfrac{1.6}{2.9}\right)$ $a = 7 - 0.12(73)$

   $b = 0.12$ $a = -1.76$

   $y = a + bx$

   $y = (-1.76) + .12x$

4. $\text{SEE}_{0.05} = \sigma_x\sqrt{1 - r^2} = 12.9\sqrt{1 - 0.9025} = (12.9)(0.31) = 4(1.96) = \pm 8$

5. $7 = (-1.76) + 0.12(x)$

   $x = \dfrac{8.76}{12} - \text{SEE}$

   $x = 73 - 8$

   $x = 65$

NOTES

[1]Maxine Kurtz, "Bottom Line Discrimination Defense Voided," *Public Administration Times* (October 1, 1982), p. 3.

[2]Frank L. Schmidt, et al., "Statistical Power in Criterion-Related Validation Studies," *Journal of Applied Psychology*, Vol. 61, No. 4 (1974), 473–85.

[3]The Civil Rights Act of 1964, P.L. 88-352, 78 Stat. 241, 28 U.S.C. s. 1447 [1976].

[4]*Albemarle Paper Company v. Moody*, 422 U.S. 405, 10 FEP 1181.

[5]Edward L. Levine and Abram Flory III, "Evaluation of Job Applications—A Conceptual Framework," *Public Personnel Management* (November-December 1976), pp. 378–85.

[6]Edwin E. Ghiselli, "The Validity of Aptitude Tests in Personnel Selection," *Personnel Psychology*, vol. 26 (1973), 461–77.

[7]Craig C. Pinder, "Statistical Accuracy and Practical Utility in the Use of Moderator Variables," *Journal of Applied Psychology*, vol. 97, no. 2 (1973), 214–21.

[8]William Jasper, "Results of Study of Fairness of Written Tests," *The Personnel Research Reporter* V, vol. 2, no. 3 (July 1972), 1–6.

[9]I. von Raubenheimer and Joseph Tiffin, "Personnel Selection and the Prediction of Error," *Journal of Applied Psychology*, vol. 55, no. 3 (1971), 229–33; and Herbert S. Field, Gerald A. Bayley, and Susan M. Bayley, "Employment Test Validation for Minority and Nonminority Production Workers," *Personnel Psychology*, vol. 30, no. 1 (1977), 37–46.

[10]Robert L. Ebel, "Comments on Some Problems of Employment Testing," *Personnel Psychology*, vol. 30, no. 1 (1977), 55–63.

[11]P.L. 93-380, 88 Stat., 20 U.S.C. s. 1232g.

[12]Robert E. Carlson, et al., "Improvements in the Selection Interview," *Personnel Journal* (April 1971), pp. 268–75ff.

[13]S.W. Constantin, "An Investigation of Information Favorability in the Employment Interview," *Journal of Applied Psychology*, vol. 61, no. 6 (1976), 743–49.

[14]Neal Schmitt and Bryan W. Coyle, "Applicant Decisions in the Employment Interview," *Journal of Applied Psychology*, vol. 61, no. 2 (1976), 184–92.

[15]Robert L. Dipboye, Howard L. Fromkin, and Kent Wiback, "Relative Importance of

Applicant Sex, Attractiveness and Scholastic Standing in Evaluation of Job Applicant Resumes," *Journal of Applied Psychology*, vol. 60, no. 1 (1975), 39–43; Manuel London and John R. Poplawski, "Effects of Information on Stereotype Development in Performance Appraisal and Interview Contexts," *Journal of Applied Psychology*, vol. 61, no. 2 (1976), 199–205.

[16]Enzo Valenzi and I. R. Andrews, "Individual Differences in the Decision Process of Employment Interviews," *Journal of Applied Psychology*, vol. 58, no. 1 (1973), 49–53; Glen D. Baskett, "Interview Decisions as Determined by Competency and Attitude Similarity," *Journal of Applied Psychology*, vol. 57, no. 3 (1973), 343–45.

[17]Milton D. Hakel, "Similarity of Post-Interview Trait Rating Intercorrelations as a Contributor to Interrater Agreement in a Structured Employment Interview," *Journal of Applied Psychology*, vol. 55, no. 5 (1971), 443–48.

[18]Ed Yager, "Assessment Centers: The Latest Fad?," *Training and Development Journal*, vol. 30, no. 1 (1976), 41–44.

[19]Alan L. Gross and Wen-huey Su, "Defining a 'Fair' or 'Unbiased' Selection Model," *Journal of Applied Psychology*, vol. 60, no. 3 (1975), 345–51.

[20]Yoash Wiener and Mark L. Schneiderman, "Use of Job Information as a Criterion in Employment Decisions of Interviewers," *Journal of Applied Psychology*, vol. 59, no. 6 (1974), 699–704.

8

Human Resource Planning

In 1981 President Reagan's Omnibus Budget Reconciliation Act reflected the policy of New Federalism that he had previously proposed as a means of reducing the size of the federal bureaucracy and returning control of federal programs to state and local governments. Regardless of its effects on the federal budget or budget deficit, the New Federalism had dramatic effects on state and local government programs. Florida's share of the $35 billion reduction in federal spending was $214 million, primarily reductions in Medicaid payments, CETA-funded positions, sewerage treatment, and highway construction. This in turn caused the state's human service agency, the largest state department, to lose several hundred positions.

This example relates the effect of changing federal budget priorities on one state's federally funded programs. But how does budgeting relate to public personnel management in general, and to human resource management in particular? First, budgeting is the heart of the junction between politics and public administration. It is the process by which value conflicts are resolved and translated into concrete programs through the allocation of scarce resources toward program objectives. Through programmatic authorizations and monetary appropriations, the legislature exercises joint control with the chief executive over agency priorities.

Second, because pay and benefits constitute about 50 to 70 percent of all public agency expenditures, the most vital budgetary items proposed by the chief executive, or funded by the legislature, are expenditures for pay and benefits. The most common tool used by the legislature to influence the magnitude and direction of agency programs is budgetary restriction on the number of positions allocated to an agency, and the levels of pay and benefits attached to public agency positions. Therefore, the budget preparation and approval process is the means by which the field of public personnel management relates to the larger political context.

Third, human resource planning is that aspect of public personnel management which mediates between this external political environment and those core activities such as job analysis, job classification, job evaluation, and compensation. In brief, human resource planning matches "wish lists" proposed by agency managers with political realities established by legislative priorities and revenue forecasts. It begins with a request to these managers from their executive-level supervisors: "How many positions, and what kinds of positions, do you need to meet your program objectives?" It ends with a legislative authorization of these programs and the appropriation of funds to fill the new (or existing) positions.

The predominant relationship between human resource planning and political responsiveness is also shown by the way in which revenue cuts affect public agencies. During a "cutback management" crisis, management's first step is usually to stop or restrict hiring, thereby refraining from filling existing positions as they become vacant. If the situation is more serious, low priority positions are abolished, meaning that they are permanently removed from the agency and the pay and benefits allocated to them are returned to the legislature. Or a serious cutback situation can also be met by reducing the pay and benefits of all employees, either through direct legislative action or through the negotiation and ratification of collective bargaining agreements.

Thus, the dominant value enforced through the mediation of human resource planning between the external environment and core allocation activities is *political responsiveness*. This value signifies the requirement that the number of positions established, and the level of pay and benefits attached to each position, be determined politically rather than administratively.

Yet issues such as job classification, evaluation, and pay involve other values besides political responsiveness. For example, social equity requires that men and women be classified and paid equally if they perform substantially the same duties under substantially similar conditions. Second, pay and benefits are determined not only legislatively, but also often through a collective bargaining process which reflects the importance of the value of individual rights through the sanctions process.

At bottom, however, political responsiveness is the dominant value. Courts may require equal compensation, or a compensation package may be negotiated through collective bargaining. But neither of these decisions can be implemented until a legislature, through the budget preparation and approval process, appropriates funds to effectuate these decisions.

By the end of this chapter you will be able to:

1. Describe the relationship between human resource planning and the budgetary and financial management process
2. Discuss why human resource planning serves as a mediating activity between the environment of public agencies and other personnel activities such as job analysis, job classification, compensation and benefits
3. Describe alternative techniques for forecasting the demand for, supply of, and need for human resources in public agencies
4. Discuss the relationship between human resource planning and other personnel management programs, including the option of "contracting out"
5. Discuss the comparative advantages and disadvantages of alternative techniques for reducing personnel expenditures, such as attrition or a reduction in force (RIF)

BUDGETING AND FINANCIAL MANAGEMENT

A budget is a document that attempts to reconcile program priorities with projected revenues. It combines a statement of organizational activities or objectives for a given time period with information about the funds required to engage in these activities or reach these objectives. A budget has many purposes: information, control, planning, or evaluation.[1]

Historically, the most important purpose of a budget has been external control, that is, to limit the total resources available to an agency and to prevent expenditure for activities or items nor allowed by law. This control has applied to both money and jobs. The type of budget used for control purposes is called a *ceiling budget*. It controls an agency directly by specifying limits to expenditures through appropriations legislation, or indirectly by limiting agency revenues to a source of known and limited size.

Other types of budgets have been developed for different purposes. A *line-item* budget, which classifies expenditures by type, is useful for controlling the types of expenditures as well as their total amount. *Performance and program* budgets are useful for specifying the activities or programs upon which funds are spent, and thereby assist in their evaluation. By separating expenditures by function (such as health or public safety) or by type of expenditure (such as personnel and equipment (or by source of revenue such as property tax or user fees), administrators and legislators can keep accurate records of an agency's financial transactions, for maintenance of either internal efficiency or external control.

Budgeting is like a game in that its participants, rules, and time limits are known in advance by all players.[2] The primary budget game participants are interest groups, public agency administrators, the chief executive, and legislative committees.

Although each participant's "game plan" will differ with circumstances, each participant has a generally accepted role to play. Interest groups exert pressure on administrators to propose or expand favorable programs. Department administrators use these pressures and their own sense of their department's goals and capabilities to develop program proposals and specify the resources (money, time, and people) needed to accomplish them. Chief executives coordinate and balance the requests of various departments.[3] After all, resources are limited and departmental objectives should be congruent with the overall objectives of the city, state, or national government. In many cases, the chief executive has a staff agency responsible for informing departments (or agencies) of planning limitations, objectives, and resource limits. The chief executive presents the combined budget request of all departments within the executive branch to a legislature (city council, county commission, state legislature, or Congress).

Legislative action on appropriations requests varies, depending on the legislature's size and the staff's capabilities. At the national and state levels, different committees consider funding requests from different types of agencies. These committees examine funding requests in the light of prior expenditures, hear testimony from department heads and lobbyists, and listen to committee members' own feelings about the comparative importance of the agency's programs and objectives. Appropriations requests are approved (reported out of committee) when the committee agrees on which programs should be funded, and on the overall level of funding.

The entire legislature usually approves committee proposals, unless the funding relates to programs that affect the interests of groups not having expressed their opinions adequately during committee hearings. Legislation authorizing new programs is usually considered separately from bills that appropriate funds for those programs.

In an elementary view, after new programs are authorized and funded, the executive branch is responsible for executing them. The chief executive is responsible for administering the expenditure of funds to accomplish the objectives intended by the legislature; and department administrators are responsible for managing their budgets and programs accordingly. *Financial management* is the process of developing and using systems to ensure that funds are spent for the purposes for which they have been appropriated. Through an accounting system, each agency keeps records of financial transactions. These systems compare budgets with actual expenditures. Agency managers engage in budget management when they take steps to limit expenditures, or transfer funds from one budget category to another to meet program priorities.

The process of budget preparation, approval, and management is shown in Figure 8–1. This process is a recurrent ritual whose frequency depends on the length of the appropriations cycle. Most governments bud-

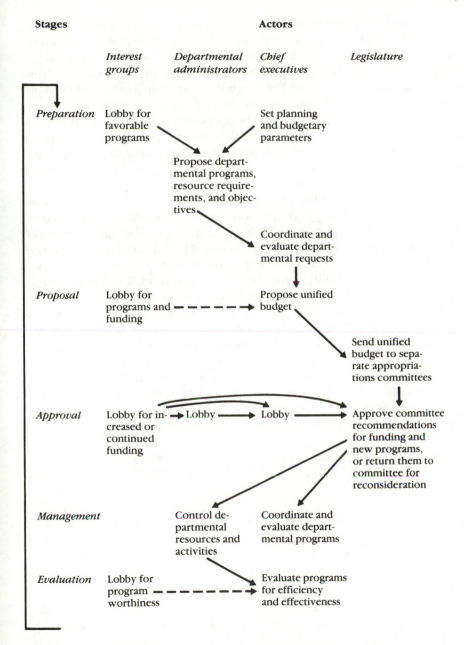

Stages

Actors

Interest groups — *Departmental administrators* — *Chief executives* — *Legislature*

Preparation — Lobby for favorable programs — Set planning and budgetary parameters

Propose departmental programs, resource requirements, and objectives

Coordinate and evaluate departmental requests

Proposal — Lobby for programs and funding — Propose unified budget

Send unified budget to separate appropriations committees

Approval — Lobby for increased or continued funding — Lobby — Lobby — Approve committee recommendations for funding and new programs, or return them to committee for reconsideration

Management — Control departmental resources and activities — Coordinate and evaluate departmental programs

Evaluation — Lobby for program worthiness — Evaluate programs for efficiency and effectiveness

FIGURE 8–1. The Budget Process (Source: Donald E. Klingner, *Public Administration: A Management Approach.* © 1983 by Houghton Mifflin, Boston, Mass. All rights reserved.)

get annually, although the problems associated with continually developing and evaluating programs have led many state legislatures to develop biennial budgets (every two years). In the typical annual budget cycle, however, an agency or a department normally is developing the next year's budget a year in advance of the period for which it is requesting funds. At the same time, it is also evaluating programs in the prior year. Figure 8–2 represents the time frame within which annual budgets occur. Although most governments follow an annual budget cycle, their budget years begin and end on different dates. Most state governments use a fiscal year beginning July 1 and ending June 30, while the federal government's fiscal year begins October 1 and ends September 30.

Budgeting, then, is the process by which general policy objectives are translated into specific programs, with funds allocated for their accomplishment. Financial management and auditing are the means by which expenditures are limited to those purposes. These practices are therefore at the heart of the resource allocation process, and they constitute the key relationship between politics and public administration. The budget preparation and approval process is complex. It can be viewed politically as a contest among opposing agencies for scarce resources; organizationally as the formal set of policies and procedures that govern the approval process; or informally is a ritualized interaction among the conflicting expectations of program managers, chief executives, legislators, and lobbyists.

The role that public personnel managers play in the budget preparation and approval process combines their staff responsibility of assisting other department heads, and their line responsibility of directing their own departments. Their staff responsibility is to work with department heads so

FIGURE 8–2.   The Budget Cycle   (Source: Donald E. Klingner, *Public Administration: A Management Approach.* © 1983 by Houghton Mifflin, Boston, Mass. All rights reserved.)

| | | Prior year | | | | Current year | | | Proposed year |
	Jan.	Apr.	Jul.	Oct.	Jan.	Apr.	Jul.	Oct.	Jan. Apr. Jul. Oct.
Prior year's budget	Management				Evaluation				
Current year's budget	Preparation	Proposal	Approval		Management				Evaluation
Proposed year's budget					Preparation	Proposal	Approval	Management	

that the budget proposals of these departments will include sufficient funds to hire the employees needed to meet agency objectives. For example, a city police chief may have received a mandate from the city council to "stop crime." Translated into budgetary terms, this means that the council is willing to spend an additional $200,000 on uniformed personnel (pay and benefits). The city's personnel director will meet with the police chief (or his director of administration) to determine how many additional officers can be hired for this amount. Assuming a starting pay of $16,000, and benefits equal to 50 percent of salary, it is agreed that eight new officers should be added. But the cost of uniforms and equipment is $25,000, so this reduces the number to seven. The police chief can then propose this formally, and the request will either be accepted or modified by the city manager (or mayor) and the council. In addition, the personnel director will be responsible for ensuring that department directors include in their budget requests sufficient funds for recruiting and training new employees, if these functions are done by departments rather than by the central personnel department.

The second major budget preparation function of a personnel director is to develop and defend the budget needed to provide support services to other departments: human resource planning, job analysis and classification, operation of the payroll and benefits system, training and orientation, performance evaluation, grievances and disciplinary action, and collective bargaining. For example, in a metropolitan area comprised of many local governments, personnel managers will commonly conduct an annual or semiannual wage and salary survey to determine the pay scales for certain positions common to all jurisdictions. These data will then be used to make recommendations to the city manager concerning whether or not pay rates should be changed, or to support the government's position in salary negotiations with a union. Or the city may need to develop new job descriptions or testing procedures as a result of affirmative action pressure. The cost of these activities, including the rationale for them, is presented by the personnel director to the city manager. In this respect, the personnel director functions as a line manager.

Because pay and benefits constitute such a large proportion of an agency's budget, human resource managers are heavily involved in budget management. In this instance, agency managers and supervisors play the primary role in that they are responsible for controlling and reallocating human resources to meet program priorities within budgetary limitations. Agency personnel managers respond to the priorities set by managers by filling positions, paying employees, and otherwise implementing their decisions. In a cutback situation, however, agency personnel managers may take the initiative by declining to fill positions, by postponing promotions, and by other methods of reducing personnel expenditures. These will be discussed later in this chapter.

THE MEDIATING ROLE OF HUMAN RESOURCE PLANNING

From this discussion of the budget process in public agencies, it is evident that it has an important effect on human resource planning. The budget preparation and approval process is, in effect, the "driver" that forces legislative and executive consensus on programs and expenditures.

It is also clear that human resource planning is the personnel activity most closely related to this process. Given the extent to which public agency expenditures comprise pay and benefits, and the use of ceiling budgets or personnel ceilings to control agency activity, human resource planning is the means by which agency officials use the legislative budget to allocate resources among competing priorities and programs.

In addition, human resource planning relates to two other important allocational activities: job analysis and classification, and compensation and benefits, which will be discussed in the following two chapters. By establishing the duties and qualifications for positions, job analysis allows positions to be classified by type of occupation and level of difficulty. This, in turn, enables uniform and equitable pay and benefit programs to be established for each position. Without these two additional steps, it would not be possible for human resource planners to use human resource forecasts to estimate human resource costs.

HUMAN RESOURCE FORECASTING

The public personnel manager works with department heads to help them forecast their future human resource needs and then uses these combined estimates (for all departments) to develop a coordinated staffing program for the agency.

Incrementalism (or *decrementalism*) is a forecasting method that projects straight-line changes in personnel needs based on budget fluctuations. For example, an incremental human resource plan might call for a 5 percent increase in the number of positions allocated to each organizational unit for each 5 percent increase in the agency's budget (adjusted for cost-of-living). A decremental plan might call for a 5 percent reduction in personnel for each 5 percent reduction in the agency's budget. Neither one is very effective as a forecasting technique because they both ignore the shift in skill needs that results from changes in program emphasis, as well as the long lead time required to acquire and develop human resources.[4]

The most widely used forecasting technique is *collective opinion*. It first involves the gathering of information from a variety of sources inside and outside the agency and then reaching a group consensus about the interpretation of these data. Some utilized information sources are shown in Table 8–1.

This information could relate to such external factors as enabling legislation, budgetary and personnel ceilings, changes in agency structure or objectives, affirmative action goals, collective bargaining, or pressures for political responsiveness. Internal factors might include current human resource utilization, projected staffing needs, or shifts in program priorities. For example, a group of agency personnel directors might conclude that a new state law requiring the issuance of environmental impact permits for beach-front developers, and the funding of the program for a certain dollar figure would require a 20 percent increase in employees for the state environmental management agency over the next three years.

Usually this human resource "planning" process is not a rational one. That is, new positions are created and abolished as a reaction to legislative funding priorities rather than to managerial efficiency or employee rights. Given the importance of these two objectives, one of the roles the personnel manager is likely to play in the future is in working with line managers to rationally forecast human resource needs. Two rational approaches to human resource planning are available.

First, macrolevel forecasting techniques such as *categorical* and *cluster forecasting* may be used. Categorical forecasting estimates further needs for separate occupational groups, such as doctors, lawyers, or personnel managers. Cluster forecasting groups together those occupations with common skill requirements and those that are required for other positions to function. It is most often used by larger organizations. For example, a personnel manager may estimate that he or she needs to add one job analyst to the personnel department for every 1000 new employees in the organization, because this is the ratio of analysts to employees needed to handle routine requests for reclassification.

TABLE 8–1. Sources of Information

LOCATION OF SOURCE	RELATIONSHIP	SOURCES OF INFORMATION
Outside agency	Personal	Clients, legislators, lobbyists, other agency administrators
	Impersonal	Newspapers, budget hearings, professional conferences, polls
Inside agency	Personal	Subordinates, supervisors, coworkers
	Impersonal	Meetings, conferences

Modeling, or simulation, is a second forecasting technique. Though some applications of this require the use of mathematics and computers, others do not.[5] The simulation process requires developing a model that duplicates reality with respect to the crucial environmental, organizational, or interpersonal factors affecting a particular agency goal. Thus, a model specifies the conditions that affect the relative feasibility of alternative solutions. A model requires that guidelines be established, current programs identified, and their outputs determined. Next, it requires that possible alternative programs be substituted to determine their effect on outputs.

For example, a personnel director seeking to estimate future personnel costs for a department might review the turnover data for secretarial positions. If the turnover rate was 33 percent annually, he or she would conclude that if the number of positions in the agency were to remain constant, one-third of the secretarial positions would need to be filled annually. Anticipated costs for this activity could then be projected by computing the cost of recruitment, selection, orientation, and training for new employees, minus any salary dollars saved for the time the positions were vacant.

Further, the personnel director might assist a county welfare administrator by using modeling to predict how many employees will be needed. The model might be stated in this way:

1. Currently, with unemployment at about 9 percent, welfare applications can be processed within time standards by three full-time employees, using a manual index card system.
2. However, if unemployment increases to 12 percent, the office will need to add two more employees to handle the additional increase in workload, or change to a computer system in order to process welfare applications more efficiently.

Which forecasting technique should be used? Although most organizations will continue to use nonrational methods, rational techniques may be adopted fairly easily by many agencies, particularly those that have adequate and competent staff, sufficient data on current programs and resource requirements, receptive management, and access to computer facilities.[6] The administrator's skill and commitment to seeking the best solution determines the technique used and its effectiveness in forecasting.[7]

Having used a variety of techniques to forecast the *demand* for human resources within the agency, managers must use the same techniques to forecast the *supply* of qualified applicants—the potential labor market from which the agency can recruit. This is influenced by a number of factors inside and outside the agency, and among them are the state of the economy, the level of technology, the educational system, competing employers, the nature of the labor market, the agency's compensation system, number of vacancies, and the agency's recruitment practices.

By subtracting the aggregate *supply* of human resources from the aggregate *demand* for these resources within the organization, human resource planners compute the *need*. This figure is then used to develop programs for acquiring, developing, and utilizing human resources.

HUMAN RESOURCE PLANNING AND OTHER PERSONNEL ACTIVITIES

Human resource planning relates most strongly to the allocation function, that set of human resource management activities closest to external legislative control over resources and program priorities. These include job analysis, classification, and evaluation. But before any of these functions can be related to human resource planning, a more basic question must be addressed, namely, whether a government will perform services with its own employees, contract them out to private or governmental subcontractors, or not perform them at all.

The current emphasis on "cutback management" creates a dilemma for elected officials. Citizens continue to demand a variety of high-quality public services, such as schools, law-enforcement, and transportation, but they continue to push for lower taxes and smaller public payrolls. A dilemma differs from a problem in that it has no apparent solution; resolving one problem makes the other one worse. Yet legislators and agency heads often choose to "contract out" services as a solution to this dilemma. For example, the City of North Miami Beach recently abolished its park maintenance division of the Parks and Recreation Department, and hired a private contractor to provide the same services. Other cities hire private contractors to provide trash pickup; state and federal agencies rely heavily upon private nursing homes and hospitals to provide health care to individuals.

Contracting out means that public personnel managers have no role in providing these services. Rather, public control is through financial management, contract compliance, and oversight by elected officials. This creates a problem; it is often easier to control one's own employees than those of an outside organization. In addition, it is often difficult to predict the costs of contracted-out services because of the vagaries of the competitive bidding process.

If governmental services are not contracted out, then the human resource manager will use human resource planning to develop a resource budget for the agency. This requires that needed positions not only be identified but also analyzed and evaluated to determine their appropriate salary and benefits. Combining this information with human resource forecasts, managers can project future budget needs for presentation to the city manager, governor, or Congress. If collective bargaining is provided for under federal or state laws, then the legislature also has a role in determining salary and benefits through its decision to ratify or not ratify a negotiated collective bargaining agreement.

Human resource managers must also relate forecasts to other personnel activities—recruitment, performance evaluation, training, selection and promotion, affirmative action, compensation, labor-management relations, and career development.[8]

If anticipated needs are to be met from outside the organization, recruitment must occur far enough in advance to be completed by the time a program needs to be operational. Given the nature of the labor market for the particular position, this may require that recruiters be given several years "lead time."

If the labor market is a difficult one to recruit in, test-validation specialists may need to assist in developing selection or promotion criteria that screen out unqualified applicants or employees without also screening out qualified ones as well.

If anticipated needs are to be met from within the agency, the personnel department must develop a performance evaluation system to identify qualified employees for these positions, and possibly training programs to qualify people for them.

If career development is important to employees, the personnel department can assist by identifying "model career patterns" that employees can use to plan their future in the organization. Having identified these model career patterns, it is then up to the agency to follow through by utilizing its performance evaluation, training, and affirmative action programs to see that employees have a substantial and equitable opportunity of achieving their objectives.

The level of compensation for a position determines the size and quality of the applicant pool. A position characterized by both low salary and benefits in relation to market conditions will be hard to fill with qualified employees, or it will evidence high turnover as unqualified employees become sufficiently qualified to compete for jobs in the private-sector market. The personnel manager can often justify higher salaries by showing that the cost of replacing and training new employees is greater than the cost of a proposed boost in pay and benefits. Compensation and benefits have to be adjusted to meet conditions in the external labor market, or the terms of a negotiated collective bargaining agreement. This is particularly true if the employer bargins collectively with multiple employee associations, or if the union representing a group of employees also represents similar employees in nearby competing organizations.

If certain groups are underutilized, and this is reflected in the affirmative action objectives of the agency, human resource supply forecasts will have to consider not just the aggregate supply of employees in a particular type of job, but the similarities and differences between this general labor market and the specific market for female or minority-group employees and applicants.

HUMAN RESOURCE PLANNING AND CUTBACK MANAGEMENT

A realistic appraisal of the future indicates that public agencies will be expected to do more with less funds: to practice cutback management. As cuts in federal taxation and spending occur, demands on state and local governments will escalate. At the same time, taxpayers will resist overly large raises in state and local taxes to pay for these services. This problem will be worsened by the regressive nature of state and local taxes; sales and property taxes do not increase proportionately with income.

Because most expenditure cuts are targeted to social programs, the poor and the middle class bear the brunt of lowered budgets most strongly, both in terms of the taxes they pay and the services they receive. For example, Florida legislators estimated that President Reagan's $35 billion reduction in federal spending for fiscal year 1982–1983 cost that state $214 million in federal funds. In terms of specific grant-in-aid programs, this cut reduced Medicaid payments by $17 million, CETA-funded positions by 13,000 jobs, sewerage-treatment plant construction by $100 million, and highway construction by $10 million.[9]

The social equity implications of cutback management will also mean changes in the demographic composition of a work force. As fewer employees are hired or as RIFs (reductions-in-force) lay off those with little seniority, the work force tends to become older. If the agency has been hiring a high percentage of minorities and/or women to redress previous patterns of discrimination, RIFs will mean that they are the first to be let go, because they have, on the whole, less seniority than their white male counterparts. As the seniority of the average employee increases, this has consequences on compensation and retirement benefits. Since most employees laid off are at the bottom of the organization, the average grade level of employees also tends to increase.

Such losses in funds mean that public agencies will be required to practice cutback management. In reality, this means that agencies will hire fewer employees, because an average of 70 percent of the typical public agency's budget goes for salaries and benefits. This creates problems. Cuts in the school board's budget mean fewer teachers, larger classes; cuts in the public works department mean unpatched streets or less frequent trash pickups.

At an agency level, the cutback process also has ramifications. First, it is difficult to cut an agency's programs equitably. Both the contributions of each program to agency goals and the comparative effects of alternative cuts on public services are difficult to measure without resolving the problems related to productivity measurement and program evaluation.

A second problem, one closely related to the responsibilities of the public personnel manager, is that the easiest methods of reducing agency expenditures are seldom the most appropriate from a productivity or effectiveness standpoint.[10] Such methods involve across-the-board cuts, hiring freezes, a reduction-in-force, or attrition.

Across-the-board cuts, like the incremental or decremental methods discussed earlier in this chapter, are an irrational method of reducing expenditures in the absence of more definitive program evaluation information.

Hiring freezes prohibit an agency from filling vacated positions and authorizing new ones. Though this may result in a reduction of costs in pay and benefits, the long-term consequences are harmful. Jobs with high turnover rates (clerical, service delivery, or technical positions) go unfilled because of hiring prohibitions, while career administrators tend to stay with their jobs. Unless the agency can subvert the intent of a freeze by increased hiring out—and this is likely to attract strong opposition from the legislature and unions—attrition is likely to trigger productivity decreases.

Conversely, a reduction-in-force has disadvantages as well. A RIF, as it is called, is the laying off of employees within those occupational groups and organizational units determined to be of lowest priority to the agency's mission. This is usually done on the basis of seniority, but it may also be based on other factors such as social equity or productivity. As might be expected, the threat of a RIF causes a drop in agency morale coupled with intense internal politicking to have one's own organizational unit or job category exempted from the reduction. In addition, a RIF has hidden costs that tend to offset the immediate benefits of a reduction in personnel expenses. These are the costs of lump-sum leave and retirement payouts, counseling, maintenance of a call-back system for employees affected by a RIF, increases in unemployment compensation charge-backs, and other hidden costs.[11]

A RIF exacerbates the conflict between three fundamental values in human resource management: managerial demands for efficiency, union demands for protection of employee rights through seniority, and affirmative action demands for protection of the rights of minority and female employees. As the effects of a RIF on organizational efficiency have already been discussed, let's consider their effects on the other two variables. If members of a particular group lack seniority because of previous patterns of discrimination, this can be remedied (as discussed in Chapter 5) through such devices as "fictional seniority." However, in a layoff, the last hired are the first fired. The implications of this for affirmative action are ominous, as a recent report by the New York City Commission on Human Rights indicated. The report, which analyzed the disproportionate impact of austerity-induced layoffs on women and minorities, concluded that "... it is difficult to believe that the remainder of the city's three-year austerity program, if it is to involve still more layoffs, can avoid virtually wiping out the city's minority workforce and crippling female representation as well."[12]

Given the problems engendered by all "solutions" to cutback management, it can only be expected that public personnel managers will find it difficult to find appropriate answers. However, it is necessary that they recognize that they will probably play the mediating role in arranging compromises among the competing values that conflict in this situation. The pressure for cutbacks can be resisted by encouraging the agency to maintain and broaden its base of support by providing services to those clients who are most influential. If cuts are inevitable, their impact can be minimized by examining the organizational mission and limiting activities to those programs required by law; eliminating programs that serve an isolated or politically unresponsive clientele; or installing rational choice mechanisms such as cost-benefit analysis or program evaluation.[13]

Perhaps more vital than these strategies, however, is maintaining communication with clients and employees. They should be so informed as to view cutbacks as a problem that they can help solve. Problems should not be hidden. When clients and employees find out, as they must, concealment will be seen as a sign of weakness and mistrust on the personnel director's part.

SUMMARY

Human resource planning is important to public personnel management because it represents the impact of the value of political responsiveness on the field, through the cyclical mechanism of the budget process. This process, and the appropriations that result from it, function as an externally imposed ceiling on the number of employees and the level of expenditures of public agencies.

Human resource forecasting also serves to mediate between the politics of the budgetary process and the other allocational personnel activities, namely, job analysis and classification, and compensation and benefits.

Public personnel managers can adopt a variety of approaches to human resource planning, ranging from the nonrational to the rational. Rational approaches such as modeling, and composite and cluster forecasting are recommended because they lead to greater efficiency and protection of employee rights.

Once human resource needs are forecast by comparing demand and supply, the personnel manager will need to integrate this activity with others: recruitment, selection and promotion, training, performance evaluation, compensation, labor-management relations, and career development. In this fashion, the human resources needed by the agency can be acquired, maintained, and utilized.

Given current pressures for increased government services at a time of reduced government revenues, it is inevitable that public personnel managers will be confronted with the necessity to cut back. This involves the use of a variety of techniques—reduction-in-force, across-the-board cuts, attrition, or a hiring freeze—none of which has a favorable impact on the agency. Under these circumstances, it is important that the public personnel manager resist these cuts as long as possible and accommodate to them if and when it becomes necessary. Although it is likely that the manager will play a central role as mediator among conflicting values in the cutback management process, it is also important to remember that this responsibility, and its consequences, will be shared with other managers, employees, and clients.

DISCUSSION QUESTIONS

1. Why does budgeting epitomize the impact of the value of political responsiveness on public personnel management?
2. How is human resource planning in public agencies related to the budget process?
3. Why does human resource planning serve as a mediating activity between the budgetary process and other personnel activities such as job analysis and classification, and compensation and benefits?
4. How do public personnel managers assist in budget preparation, both as staff assistants to other managers and as managers of their own departments?
5. How is human resource planning related to the allocation function, and to other human resource management activities?
6. What are the effects of cutback management on a workforce, and how should the human resource manager respond to them?

KEY TERMS

budget
ceiling budget
human resource forecasting
cutback management

reduction-in-force (RIF)
attrition
across-the-board cuts
decremental budgeting
incremental budgeting

EXERCISE: CUTBACKS IN A HUMAN SERVICE AGENCY

Prosperity is a city in the Midwest with a population of 500,000. It is governed by an elected mayor and a city council that oversees the operations of seven city departments.

One of these, the Department of Manpower Training (DMT), has been responsible for the administration of between $3 million and $5 million annually in grants to the city as a prime sponsor under the Comprehensive Employment and Training Act (CETA). The DMT is responsible for the following functions:

Intake Counseling: screening applicants for positions; and referring qualified applicants for testing, job counseling, or training necessary for job placement

Job Development: contacting potential employers and developing suitable job placements for CETA employees

Placement Counseling: counseling CETA program participants as they move through training and are placed on the job, to ensure that they stay in the program

Data Base Management: keeping records on all participants, from intake through successful job placement

Contract Administration: administering subcontracts with organizations that test and train CETA program participants to ensure that the contracts are in compliance

Program Planning and Evaluation: coordinating and reviewing all of the other five functions to ensure that requests for continuing funds are approved, and that the DMT meets evaluation standards of the U.S. Department of Labor.

All employees of the DMT, with the exception of the six unit heads, the director, and the assistant director, are covered by civil service rules. But positions for civil service employees may be abolished for either lack of work or lack of funds. Employees have "bumping rights" only within DMT, not between DMT and other departments. DMT employees are also covered by a collective bargaining agreement.

This year, however, Prosperity's mayor received two disturbing bits of news. First, the Department of Labor was rumored to be considering a formal audit of his city's CETA program because of widespread rumors that CETA jobs had been used to finance the dominant political party's base of support within the city. Second, there was a widespread expectation that federal funds to the city would be cut because of the Reagan Administration's pressure on Congress to cut human services programs. Last week, both of these rumors materialized: the Regional Office of the Department of Labor in St. Louis announced that it would be conducting a full-scale investigation of Prosperity's CETA program, and the office of the Secretary of Labor in Washington announced that funds to Prosperity's CETA program, among others, would be reduced approximately 20 percent during the next fiscal year.

You are the assistant director of the DMT. Your first reaction is, "Isn't that just like the federal government! First they drop tons of money on us in the seventies and tell us to spend it as fast as we can. Then a few years later they cut our budget and say they're planning to investigate us for fraud and waste! Why don't they make up their minds whether they want this program or not? If they don't, kill it now. If they do, give us a chance to do long-range planning and program development." Your second reaction is to do what you can to meet these twin pressures. Your boss, the director, wants you to come up with a reorganization plan designed to increase the capacity of the DMT to detect and control fraud and waste, either by CETA program participants or subcontractors. The director also wants you to develop reduction-in-force policies and procedures that will enable the DMT to reduce the total number of its employees by 20 percent.

The current DMT organizational chart, along with the number of employees in each organizational unit, is shown in Figure 8–3.

Your first assignment as a class is to determine what the new structure and staffing pattern for the DMT will be, and how many positions will be allocated to each organizational unit. Will all of the old functions be retained, or will some be eliminated? If they are all retained, will they have the same proportion of employees as they did before, or will the 20 percent

FIGURE 8–3 Current DMT Organization Chart

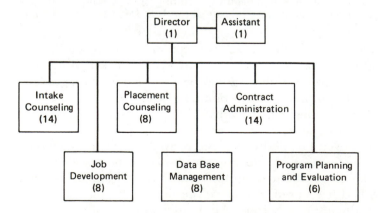

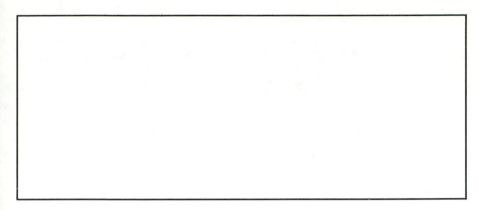

New DMT Structure and Staffing

cut fall more heavily on some functions than others? Make a group decision about these issues. In the above space, draw the new organizational chart for the DMT, and indicate the number of employees in each organizational unit.

Second, split up into working groups of three to five students so that one group is assigned to each of the units in the reorganized DMT (job development, contract administration, data base management, program planning and evaluation, and so on). Within each group, decide what types of occupations will be needed to perform the unit's functions. On the basis of this analysis, and after reviewing the current employee roster found on pages 145–47, decide which positions will stay in the unit.

Third, assume that employees will be given priority to apply for available jobs on the basis of one or more of the following criteria: seniority, performance evaluation, party loyalty, education, age, race and/or sex. Based on your understanding of the organization's situation, and your study of public personnel management, rank these factors in order of importance for employee retention during the reorganization and RIF. Do this individually at first, and then reach a consensus within your group.

Use this criteria to prepare a roster for the unit of the organization to which your group has been assigned. To make it easy on yourselves, and to conserve space on the blackboard, write only the names of the employees who have been added to or deleted from the work unit, using a format similar to Figure 8–5.

Remember, employees must be retained in a job for which they are qualified on the basis of education or experience. Granted it is not possible to develop firm conclusions about the nature of jobs since job descriptions are not provided. But exercise some judgment if you wish to retain "good" employees by reassigning them to other positions.

FIGURE 8–4.   DMT Employee's RIF Retention Criteria

CRITERION	GROUP A	GROUP B	GROUP C	GROUP D	GROUP E	GROUP F
Seniority						
Performance Evaluation						
Party						
Education						
Age						
Race/Sex						

Compare your responses in "New DMT Structure and Staffing," and Figures 8–4 and 8–5 with those of the other groups in the class. As you evaluate each other's work, consider the following questions:

1. What factors in the external and internal environment or your unit of DMT made you decide on the particular staffing pattern of your unit?
2. Did you follow, in Figure 8–5, the theoretical criteria for RIF retention that you established in Figure 8–4? If you did not, what factors precluded you from doing so?
3. Why did you rank the retention criteria in the order you did in Figure 8–4? How will you justify your criteria if the process becomes publicized or scrutinized by the city commission or the Department of Labor?
4. How would you justify the cutback to individual employees who must be RIFed?
5. What were the characteristics (age, education, race, sex, etc.) of this work force prior to the cutback? Are they significantly different following the layoff? What are the implications of this new work force profile for human resource management in the agency?

FIGURE 8–5.   Revised Roster for _____

Employees Added:

Employees RIFed:

TABLE 8–2. Current DMT Roster

(1) INTAKE COUNSELING (14 EMPLOYEES)

Name	Position	Years	Education	Party	P	A	S	R*
1. Geraldine Angelo	Intake Counselor I	3	BA—Personnel	R	Sat	29	F	H
2. Tony Dunn	Intake Counselor I	5	BA—Sociology	D	Sat	32	F	B
3. Clay Ellis	Intake Counselor I	8	HS	R	Sat	49	M	B
4. Ralph Frey	Intake Counselor I	1	BS—Psychology	R	Sat	24	M	W
5. Stephen Gide	Intake Counselor I	1	BS—PoliSci	R	Sat	27	M	W
6. Roberta Heid	Clerk Typist II	4	HS	D	Sat	47	F	B
7. Larry Hilman	Intake Counselor I	3	BS—Economics	R+	Sat	32	M	W
8. Carla Kantner	Clerk Typist III	11	HS	D	Sup	40	F	W
9. Fred Kranpe	Intake Counselor I	5	HS	D	Sup	34	M	B
10. Frieda McAllister	Intake Counselor I	3	BS—Pub. Admin.	R+	Sup	30	F	W
11. Diane Meredith	Clerk Typist II	6	HS	R	Sat	36	F	B
12. Carla Mueller	Clerk Typist I	1	HS	R	Unsat	22	F	W
13. Robin Reed	Clerk Typist IV	13	HS	R	Sat	52	F	B
14. Nancy Slocum	Clerk Typist II	3	BS—Home Econ.	R	Sup	26	F	W

(2) JOB DEVELOPMENT (8 EMPLOYEES)

Name	Position	Years	Education	Party	P	A	S	R
1. Betsy Ault	Clerk Typist II	4	HS	R	Sat	28	F	W
2. Ron Bates	Job Developer	3	BS—Soc. Serv.	R	Sat	28	M	W
3. Jerry Boswell	Job Developer	3	BS—History	R	Sat	28	M	B
4. Anthony DeBonis	Job Developer	3	BS—Economics	R	Sat	27	M	W
5. Jan Gunn	Clerk Typist I	2	HS	R	Sat	24	F	W
6. Sara Keasley	Clerk Typist I	1	HS	R	Sat	19	F	W
7. Marvin McCann	Job Developer	2	BS—Sociology	R	Sat	28	M	W
8. Yvonne Rawls	Clerk Typist II	7	HS	D	Sat	36	F	B

*P = performance rating; A = age; S = sex; R = ethnicity. Under "R," W = white, B = black, and H = Hispanic.

(continued)

TABLE 8–2. (Continued)

(3) PLACEMENT COUNSELING (8 EMPLOYEES)

Name	Position	Years	Education	Party	P	A	S	R*
1. Al Anastasi	Placement Counselor I	6	BS—Counseling	D	Sat	32	M	W
2. Felix Dean	Placement Counselor II	2	BS—Bus. Admin.	R+	Sat	27	M	W
3. Todd Gambell	Placement Counselor II	1	BS—Accounting	R	Sat	24	M	W
4. Martha Hicks	Clerk Typist II	8	HS	R	Sat	38	F	B
5. Don McIntosh	Placement Counselor I	5	BS—Soc. Serv.	D	Sat	33	M	W
6. Arthur Murray	Placement Counselor I	2	HS	R+	Sat	63	M	W
7. Charles Proctor	Placement Counselor I	7	HS	D	Unsat	36	M	B
8. Carl Sharpe	Placement Counselor I	4	BS—Soc. Serv.	D	Sat	38	M	B

(4) DATA BASE MANAGEMENT (8 EMPLOYEES)

Name	Position	Years	Education	Party	P	A	S	R*
1. K. P. Areson	Systems Analyst	6	MS—Comp. Sci.	D	Sup	36	M	W
2. Kim Caldwell	Keypuncher	1	HS	?	Sat	19	F	B
3. James Harris	Keypuncher	2	HS	?	Sat	21	M	B
4. Ruth Hill	Keypuncher	1	HS	?	Sat	20	F	B
5. Karen Laine	Keypuncher	0	HS	?	Sat	19	F	B
6. Craig Pettibone	Clerk Typist I	3	HS	R+	Sat	58	M	W
7. Gary Seward	Programmer	3	BS—Comp. Sci.	R	Sat	29	M	W
8. Ray Wilcox	Systems Analyst	2	BS—Math	D	Sup	25	M	B

(5) CONTRACT ADMINISTRATION AND COMPLIANCE (14 EMPLOYEES)

Name	Position	Years	Education	Party	P	A	S	R*
1. Alonzo Allen	Contract Negotiation	3	BS—Bus. Admin.	R	Sat	42	M	H
2. Roger Birkle	Accountant	3	MBA	R	Sup	27	M	B
3. Barbara Clint	Accounting Clerk	2	HS	R	Sat	22	F	B
4. Audrey Drury	Accounting Clerk	2	HS	R	Sat	49	F	W
5. Iris Floyd	Clerk Typist I	1	HS	R	Sat	41	F	W
6. Patricia Gibson	Clerk Typist I	2	HS	R	Sat	37	F	W
7. Denny Groves	Clerk Typist I	1	HS	R	Sat	24	F	W
8. Albert Hyde	Contract Administration	1	MBA	R	Sup	30	M	B
9. Mary Keene	Accounting Clerk	1	HS	R	Sat	32	F	W
10. Geraldine Maples	Clerk Typist I	1	HS	R	Sat	31	F	W
11. Donna Newman	Accounting Clerk	1	HS	R	Sat	30	F	W
12. Rosa Rath	Clerk Typist I	1	HS	R	Sat	23	F	H
13. Victor Sahn	Contract Negotiation	2	BS—Engineering	R	Sat	46	M	W
14. Larry Singh	Contract Administration	3	BS—Bus. Admin.	R	Unsat	26	M	W

(6) PROGRAM PLANNING AND EVALUATION (6 EMPLOYEES)

Name	Position	Years	Education	Party	P	A	S	R*
1. Laura Bennett	Clerk Typist I	1	HS	R	Sat	29	F	W
2. Sharon Cole	Clerk Typist I	1	HS	?	Sat	27	F	W
3. Floyd Hale	Program Development	3	HS	R+	Sat	47	M	W
4. Belinda Hughes	Clerk Typist I	1	HS	R	Sat	22	F	W
5. Audri Jones	Management Analyst	7	BS—Soc. Serv.	R	Sup	38	M	B
6. Martha Nicholson	Clerk Typist I	1	HS	R	Sat	44	F	W

NOTES

[1]Richard W. Lindholm, et al., "The Budgetary Process," in J. Richard Aronson and Eli Schwartz (eds.), *Management Policies in Local Government Finance* (Washington, D.C.: International City Management Association, 1975), pp. 63–64.

[2]Aaron Wildavsky, *The Politics of the Budgetary Process* (Boston: Little, Brown, 1974).

[3]Larry Berman, "OMB and the Hazards of Presidential Staff Work," *Public Administration Review*, Vol. 38, No. 6 (Nov.–Dec. 1978), 520–24.

[4]Albert C. Hyde and Torrey Whitman, "Workforce Planning—the State of the Art," in Jay M. Shafritz (ed.), *The Public Personnel World: Readings in the Professional Practice* (Chicago: IPMA, 1978), pp. 65–73.

[5]Milton Drandell, "A Composite Forecasting Methodology for Manpower Planning Utilizing Objective and Subjective Criteria," *Academy of Management Journal*, Vol. 16, No. 3 (September 1975), 512.

[6]Drandell, 512–18.

[7]Steven C. Wheelwright and Darral G. Clarke, "Corporate Forecasting: Promise and Reality," *Harvard Business Review* (Nov.–Dec. 1976), 64–70.

[8]Ernest C. Miller, "The Human Resource Executive and Corporate Planning: A Personnel Symposium," *Personnel*, Vol. 54, No. 5 (Sept.–Oct. 1977), 12–22.

[9]Stephen K. Doig, "Federal Budget Cuts Appear Not So Deep," *The Miami Herald*, September 6, 1981, p. D6.

[10]Charles H. Levine, "More on Cutback Management: Hard Questions for Hard Times," *Public Administration Review*, Vol. 39, No. 2 (March–April 1979), 179–83; and I. Rubin, "Preventing or Eliminating Planned Deficits: Restructuring Political Incentives," *Public Administration Review*, Vol. 40, No. 6 (Nov.–Dec. 1980), 575–84.

[11]Leonard Greenhalgh and Robert McKersie, "Cost-Effectiveness of Alternative Strategies for Cutback Management," *Public Administration Review*, Vol. 41, No. 6 (Nov.–Dec. 1980), 575–84.

[12]"New York City Layoffs Reverse Equal Opportunity Gains," *The Spokeswoman*, Vol. 6, No. 11 (May 15, 1976), 2.

[13]Charles H. Levine (ed.), "Symposium on Organizational Decline and Cutback Management, *Public Administration Review*, Vol. 38, No. 4 (July–August 1978), 315–57; especially Charles H. Levine, "Organizational Decline and Cutback Management," 316–25.

9

Job Analysis
and Classification

The previous section analyzed the impact of affirmative action on recruitment, selection, and promotion. Yet these activities do not occur in a vacuum. Before a position can be advertised and filled, its duties and qualifications must be established.

This creates an initial controversy, between the needs of personnel managers and those of employees and supervisors, that often proves insurmountable. For their part, supervisors want job descriptions that can be used to increase productivity. Employees want a description of their duties that makes the job more understandable, and the relationship between job performance and rewards more predictable. But job descriptions are not always seen as useful for these purposes. Many people consider job descriptions irrelevant to good management. However, a brief example will illustrate their necessity.

In the early 1970s, a mysterious bank robber named "D. B. Cooper" captured the attention of the country when he escaped by parachuting from a skyjacked airplane over a remote area of Oregon's Cascade Mountains. Shortly thereafter, this fascination changed to alarm when political malcontents began skyjacking commercial flights, forcibly rerouting them to desired destinations and holding passengers and crew hostage.

The federal government responded to this challenge by establishing a task force. One of its preliminary recommendations was that skyjackings be deterred or prevented by placing specially trained "antiskyjackers" on selected high-risk flights. The task force initially recommended that these people be qualified in both clinical psychology (in order to talk mentally deranged skyjackers into surrendering) and hand-to-hand combat (in order to disarm them without endangering passengers or the aircraft's pressurization). Based on a realistic assessment of the salary commanded by people with this unique combination of skills, the task force initially recommended a pay level of GS–13—equivalent to about $42,000 at this writing.

When these initial recommendations were "leaked" to top administrators and Congressional leaders to get their reaction, the response was negative. Understandably, no one wanted to take the "heat" for approving this high a salary for someone whose main function would be riding around on airplanes on the chance that (a) a skyjacking would occur, and (b) the skyjacking could be deterred or overcome. When the final report was published, it called for the position of sky marshal, but the qualifications (and the salary) were only GS–7—the same grade as for the federal marshals responsible for transporting prisoners from one location to another. Within two years, skyjackings had decreased and the program was abandoned.

This example shows that job analysis and classification are a necessary link between human resource planning and the management of human resources. Once human resource needs are forecast, it is still necessary to define the duties of the position and to develop a realistic set of qualifications required to ensure that the applicant can perform those duties adequately. Otherwise, pay levels cannot be set, meaning that a budget estimate cannot be prepared for submission to the chief executive or the legislature. In addition, recruitment and selection cannot occur.

By the end of this chapter you will be able to:

1. Describe the history of job analysis and classification
2. Discuss traditional methods of job analysis
3. Evaluate the comparative advantages and disadvantages of results-oriented job descriptions as an alternative
4. Write a job description for a position
5. Describe the purposes and methods of job classification
6. Discuss the politics behind job reclassification

HISTORY OF JOB ANALYSIS AND CLASSIFICATION

In large measure the history of public personnel management is synonymous with the development of job analysis and classification. Personnel management, as a branch of administrative science, is based on the bureaucratic model developed by the German sociologist Max Weber. According to this model, bureaucratic organizations, at least in theory, are characterized by a hierarchy of authority, a division of labor, reliance on rules as the basis for decision making, and selection and promotion on the basis of merit. These are also the objectives of job classification and evaluation.

Organizational applications of the bureaucratic model were developed by the *administrative science* school of management. This school originated in the early 1900s with the work of Frederick W. Taylor, an industrial engineer who believed that there was "one best way" to do a job or run an organization. Given this rational, engineering-oriented approach to management, it followed that the manager's primary function was to plan and organize work in the most technically efficient manner.

With respect to jobs, this involves the first principle of any natural science: classification of jobs into distinct groups on the basis of their characteristics and level of responsibility. This was first embodied in the Classification Act of 1923, which provided for job analysis and classification for some federal positions. It is important to realize that classification developed because, like positivism, it was based on a scientific principle augmented by morality. That is, classification was considered beneficial not only because it carried the principle of description over from the natural sciences, but also because it supported the twin values of agency efficiency and individual equity. On the one hand, classification helps the line manager and the personnel manager to divide labor more efficiently. On the other, it provides for the equitable compensation of employees according to the true worth of their jobs. Lastly, it decreases the opportunity for political favoritism by providing that pay be based on a realistic assessment of duties and qualifications, rather than as a reward for political responsiveness.

The concept of public management as an efficiency-oriented administrative science was augmented by a second philosophical orientation—the "politics-administration dichotomy." This school of thought, first developed in some detail by Frank J. Goodnow, proposed the existence of a clear distinction between politics and administration.[1] According to this model, politics is the art of gaining agreement on policy objectives through executive or legislative action, whereas public agencies and administrators perform purely technical or professional functions relating to policy implementation. Once policy is agreed on and enacted into law under this model, administrators carry out that policy impartially and efficiently according to principles of technical rationality.[2]

For a number of reasons, this amalgam of administrative science and the politics-administration dichotomy is no longer considered a realistic model of public administration. First, current models of public administration derived from functional analysis or public policy analysis tend to emphasize the role that administrative agencies play in making policy when they implement legislation. Second, organization theory has demonstrated that the assumption of a closed-system, rational, technically oriented organization is unwarranted. In its place contingency theorists have developed models of organizations that emphasize the constant interaction between managerial desires for predictability and efficiency, and the essential unpredictability of their environments. Third, administrative behaviorists have concluded that managerial behavior arises out of the interplay of conflicting role expectations rather than out of a single value such as efficiency.

In sum, job analysis and position classification arose from a heritage of civil service reform, administrative science, and the politics-administration dichotomy. Although these values are no longer ascendant, the personnel functions remain important as methods of achieving external political responsiveness. And, as we shall see, they can also be useful for achieving managerial efficiency and employee satisfaction.

TRADITIONAL JOB ANALYSIS

Job analysis is the process of recording information about the work performed by an employee. It is done by observing or interviewing the worker, with the corroboration of the supervisor. It results in a *job description*—a written statement of the employee's duties. It may also include a *qualifications standard,* which specifies the minimum education and/or experience an employee needs to be able to perform the position's duties satisfactorily.

Figure 9–1 is an example of a traditional job description. Note that it specifies the organizational unit to which this position is responsible, the general duties performed by the incumbent, and the minimum qualifications required for eligibility.

FIGURE 9–1. Traditional Job Description

Responsibilities:

Works under the direction of the supervisor, Operations Control section

Duties:

Types correspondence and reports
Compiles reports
Maintains inventory of supplies
Arranges meetings and conferences for the supervisor
Handles routine correspondence
Other duties as assigned

Qualifications:

High school degree or equivalent
Typing speed of 40 wpm
Two years experience in a secretarial position or equivalent education

---

If the goal of the job description is to promote managerial efficiency, this job description is deficient in two respects. It does not specify the performance expected of the employee; nor does it specify the linking or enabling relationship among standards, skills, and minimum qualifications. What do these deficiencies mean?

This job description lists the general duties performed by any number of administrative assistants. Because it applies to a range of positions, it is necessarily vague concerning the nature of the typing, reports, meetings, and correspondence involved. The employee may be working in a foundry, a personnel office, or a chemical supply house. In each case, specific duties will differ. The entry "Other duties as assigned" leaves the job description open to any additions the supervisor may propose.

However, there are no clues provided concerning the conditions under which the job is to be performed. Is an electric typewriter available or not? How large is the filing system, and is it current and accurate? How much correspondence is there to answer? Do all duties occur continuously, or do some require more work at certain times? What written guidelines or supervisory instructions are available to aid the employee? What conditions make task performance easier or harder? Thus, from the applicant or employee's point of view, there is not enough useful information for orientation purposes. The employee or applicant's query, "What is expected of me in this job?" is not answered.

More critically, there are no standards set for minimally acceptable employee performance along each of the job's duties. This omission is basic to the distinction between job evaluation and performance evaluation. The former is the process of evaluating job worth, while the latter is the process of measuring the performance level of an employee in that job. While this distinction is accepted by most personnel managers, most managers and employees feel that in practice it is difficult to separate an abstract "job" from the concrete performance of its incumbent. The above job description does not specify the quantity, quality, or timeliness of service required, nor does it set these standards in the light of varying conditions. For example, it may be easier for a salesperson to increase sales 10 percent annually in an industry growing by 20 percent annually than to achieve the same rate of increase in a declining market.

Moreover, traditional job descriptions specify a general set of minimum qualifications for each position. If jobs have been classified according to the type of skill required, these minimum qualifications may be based on skills required to perform duties. In general, however, traditional methods blur the following logical sequence of relationships between tasks, standards, skills, and qualifications:

1. Each job task must be performed at certain minimum standards for the organization to function well.

2. Certain skills, knowledge, and abilities enable the employee to perform a task up to standard.
3. Certain minimum qualifications ensure that the employee will have these skills, knowledge, and abilities.

Thus, even though job analysis is traditionally seen as a cornerstone of public personnel management, its links to other functions such as selection and performance evaluation are indistinct because it is deficient in the above respects. These two problems—the lack of a clear relationship among tasks, skills, and qualifications, and the lack of clear information about the nature of the job—clearly reduce the usefulness of job descriptions for organizational planners, program managers, and employees. Indirectly, but perhaps most significantly, they affect the perception that all these groups have for the personnel management profession itself.

Organizational planners are handicapped because such traditional job descriptions describe only the personnel inputs into a job and not the resultant outputs. That is, they do not specify how many employees would be needed to produce outputs at a given level of quantity, quality, or timeliness. Because traditional job descriptions do not lend themselves to output analysis, they are not useful for human resource planners who need to establish a link between human resource inputs and organizational outputs. This makes it more difficult for them to assume a proactive role in the human resource planning process. Output-oriented job descriptions are a microcosm of program-oriented budgets, while traditional job descriptions more closely resemble ceiling or line item budgets. While the latter is more useful for external control purposes, the former is better suited for productivity improvement.

Managers are handicapped because they cannot readily use such job descriptions for recruitment, orientation, MBO (Management by Objectives) goal setting, or performance evaluation. If new employees are recruited on the basis of the brief description of duties and qualifications given in the traditional job description, then extensive interviewing by managers may be needed to select those applicants most qualified for a particular job. Orientation will require clarification of the job description to fit the particular organizational context, and it may be incomplete because of other demands on the manager's time. If the organization uses MBO goal setting and evaluation procedures, these will occur independently of the position's job description. This means that job descriptions will be used only by the personnel department for human resource planning, recruitment, position management, and other external control-oriented activities, while managers will control and evaluate employee performance by an unrelated set of MBO procedures. If MBO is not used, then performance evaluation will be based on employees' job-related personality traits rather than on outputs.

Employees are generally unable to use traditional job descriptions for orientation, performance improvement, or career development. Because job descriptions give only a brief outline of duties, employees must wait to learn about working conditions and standards until they have been hired. Yet this may be too late; unclear or inequitable psychological contracts are a cause of much unrest between employees and organizations. Evaluating employees without giving them clear performance expectations is a sure way to increase anxiety and frustration.[3]

Moreover, employees cannot use traditional job descriptions for career development because they do not specify how increases in minimum qualifications are related to increases in skills required for satisfactory task performance. It is easiest for employees to accept the qualifications for a position and to strive to meet them through upward mobility programs, if these linkages are more apparent.

But personnel managers, and the personnel management function itself, are most seriously affected by the limited usefulness of traditional job descriptions. Because traditional job descriptions are best suited to cataloguing and managing positions, they are regarded as irrelevant to productivity improvement by program planners, managers, and employees.[4] Inevitably, job descriptions tend to be regarded in the same light as inventories of office equipment or the updating of civil defense plans—something that must be maintained as a bureaucratic necessity, but which is not a useful tool for accomplishing primary organizational or employee goals. This perceived uselessness of job descriptions affects other personnel activities as well. If personnel managers consider job descriptions to be one of the most important personnel activities, and if job descriptions are perceived by managers and employees to be useless for their own purposes, then it follows logically that other personnel activities are equally unimportant. This logic is frequently used to belittle performance evaluation, job analysis, training needs surveys, and other items from the personnel manager's stock in trade.[5]

Consequently, the primary result of these deficiencies in traditional job evaluation is to divorce personnel management from those organizational activities concerned with outputs and environmental relationships—primarily program planning, budgeting, and program evaluation. As a result, personnel management is viewed as a series of low-level, operational techniques used mainly for external control or system maintenance purposes.

HOW TO IMPROVE TRADITIONAL JOB DESCRIPTIONS

Job descriptions would be more useful if they clarified the organization's expectations of employees and the linkages between tasks, standards, skills, and minimum qualifications. These improved, results-oriented job descriptions would contain the following information:

1. *Tasks*: What behaviors, duties or functions are important to the job?
2. *Conditions:* What things about the nature of the job, or the conditions under which tasks are performed, are particularly easy or difficult? What written guidelines or supervisory instructions are available to aid the employee in performing a task?
3. *Standards*: What objective performance expectations are attached to each task, expressed in terms of standards of quantity, quality, or timeliness, which are meaningfully related to organizational objectives?
4. *SKAs*: What *s*kills, *k*nowledge, and *a*bilities are required to perform each task at the minimally acceptable standard?
5. *Qualifications*: What education, experience, and/or other qualifications are needed to ensure that employees will have the necessary SKAs for task performance?

Two examples of results-oriented job descriptions (RODs) are shown in Figure 9–2.

FIGURE 9–2.   Results-Oriented Job Descriptions

---

a. Typist/Receptionist

Tasks	Conditions	Standards
Type letters	when asked to by supervisor; using an IBM Selectric typewriter; according to the office style manual	all letters error-free, completed by 5 P.M. if assigned before 3 P.M.
Greet visitors	as they arrive, referring them to five executives with whom they have scheduled appointments	no complaints from visitors referred to the wrong office, or waiting before being referred

Skills, knowledges, and abilities required:

ability to type 40 wpm
ability to use Selectric typewriter
knowledge of office style manual
courtesy

Minimum qualifications:

high school degree or equivalent
six months experience as a typist or an equivalent performance test

---

(continued)

b. Juvenile Probation Officer

Tasks	Conditions	Standards
Meet with probationers weekly to assess their current behavior	caseload of not more than 60 appointments scheduled by receptionist; supervisor will help with difficult cases; use procedures stated in rules and regulations	all probationers must be seen weekly; those showing evidence of continued criminal activity or lack of a job will be reported to your supervisor
Prepare presentence reports on clients	when requested by the judge; average of five per week, according to instructions issued by judge; supervisor will review and approve	your reports will be complete and accurate as determined by the judge; he or she will accept 75 percent of your presentence recommendations

Skills, knowledges, and abilities required:

knowledge of the factors contributing to criminal behavior
ability to counsel probationers
ability to write clear and concise probation reports
knowledge of your judge's sentencing habits for particular types of offenders and offenses
knowledge of law concerning probation

Minimum qualifications:

high school degree or equivalent plus four years of experience working with juvenile offenders, or a BS degree in criminal justice, psychology, or counseling
able to pass a multiple-choice test on relevant probation law
possess a valid driver's license

FIGURE 9–2. *(continued)*

These results-oriented job descriptions provide clearer organizational expectations to employees. They encourage supervisors and employees to recognize that both standards and rewards can be contingent upon conditions. For example, a secretary can type neater copy more quickly on an electric than on a manual typewriter. In the second example, an increase in the local crime rate might cause a temporary increase in each probation officer's caseload from 60 to 75 clients. If this happens, it could be expected that the quality, length, or frequency of weekly visits would be reduced and that the judge would accept fewer than 75 percent of their presentence recommendations.

SKAs are tied to task performance, and minimum qualifications are related to them using content validation methods. As performance standards vary, it is probable that SKAs would vary in corresponding fashion, as would minimum qualifications. For example, a probation officer handling difficult cases and working without direct supervision would need more skill in counseling probationers and writing presentence investigation reports. This would probably require more experience, more related education, or a more successful counseling record.

Results-oriented job descriptions focus on performance standards, the conditions that differentiate jobs, and the linkages between standards, SKAs, and qualifications. In so doing, they resolve many of the problems attributed to traditional job descriptions:

> They give the program planner a means of relating personnel inputs to organizational outputs.
>
> They give managers a means of orienting new employees to performance expectations, setting MBO goals, and evaluating employee performance objectively.
>
> They give employees a clearer idea of organizational performance expectations and of the minimum qualifications for promotion or reassignment.
>
> They increase the impact of personnel managers on organizational and employee productivity, rather than limiting their impact to position management and enforcement of external legislative control.

While they are useful for these purposes, RODs appear to have some serious disadvantages:

1. Changes in conditions and standards require constant rewriting of RODs.
2. Each position requires a different ROD.
3. Some positions do not have measurable performance standards.
4. RODs cannot be used to classify or evaluate positions.

First, it is inevitable that conditions affecting task performance will change. Won't this require that RODs be rewritten frequently to specify these changed conditions and standards, thereby causing an unmanageable paperwork load for supervisors and the personnel department? Possibly. On the other hand, most communication between employees and supervisors concerns unforeseen changes in organizational goals, employee tasks, environmental conditions, and performance standards. Integrating RODs into the organizational planning and evaluation system does mean an increase in time spent on writing job descriptions, but it may not mean an increase in time spent on organizational communications. What will occur, in fact, is a new focus of communications on those changes in goals or conditions that affect employee performance standards. Moreover, most organizations do not change objectives frequently.[6] Moreover, the use of new job description methods will not in itself increase the rate of organizational change.

Second, much of the previous analysis has emphasized that different positions within a job will have different conditions and standards. Won't this lead to a proliferation of different position descriptions for similar positions? The answer to this question depends on the position. It will not do so where groups of employees perform similar tasks under similar conditions. It will where they do not. For example, a group of claims examiners assigned to clients on a random basis, using identical methods and equipment, and working in the same location, could be classified in the same job classification and evaluated against the same performance standard.

Third, many supervisors and job analysts consider it difficult to establish individual performance expectations where groups of employees must work closely together. There are two possible responses to this problem: to establish, as part of the "conditions" statement attached to each task, the nature and extent of support needed from other employees for successful task performance; or to develop group performance standards and reward systems that assume that such interdependencies exist.

The last objection is the most serious from the personnel manager's viewpoint. Job descriptions are used not only to clarify expectations for each position but also to classify jobs for human resource planning purposes, and to evaluate them for pay comparability purposes. How could these vital functions be accomplished using RODs? The answer is to continue using those aspects of traditional job analysis that are necessary for these purposes. Personnel managers could continue to group jobs into occupational classes based on the type of work performed. Traditional job evaluation methods could then be used to determine the pay ranges appropriate to each position, and employee performance relative to objectives specified in the ROD would be used to "fine-tune" the system within pay ranges. That is, the pay range for a position could be established through traditional job evaluation methods, and increments (or decrements) from this midpoint could be allocated on the basis of an individual employee's performance in the position.

By tying skills, knowledge, and abilities to tasks and validating minimum qualifications as enablers to task performance, linkages could be established between positions to aid in career development planning, promotion potential assessment, and upward mobility. Here again, the relationship between RODs and traditional evaluation methods would be complementary. Traditional methods would show an organization's job structure, and clusters of RODs (grouped by occupation) would show how increasing qualifications were related to SKAs and SKAs to task performance.

Adopting RODs means that organizations will use two types of job descriptions: traditional and performance-oriented. There is a justifiable tendency to reject proposed solutions that are more complicated than current techniques. However, this tendency also reflects a desire to return to an era when public personnel management techniques were simpler and more uniform than they are today. Yet our experience usually shows that diverse techniques are necessary.[7] Most authorities recommend different performance evaluation methods for different purposes (for example, performance improvement or reward allocation).

They also recommend a variety of selection methods—performance tests, review of biographical data, or interviews—for different types of positions. Because job analysis and evaluation are used for several purposes, among them external control, employee orientation, and managerial performance improvement, we need to accept the validity of different job evaluation methods for these purposes.

JOB CLASSIFICATION

Job classification is the process of categorizing positions according to the type of work performed, the type of skill required, or any other job-related factor. Classification simplifies job analysis, for it means that a standardized job description and qualifications standard can be written for an entire group of positions. A job, therefore, is actually a group of positions sufficiently alike with respect to their duties and qualifications to justify their being covered by a single job description. For example, a government agency may employ several hundred secretaries. Although some details of their positions differ, the job duties (typing, filing, and handling phone calls and walk-in visitors) are sufficiently similar to be classified as one occupation (secretary), or several types of secretarial positions based on the difficulty of work or its level of responsibility (Secretary I, Secretary II, and so on).

Two types of classification are commonly used. First, jobs are divided into generic occupational classifications. Second, within each generic occupational classification, jobs are differentiated according to the level of responsibility. The first of these classification methods will be discussed here; the second will be examined in the following chapter on job evaluation and compensation.

Classification systems for all jobs, both public and private, are based on a variety of factors:[8]

Information input: Where and how does the worker get information used in performing the job?

Mental processes: What reasoning, decision-making, planning, and information-processing activities are involved in performing the job?

Work output: What physical activities does the worker perform and what tools or devices does the worker use?

Relationships with others: What relationships with other people are required in performing the job?

Job context: In what physical and social context is the job performed?

Work methods: What methods or techniques are used to perform the job?

Worker traits: What personality characteristics or aptitudes are needed for job performance?

Generally, jobs are classified into different categories depending on the level of government. Federal jobs are classified into GS (general schedule)—clerical and professional positions—and WG (wage grade)—technical and laborer positions. In addition, jobs not covered by the merit system protections that apply to GS or WG positions are classified separately. Schedule C appointments are political appointees; and the SES (Senior Executive Service) is composed of several thousand top-level career bureaucrats who have voluntarily given up some civil service protections in return for the opportunity of earning merit pay for meritorious performance.

State jobs are generally classified into administrative, clerical, protective (law-enforcement), health professionals, and laborers. Local government employees are usually classified according to the development of collective bargaining units—firefighters; police officers; administrative and clerical; sanitation; and exempt (those not covered by a collective bargaining agreement or not subject to civil service protection). Again, classification systems are not developed solely by job analysts, but out of the admixture of historical practice and the relative power of employee groups, and their relative influence on the collective bargaining process.

THE POLITICS OF RECLASSIFICATION

In the previous chapter it was stated that three personnel activities—human resource planning, job analysis and classification, and job evaluation—related most closely to the allocation function, and hence most closely to the value of political responsiveness. This section will explore the allocative functions of job analysis by describing the political ramifications of two types of reclassification decisions, namely, the reclassification involving a change in pay, and the reclassification involving a change in status from a classified civil service position inside the collective bargaining unit, to an exempt (unclassified) position outside the bargaining unit.

The political implications of a "change in pay" reclassification are illustrated by the following example. Recently, a major county government centralized fire and rescue service by consolidating all municipal fire departments into one central county agency. One of the major obstacles related to this consolidation was the differences in duties and pay of various fire and rescue personnel in different municipal governments, and the desire of municipalities to keep control over their own systems. Most of these differences were resolved at the municipal level because city council members could see that county-wide consolidation would reduce equipment costs and provide greater economies. Second, most local unions (all municipal fire departments involved had the International Organization of Fire Fighters (IOFF) as their bargaining agent) and their members welcomed the greater stability of pay, benefits, and pensions that would result from consolidation.

However, several cities had required that their firefighters also be trained and certified as paramedics. The employees involved believed that possession of the SKAs symbolized by this certification made them essentially different from other firefighters, and hence entitled to a separate classification and a higher rate of pay. The county, for purposes of administrative efficiency and to save money, did not wish to create a special classification. Because the overwhelming majority of IOFF members did not have these skills, the union was more interested in protecting the rights of this majority than in insisting on the establishment of a special classification. Thus, IOFF locals representing those firefighters with paramedic training were unsuccessful in their efforts to establish a separate classification and pay grade.

They then appealed to the state collective bargaining regulatory agency, which was responsible for deciding which party—unions or management—was guilty of unfair labor practices. When the state-appointed arbitrator refused to order the establishment of a special classification, the involved IOFF locals and their employees took the case to state court. They also made it a subject of local politics by campaigning for those county commissioners who favored the creation of the special job class, and against those who opposed it. The issue has not been resolved at this writing.

A second type of reclassification issue occurs when employees are reclassified from classified (civil service) positions to exempt positions—those not covered by civil service protections or excluded from the bargaining unit. Traditionally, management has sought greater flexibility in hiring, disciplining, and transferring managerial employees by requiring them, as a condition of employment, to give up certain civil service protections. Unions, on the other hand, have resisted these efforts because exempt employees, as managers, are also excluded from the bargaining unit.

Likewise, civil service advocates resist managerial pressures to transfer employees to exempt positions because this makes these employees more susceptible to political pressure.

A classic example of the conflicts inherent in this type of reclassification occurred when the federal Civil Service Reform Act was implemented in 1980. Under the provisions of this Act, several thousand top-level federal administrators (in grades GS-15–18) were offered the option of either continuing in civil service positions or transferring into exempt positions, which provided more opportunity for merit pay for productive performance (the Senior Executive Service, or SES).

To date, those federal administrators who elected to remain in the classified service as well as those who chose to join the SES are uncertain about the advantages and disadvantages of each option. In favor of the SES, it can be stated that some administrators have received performance bonuses, and a larger group consider the system to have increased managerial flexibility without loss of employee rights. On the other hand, a large number of federal administrators have concluded that their switch to the SES has made political reprisals against them easier and has not resulted in the performance bonuses they had anticipated, particularly in those human service agencies whose objectives have a relatively low priority in the current administration.

Both these reclassification actions illustrate the link between politics and job classification. This link is either direct, in that changes in classification cause changes in the allocation of resources to groups of positions; or it is indirect, in that shifting groups of positions into or out of civil service protection and eligibility for bargaining unit membership affects their political influence.

SUMMARY

After human resource needs are forecast, jobs must be analyzed and classified before funds can be appropriated or allocated for them. Therefore, job analysis and classification are at the heart of public personnel management. Not only are they important in tracing the historical development of the discipline, but they show its relationship to the budget process and the value of political responsiveness. In addition, they can be related to the other objectives of employee orientation and managerial efficiency if traditional job analysis methods are augmented by a results-oriented job description (ROD).

Job classification, either by level of responsibility or by type of work, is a second major activity required for external control, salary equity, and managerial efficiency. As the case studies of reclassification have shown, job classification is related to politics either directly (in that changes in classification affect the pay allocated to groups of positions) or indirectly (in that reclassification of employees to noncivil service or exempt positions can increase their political responsiveness).

DISCUSSION QUESTIONS

1. How are job analysis and classification related to resource allocation?
2. What are the objectives of job analysis?
3. How is job analysis related to the historical development of public personnel management?
4. What are the characteristics of traditional job descriptions?
5. What are the disadvantages of traditional job descriptions?
6. What are the characteristics, advantages, and problems associated with results-oriented job descriptions (RODs)?
7. What criteria are used to classify jobs?

KEY TERMS

job analysis
job classification
administrative science
division of labor
"politics-administration dichotomy"
job description
qualifications standard
SKAs
tasks
conditions
standards
qualifications
job reclassification
exempt position
results-oriented job description (ROD)

EXERCISE: A RESULTS-ORIENTED JOB DESCRIPTION FOR CORRECTIONAL OFFICERS

In 1974, the Department of Correction in the state of Indiana became concerned about the need for prison reform. The Governor and the department director appointed a task force to investigate the problem. Among the issues raised by the task force was the need for more qualified prison guards. In place of the traditional role of the guard (applying "boot leather" therapy to recalcitrant prisoners), the task force proposed a model that combined this traditional role with an additional one—informal counseling of inmates.

The task force proposed the following job description for the position of correctional officer:

I. Duties

Ensures maintenance of order and supervises inmates in a state correctional institution. Advises and counsels inmates in their adjustment to institutional living. The correctional officer also:

Remains alert for signs of disorder or tension.

Patrols assigned areas at various intervals for security of inmates, count of inmates, and security of buildings and grounds.

Supervises inmates in various work details, including general cleanup of institutional grounds and buildings.

Escorts inmates to and from the visiting room and dining room, and on various trips away from the institution.

Counsels inmates when necessary, discussing inmate's problems in an informal and unofficial capacity.

Keeps records and makes reports on such matters as inmate movements and progress, as well as violations of rules.

Works in shakedowns of cell blocks, searching for possible contraband.

Encourages inmates to accept professional assistance from staff.

II. Conditions

Like many states, Indiana does not choose to spend a great deal of money on prisons. Its primary maximum security prison is located in Michigan City, east of Chicago on the shores of Lake Michigan. Although this building is sturdy, it is antiquated and lacks up-to-date heating and air-conditioning systems. These physical conditions, when compounded by the geographic isolation of the site and the normal variations in climate that occur over the course of the year, make the work location uncomfortable. To this must be added the additional dangers that come from supervising inmates, and the boredom that normally characterizes the job of corrections officer.

Work is performed indoors in a cell house atmosphere or outside in various weather conditions while patrolling the institutional grounds and performing normal custodial duties. It requires an extensive amount of standing, walking, and climbing of steps. Above-average strength is required when defending against one or more irate inmates.

On the other hand, several things make the work easy. A multitude of rules and regulations covers ever aspect of inmate behavior. Training is provided to all new officers (they must complete this training within the first year on the job in order to keep their position). While their control over inmates is never absolute, they are supported both by regulations, by other officers, and by the entire character of the institution.

III. Skills, Knowledge, and Abilities

Working knowledge of and familiarization with appropriate Department of Correction and institutional rules and regulations

Ability to supervise effectively and obtain results from inmates who may not be work-motivated

Some knowledge of psychology, sociology, alcoholism, drug addiction, and criminology

Ability to defend oneself physically

Ability to operate cell house range controls

Ability to prepare reports of unusual happenings, accidents, or violations of rules

Alertness and ability to act quickly and effectively in an emergency

Ability to keep abreast of progress and study in the field of corrections

Ability to understand the proper use of firearms

Ability to work with inmates from different cultures and backgrounds (Note: although Michigan City is rural, most inmates are urban blacks and Hispanics)

Your assignment is to write a results-oriented job description for this position, using the information provided in the above job description. Using the following format, specify the tasks, conditions, SKAs, and qualifications for the position.

1. *Tasks*: What are the four most important tasks of the position? Use plain, simple language to describe them in a few words each.
2. *Conditions*: What conditions make the job easy or difficult?
3. *Standards*: What objective performance standards (quality, quantity, or timeliness) could be used to measure whether each of the above tasks had been satisfactorily accomplished?
4. *SKAs*: What skills, knowledge, and abilities are needed to perform the above tasks, at the above standards, under the above conditions?
5. *Qualifications*: What education, experience, and other qualifications would be required to ensure that applicants possess the minimum SKAs described above?

Tasks
(example: maintain order)

Conditions
(examples: Job is *hard* because: prisoners are dangerous; Job is *easy* because: regulations tell you
what to do)

Standards
(example: no escapes, deaths, or reportable injuries or incidents)

SKAs
(example: ability to work with inmates from different backgrounds)

Qualifications
education:
experience:
licenses or credentials:
other qualifications:

FIGURE 9–3. Correctional Officer Job Description. (Adapted from Correctional Officer job
description, Personnel Division, State of Indiana. All rights reserved.)

NOTES

[1]Frank J. Goodnow, *Politics and Administration* (New York: Macmillan, 1900).

[2]Nicholas Henry, *Public Administration and Public Affairs* (Englewood Cliffs, N.J.: Prentice-Hall, Inc., 1975), pp. 6–8.

[3]Frank P. Sherwood and William J. Page, Jr., "MBO and Public Management," *Public Administration Review*, vol. 36, no. 1 (January–February 1976), 29; and John C. Aplin and Peter P. Schoderbek, "How to Measure MBO," *Public Personnel Management* (March 1976), 89.

[4]Bernard H. Baum and Peter F. Sorensen, Jr., "A 'Total' Approach to Job Classification," *Personnel Journal* (January 1969), 31–32.

[5]Robert L. Malone and Donald J. Petersen, "Personnel Effectiveness: Its Dimensions and Development," *Personnel Journal* (October 1977), 498–501.

[6]Patricia Cain Smith and L. M. Kendall, "Retranslation of Expectations: An Approach to the Construction of Unambiguous Anchors for Rating Scales," *Journal of Applied Psychology*, Vol. 47, No. 2 (1963), 149–55.

[7]Edgar H. Schein, "Changing Role of the Personnel Manager," *Journal of the College and University Personnel Association*, Vol. 26, No. 3 (July–August 1975), 14–19.

[8]Sidney A. Fine, "Functional Job Analysis: An Approach to a Technology for Manpower Planning," *Personnel Journal*, Vol. 53, No. 1 (November 1974), 813–18; U.S. Employment Service, *Dictionary of Occupational Titles* (Washington, D.C.: U.S. Government Printing Office, 4th ed., 1977); Ernest J. McCormick, Joseph W. Cunningham, and George G. Gordon, "Job Dimensions Based on Factorial Analyses of Worker-Oriented Job Variables," *Personnel Psychology*, Vol. 20 (1967), 417–30.

10

Job Evaluation and Compensation

How much are you worth to your employer? At bottom, the answer to this question is simple: you are worth what the employer is willing to pay for your services. But arriving at the specific dollar amount the employer will pay is not simple. Rather, it is a complex process which reflects not only market conditions, but other factors as well—societal values, judgments concerning job evaluation criteria, and political realities.

Initially, of course, public employees' pay is based on market conditions, and therefore reflects what other employers pay for employees with similar qualifications. But salary is also heavily influenced by values as well as economics. The dominant value is *political responsiveness* in that pay rates are either established directly by a legislature, or indirectly through collective bargaining agreements subject to legislative ratification. This in itself can cause inequities. For example, state agencies in urban areas often have trouble recruiting or retaining qualified applicants if the state capital is located in a rural area. Why? Because legislators' perceptions of the "fair" prevailing wage rate reflect salaries in rural areas, where the cost of living is likely to be lower. In addition, intangible benefits such as greater job security have frequently been used as a justification for paying public employees less than prevailing wage rates.

Even though political responsiveness is the dominant value affecting compensation, the other three values affect it as well. First, it requires not only that all groups be fully represented in the work force, but that they be equally represented in different occupations (especially higher-paying professional and managerial jobs). Traditionally, minorities and women have been underutilized in these occupations, and have therefore earned lower average salaries than have white males. Thus, concern for the value of social equity demands that job evaluation and compensation look at job worth not solely in economic terms, but also in light of its implications for affirmative action compliance.

Second, the value of *administrative efficiency* dictates that public agency managers get the most value from scarce resources. Since pay and benefits constitute between 50 and 70 percent of total government expenditures, efficiency requires that pay and benefits be kept high enough to ensure an adequate supply of qualified applicants, but no higher than that level in order to conserve resources. Because budgets are prepared (and collective bargaining agreements renegotiated) annually, managers frequently find that their flexibility to adjust pay rates to fit their needs is more limited than it would be in private industry.

Third, the value of *individual rights* influences compensation in that everyone wants to be paid "a fair day's pay for a fair day's work." Yet because individual standards of equity differ, some method must be found for equating employee contributions based on employee characteristics (such as seniority or performance) and job worth factors (such as the inherent difficulty or responsibility of the work). These equity issues are not only the subject of individual discussions between employees and managers, they are also resolved through internal grievance procedures and external affirmative action compliance mechanisms. The collective bargaining process also provides a means by which groups of employees may assert claims of increased job worth.

Because ours is a materialistic society, we have a tendency to measure our own worth and that of our friends in terms of salary. The importance of pay and benefits to self-esteem, and the conflicts which occur among the four values that influence job worth, serve as a continual reminder that salary reflects not only market conditions, but also political assumptions and societal values.

By the end of this chapter you will be able to:

1. Discuss the objectives of job evaluation and compensation
2. Discuss the laws regulating pay and benefits for classified and unclassified employees
3. Describe the point-factor method of job evaluation
4. Discuss the ways of measuring employee contributions
5. Discuss the inducements-contributions contract
6. Discuss the types of rewards organizations can offer employees
7. Discuss the criteria for designing, implementing, and evaluating compensation systems
8. Discuss the relationship between cutback management and employee benefit systems

9. Discuss the need for reform of public pension systems
10. Discuss some specific allocational issues raised by job evaluation and compensation, namely, seniority and comparable worth

OBJECTIVES OF JOB EVALUATION AND COMPENSATION

As the introduction indicated, job evaluation and compensation have diverse objectives. Elected officials want clearly established salaries that make budget projections possible, without those salaries or benefits being "excessive" in comparison with private sector rates. Agency managers want compensation and benefit systems that enable them to recruit and retain employees well enough to accomplish program objectives; that provide benefits that are predictable enough for ease in budget management, yet flexible enough to reward productive employees. Employees want equity in comparison with other employees and in terms of the nature of the work.

Elected officials use the predictability of pay and benefit systems for several purposes related to external control. First, accurate estimation of proposed expenditures is required to keep them within receipts. Second, the "costing" and evaluation of proposed collective bargaining agreements requires that the legislature, which has the responsibility of approving or disapproving negotiated contracts, have accurate estimates of the costs of proposed changes in pay and benefits. Third, legislators and managers tend to compare public sector pay and benefits with those offered for similar work in the private sector. This enables them to determine the fairness of compensation as well as the comparative advantages and disadvantages of "contracting out"—that is, purchasing the same services in the private sector rather than having them performed by government employees.

For example, the manager of a school district cafeteria system recently concluded that it was more cost-efficient to hire an outside contractor to provide food service workers than to have the service performed by district employees. Why? Cutbacks in the school budget had forced the district to cut its food service allocation. A high percentage of this expenditure was labor costs. Since food services are normally provided at noon, the obvious solution was to cut every employee's hours (from eight to six hours per day, for example) so that full staffing was provided at peak hours. Yet the contracts with the food service employees' union required that, in the event of budget cuts, employees be laid off on the basis of seniority, while those remaining employees be entitled to work a full shift (eight hours). Management therefore concluded that it had to ask for a contract revision. But this created another problem. Even if each employee's hours were reduced equally so as to retain full staffing during peak service hours, benefit costs would increase from about 30 percent to 40 percent of salary. Why? Because management was required to pay certain minimum benefits to all employees (health services, workmen's compensation, life insurance) regardless of the number of hours they worked per pay period. In sum, management concluded that it was cheaper and easier to abolish its food service positions, and it made arrangements to have the work done by a private contractor.

This example also illustrates management's interest in being able to predict the cost of pay and benefits so as to project human resource costs, and to develop strategies to meet agency objectives within resource constraints. In this case, the options began with a choice between two cutback management techniques (seniority-determined layoffs, or proportionate reduction of all employees' hours) and culminated in a decision to contract out rather than to perform work in-house. Managers want *predictability* of rewards so that they can deal knowledgeably with legislators and chief executives concerning budgetary needs; they want *flexibility* so that they can reward productive employees to a greater extent than unproductive ones.

Employees are interested in the predictability of rewards, though for different reasons than managers. Employees want to be able to count on future paychecks or benefits so that they can make personal financial decisions, plan vacations, or look forward to retirement. Employees also want to be able to assess whether the rewards they receive are fair (in comparison with those of other employees). This means they want disclosure of salaries and benefits within the organization, and disclosure of the criteria used to determine job worth and employee performance. Lastly, employees want to maximize pay and benefits. Historically, at least, they have felt that the relatively lower pay of public sector jobs should be counterbalanced by greater job security and a more attractive benefits package (particularly health care and retirement).

LAWS REGULATING COMPENSATION

Several types of laws affect public sector compensation and benefits. These relate to procurement, allocation, employee development, and sanctions. With respect to procurement, affirmative action laws require that people be paid equally for equal work, and in particular that women and minorities be paid equally with white males. The pertinent legislation here is the Equal Pay Act of 1963 and the 1972 Equal Employment Opportunity Act, both of which were discussed in Chapter 7.

Yet these statutes all assume that funds are available to hire and pay employees. Therefore, allocational laws are the most fundamental to pay and benefits. For example, in order for employees to be paid, funds must be appropriated on the basis of a pay schedule or collective bargaining agreement. Both substantive and appropriations bills will require legislative approval before they are enacted. In those state and local governments that bargain collectively, the refusal of a legislature to ratify a negotiated collective bargaining agreement is not a breach of "good faith bargaining"; indeed, it is usually contrary to the state constitution for a state legislature or local governing body to ratify such an agreement without having identified a source of funds for the pay and benefits it establishes.

A number of laws tie compensation and benefits to employee performance, and several personnel systems in the past few years have attempted to tie pay increases to the performance appraisal system. Thus, employees rated "outstanding" are eligible for a greater merit increase than employees whose performances have been "satisfactory."

The sanctions process relates to the method used to resolve disputes concerning public personnel management activities. As was stated previously, the legislature has an almost exclusive right to adjudicate differences of opinion concerning pay and benefits since it must appropriate funds and ratify collective bargaining agreements. An important Supreme Court case (*National League of Cities* v. *Usery*) determined that the 1976 amendments to the Fair Labor Standards Act of 1938, which extended the Act's minimum wage and maximum hour provisions to employees of state and local governments, are unconstitutional. This obviously has had a critical impact on local governments, which otherwise would be unable to operate fire departments on a 24-hour on, 48-hours off schedule, to avoid paying time-and-one-half for overtime, or to avoid paying minimum wages. This landmark court case established that, at least for the time being, control of allocational policies would be considerably decentralized to state and local governments. Yet because this issue is so controversial and central to the interests of both employees and agencies, this question has been a topic of continued debate since then.[1] In addition, in *Wyoming* v. *EEOC* (1983), the Supreme Court found that the Age Discrimination in Employment Act also applied to state and local governments.[2]

The specific methods by which public employees' salaries are set differ by type of job. As described in Chapter 9, public positions can be grouped into two categories—*classified* and *unclassified*. Wages or salaries for classified positions are usually established by a formal method of job evaluation, or by collective bargaining agreements. The bulk of positions falls into this category. Salaries for unclassified positions—those not covered by civil service protections or collective bargaining agreements—are set by the much less formal process of political negotiation.

For example, in a county government with 10,000 employees, several hundred positions will normally be unclassified. These are filled by the county administrator, department and division directors, administrative assistants, and employees of the county commission and judiciary. Because these positions usually fall outside the civil service system, they traditionally have not been classified or evaluated within civil service systems. The people who occupy these positions, from the county manager down, negotiate their salaries with their supervisors (and ultimately with the local governing body). In this process, all of the factors used to determine compensation are used—market conditions, social equity, individual performance, seniority, and the salaries of classified employees.

POINT-FACTOR JOB EVALUATION

Job evaluation is a comparison of classified jobs in order to determine how much money they are worth. Although several methods have been used, the most prominent today is the point-factor method. It compares jobs on an absolute scale of difficulty, using several predetermined job worth factors which are quantified to make numerical comparisons easier. The following methodology is used in developing a point factor job evaluation:

1. Analyze all jobs in the organization.
2. Select factors that measure job worth across all positions. (It may be necessary to break jobs into broad occupational classes first, and to develop separate compensable factors for each class.)
3. Weight job worth factors so that the maximum possible value is 100. (For example, there could be five job worth factors, each with a maximum value of 20 points; or four factors worth 15 points each and one worth 40 points.)
4. Develop quality levels for each job worth factor, and apportion points within that factor to each quality level. (For example, if "working conditions" is selected as a job worth factor, with a total value of ten points out of 100, then three quality levels might be established for this job worth factor:
   a. no points: working in an office
   b. three points: occasional outside work; walking or standing required
   c. ten points: outside work in bad weather required; much heavy lifting required)
   Evaluate each job along each job worth factor, and compute the point total.
5. Establish realistic pay ranges for "benchmark" jobs based on market comparisons with similar jobs elsewhere.
6. Pay benchmark jobs the market rate, and pay other jobs in proportion to their comparative point totals.

Point-factor methods of job evaluation are extremely stable and reliable. Provided that care has been taken in the choice and weighting of job worth factors and quality levels, they are potentially the most valid of job evaluation methods. Not surprisingly, their primary drawbacks are the complexity and development costs associated with the method. Table 10–1 shows how the point-factor job evaluation method works in practice.

It can immediately be seen that this initial attempt to create a point-factor evaluation format has resulted in some apparent pay inequities:

police lieutenants would make more than the police chief, and police officers would make more than the sergeants who supervise them. Note, however, that this is entirely due to the choice of job worth factors, their relative weight, the choice of quality levels, and their relative weight. Each of these four choices is up to the discretion of the job analyst, except when it comes out like this! When this happens, other groups such as unions would quickly become involved.

Their involvement would probably result in alterations of job worth factors or the point values of quality factors to more acceptable levels. For example, the relative value of the above five jobs could be altered by changing the value of the job worth factor "responsibility" from 40 to 60 points, and by reducing the value of the other two factors to 20 points each. This would necessitate changing the quality factors' point values, and perhaps dividing "responsibility" into five factors rather than four. This would result in the point-factor job evaluation chart shown in Table 10–2.

While there might be some difference of opinion concerning the relative value of these jobs, it is clear that the point-factor evaluation method can be used to arrive at clear and consistent job evaluations. This is necessary not only for rational planning of personnel expenses, but also for pay equity and affirmative action compliance.

But job evaluation has a flaw. Even if the system is well designed and equitably applied to all positions, it will not pay people equally for equal

TABLE 10–1. Point-Factor Job Evaluation Method

JOB WORTH FACTORS   skill (30 points), working conditions (30 points), and responsibility (40 points) = 100 points total

QUALITY LEVELS

Skill:	30—professional knowledge and independent judgment
	20—technical knowledge under supervision
	10—some technical skill under close supervision
Working Conditions:	30—constantly unpleasant and dangerous
	20—occasionally unpleasant or dangerous
	0—office work
Responsibility:	40—makes decisions affecting a major program area
	25—makes decisions affecting a department
	10—makes decisions affecting service to individual clients

COMPENSABLE FACTORS

Position	Skill	Conditions	Responsibility	Total	Salary
Mayor	30	0	40	70	$35,000
Police Chief	30	0	25	55	27,500
Lieutenant	30	10	25	65	32,500
Sergeant	20	10	10	40	20,000
Police Officer	10	30	10	50	25,000

TABLE 10–2.   Revised Point-Factor Job Evaluation

JOB WORTH FACTORS   skill (20 points), working conditions (20 points), and responsibility (60 points) = 100 points total

QUALITY LEVELS

Skill:	20—exercises professional judgment independently
	14—exercises judgment with some supervision
	7—exercises technical skill under supervision
Working Conditions:	20—constant danger and discomfort
	10—occasional danger or discomfort
	0—office work
Responsibility:	60—in charge of a large organization
	45—in charge of a major department
	30—supervises more than ten employees
	15—supervises less than ten employees
	0—no supervisory responsibilities

POINT-FACTOR EVALUATION

Position	Skill	Conditions	Responsibility	Total	Salary
Mayor	20	0	60	80	$60,000
Police Chief	20	0	45	65	48,750
Lieutenant	20	10	30	60	45,000
Sergeant	14	20	15	49	36,750
Police Officer	7	20	0	27	20,250

work. Why not? Because job evaluation systems only compensate people based on the relative worth of their *jobs* rather than according to the relative *quality of their performance* in those jobs. Obviously, different people perform the same job with different degrees of skill. In order to measure the impact of the person on the job, either job-related traits or performance must be used, in addition to job worth, as criteria for setting salaries.[3]

MEASURING EMPLOYEE CONTRIBUTIONS

Job worth is only one of several factors that are used to compensate employees. Two others are personal characteristics (such as seniority or education) and the quality of an employee's performance.

The most frequently used employee characteristic is seniority, both because it has a logical relationship to quality of performance, and because it is easy to measure from the date the employee assumed the position or entered the organization. It is also common for employees to be compensated on the basis of education. Employees—particularly police officers and school teachers and administrators—are often given bonuses beyond the base pay rate for their positions.

Performance is also an important criterion for allocating rewards, for it is obvious that two different employees can perform the same job at different levels of competence.

An optimal solution seems to be a combination of job-oriented and person-oriented compensation factors, similar to the RODs approach suggested in Chapter 9. Once the pay range for a job has been established according to one of the four job-evaluation methods discussed previously, the pay of individuals within that range should be set on the basis of the person's job-related characteristics or performance. This compromise would have some of the advantages of both systems. The job-oriented approach would offer administrative ease, standardized pay ranges, and uniformity of compensable factors; the person-oriented approach would allow compensation on the basis of seniority, education, and performance.[1]

Unfortunately, most public agencies would apparently rather have the predictability of rewards by developing and implementing uniform pay plans based on job worth and/or seniority than bother with trying to allocate rewards on the basis of performance. Part of this is due to managerial and supervisory reluctance to deal with the problems of objective performance evaluation; another part must be attributed to union opposition to the concept of productivity bargaining. Yet changes are occurring that augur a reduction in the strength of this opposition. These factors will be discussed in the chapters on performance evaluation and labor-management relations.

THE REWARDS-CONTRIBUTIONS CONTRACT

When individuals are recruited by an organization, each party views the other in terms of a *rewards-contributions* contract. In other words, applicants gather data about the organization's expectations and rewards, while the organization gathers data on each applicant's capabilities and expectations. Rewards-contributions contract models draw upon several concepts, notably Barnard's inducements-contributions model.[5]

Figure 10–1 reconstructs the logic by which individuals develop the explicit contracts that are a part of everyday economic and social relationships. Each party determines its objectives, clarifies the behaviors it must engage in to achieve its goals, and determines whether the goals are feasible. If not, it redefines goals until they are feasible. Next, the parties agree on their respective behaviors and expectations. Following performance, they review their contributions to and rewards from the contract. This review of outcomes results in the contract being renewed, revised, or termi-

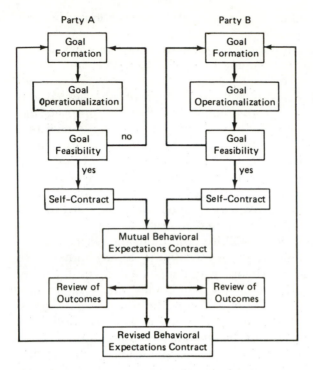

FIGURE 10–1. Inducements-Contributions Contract Process

nated. Individuals and organizations undergo the same process, with some differences. Organizations do not make decisions; therefore, the organization's choices are made by individuals acting in organizational roles. Both the employee and the organizational representative set objectives, establish the behaviors necessary for them to achieve these objectives, and determine the feasibility of these behaviors. If the behaviors are feasible, the result is an implicit rewards-contributions contract by which the organization determines the specific levels of performance it can expect from each employee, and what rewards it will have to offer in return.

Potential problems occur when either the organization or the individual feels that the terms of the contract have not been fulfilled. Typically, the organization will react to this by initiating disciplinary action or withholding scheduled rewards. The employee may react to this by seeking a formal revision of the contract by adjusting performance downward to match perceived rewards. It is the latter alternative that is most troublesome to public personnel managers, for substandard employee performance is a major cause of poor client service.

CRITERIA FOR DESIGNING A COMPENSATION SYSTEM

To be useful, a compensation system must meet the needs of both employees and the organization. That is, it must provide equity, be easy to administer, and be flexible. Unfortunately, these characteristics seem to contradict one another in practice. Thus, it is the job of the public personnel manager to reconcile them.

The usual reasons given by the organization for inflexible reward systems are legal requirements for equity and budgetary requirements for predictability. For instance, equity demands that identical life insurance benefits be provided to all employees in the same type of work in the same agency; and predictability of resource allocation demands that the pay and benefits attached to a position be easily calculable.

Given the lack of flexibility in economic rewards, it is still the responsi-

TABLE 10–3. Possible Public Agency Rewards

	INFLEXIBLE	FLEXIBLE
Economic	pay unemployment compensation hospital insurance life insurance retirement company vehicles clothing and equipment allowance (law enforcement) worker's compensation insurance commissary privileges (military) medical and health services (military)	promotion overtime pay parking education perquisites
Social	sports parties cafeteria or lounge newsletter	conferences management-oriented parties
Growth and recognition	none	training on-the-job training education "stand-in" supervisor autonomy outstanding performance evaluation recommendation for promotion quality step increase "employee of the month" letter of commendation

bility of the public personnel manager to encourage supervisors to recognize employee contributions through greater use of social and growth-oriented rewards. While most employees consider financial rewards important, other types of rewards are just as much in demand, and are equally useful in improving performance.[6] Table 10–3 summarizes some of the rewards that supervisors can use for this purpose.

PENSION PLANS

Recent concern over the financial soundness of the Social Security System has begun to focus the attention of taxpayers, employees, and elected officials on the condition of other public pension systems. There are over 3500 such systems, although 120 large municipal and state systems include over 90 percent of those employees covered. The assets of these systems are immense; they received over $43 billion in contributions in 1979, and they have assets of over $210 billion.[7]

Three primary issues have emerged that relate to public pension systems: (1) inadequate standards of disclosure, (2) inadequate actuarial standards, and (3) low recognition of the systems' potential for strategic investment.

Unlike private pension plans, for which minimum standards of disclosure and actuarial soundness have been established by the Employee Retirement Income Security Act (ERISA) of 1974, state and local pension systems are not regulated by federal law. Consequently, there is widespread agreement that they frequently do not inform beneficiaries, taxpayers, or elected officials concerning their financial condition. In response to this problem, and the threat of federal PERISA legislation, several states have passed disclosure laws that apply to state and local pension systems under their jurisdiction.

Much confusion also exists about the actuarial standards to which public pension systems should conform. These standards are assumptions about the rates of employment, death, inflation, etc., that are used to calculate the relationship between payments into the system and benefits drawn from it. Two types of systems are used—*fully funded* and *pay-as-you-go*. In a fully funded system, contributions of current employees are adjusted to meet the demands on the system by retirees, so that the system always remains solvent. Under a pay-as-you-go plan, employee contributions bear no necessary relation to payments, and funds are appropriated from general revenues to pay retirees' pensions.

However, there is no federal requirement that public pension funds be operated in conjunction with generally accepted accounting principles applicable to private pension plans as set forth in ERISA. This lack of uniform accounting, auditing, and actuarial standards led the General Accounting Office (GAO) to report that about 56 percent of the 72 pension plans it reviewed were not actuarially funded.[8]

Perhaps the most neglected aspect of public pensions is the potential for using these funds for strategic investment purposes. Traditionally, the administration of state and local pension systems has been burdened by laws that were either too lax or too restrictive. That is, they either allowed use of pension funds to subsidize favored groups of employees, or they restricted pension fund investments to low-interest, low-risk assets. Today, however, some states are recognizing the impact that pension funds can have on economic development. In Minnesota, for example, the Minneapolis Employee Retirement Fund (MERF) recently formed an investment corporation that lent money to high-tech industries wishing to relocate to the state. In Ohio, a recent change in state law allows the state's public pension funds to invest 5 percent of their assets in high-risk local investments (such as proprietorships and corporations), which formerly had been prohibited as investments. The pressure for this increased adoption of strategic investment has come not only from special interest groups but also from unions, who see it as a means of stimulating investment and creating jobs within the region.

COMPARABLE WORTH AND SENIORITY

Two issues that illustrate the impact of job evaluation and compensation on public personnel management are *seniority* and *comparable worth*.

Seniority is important because it is frequently used as a basis for allocating pay or allocating differential vacation benefits. Yet because it benefits those who have been with an employer longest, the issue of seniority creates allocational conflicts between older and younger workers.

Seniority is also important because of its potential for conflict with affirmative action. The Supreme Court has ruled that employees who previously have been discriminated against in selection should be given "fictional seniority" retroactive to the date of their original job application. However, in two similar cases, the Court has narrowed the impact of retroactive seniority by holding that plaintiffs seeking relief from seniority systems established prior to 1964 are not eligible for redress under Title VII of the 1964 Civil Rights Act.

One would expect affirmative action and seniority to conflict with respect to retention of employees as well. This is the case, as we have seen from the discussion in Chapter 5. Particularly in a cutback situation, seniority creates conflicts between senior employees and unions (who want retention rights to be allocated on this basis) and between managers and junior employees (who want discretion to allocate retention rights on the basis of productivity, social equity, or other criteria).

Job evaluation is also an allocational issue because of the continuing gap between average salaries for men and women. In 1930, women earned about 60 percent of the salary of men of similar race and education. By 1980, despite the passage of numerous affirmative action laws and a societal revolution in the working habits and educational accomplishments of women, this gap still existed. Those who argue that this difference is a continuing sign of illegal discrimination base their case on the assumption that a broader definition of equity is needed. The legal requirement of "equal pay for equal work" established by the 1963 Equal Pay Act—long a key principle of merit systems—should be considered too limited because, to apply, it requires that jobs involve equal duties performed under equal circumstances. In its place, critics reason that *comparable* jobs—those involving skills or abilities of equivalent value—should be compensated equally. This has thrown the decision into the hands of the job evaluators, who make comparability judgments after analyzing jobs, developing job worth factors and quality levels, and weighting them so that points can be attached to them. As we saw earlier, these decisions are judgmental ones about which job evaluators are not likely to agree.

The judgmental nature of job evaluation, and its relationship to allocation, means that comparable worth is a political issue as well as an administrative one. The U. S. Equal Employment Opportunity Commission (EEOC) promoted two national reports which in 1979 began to turn women's concern from hiring and promotions to job evaluation.[9] Several states have passed legislation establishing comparable worth as policy, several state court decisions have supported it, and many unions and professional organizations have advocated job re-evaluation.

Not surprisingly, most business and managerial interests oppose the concept as inimical to the external market system or internal wage stability.[10] At least before the election of Ronald Reagan, the business community was clearly alarmed that the EEOC might support a position of comparable worth, thus leaving employers no defense (other than absolute salary equality between men and women) against charges of sex discrimination.

Several strategies appear to be useful for groups concerned about achieving comparable worth or about its negative effects on organizations. Initially, it is necessary to realize that the determination of job worth depends not on intrinsic evaluation factors, but on the assumptions and power relationships of the parties involved. Next, it is important to consider that market considerations cannot be disregarded, but they can be modified if it is granted that they have acted to discriminate against the allocation of pay to women.

SUMMARY

Job evaluation and compensation affect the allocation of resources to public jobs in that they regulate the pay and benefits attached to each position. The objectives of equity, flexibility, and administrative efficiency often conflict in the design and administration of these programs.

From the perspective of the individual employee, job evaluation and compensation are key elements in the rewards-contributions contract, for they establish the economic and noneconomic rewards that the organization offers in return for participation and performance.

Among some managers and supervisors, it has become popular to lament that the lack of flexibility in reward allocation "ties their hands" so that productive employees cannot be rewarded. While equity considerations make some uniform benefits necessary, sufficient discretionary benefits exist so that managers can vary extrinsic rewards to match employee productivity.

Public pension plans have recently come under fire for problems relating to inadequate disclosure, poor actuarial safeguards, and insufficient utilization for strategic investment purposes. However, through increased pressure by unions, interest groups, taxpayers, and elected officials, these problems are being corrected.

Two controversial issues that illustrate the value conflicts involved with allocational functions are seniority and comparable worth. Particularly during a cutback situation, seniority pits older workers against younger ones, and unions against managers who wish to use alternative criteria (such as social equity or productivity). Likewise, comparable worth focuses attention on the fact that women's salaries are lower than men's and that this gap is not decreasing. This continued debate serves as a reminder that job-evaluation criteria are judgmental, and that they reflect not only market realities but also political assumptions and societal values.

DISCUSSION QUESTIONS

1. What are the objectives of job evaluation and compensation?
2. Why are different methods sometimes used to set salaries for classified and unclassified employees?
3. Describe point-factor job-evaluation methods.
4. Why should seniority and performance affect salary?
5. What is the rewards-contributions contract, and how is it related to pay and benefit systems?
6. What types of rewards can public agencies offer productive employees?

7. What is the relationship between cutback management and employee pension and benefit systems?

8. How are "comparable worth" and "seniority" related to compensation?

KEY TERMS

job evaluation
equity
psychological contract
point-factor evaluation
benchmark
job worth factor
seniority
social rewards
growth-oriented rewards
actuarial standard
strategic investment
comparable worth

EXERCISE: EQUITABLE PAY FOR PSYCHIATRIC ATTENDANTS

In 1977, a psychologically troubled real estate speculator named Tony Kiritsis walked into an Indianapolis bank and took one of its officers hostage. The officer was John Hall, a vice-president in charge of real estate loans. From the story that unfolded later, it was apparent that Mr. Kiritsis was in imminent danger of foreclosure on a tract of land that he wished to hold until investors purchased it to build a proposed shopping center. He felt that the bank, which held the mortgage on the property, was deliberately steering buyers away from his property so that it could repossess the land at a bargain price and sell it to potential buyers itself. He attempted to dissuade the bank from this course of action by kidnapping Mr. Hall, wiring a shotgun to his neck, and holding him hostage for several days until police managed to rescue Mr. Hall and imprison Mr. Kiritsis.

Following his arrest, Mr. Kiritsis was held in the Forensic Unit at Larue Carter, a state-run mental institution in Indianapolis. The Forensic Unit was reserved for people who had committed (or had been accused of committing) crimes, but who were also not considered sane enough to stand trial. At the time of his arrest, the Forensic Unit had approximately 100 inmates. The existence of this group of people was a byproduct of Indiana's unique insanity law. Briefly, the state's penal code requires that the prosecution prove that a suspect is sane in order for the suspect to be tried on criminal charges, rather than for the defense to prove the suspect insane during the course of the trial.

Mr. Kiritsis responded to this situation by refusing to undergo any of the psychiatric tests ordered by the court. As of this writing, the situation has not changed. Until he undergoes these tests, he remains in the Forensic Unit.

The Kiritsis case brought to a head several other developments that were occurring in the Indiana Department of Mental Health, which was responsible for the administration of 12 mental hospitals and numerous community mental health centers throughout the state. On the one hand, the movement to de-institutionalize the care of mental patients was gaining support, due both to the costs of institutionalized care and consideration for the legal rights and medical welfare of patients. On the other hand, the adverse publicity resulting from the Kiritsis case made the public—and legislators—aware of the potential risks of housing mentally unstable and dangerous people in the middle of the capital of the state.

These twin pressures culminated in a decision by the legislature and the Department of Mental Health to move all patients in the Forensic Unit to Logansport State Hospital. This facility was considered a better location because it was located in a rural area halfway between Indianapolis and Chicago. It also enjoyed considerable local support as an employer of many people in the area.

The proposed move drew a strong and immediate response from the head of the local chapter of the Indiana State Employees Association. His response was that the state's Personnel Department should not expect that the psychiatric attendants currently working at Logansport State Hospital, or any new ones hired to care for the inmates in the new Forensic Unit, would be willing to handle the increased hazards unless their positions were reclassified upward and/or they were given an additional increment of "hazard pay."

The state's personnel director was unwilling to support either of these demands. First, he contended that psychiatric attendants working in the Forensic Unit at Larue Carter had never received reclassification or hazard pay. Why should this occur now that the Forensic Unit was being transferred to Logansport State Hospital? Second, he believed that the creation of an additional classification would increase requests by personnel for transfer from other state mental hospitals to Logansport. This was because several hundred psychiatric attendants throughout the state had already reached the top step in their pay structure, and there were no jobs to which they could transfer laterally. That is, in order to be promoted they would first have to take a *demotion* to a lower grade in another field (such as rehabilitation therapist or psychiatric technician), work several years before being eligible for promotion back to their same pay grade in the other field, and then be eligible for further promotion. Though the desire for upward mobility among psychiatric attendants was great, their unwillingness to take a pay cut for several years to achieve it was also understandable.

TABLE 10–4.   Psychiatric Attendant Job Description

1. *Duties:* Responsible for supervising and transporting patients, and assisting medical and nursing personnel in carrying out patient care.

2. *Conditions:* Patients are disordered; the facility suffers from chronic underfunding, under-staffing and employee turnover; the work is generally not difficult; it is repetitious and closely regulated by rules and supervisory instructions.

3. *Standards:* Patients are not to escape, to cause reportable incidents, to injure or kill themselves or others, or to damage the facility; medical care instructions are to be followed precisely; written reports are to be accurate, complete, and timely.

4. *SKAs:* To perform these duties up to these standards under these conditions, psychiatric attendants must be alert to changes in patient disposition, possess an even temperament, be able to lift and carry other people, be able to follow orders, and be competent in handling routine and sometimes unpleasant job duties.

5. *Qualifications:* Six months' experience in any job working with other people; ability to pass a psychiatric screening examination; healthy; a high school diploma or its equivalent (GED, or passing score on a performance test of reading and writing ability).

Table 10–4 is a condensed job description for the position of psychiatric attendant.

As could be expected, the pay range for psychiatric attendants was relatively low compared with the median salaries paid by employers in Cass County, where Logansport State Hospital was located. The average weekly wage in Cass County (1982) was $222, and the average weekly manufacturing wage was $287, compared with a weekly pay range for psychiatric attendants of $156 to $244. The total Cass County labor force (1982) was 18,600, of whom 17,900 were employed; the projected unemployment rate is 7 percent.

The following options are possible solutions to the problem. Working in groups of four or five people each, decide which option(s) you would select if you were director of the Logansport State Hospital. Next, tell why you think it would be an appropriate solution to the problem. Tell how you would go about implementing it. Lastly, describe the technical, professional, or political problems your proposed solution(s) would encounter, and how you would go about overcoming them.

Possible Solutions

1. Make no policy changes.   Use the existing job classification, pay structure, and selection criteria for the position of psychiatric attendant. This solution relies on intensified recruitment through the Indiana Office of Occupational Development and the Indiana State Employment Service. It may result in some recruitment problems because of the relatively low pay rate, some union grievances based on employees allegedly working out of their job classification, and some risk to employees because of the Personnel Division's inability to tailor selection factors to the needs of the Forensic Unit.

2. Use "desirable" selection criteria as "merit ranking factors."

Without altering existing job classifications or pay rates, rank eligible applicants for the psychiatric attendant position on the basis of additional desirable qualifications (such as physical strength or ability measures). This might result in the selection of more qualified people as psychiatric attendants on the Forensic Unit, with a resultant decrease in risk to patients or employees. On the other hand, it does not resolve the recruitment or pay problems identified in solution 1; the union will probably object to the use of quality ranking factors without a commensurate pay increase; and the Personnel Division may object to the use of quality ranking factors as an implicit increase in minimum qualifications for the position (and therefore an undesirable fragmentation of the classification system).

3. Reclassify the Forensic Unit psychiatric attendant positions.

Request the State Personnel Division that the position of psychiatric attendent on the Forensic Unit be reclassified upward to one of two existing classifications in the state classification system: special attendant or trainee special attendant. Special attendants earn up to $580 biweekly, and trainees earn up to $410 biweekly. The additional salary cost of reclassifying these positions would be about $50,000 annually for the first year, and an additional $50,000 annually for the next eight years, up to a maximum of $450,000. This is because there are nine steps in the pay scale for both special attendant or trainee special attendant positions, and it would take nine years for the 100 psychiatric attendants on the Forensic Unit to reach the top step of either pay range in their new positions. The reclassification could be justified by the argument that supervision of dangerous patients requires additional skills and qualifications. It would be supported by the Indiana State Employees Association. Among the disadvantages of this solution, however, are legislative opposition to pay increases; State Personnel Division opposition to upward reclassifications in general; increased pressure for transfer to the Forensic Unit by other psychiatric attendants at Logansport and other state facilities; and the inability of administrators at the Logansport State Hospital to "detail" or transfer psychiatric attendants in and out of the Forensic Unit without changes in their classification, the filing of grievances, and other internal management problems.

4. Increase the pay range of the psychiatric attendant position.

Using the existing classification system, Logansport State Hospital could request the State Personnel Division to authorize a two-step pay increase for psychiatric attendants on the Forensic Unit. The justification for this request would be that supervision of Forensic Unit patients involves duties and skills beyond those required of other psychiatric attendants, but not sufficiently so to justify a reclassification and a major pay increase. The differential would be limited to psychiatric attendants on the grounds that, while other employees might have patient contact with inmates on the Forensic Unit, only psychiatric attendants would be responsible for direct patient care. This two-step pay increase is used at a similar Forensic Unit in Norman Beatty State Hospital, where psychiatric attendants who receive this additional increment function as "work leaders" and supervise other attendants. Because this pay increase is a temporary administrative decision that takes place only as long as attendants function as "work leaders," hospital administrators at Beatty can transfer attendants in and out of positions as needs dictate, without the necessity for reclassifications or grievances. Adoption of a two-step differential for Forensic Unit psychiatric attendants would cost an additional $110,000 above regular pay annually. This solution would encounter some legislative opposition on economic grounds, some State Personnel Division opposition as a *sub rosa* reclassification, and potential union opposition because of the possibility that management would use the two-step differential as an inequitable reward or punishment, rather than as equitable compensation for working with Forensic Unit patients.

5. Establish career lattices for psychiatric attendants.   One possible solution is to improve promotion or reassignment potential for psychiatric attendants without altering their pay, classification, or job description. For example, attendants could be given training and educational subsidies to encourage them to meet minimum qualifications for special attendant, attendant supervisor, rehabilitation therapy assistant, or other lateral or upward positions. While the existence of career lattices is an important aid in retaining attendants, it is doubtful that this solution by itself would be sufficient. There are only 21 positions identified in the Logansport State Hospital's manning table for lateral or upward mobility by psychiatric attendants; and there are over 100 attendants on the proposed Forensic Unit at the Hospital, plus others in other units.

NOTES

[1]*National League of Cities* v. *Usery*, 96 S.Ct. 2465 (1976).

[2]*Wyoming* v. *EEOC*, U.S. S Ct 81-554, 75 LEd2d 18-103.

[3]Ned R. Brown, "Improving, Measuring and Rewarding Performance," *Management by Objectives*, Vol. 40, No. 4 (1974–75), 31–39; William H. Mobley, "The Link Between MBO and Executive Compensation," *Personnel Journal*, Vol. 53, No. 6 (June 1974), 423–77.

[4]Edwin S. Mruk and Edward J. Giblin, "Compensation as a Management Tool," *Management Review* (May 1977), 50–58; Scott Lefaver and Ralph Jaeck, "Compensation for Public Managers: A Different Way," *Public Personnel Management* (July–August 1977), 269–75; Rich-

ard D. Ferrante, "Compensating Creative Personnel," *Personnel Journal* (December 1977), 598–99.

⁵Chester Barnard, *The Functions of the Executive* (Cambridge, Mass.: Harvard University Press, 1938).

⁶J. H. Foegen, "Fringe on the Fringe," *Personnel Administration* (January–February 1972), 18–22.

⁷U.S. Congress, Senate Joint Committee on Taxation, "Description of S. 2105 and S. 2106 Relating to State and Local Public Employee Benefit Plans" (Washington, D.C.: U.S. Government Printing Office, 1982).

⁸U.S. General Accounting Office, *An Actuarial and Economic Analysis of State and Local Pension Plans,* PAD-80-1, February 26, 1980.

⁹Steven A. Neuse, "A Critical Perspective on the Comparable Worth Debate," *Review of Public Personnel Administration,* Vol. 3, No. 1 (Fall 1982), 1–20.

¹⁰E. R. Livernash (ed.), *Comparable Worth: Issues and Alternatives* (Washington, D.C.: Equal Employment Advisory Council, 1980).

11

Productivity

Of the core personnel functions—procurement, allocation, development, and sanction of human resources—the development of employees historically has received the least emphasis. The development function focuses on increasing the ability and the motivation of public employees to perform. In many ways it complements the procurement function, which represents an employer's initial attempt to select people according both to their ability and to other factors that will contribute to their subsequent performance. Traditionally, the field of employee development in the public sector has confined itself to training programs to increase the employee's ability to perform work, and to the appraisal function, where employee performance deficiencies are noted and the motivation of employees to improve upon their performance is somehow sparked.

Recent economic and political conditions have forced public employers to pay more attention to the development of their employees. With economic inflation, recession, and cutbacks in personnel allocations, the value of administrative efficiency has emerged with a powerful influence on managing public sector operations. This ascendancy of the efficiency value in comparison with other values, namely, social equity, political responsiveness and effectiveness, and employee rights, has affected the development function through the now familiar call for increased productivity in government. The search for productivity improvements has forced upon public employers a more sophisticated understanding of employee motivation and satisfaction, the complex relationship between person and job through the design of work, the impact of health and safety on em-

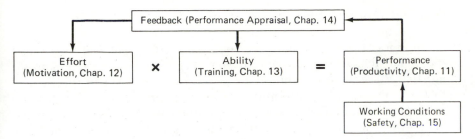

FIGURE 11–1. Development Factors Affecting Individual Performance

ployee performance, and the recognition that in labor-intensive work turn-over and absenteeism can significantly affect productivity.

Figure 11–1 focuses on an individual employee's performance, and it suggests that both the effort that the individual expends, and the individual's ability, influence employee output.

By the end of this chapter you will be able to:

1. Identify the relationships between efficiency and the other values that affect the design and dynamics of public personnel systems—social equity, responsiveness, and individual rights
2. Differentiate between a goal model of organizational effectiveness and an open-systems model
3. Define the meaning of the term *productivity*
4. Give examples of productivity-improvement activities
5. Discuss the influence of the personnel department, line managers, and the legislature on employee performance
6. Identify three opportunities public personnel officers have to expand their role in productivity programs
7. List the costs associated with replacing an employee
8. Describe a model of the employee-turnover process

PRODUCTIVITY AND ADMINISTRATIVE EFFICIENCY IN PUBLIC PERSONNEL MANAGEMENT

The governmental response to the push for administrative efficiency has produced attempts to increase the productivity of public employees. For example, in the personnel field the Civil Service Reform Act of 1978 included a pay-for-performance provision designed to motivate and reward superior performance. In addition, experiments with alternative work schedules, assistance programs for employees with drug and alcohol problems, and the innovative design of work to capture the motivation of employees all represent the impact of the efficiency value on employee development.

In times of economic hardship or, in response to political corruption, the demand for administrative efficiency in government increases to the point that it seems to contain virtue beyond dispute. But in the field of public personnel administration there are competing value claims that frequently weaken initial enthusiasm for productivity. More specifically, administrative efficiency clashes with claims to social equity and employee rights as seen in the Boston police case at the end of Chapter 2. Here budget cutbacks produced layoffs that brought affirmative action goals into conflict with union advocacy of seniority systems. Administrative efficiency may represent a threat to employee rights in other ways as well. For example, with the majority of employees at the local level of government working for school districts, it makes sense for major public sector productivity advances to focus on the teaching profession. This is exactly what the Reagan Administration advanced in 1983 with its endorsement of salary increases based on merit rather than seniority or advanced educational credits. As might be expected, this initiative met with resistance from both the National Education Association and the American Federation of Teachers who claim that effective teaching is difficult to measure and attempts to differentiate teaching performance would inevitably result in arbitrary salary allocations.

With these competing value claims, why has productivity in government received so much attention in the late 1970s and 1980s? Contemporary economic conditions represent one answer. Where citizens want or need government services but money is not available to provide them at existing levels, public employers are forced to hold the line in the provision of services while reducing available resources. The other answer is that the search for administrative efficiency has become a political issue as well as an economic one. In other words, for government to respond to public demands, it must become efficient. Recall that both efficiency and responsiveness are among the central values that drive the world of public personnel management. In the early 1980s, in order to be politically responsive government leaders endorse the value of administrative efficiency even if the cost is reduced emphasis on social equity and employee rights. To be efficient is to be responsive. In the 1970s Proposition 13, placing limits on property tax levies in California, led the way to the politicization of productivity in the public sector. Proposed constitutional restrictions against deficit spending also reflect this trend toward the merging of efficiency and responsiveness.

In sum, productivity has become a major interest in the public sector due to both the merger of efficiency with the value of political responsiveness and to adverse economic conditions.

THE CONCEPT OF ORGANIZATIONAL EFFECTIVENESS

Despite the upsurge of interest in productivity in government, a simplistic view of the way organizations operate frequently leads to high expectations and resultant disappointment that public employees are not more efficient. An unsophisticated view holds that public organizations have clear-cut missions and objectives specified by law, that the objectives are compatible, that goal accomplishment is measurable, and that the methods to accomplish the goals are known.

The *goal model* assumes that any organization, public or private, is the instrument whose parts can be arranged in order to meet the organization's goals. Organizing principles, allocation of staff, operating procedures, and staff responsibilities are developed with the organization's goals in mind.

Another perspective views an organization as an *open system,* constantly attempting to minimize its dependencies on environmental forces while maximizing the resources it can gain in its environment from other organizations like legislatures, lobbying interests, and unions or professional associations. In other words, an organization attempts to maintain for itself a necessary degree of flexibility so it can adapt to changes in either its internal or external surroundings.

The open-systems approach views efficiency and effectiveness measures simply as two elements of information utilized in organizational assessments and subsequent resource allocation. Gaertner and Ramnarayan[1] state this case succinctly:

> Effectiveness in organizations is not a thing, or a goal, or a characteristic of organizational outputs or behaviors, but rather a state of relations within and among relevant constituencies of the organization. An effective organization is one that is able to fashion accounts of itself and its activities in ways in which these constituencies find acceptable. . . . A fuller apprehension of [effectiveness] requires an understanding of why and for whom [any] particular set of bottom line figures was produced, and of the institutional vision and logic that supports this account to its constituents. (p. 97)

This view conceives of effectiveness as a continual process of negotiation rather than something that is produced. The question "Is the organization effective?" frequently defies an adequate response. A more relevant question is: "Who values which organizational outputs?" The process agency executives use to establish an organization's effectiveness involves continual surveillance of an environment to ensure that the organizational outputs one constituent group finds acceptable will not alienate another that has resources the organization must rely upon for its future well-being. In short, the capacity of a complex public agency to fulfill its legislative mandates requires continued enhancement of the many different reputations it will have among its many different constituent groups, each of which frequently focuses on an isolated aspect of the agency.

This view of effectiveness as a process casts a political rather than an economic aura over the field of productivity. This coincides with the view that productivity is a mediating activity in the public personnel field. Each mediating activity we have identified—affirmative action, human resource planning and cutback management, productivity, and labor relations—has a political side to it. It is also clear from this perspective that the forward movement in the area of productivity in the public sector is not so much due to an economic imperative as to its nature as a taxpayer or constituent demand. Again, to be productive is to be politically responsive.

But just as each mediating activity has a political side, it shows a technical side too. It is the nature of mediating functions to connect technical and political worlds.

WHAT IS PRODUCTIVITY?

Various terms like output, performance, efficiency, effectiveness, and "bang for the buck" are commonly associated with productivity. Generally speaking, productivity concerns two specific assessments of performance. First, *efficiency* is measured as a ratio of outputs to inputs. In other words, measuring efficiency requires identification of a performance outcome, such as the number of school lunches served in the cafeteria or the number of arrests made by a police officer or police department, and identification of the amount of resources used to produce the outcome, such as employee hours worked or funds allocated to meal service or wages in the police department. The efficiency ratio then becomes

$$\frac{\text{number of meals served}}{\text{number of cafeteria employee hours worked.}}$$

The resultant ratio measures meals per hours worked. Efficiency will increase in either of two ways: by increasing the number of meals served with the same number of employees, or by serving the same number of meals with fewer employees.

In the private sector and in many public sector cases, efficiency and productivity are synonymous. But what if in our example, efficiency were increased by serving more meals and making more arrests yet the meals were unappetizing and were not fully consumed and the arrests failed to lead to convictions and crowded the courts? Could one say that productivity had been improved? Probably not.

Productivity also implies an *effectiveness* measure, a concern with the quality of the output measured against some standard. Thus, a more valid productivity measure would be:

$$\frac{\text{number of meals consumed}}{\text{number of cafeteria hours worked}}$$

where consumption is distinguished from meal preparation. Similarly,

$$\frac{\text{number of arrests leading to convictions}}{\text{salary and wages of police officers}}$$

attempts to incorporate a quality-measure for the original output, number of arrests.

EXAMPLES OF PRODUCTIVITY IMPROVEMENT

Productivity programs seem to cluster into three areas. The first includes changes in organizational structure, processes, and operating procedures.

Flexibility in civil service procedures

Centralization of management support services like typing, payroll, purchasing

Pooling fiscal accounts to increase interest revenue

Selective decentralization or reorganization into homogeneous units

Increased use of performance measures and work standards to monitor productivity

Consolidation of services

Use of economic-rational decision models for scheduling and other problems

Energy conservation

Recycling projects

A second set of projects and innovations involve increased use of technology.

Labor-saving capital equipment—shifting from three- and two-person sanitation crews to a one-person sideloaded truck

Automation in areas like record keeping, payroll, and billing

Electronic data processing for scheduling, tracking of projects, and early warning of problems

The last area includes personnel-related activities.

Job simplification

Incentive awards

Increased sophistication in training

Job-related performance appraisal methods

Specification of work standards

Increased office communication, team building, and organizational development

Alternative work schedules

These represent the kinds of activities undertaken to increase productivity in the public sector. A significant number of these relate directly to the managing of personnel and the performance of individual employees and work units. Most of the personnel-related improvements are described in some detail in Chapters 12–15. For now, we will describe how the personnel department, supervisors and department heads, and administrative executives and legislators all affect the performance of the employee.

ROLE OF THE PERSONNEL MANAGER, DEPARTMENT HEADS, AND EXECUTIVES AND LEGISLATORS IN PRODUCTIVITY IMPROVEMENT

Figure 11–1 showed that an employee's performance basically depends on effort and ability. We have expanded that view here to include two other factors indicated in the following questions. Has the organization provided the employee with the opportunity to perform at a desired level? Has the organization adequately communicated performance goals to the employee? Focusing on these four factors, Table 11–1 provides examples of the ways various individuals interested in productivity improvement can affect an employee's performance.

Legislatures and administrative executives have the most significant affect on the ability of the worker through the wage-setting process. The more money allocated to salaries the more competitive a governmental employer will become in the labor market and the more talent it will attract to government service. Similarly, salary level and working conditions affect an employee's intention to stay with an employer. At the departmental level, the most significant impact is felt in the selection of employees. Assuming that a market wage will attract talent to the public employer, it is now necessary to select those potential employees with the most ability to perform and to learn new methods as well. Other important departmental influences on the employee's ability to perform include the quality of on-the-job training, coaching in the use of appropriate work methods, and the

TABLE 11–1. Legislative/Executive, Departmental, and Personnel Department Influences on Employee Performance

	LEGISLATIVE/EXECUTIVE	DEPARTMENT/SUPERVISION	PERSONNEL DEPARTMENT
Employee Ability to Perform	Establish competitive salary structure and working conditions	Utilize valid selection procedure Provide on-the-job training Match employee and job	Conduct training needs assessment Validate selection procedures Train supervisors in selection methods and performance appraisal
Employee Motivation to Perform	Provide incentive plan Adopt equitable human resource policies	Link rewards/punishment to performance Provide challenging jobs Treat employees fairly Provide performance feedback to employees Provide career ladder	Train supervisors in dynamics of motivation and equity Design and maintain equitable yet flexible pay and classification plans Design career ladders
Opportunity to Perform	Provide adequate resources Establish reasonable program expectations Invest in safe working conditions Promote modern personnel procedures	Match resources to program objectives Establish reasonable work goals Provide safe working conditions	Reduce rigidities in personnel system Monitor compliance with safety goals Establish employee assistance programs
Goal Clarity	Specify program priorities Define program goals	Specify individual and work unit goals Provide constructive feedback	Conduct job analyses Train supervisors in goal setting Train supervisors in assessment process

quality and timeliness of feedback regarding performance. The personnel department has a significant affect on the ability factor as well by conducting training needs assessments and locating training opportunities, by emphasizing and researching the validity of selection methods, by working with supervisors and employees to develop performance-based appraisal methods, and by increasing supervisory skill in communicating constructive feedback to employees. In some cases the personnel department may keep track of labor market conditions and gather data on prevailing wages for input into legislative decisions regarding allocations.

Employee motivation is similarly affected by an array of organizational and environmental factors. At the legislative-executive level, provision of incentives for superior employee performance and, importantly, a commitment to fair and equitable human resource management will influence employee motivation to perform. In addition, endorsement of fair but streamlined disciplinary procedures will carry the message to managers as well as employees that unsatisfactory performance will not be overlooked. At the departmental level, linking incentives to desired performance will critically affect the employee's belief that high performance will be rewarded and poor performance dealt with. The creation of challenging jobs will tap the intrinsic desire people have to master their work and avoid boring, fatiguing activities that hold few positive outcomes. Perhaps the greatest influence on employee performance involves the fairness with which employees feel they are being treated. It is difficult for employees to commit a high level of effort to a job when they believe their employer is not according them fair treatment. Last in this list of examples, we repeat the provision of feedback. Employees need to know how they are doing in order to calculate the amount of effort they will expend in the future. Moreover, establishing career paths allows employees to look ahead to a future with their employer. The personnel office can affect an employee's motivation indirectly by providing to supervisors knowledge of employee motivation and the dynamics that affect perceptions of equity in the work place. Further, they can monitor pay and evaluation processes to assure no obvious abuses are occurring. They can assist departments in the design of challenging jobs and can work toward developing classification and compensation plans that foster innovative work design, assignments, and availability of monetary incentives. Also, they can work with various departments to develop career opportunities for employees.

Frequently overlooked among the factors connected to productivity is the employee's opportunity to perform well. For example, the availability of an on-line electronics file is likely to allow an employee to perform better work than a manual file of 3-by-5 note cards. The availability of the tools of one's trade, whether they be reliable snowplows or electronic spread sheets, is essential to satisfactory employee performance.

Similarly, employees must be given reasonable performance expectations. Included here is not so much the clarity of goal statements but the feasibility of the goal at all. For example, measuring police officers' performance by variations in the crime rate discounts the variety of factors not under a police department's control but which influence crime in a community. Similarly, the National Education Association and American Federation of Teachers have hotly criticized what they feel is the simplistic notion that incentive pay for teachers will increase student performance in class. They cite a host of factors outside the classroom that have more effect on student performance than teacher behavior.

Another factor related to productivity involves attention to safe equipment and working conditions. Sick leave or workmen's compensation cost public organizations a considerable sum of money, and unsafe working conditions reduce the employee's opportunity to work efficiently and effectively.

A last factor at this level has to do with the personnel system itself. If a system is too rigid there may be few opportunities for flexibility in work assignments, career mobility, and implementation of incentive plans. On the other hand a system too flexible might encourage favoritism, capricious personnel actions, and an undermining of morale and confidence in the overall merit concept.

At the departmental level, opportunity is made available to employees with the appropriate allocation of resources to jobs and with the specification of feasible performance objectives. Safety in the workplace often depends on its emphasis at this level. The personnel department, through its interpretation of personnel rules, enhances the employee's opportunity to perform. This, of course, is a tricky area because too much flexibility in rule application leads to favoritism and erosion of the merit concept, while too rigid interpretation stifles innovation in the awarding of incentives, work assignments, and career mobility. The personnel department also bears the responsibility of monitoring safety goals and establishing employee assistance programs.

Another factor that advocates of productivity in government easily overlook is goal clarity. Measurement of productivity in the provision of social services is often impeded by ambiguous notions of what constitutes acceptable output. Yet an employee must know what the organization considers a satisfactory performance in order to do well. At the legislative-executive level this means specification of legislative priorities and program objectives. At the departmental level, manager and supervisors must translate these priorities into specific work unit and individual objectives and must provide feedback to employees about their performance. The personnel office can contribute to goal clarity by conducting timely job analyses and by training supervisors in the writing of performance standards and in the assessment process.

In sum, at the legislative and agency executive level, productivity of employees will be enhanced by the allocation of wages and working conditions competitive with other employers, by provision of incentives, and by adoption of equitable human resource management policies. Elected officials, political and administrative executives must provide adequate resources to accomplish feasible objectives, as well as establish program priorities.

At the departmental and supervisory level, factors influencing employee performance include attention to selection methods, on-the-job training, connection of rewards to performance, equitable treatment of employees, challenging job design, and career ladders that indicate an employee may grow with the same employer. In addition, providing employees with adequate tools of their trade, ensuring safe working conditions, specifying performance standards, and giving employees information so they can make adjustments in performance will also influence productivity.

The personnel department, as we have stressed throughout, essentially takes on a supporting role in efforts to improve productivity. Activities connected with this role include training needs assessments, location of training opportunities, providing supervisors with knowledge of the factors affecting employee motivation and perceptions of fair treatment, assisting in the development and maintenance of an equitable pay plan and jobs that are challenging to employees, monitoring safety goals, setting up an employee assistance program, and training of supervisors in writing performance objectives and in the communication of constructive feedback to employees.

EXPANDING THE PUBLIC PERSONNEL MANAGER'S ROLE IN PRODUCTIVITY PROGRAMS

Table 11–1 summarizes what one might consider to be a more traditional role the personnel department plays in productivity enhancement projects; many of the activities simply comprise the day-to-day work of personnel departments. But the enthusiasm for productivity improvement in government opens opportunities for an expanded role.

Mediating activities aimed at productivity improvements affect core personnel functions but do not necessarily fall within the formal responsibilities of the personnel department. This statement is illustrated in the productivity area where line managers and fiscal analysts consistently play a larger role than personnel specialists. In a way this role assignment is understandable since line managers are most familiar with the nuts and bolts of daily operations and because the primary motive of productivity enhancement in the public sector is saving money. In addition, the line manager and fiscal analyst are familiar with numbers and ratios and tracking production figures and budgetary accounts throughout the year. Thus, it is very easy for the personnel department to be shut out from the productivity action.

The price for entering the productivity field is expertise that those initially involved in productivity projects will value and subsequently search out. The personnel department has an opportunity to contribute in at least three areas. First, many projects involve some kind of management by objectives and the writing of job standards that specify that minimally acceptable employee work performance. When performance appraisal systems measure what employees actually do rather than the kinds of people they are (dependable, reliable, trustworthy, and so on), there is probably no one more competent to advise on the writing of these performance objectives or standards than the personnel department. The use of the results-oriented job descriptions described in Chapter 9 clearly shows this kind of connection between the formal aspects of personnel administration and productivity improvement. Along similar lines, the personnel department is in a unique position to compare and suggest adjustments in performance standards from different departments in a government jurisdiction. There is nothing that lowers morale more than the employee's perception that two people who are doing the same kind of work and who are paid the same are operating under different job standards.

The second area focuses on productivity improvements directly relating to the motivation of employees. In grouping productivity projects, one cluster centers around issues like work incentives, job design, job-related performance assessments, realistic training goals and workable designs, and alternative work schedules. These kinds of projects are aimed directly at enhancing both the employee's motivation and his or her ability to work. To develop programs in these areas and to anticipate their consequences requires a sophisticated understanding of employee motivation, the factors contributing to job satisfaction, equity theory, how people learn, and how organizations and work units change as well as resist change. In the vast majority of organizations, public and private, this knowledge does not exist in a way that is readily accessible to line managers and planners who might value it. Academically, this knowledge is found in other disciplines: psychology, sociology, anthropology, social psychology, communication studies, and political science. The application of social science knowledge to real-life problems often is referred to as applied behavioral science (ABS).

The third area of expertise extends knowledge of the applied behavioral sciences into the fiscal arena. Successful programs designed to boost the motivation of employees must develop out of expert knowledge of motivation, and expertise in the fiscal assessment of program results. Thus, anyone who can develop models that include the fiscal implications of projects that apply behavioral science knowledge will be valued. For example, the cost of hiring and training a new employee and the time it takes before that employee is performing satisfactorily represent dollar costs to an organization. The sooner that employee leaves the organization the less time the organization has to recover its costs. Given that the greatest turnover occurs among employees with a short time on the job, knowledge of how to retain good employees, for example through realistic job interviews,[2] can translate into cost savings. As another example, it is commonly known that dissatisfied employees are more likely to quit than satisfied employees.[3] Once one can establish the cost of turnover, it is statistically possible through regression analysis to determine the fiscal implications of variations in the morale of a work force. The design of such an evaluation is complex, but the point to be made here is that knowledge of the applied behavioral sciences allows one to develop models assessing the costs of productivity projects that will affect employees.

ABSENTEEISM AND TURNOVER

The areas of employee absenteeism and turnover deserve attention because they illustrate the ABS and fiscal expertise personnel officers of the future might need to develop. When an absent worker is paid for time not at work, productivity is negatively affected. This is true whether the absence is a legitimate one or not. For example, when workers take a sick day they are paid even though they contribute no work. Referring back to productivity in terms of an input/output ratio one can see that even a poor performer who is on the job adds more to a work unit's productivity than an excellent worker who is absent. In terms of its impact on day-to-day productivity, one might be justified in arguing that the emphasis most public employers place on attendance is understated.

Abuse of sick time not only has real dollar costs to an employer, but productivity further suffers if untrained workers must substitute for an experienced one who is absent; longer waiting times for clients may trigger complaints; poorer quality service may result in the need for additional staff time in the future to rectify problems; and increased supervision may be required. Supervisors may even have to assume some of the absent worker's duties and fall behind in other areas.

Employee turnover, which averaged 22 percent per year in the private sector from 1976–1979,[4] represents another potential employer cost easily overlooked in the public sector. According to Flamholtz,[5] replacing an employee involves three kinds of costs, which are summarized in Table 11–2.

Acquisition costs refer to those activities needed to acquire a new employee. Learning costs are those incurred while the new employee de-

TABLE 11–2. Human Resource Replacement Costs

ACQUISITION COSTS	LEARNING COSTS	SEPARATION COSTS
Recruitment	Formal training and orientation	Separation pay
Selection	On-the-job training	Loss of efficiency prior to separation
Hiring	Cost of trainer's time	
Placement		Loss of production while position is vacant
Promotion or transfer costs		

velops the proficiency of the employee being replaced. Separation costs are those involved in the outprocessing and the decline in performance often characteristic of a "short timer." These, then, are some of the costs associated with replacing an employee. Naturally they vary according to employer and the job where the turnover occurs.

Attending to the costs of turnover, however, should not detract from the benefits. Table 11–3 identifies both costs and benefits of employee turnover from several perspectives.

The potentially costly nature of absenteeism and turnover invites analysis of their causes. Mobley, Griffith, Hand, and Meglino[6] have developed a model of the employee turnover process, which Figure 11–2 summarizes.

This model suggests that an employee's evaluation of the present job situation results in feelings of satisfaction/dissatisfaction. If dissatisfied, the employee may begin thinking about quitting, but if rational, he or she will first consider the alternatives. These boil down to two sets of factors. The first set centers on changing jobs. Are alternative jobs available? Is it worthwhile to search them out? What will be the drawbacks of leaving my present job? What is the likelihood I will be more satisfied in a different job than I am now? These questions may result in an employee's search for actual alternatives. The information gained in a search will be compared against a second set of factors involving speculation about what the employee can expect by not quitting. Will the present situation improve? Is it really that bad? Are my expectations too high? The comparison of these two factors may lead the employee to decide to quit. On the other hand, if the employee is dissatisfied with the present job and fails to see the possibility of leaving as a realistic alternative, absenteeism or apathy may result. Mobley and his colleagues caution, however, that while absenteeism expresses an employee's withdrawal from work, this is not always the case with turnover. Satisfied employees who associate highly positive expectations with a job change that fails to materialize are not likely then to find alternate ways of withdrawing from their present job.

TABLE 11–3.   Some Possible Positive and Negative Individual and Organizational Consequences of Employee Turnover

ORGANIZATION	INDIVIDUAL (LEAVERS)	INDIVIDUAL (STAYERS)
Possible Negative Consequences		
Costs (recruiting, hiring, assimilation, training)	Loss of seniority and related prerequisites	Disruption of social and communication patterns
Replacement costs	Loss of nonvested benefits	Loss of functionally valued coworkers
Out-processing costs	Disruption of family and social support systems	Decreased satisfaction
Disruption of social and communication structures	"Grass is greener" phenomenon and subsequent disillusionment	Increased work load during and immediately after search for replacement
Productivity loss (during replacement search and retraining)	Inflation-related costs (e.g., mortgage cost)	Decreased cohesion
Loss of high performers	Transition-related stress	Decreased commitment
Decreased satisfaction among stayers	Disruption of spouse's career path	
Stimulate "undifferentiated" turnover control strategies	Career path regression	
Negative PR from leavers		
Possible Positive Consequences		
Displacement of poor performers	Increased earnings	Increased internal mobility opportunity
Infusion of new knowledge/ technology via replacements	Career advancement	Stimulation, cross-fertilization from new coworkers
Stimulate changes in policy and practice	Better "person-organization fit," thus (for example) less stress, better use of skills, interests	Increased satisfaction
Increased internal mobility opportunities	Renewed stimulation in new environment	Increased cohesion
Increased structural flexibility	Attainment of nonwork values	Increased commitment
Increased satisfaction among stayers	Enhanced self-efficacy perceptions	
Decrease in other "withdrawal" behaviors	Self-development	
Opportunities for cost reduction, consolidation		

From William H. Mobley, "Some Unanswered Questions in Turnover and Withdrawal Research," *Academy of Management Review*, 7 (1982), p. 113. Reprinted by permission of the Academy of Management.

Mobley[7] also points out the costs of turnover may be worth bearing if the employees who leave are the poor performers, and they can be replaced with better workers. But according to Mobley, the relationship between work performance and turnover is an area where considerable study is needed.

FIGURE 11–2. Employee Turnover Process

SUMMARY

The emphasis on productivity in the public sector is the metaphorical bridge along which the value of administrative efficiency meets the developmental function in public personnel administration. Economic conditions have fostered the concern with productivity, but its real momentum occurred when administrative efficiency became a political issue.

Productivity projects cluster into three categories: operations, technology, and personnel. Many of these projects involve the formulation of work objectives and performance standards that personnel departments are familiar with. Others require a sophisticated understanding of the applied behavioral sciences, knowledge which personnel departments might seek to master as a way of gaining influence over the productivity-mediating function.

Finally, the last section of the chapter discussed employee absenteeism and turnover to illustrate the way knowledge of the applied behavioral sciences could affect fiscal analyses of work-force productivity.

KEY TERMS

productivity
efficiency
effectiveness
goal model of effectiveness
open-systems model of effectiveness
applied behavioral sciences (ABS)
absenteeism
turnover

DISCUSSION QUESTIONS

1. What are the relationships between administrative efficiency and the other values that affect public personnel systems?
2. What are the differences between a goal model of organizational effectiveness and an open-systems model? As an analyst of organizations, under what conditions would a goal model be appropriate? An open-systems model?
3. Can an organization or work unit be efficient without being effective?
4. What are the basic differences in perspective toward productivity taken by legislators, department heads/supervisors, and the personnel department? What do you think the employee's perspective might be with regard to productivity improvements?

FIGURE 11–3. Total Estimated Cost of Employee Absenteeism. (From Wayne F. Cascio, *Costing Human Resources: The Financial Impact of Behavior in Organizations* (Boston: Kent Publishing Company, 1982), p. 48. © 1982 by Wadsworth, Inc. Reprinted by permission of Kent Publishing, a division of Wadsworth, Inc.)

1. Compute total employee hours lost to absenteeism for the period.

2. Compute weighted average wage or salary/hour/absent employee.

3. Compute cost of employee benefits/hour/employee.

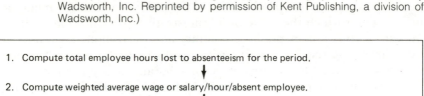

4a.   Yes   Are absent workers paid?   No   4b.

Compensation lost/hour/absent employee = wage/salary + benefits   Compensation lost/hour/absent employee = benefits only

5. Compute total compensation lost to absent employees (1. x 4a. or 4b. as applicable).

6. Estimate total supervisory hours lost to employee absenteeism.

7. Compute average hourly supervisory salary + benefits.

8. Estimate total supervisory salaries lost to managing absenteeism problems (6. x 7.).

9. Estimate all other costs incidental to absenteeism.

10. Estimate total cost of absenteeism (Σ 5., 8., 9.).

11. Estimate total cost of absenteeism/employee (10. ÷ total no. of employees).

5. What three areas of knowledge provide opportunities for the personnel professional to influence the productivity movement?
6. What costs are involved in replacing an employee?
7. Describe the employee turnover process. What factors would you add to make the model more accurate or complete?

EXERCISE

The municipality of Cityville employs 500 people. Last year, excluding vacation time, which averages two weeks per employee per year, the rate of absenteeism was calculated at 3 percent. This 3 percent loss in scheduled work time is attributed to clerical workers (55 percent), blue collar workers (30 percent), and professional staff (15 percent). The average hourly wage for clerical workers is $5.76 with an additional 30 percent in fringe benefits; for blue collar workers $9.62 with an additional 35 percent fringe benefits; and for professional employees $14.42 with 33 percent fringe benefits.

Twenty-five supervisors, whose average wage and fringe benefits total $12.50 per hour, handle most of the absentee worker problems and estimate they spend about 30 minutes a day rearranging schedules and trying to organize work to compensate for the unscheduled absences. Cityville's finance director indicates that some $30,000 in incidental costs are associated with absenteeism. These include items like overtime, temporary help, and even an educated guess as to the costs attributed to lower quality of work done by the replacement workers. Problem: Using these amounts and the guide in Figure 11−3, estimate the total cost of absenteeism to the taxpayers of Cityville.

NOTES

[1]Gregory H. Gaertner and S. Ramnarayan, "Organizational Effectiveness: An Alternative Perspective," *Academy of Management Review,* 8 (1983), p. 97.

[2]John P. Wanous, *Organizational Entry: Recruitment, Selection and Socialization of Newcomers* (Reading, Mass.: Addison-Wesley, 1980).

[3]William H. Mobley, *Employee Turnover: Causes, Consequences, and Control* (Reading, Mass.: Addison-Wesley, 1982).

[4]Wayne F. Cascio, *Costing Human Resources: The Financial Impact of Behavior in Organizations* (Boston: Kent Publishing Co., 1982), p. 17.

[5]E. G. Flamholtz, *Human Resource Accounting* (Encino, Calif.: Dickenson, 1974).

[6]William H. Mobley and others, "A Review and Conceptual Analysis of the Employee Turnover Process," *Psychological Bulletin,* 86 (1979), 493−522.

[7]Mobley, *Employee Turnover: Causes, Consequences, and Control.*

12

The Motivation to Work

Early assumptions about the kinds of rewards that would motivate people at work centered on economic inducements. Not only did this assumption underpin Frederick Taylor's school of scientific management (described earlier in this book) but along with the search for job security it has characterized the focus of labor union interest in the United States for some time. Since the 1930s, analyses of employee behavior by both managers and academicians have led to a sophisticated understanding of the person-job relationship. The recent emphasis on productivity in government has renewed interest in channeling the motivation and commitment of public employees toward their work.

A myriad of forces peripheral to the effort employees expend at work affect the efficiency and quality of a government's operations, and they often become the hub of productivity improvements. For example, moving to a centralized purchasing operation, keeping better track of inventory, more economic and rational fleet maintenance scheduling, and more efficient money management have little to do with employee performance directly. A more concentrated analysis of employee performance itself would be concerned with two main factors: the willingness or motivation of the employee to perform, which produces employee effort, and the employee's ability to perform. In other words,

$$P = f(m \times a)$$

where p = performance
m = motivation
a = ability

A personal example will illustrate these factors. A few years ago the son of one author professed a willingness to mow the lawn, attracted apparently by the prospect of earning a few extra dollars to support his video game habit. Unfortunately, he was not yet strong enough to perform this chore. The father, who was able to mow the lawn, found it difficult to associate any benefits from doing so, but the anticipated scorn of the neighbors along with his own sense of homeowner obligation provided the motivation if not the commitment to perform the task. The result? The father cut the lawn when it was badly needed and did a minimally acceptable job.

More recently the son, now a young teenager, has taken on the job. Following some training to show him how to cut the lawn according to minimal quality and safety standards, not only does he cut the grass but he clips the edges according to a workload-for-pay schedule; that is, the more he clips the more he gets paid! The parents hold no hopes that this satisfactory scheme will last, however. As the work itself becomes boring, as other activities become more attractive to the boy, and as his need for money grows beyond the economic potential of lawn mowing, his motivation to perform the task will decline, and once again the father's labor will be needed.

This chapter concentrates in more detail on the motivation of employees to perform their work. The next chapter deals with developing the ability of employees to perform their work and includes a discussion of training methods.

By the end of this chapter you will be able to:

1. Define the terms *job satisfaction* and *motivation*
2. Describe the factors affecting an employee's satisfaction with work
3. Describe the factors affecting an employee's motivation to work
4. Discuss the work outcomes people value
5. Identify the effect that job design has on a worker's satisfaction and motivation
6. Discuss the impact that *opportunity to perform* and *goal clarity* have on employee performance.
7. Identify various quality of working-life experiments

SATISFACTION AND MOTIVATION

Frequently, the terms *satisfaction* and *motivation* are mistakenly interchanged. The following definitions may clarify the distinctions. An individual employee's satisfaction or dissatisfaction with work is a subjectively derived conclusion based on a comparison of what the employee receives from working compared to what the person expects, wants, or thinks he or she deserves.

While each employee subjectively determines how satisfying the job is, job satisfaction is influenced by a social frame of reference. For example, an individual may be making less money than desired, but if the amount is similar to that made by comparable others, and if several of this person's neighbors are unemployed, only a minor dissatisfaction will result.

Job satisfaction is usually measured in an employee survey. One can ask the question, "Overall, how satisfied are you with your work?" Responses could range from "very satisfied" to "very dissatisfied." But a general question like this fails to provide the survey sponsor with much diagnostic information. It does not indicate the source of the satisfaction or dissatisfaction. Satisfaction is a multifaceted concept. An overall conclusion about satisfaction masks an employee's subjective weighting of satisfaction with pay, job security, supervision, interpersonal relations at work, future opportunities, and the work itself.

While an employee's satisfaction with work is likely to affect the person's attendance at work and desire to change jobs, it also may affect the willingness to work. An employee's willingness or motivation to work usually is indicated by sustained, goal-directed activity. Thus, a so-called motivated employee is one whose behavior is directed toward organizational goals and whose activities are not easily interrupted by minor distractions. When managers or supervisors describe an employee as lacking motivation, they may mean any of three things: (1) the employee's behavior does not appear goal directed, (2) the employee's behavior is not directed toward an organizationally valued goal, or (3) the employee is not committed to the goal, and thus is easily distracted and requires frequent supervision. As one can observe, the manager's description of an employee as "unmotivated" does not reveal to the employee or others very much more than the manager's dissatisfaction with the employee.

Figure 12–1 displays the possible relationships between satisfied and motivated employees. Employees who are both satisfied and motivated are found in quadrant I. This is the ideal situation for both employer and employee. It occurs when the contributions the employee makes to the organization are organizationally valued and where the organization in return provides the employee with outcomes he or she wants, expects, or deserves.

Employees found in quadrant II are motivated to perform well but are dissatisfied with their work. There may be several reasons for this. The employee may need the job or money, both of which may be contingent upon good performance. On the other hand the employee may feel he or she is deserving of more job security or salary than the organization is willing to give. When an employee is performing well but is dissatisfied, one can expect some evidence of employee withdrawal—in the form of a desire to change jobs or perhaps in time with a drop-off in performance or evidence of apathy.

Satisfaction

		High	Low
Motivation	High	I Positive value for organization and employee	II Positive value for organization, negative value for employee
	Low	III Negative value for organization, positive value for employee	IV Negative value for organization and employee

FIGURE 12–1.   Relationship Between Satisfied and Motivated Employees.

In quadrant III, one finds the case of the low-performing employee who is satisfied with the job. The organization is fulfilling this employee's needs, thus the employee has little to complain about. But in contrast to quadrant I, fulfillment of the needs is not contingent upon an organizationally valued behavior. For example, an employee may be very happy working in a particular geographic location, and as long as geographic assignment is not made contingent upon job performance, there is no reason to expect that because this employee is satisfied with work that he or she will also be a high performer.

The last case is a temporary scenario. The employee is not performing well and is not finding the organization's inducements satisfying either. This is the situation that will lead to the employee's intention to quit or the organization's decision to terminate the employee because no value is found by either employee or employer in the other.

The crucial observation derived from Figure 12–1 is that satisfied employees are not necessarily productive ones or vice versa. Creating a work situation characterized by high productivity and a satisfying quality of working life is a delicate endeavor that entails deliberate legislative and administrative action.

EQUITY THEORY AND JOB SATISFACTION

In order to explain more analytically the determinants of job satisfaction and employee motivation, theoretical tools are needed. In this section, *equity theory* is described with particular emphasis on job satisfaction. In the next section expectancy theory will permit a more sophisticated discussion of employee motivation.

Equity theory helps us understand how a worker reaches the conclusion that he or she is being treated fairly or unfairly. The feeling of being treated equitably is an internal state of mind resulting from a subjective calculation of what one puts into a job and what one gets out of it in comparison to some other relevant person.

An interesting observation about equity at work is that few people want to treat others unfairly, and no one wants to be treated unfairly, yet charges of favoritism, and unfair and inequitable treatment constitute major problems in supervision and thus play a significant role in determining an employee's satisfaction at work. One key to this puzzle is found in the way equity is internally calculated.

Begin with the popular saying "An honest day's work deserves an honest day's pay." Translate the saying as follows: An honest day's contribution or input of employee work deserves an equitable return of organizational rewards. In other words, inputs and outcomes should be equal, I=O. In equity theory inputs and outcomes are represented in a ratio, I/O. Because equity is subjectively calculated, inputs can include anything the employee brings to the organization that he or she thinks is deserving of some special recognition in comparison with others. Thus, inputs can include skill, position, education, type of work, difficulty of work, quantity of work, and seniority. Inputs can also include the less formally recognized but nevertheless frequently claimed credit for sex, race, or age. For example, the statement "Blacks are taking all of our job opportunities" reflects a white person's conclusion that some people are being given credit for race, a factor that should be eschewed in employment decisions. Similarly, if one says, "Blacks deserve the first opportunity for promotions," one is also using race as an input credit. Outcome credits have equal range: pay, future opportunity, promotion, recognition, working atmosphere, flexible work schedule, autonomy, a reserved parking place, a certain size and location of office.

The case of Rhonda, John, and Louisa illustrates the subjective calculation of equitable ratios. Rhonda receives ten outcome units, which we will simplify by saying she earns ten units of pay. She calculates that she deserves those ten because she contributes ten input units. These input units break down in her mind to five units for the quantity of work performed and five units for the difficulty of the work.

$$\text{Rhonda} \quad \frac{\text{Inputs}}{\text{Outcomes}} = \frac{10}{10} = \frac{5 \text{ quantity} + 5 \text{ difficulty}}{10 \text{ pay}}$$

John also receives ten units of pay and claims five input credits for difficulty of work, but can only reasonably claim three units for quantity of work performed. John makes up the difference by claiming two input units for accuracy of his work.

$$\text{John} \quad \frac{\text{Inputs}}{\text{Outcomes}} = \frac{10}{10} = \frac{3 \text{ quantity} + 5 \text{ difficulty} + 2 \text{ accuracy}}{10 \text{ pay}}$$

Louisa also receives ten units of pay and claims five input credits for quantity like Rhonda, two for accuracy like John, but her work is pretty simple so she claims no credit for difficulty. But Louisa claims three input credits for working the night shift, a shift generally regarded as undesirable.

$$\text{Louisa} \quad \frac{\text{Inputs}}{\text{Outcomes}} = \frac{10}{10} = \frac{5 \text{ quantity} + 2 \text{ accuracy} + 3 \text{ night shift}}{10 \text{ pay}}$$

These three workers each feel they are honestly earning their pay, and in a working context characterized by a high degree of trust and mutual respect each might acknowledge the legitimacy of the other's input credits. But when they all compare their ratio of inputs to outcomes they may feel they are being treated unfairly. Rhonda says, "I do more work than John and harder work than Louisa, but they get paid the same as me. Either I'm underpaid or they are overpaid."

John counters, "Granted I don't do as much work as Rhonda, but I make up for it in my accuracy. Rhonda makes so many mistakes, if she would only slow down we'd all be better off. As for Louisa, she's got the easiest work of anybody around here."

What is Louisa's response? "Sure I don't have the hardest job, but I do as much as anyone else and, besides, anytime you want to trade shifts with me, just say the word!"

These examples illustrate that equity calculations involve both a ratio of inputs to outcomes, and social comparison. Moreover, they involve disputes over what kind of credits deserve recognition and how much recognition is justified.

One other facet of equity deserves brief discussion. An input/outcome ratio need not be equal as long as the relevant comparison person has a similar ratio. In other words, if an employee feels he or she is contributing more than receiving, but so is everyone else, it is unlikely that a major equity issue will arise. Similarly, if someone receives twice as many outcome units as another, but is perceived to be contributing twice as many input units, the comparison ratio is maintained without any perceived injustice. For example, employees usually do not argue when executives are granted reserve parking spaces because their hierarchical position justifies it.

Equity issues are confronted in an organization at two levels, in terms of policies regarding human resource management and in the supervisor-subordinate relationship. At the policy level considerable attempts are made in public organizations to preclude equity issues from surfacing. For example, merit systems are built around the idea that credit is given for ability and performance, not personal or political factors. Equally relevant to a merit system is the concept of equal pay for equal work. Performance appraisal systems, which are based on sound job analyses and which set out work standards or performance objectives, minimize the types of complaints encountered in our examples of Rhonda, John, and Louisa. Finally, the establishment of grievance procedures protects employees from arbitrary personnel actions and provides a predictable and credible path for conflict resolution.

Inevitably, questions of equity will occur at the working level in any organization. There are several ways to deal with an employee's feeling of being treated unfairly. First, the supervisor must recognize that reaching a conclusion that one has been treated unfairly is the product of a person's unique internal logical processes driven in many cases by a gnawing sense of injustice. Rationally trying to settle a charge of inequitable treatment many times will fail because of the emotional energy driving the feeling of injustice. Also impeding simple resolution of equity issues is the facility human beings have to distort cognitively our input/output ratio to justify our feelings. These manipulations can be seen in the way that Rhonda, John, and Louisa responded to each other. Second, the supervisor should recognize that equity claims involve perceptions of what a person feels is deserving of reward, perceptions of what the individual has received in return for his or her contributions, and selection of a comparison person. Thus, the supervisor should attempt to ascertain the employee's perceptions in these areas to clarify the source of irritation. Third, the supervisor can attempt to forestall equity claims by making clear to others what he or she feels deserves organizational rewards and then consistently applying organizational rewards and punishments and specify reasons behind one's actions.

EXPECTANCY THEORY AND MOTIVATION

Equity theory and expectancy theory both attempt to explain satisfaction and motivation at work. In our judgment, however, equity theory best explains job satisfaction, and expectancy theory the motivation to work. Expectancy theory logically attempts to reconstruct the mental processes that lead an employee to expend a certain amount of effort in a certain direction. It assumes that the employee's effort results from:

1.   A subjective probability regarding the employee's ability
2.   A subjective probability of rewards or punishments occurring as a result of the employee's behavior and
3.   The value the employee places on the rewards and punishments

These calculations never occur as discreetly as posited here, if they occur at all. Rather, they represent the best theoretical tools to help explain what might go on inside someone's head.

Recall the formula $P = f(a \times m)$. The first probability statement expresses the ability part of the formula, while the second and third calculations constitute the motivational aspect of the formula. An example may clarify the calculations. Let's take a supervisor in the Department of Community Development whose boss has just returned from a city council meeting and has told the supervisor that the council wants all applications for community development funds to be processed by the next council meeting if possible. This deadline is two weeks ahead of the originally scheduled completion date, and the supervisor is not happy with the new deadline and does not even know whether she can meet it. Meeting the deadline may require working after hours and the cancellation of the long weekend the supervisor was planning to take prior to the next council meeting. For the purposes of analysis, assume this supervisor is thinking in terms of three options: finish the report on time, finish one week late, or meet the original deadline date, which would be two weeks later than the council would like the job done. These, then, are the three performance levels. To begin to determine what the employee will actually do, the analyst must imagine how the employee would answer the question "If I expend the effort, what is the likelihood I can achieve the performance?" The employee answers this question for each performance level with a statement of probability ranging from 0 to 1, with 0 indicating no likelihood whatsoever, and 1 indicating certainty. These calculations are represented in Table 12–1.

Table 12–1 shows that this person feels sure to finish according to the original schedule if the person makes the effort; 75 percent sure to finish one week late; a 50/50 chance that if effort is expended, applications can be finished in time for the next council meeting.

Next, the supervisor tries to identify which outcomes will be associated with the three anticipated performance levels. Table 12–2 shows the performance levels, the likelihood of the various outcomes occurring, and the attractiveness of the outcomes. Attractiveness is measured on a scale of $+10$ to -10 with $+10$ being most attractive and -10 most unattractive.

Viewing Table 12–2, one can see that the supervisor believes that if

TABLE 12–1.   Effort-to-Performance Expectancies

PERFORMANCE LEVEL	$E \rightarrow P$ PROBABILITY
Meets new deadline	0.5
One week late	0.75
Meets original deadline	1.0

TABLE 12–2. Summary of Expectancy Model

PERFORMANCE LEVEL	OUTCOME	P → O EXPECTANCY		OUTCOME ATTRACTION		E → P EXPECTANCY	E → P EXPECTANCY EFFORT
Meets new deadline	Feelings of accomplishment	0.7	×	6	=	4.2	
	Praise from department head	0.6	×	3	=	1.8	
$E \rightarrow P = 0.5$	Recognition in personnel record	0.3	×	4	=	1.2	
	Work after scheduled hours	0.4	×	−5	=	−2.0	
	Cancel long weekend plans	0.4	×	−7	=	−2.8	
						$2.4 \times .5 =$	1.2
One week late	Feeling of accomplishment	0.4	×	6	=	2.4	
	Praise from department head	0.2	×	3	=	0.6	
$E \rightarrow P = .75$	Work after scheduled hours	0.2	×	−5	=	−1.0	
	Cancel long weekend plans	0.2	×	−7	=	−1.4	
						$0.6 \times .75 =$	0.45
Meets original schedule	Criticism from department head	0.5	×	−6	=	−3.0	
	Jeopardize chances for future responsibility	0.5	×	−4	=	−2.0	
$E \rightarrow P = 1.0$	Time available for long weekend	0.8	×	7	=	5.6	
						$0.6 \times 1.0 =$	0.6

she meets the new deadline it is likely (0.7) that she will feel a sense of accomplishment that she values (6). Almost as likely (0.6) but less valued (3) is the possibility that the Community Development department head will praise her. There is some chance (0.3) that the department head would formally recognize her accomplishment, and she places a reasonably positive (4) value on this outcome. But she experiences some conflict as we attempt to construct her thinking process. She apparently has planned some vacation time, which is the most important outcome (−7) she contemplates as being affected by the new deadline. In this case, there is a moderate probability (0.4) that if she meets the deadline she will have to cancel her weekend plans. The minus sign indicates this is an outcome she would find unattractive. Equally likely is the probability (0.4) that she will have to work extra hours, which she evidently would experience in negative terms (−5).

In sum, we see an employee who takes pride in her work but who also values her leisure time. In order to estimate whether or not she will try to meet the deadline, the analyst would have to review the performance-to-outcome expectancies and valences for the other two levels of performance.

Keep in mind that this employee probably does not really make her decision in this way. We do not actually know exactly how people determine what level of effort to expend at work and in what direction, but expectancy theory provides us with a set of questions and calculations that provide some clues.

In order to compare levels of performance, the following calculations are made for each level:

$$\text{Effort} = (E{\rightarrow}P) \times \Sigma\,[P{\rightarrow}O(V)]$$

Where $E{\rightarrow}P$ is the probability that if the person expends the effort she can accomplish the level of performance being considered

$\Sigma[P{\rightarrow}O(V)]$ is the probability that a certain outcome which has a value (V) will occur if the level of performance is achieved. Since several outcomes will be connected to each performance level these $[P{\rightarrow}O(V)]$ calculations are summed before the total is multiplied by the $(E{\rightarrow}P)$ probability

Following this formula, the level of effort the supervisor will expend to meet the deadline on time is

$$(0.5) \times [(0.7)(6) + (0.6)(3) + (0.3)(4) + (0.4)(-5) + (0.4)(-7)]$$

or

$$(0.5) \times [4.2 + 1.8 + 1.2 - 2.0 - 2.8]$$

or

$0.5 \times 2.4 = 1.2$ effort expended to meet the new deadline

This figure, of course, means little unless we compare it with the result of similar calculations made for the other two levels of performance. The effort to complete the processing of applicants one week after the new deadline will tally 0.45, and the effort to meet the original deadline is a bit higher at 0.6. Table 12–2 summarizes the expectancy model.

Assuming we have accurately captured this employee's estimates of probabilities, the valences assigned to the outcomes, and have exhausted the identification of outcomes the person associates with these different performance levels, one would predict that this employee will try to process the applications according to the new deadline.

These calculations subjectively occur in anticipation of the need to act. In other words, the calculations explained so far all occur inside the person's head, and no actual effort has yet been expended. Now, an actual amount of effort or motivation will be activated in a particular direction. It will combine with a real level of ability and produce real behavior with regard to the processing of applicants. This processing will result in *real*, not anticipated, outcomes. For example, either the supervisor will or will not be able to process all the applications on time; either the department head will or will not praise her. And soon the employee will have a history to influence subsequent ability and motivational calculations for similar situations.

In other words, our hypothetical employee may find that she actually does process the applications on time and no praise follows. Subsequently, the E→P probability might increase if this person has developed confidence in her ability, and the subjective probability connecting a similar performance with praise would decrease because it was not forthcoming when originally anticipated. The value, or valence, of the praise could remain the same, however, or it might even increase because of its scarcity.

The expectancy model provides an excellent diagnostic tool for analyzing an employee's work behavior because it focuses the analyst's attention on the ways the organization affects its employees' motivation to work. First, it affects the E→P probability when it designs a job or assigns a task. The more difficult a job the less likely the employee will perceive his or her ability to complete it. The easier the job the higher this internal calculation. Unfortunately, easy jobs are boring jobs, which means from the model's standpoint that the outcomes associated with high performance are perceived to be low or negative. Boredom and fatigue usually are assigned negative valences. Challenging work is neither too hard nor too easy as reflected in the subjective E→P probability. In the example, no feeling of accomplishment was associated with meeting the original deadline because our employee knew she could meet the deadline without any trouble. Second, the organization influences the employee's perception that a high level of performance will result in a deserved outcome. An employee who does superior work and receives no recognition may decrease his or her subjective conclusion that high performance earns positive outcomes, [P→O(V)]. When average performers receive outstanding ratings in the performance appraisal process, or when everyone receives an average rating, the message to the truly outstanding employee and to the very poor one as well is that performance does not matter. In sum, the expectancy model suggests that unless an organization can provide an employee with outcomes he or she values, the employee has little incentive to achieve high performance. As one can see from the example, the more positive outcomes an employee can associate with a particular level of performance, the more likely it is that the employee will try to achieve that performance level.

The final point in this discussion of expectancy and equity theory concerns their connection. An employee may value an outcome associated with high performance but that value may decrease if the reward is not perceived to be equitably distributed. Take the following example regarding merit pay. Merit pay is supposedly awarded to employees based on performance and is usually distinguished from other pay increases due to seniority or cost of living. To act as a motivator pay must (1) be clearly associated in the minds of employees with high performance, (2) it must be valued, and (3) the public employer must have enough funds to implement such a system. Rarely is merit pay associated in the minds of employees with high performance, because performance often is difficult to measure and the merit increment is a summary reward that rarely has a specific performance antecedent. Thus, it contains little learning value. In other words, unless employees can specifically identify in terms of performance why one person received the merit raise and another did not, they do not know what they must do subsequently to earn a similar raise.

Furthermore, equity theory would suggest that not only do high performers expect more merit pay than the average or poor employee, but they also expect increments in an appropriate ratio to their performance compared to others. If one person invests in a performance twice as much as another, he or she expects twice as much in return. Is it any wonder, then, that merit pay frequently turns out not to be a motivator but often the source of equity problems? Pay has more influence over the motivation of a person to join or leave an organization than the motivation of that person to work.

EMPLOYEE NEEDS

Both equity theory and expectancy theory include work outcomes—the rewards and punishments a person associates with differing levels of performance—as a salient variable. As the example demonstrating expectancy theory pointed out, in trying to understand what motivates an employee, that person's private life outside of the work day is frequently relevant. In the example cited, two kinds of outcomes were associated with the different performance levels. The feeling of accomplishment is termed an *intrinsic contingency* or reward. It is intrinsic to the person in the sense that it is a self-reward, and in this case it comes from doing a good job. Intrinsic contingencies can also be self-punishing. For example, when someone does something and feels guilty or is in some way self-critical, he or she has self-administered a punishment. Other rewards and punishments are originated from someone else. The praise, mentioned in the personnel folder, overtime, and cancellation of the weekend plans all occur outside of the individual's mental processes. Again, these external or extrinsic contingencies can be experienced in positive or negative terms.

In the example, the contingencies identified might be quite characteristic of those a public employee would confront. Because of the desire to avoid arbitrary personnel decisions, to minimize the possibility of fraud, and to protect employee rights, the most powerful contingencies the public employer can offer often fall in the realm of the work itself, which when done well allows the employee to feel good about him or herself. Considerable attention in the literature on satisfaction and motivation has been paid to the kinds of outcomes that people value at work.

Two major theorists, Abraham Maslow[1] and Frederick Herzberg,[2] have developed multiple-factor explanations of employee job satisfaction and motivation focusing on employee needs. These theories argue that the value or valence of work outcomes depends upon the employee's level of need.

Maslow's "hierarchy of needs" theory holds that human needs can be arranged in a hierarchy of importance, with higher needs becoming predominant motivators as lower ones are satisfied. This theory is based on a relatively individualistic and optimistic view of human nature. It holds that all people have an inherent drive toward self-actualization or fulfillment and that they will seek to achieve these goals if given the opportunity to do so. People are motivated only by their own internal needs, not by those of someone else. One person or an entire organization can create conditions under which another person's needs can be fulfilled, but one person cannot actually motivate another. According to Maslow, human needs follow this progression:

1.   Physiological needs or drives

2. Safety needs for the continued fulfillment of physiological needs and psychological security
3. Belongingness and the need for love
4. Esteem needs (both the desire for a stable and positive self-concept and for the esteem of others)
5. The need for self-actualization (a term first used by Kurt Goldstein to describe the state or feeling of having achieved all that one believes oneself capable of)

These levels of needs are arranged in an interdependent and overlapping hierarchy. An important conclusion of Maslow's theory is that a satisfied need is not a motivator of behavior. Rather, it is the most urgent unsatisfied need that dominates each person's behavior.

In present-day society, it is often assumed that the safety needs and physiological needs of most people are largely satisfied. However, Douglas McGregor notes that these motivators often take a more subtle form in contemporary management practice:

> ... since every industrial employee is in a dependent relationship, safety needs may assume considerable importance. Arbitrary management actions, behavior that arouses uncertainty with respect to continued employment or which reflects favoritism or discrimination, unpredictable administration of policy—these can be powerful motivators of the safety needs in the employment relationship *at every level* from worker to vice-president.[3]

Rarely is the need for psychological security ever fully satisfied, and it is easily activated. People find feelings of anxiety punishing, and they characteristically seek to avoid anxiety-producing situations. Unfortunately, the nature of work itself can be anxiety-provoking. In this regard,

> Satisfaction of the self-esteem need leads to a feeling of self-confidence, worth, strength, capability, and adequacy of being useful and necessary in the world. But thwarting of these needs produces feelings of inferiority, of weakness, and of helplessness.[4]

These feelings often give rise to more serious neurotic problems because the typical bureaucratic organization offers little opportunity for satisfaction of esteem needs, especially for people at the lower levels of the status hierarchy.

While academicians have criticized Maslow's needs theory as vague and nonempirical,[5] it has stimulated considerable interest, particularly among practitioners. Maslow's work is noteworthy if only because it encourages an examination of what people want from their working lives, suggesting that employee needs extend beyond adequate wages and working conditions.

Frederick Herzberg's "motivator-hygiene" theory represents the second major attempt to identify work outcomes that employees value. The key to Herzberg's theory is that the factors that produce motivated and committed employees are different and distinct from those that produce job dissatisfaction. The *motivators* are related to the nature of the work itself and to the rewards that come intrinsically and directly from the performance of that work. *Hygiene factors* are related to the physical, social, and extrinsic aspects of the work environment. In brief, motivation is different from the absence of job dissatisfaction. Previous management philosophies based on the myths of humans as "economic-rational" beings or "social man" (and woman) fail to motivate workers because the management policies derived from them affect only those factors external to the work itself: company policy and administration, supervision, relationships with supervisors, relationships with peers and subordinates, working conditions, salary, status, and the like. Real job satisfaction and internal work motivation can result only when the work itself provides employees with the opportunity for growth, advancement, responsibility, intrinsic satisfaction, recognition, and achievement.

After several years, the validity of Herzberg's theory is still disputed.[6] Going beyond the question of the validity of Herzberg's theory, several attempts have been made to draw a parallel between it and Maslow's work.[7] It has been suggested that in order for the intrinsic variables to function, the extrinsic variables must first be satisfied. Table 12–3 shows this hypothesized relationship between the two theories.

JOB DESIGN AND MOTIVATION

Much of what is known about motivation and job satisfaction can be tested in the way jobs are designed. A major advance in industrial efficiency occurred in the early part of this century with the application of engineering principles to work design. The cornerstone guidelines to designing work were *simplification, standardization,* and *specialization.* Once simplified, a job could be done by anyone with a minimal amount of training. A job should be standardized, according to the one best way of performing it. This determination would be scientifically established through objective observation and analyses of work methods. And once a job was specialized, a person could develop an expertise quickly and not waste time shifting from one facet of work to another. These principles were incorporated into the dominant method of classifying jobs as well as designing them.

Unfortunately, this orientation to job design concentrated on the ability factor, in the $P = f(a \times m)$, almost to the exclusion of the motivational factor. In fact, simplistic assumptions about motivation focused on the value of economic rewards. If one utilizes an expectancy model, this method of designing jobs could be inferred to produce the following calculations. First, a high E→P probability. Second, a high P→O probability with a

TABLE 12–3.   Maslow's and Herzberg's Motivational Theories Compared

HIERARCHY OF UNMET NEEDS	DISSATISFIERS (HYGIENE FACTORS)	MOTIVATORS
Self-actualization		Achievement Recognition
Esteem		Work itself Responsibility Advancement
Belongingness	Company policy and administration	
Safety	Supervision Salary Interpersonal relations	
Physiological	Working conditions, job security	

positive valence on economic outcomes when compensation was based on piece work. Third, equally high P→O probabilities with negative valences on outcomes like fatigue, boredom, accidents, and social pressure against high producers. In addition, these conditions permitted little opportunity for satisfaction of what Maslow refers to as the "higher-order" needs, although we should recognize that during the early 1900s job security probably dominated employee needs. As working conditions improved and as economic factors ceased to play the dominant role in motivation and job satisfaction they once had, these negative valences began to make high performance in many jobs not worth the effort required.

The work of Hackman and Oldham[8] represents a significant challenge to this historically dominant approach to job design. Because public employers rarely have sufficient extrinsic rewards to use in a carrot-or-stick fashion to influence employee performance, methods of designing work to build-in intrinsic rewards seems worthy of serious attention.

Figure 12–2 summarizes Hackman and Oldham's approach to the design of work. The model depicts the following line of argument. High internal work motivation, "growth" satisfaction, general job satisfaction, and work effectiveness result when people experience their work as meaningful, where they feel responsible for the quality and quantity of work produced, and when they have first-hand knowledge of the actual results of their labor. These psychological states are likely to result from work designed to incorporate the following characteristics: variety, work with a beginning and identifiable end; work of significance; and work characterized by autonomy and feedback. Jobs that are high in these qualities are said to be enriched and to have a high motivating potential. Whether high internal motivation, satisfaction, and productivity actually do result in holders of these kinds of jobs depends on differences in the workers' knowledge and skill, their growth-need strength reflective of the kinds of

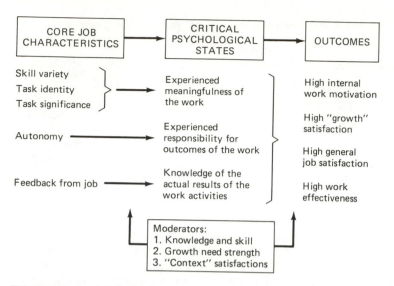

FIGURE 12–2.   Job Characteristics Model.

J. Richard Hackman and Greg R. Oldham, Work Redesign, © 1980, Addison-Wesley, p. 90.
Reprinted with permission.

higher-order needs that Maslow identifies, and by context satisfaction, which include aspects of work like pay, supervision, and working conditions.

In expectancy theory terms, the goal of job enrichment is twofold. The initial aim is to decrease E→P probabilities associated with work performance to a point where the job is experienced as challenging. Second, the critical psychological states identified in the model can be viewed as intrinsic expectancy outcomes with positive valences. The performance of work designed to include the core characteristics singled out in the model will produce these outcomes with a high degree of probability. Thus, enriched jobs lend themselves very easily to a sense of accomplishment, pride, and feelings of worth and esteem for the job holder.

Results of research into this model have been generally supportive of further work and experimentation. Hackman and Oldham's own conclusion is that research supports the general direction of the model, but examinations of the effects of the moderating variables have been mixed.[9]

THE OPPORTUNITY TO PERFORM
AND CLARITY OF PERFORMANCE GOALS

So far in this chapter the $P = f(m \times a)$ formula has guided much of the discussion. Unfortunately, individual work performance cannot be so simply explained. As Blumberg and Pringle[10] point out, a third variable influencing work performance is "opportunity." Employees who are willing to work and have the ability to perform must be given the opportunity to perform. Factors that Herzberg might include in his hygiene category and Hackman and Oldham consider as context satisfiers would be seen as affecting the opportunity of employees to do a good job at work. In addition, the design of a job itself influences the employee's opportunity to perform. Very capable employees assigned tasks they experience as routine and boring are likely to complain that they have not been given adequate opportunities to perform well.

A revised formula explaining an individual's performance at work would include the opportunity variable, Performance = f(motivation $\times$ ability $\times$ opportunity), a configuration that expands on Figure 11–1. In Blumberg and Pringle's detailed discussion of the role that opportunity plays in work performance, they cite factors like tools, equipment, materials and supplies; working conditions; behavior of coworkers; action of superiors; organizational policies, rules and procedures; information; and time. We would also include the design of the job itself.

In addition, one other variable has been shown to warrant the attention of those concerned with employee productivity. Employee performance is consistently affected by the degree of goal clarity. Frequently, people occupying roles subject to conflicting expectations find they cannot perform well because they cannot develop an adequate sense of where to aim their efforts. In other cases, supervisors assume that employees know what is expected of them and by letting employees know when they do something poorly the supervisor adequately has fulfilled his or her role. Punishing someone is not the same as specifying what the person must accomplish in order to earn rewards. Edwin Locke[11] has analyzed ostensibly competing theories of motivation and has found that in fact each theory specifies or assumes goal clarity as a necessary ingredient in effective employee performance.

Thus, the discussion of employee performance can be summarized with four basic questions:

1. Does the employee have the ability to perform well and does the employee believe he or she can meet high performance standards?
2. Is the employee motivated to do well?
   a. Does the employee connect high performance with the receipt of organizational rewards?
   b. Does the employee value the rewards the organization offers in return for high performance?
   c. Are rewards perceived as being distributed fairly?
3. Has the organization provided the employee with adequate opportunities to perform well?
4. Does the employee know what is expected of high performers?

ADDITIONAL QUALITY OF WORKING LIFE
DEVELOPMENTS

A few other attempts to improve productivity and the quality of working life by focusing on the human dimensions of work deserve brief mention.

Quality circles.   Quality circles are the latest phase in the theme of participative management.[12] Essentially, quality circles consist of small groups of employees who volunteer to meet regularly and identify, analyze, and solve problems in their common area of expertise. Most frequently, quality circles seem to involve blue collar workers. Meetings may take place during regular working hours or during nonwork hours where overtime would be paid. The circles, which are most widely utilized in Japanese industry, are responsible most frequently for quality control, production, and cost problems, and consideration is also given to accident prevention. Frequently, quality circle participants are trained in problem-solving techniques, including the development of communication and problem-identification skills, and data gathering and analysis.

Compressed work week.   A compressed work schedule involves reduction in the number of days worked per week with an increase in the number of hours worked per day. A typically compressed work schedule might consist of four ten-hour days. These schedules are staggered among employees so access for customers or clients is not negatively affected. Ronen and Primps[13] reviewed 14 reports of compressed work week experiments and concluded that employees express a generally positive attitude toward the compressed work week, particularly as it affects their home and personal life and leisure. While employee reports on performance improvements attributable to introduction of a compressed work schedule are positive, objective measures show little effect on production. Increased worker fatigue is consistently attributed to implementation of the compressed work week.

Flextime.   One of the most popular areas of experimentation in work scheduling involves *flextime*. Typically, flextime establishes core working hours, say, 9:00 A.M. to 3:00 P.M., when everyone is required to be at work, and then sets 6:00 A.M. to 9:00 A.M. and 3:00 P.M. to 6:00 P.M. as variable working hours. Thus, an employee could come to work at six in the morning and leave at three in the afternoon, with a one-hour lunch break. Or the employee could work from 7:00 A.M. to 4:00 P.M. with an hour lunch. Some schedules permit variable lunch times ranging from 30 to 90 minutes. Usually schedules are worked out in advance, or workers themselves develop their own regular shift.

Research on flextime experiments in both the public and private sectors generally reveal positive results both in employee attitudes toward flextime and in the reduction of absenteeism, tardiness, and in some cases even increases in productivity.[14] Flextime interventions are unlikely, however, to compensate for otherwise unacceptable working conditions, inadequate pay, or inadequate supervision.

EMPLOYEE PERFORMANCE AND PUBLIC PERSONNEL ADMINISTRATION

Many personnel functions already described in this book and several yet to come have a significant impact on employee performance, which depends on an employee's ability, motivation, the opportunity to work, and goal clarity. The more important an employee's ability becomes in the performance of a job, the more attention valid selection procedures and training methods warrant. Similarly, the motivation to perform is impacted by the compensation system, which in turn may be affected by collective bargaining. The design of jobs, which frequently influences the employee's opportunity to find challenges in work, will be influenced by the flexibility the classification system permits. The idea of goal clarification directly relates to adequate job analysis methods as well as formal and informal performance appraisal methods that enable employees to know how well they are meeting authoritative expectations. Thus, it is clear that employee productivity, particularly with regard to motivation, is strongly affected by the way an organization fulfills its core personnel functions other than employee development.

As with so many of the other personnel activities described earlier in this book, the personnel department itself has much less control over employee motivation and satisfaction than do legislators, agency administrators, and first-line supervisors. As seen in Table 11–1, legislatures influence salary levels, and frequently the formula for salary distributions; administrators influence goal clarity in their interpretation of legislative desires, and first-line supervisors critically affect the employee's perception of fair treatment. These examples illustrate and do not exhaust the influence that nonpersonnel staff have over employee motivation and satisfaction.

In addition, it should be clear that while improving employee productivity seems a virtuous goal, productivity programs can conflict with other values like social equity, political responsiveness, and employee rights. For example, affirmative action efforts ostensibly designed to increase the relevance of selection criteria to job performance in practice can lead to charges that selection on the basis of ability is being undermined. In this regard, *The New York Times*[15] reported in 1983, after riots broke out in Miami, that police incompetence, according to some interpretations, could be traced to a rapidly implemented affirmative action program that led to inexperienced minority officers training other newly recruited police officers. Political responsiveness affects the motivation of employees in the area of resource allocation. As another example, while public employers talk about using money as a performance incentive, the realistic observation is that taxpayers will not permit legislators to allocate enough tax dollars to public employment compensation systems to create incentives. Finally, protection of employee rights limits the effect of timely disciplinary action in many sectors of public employment. The procedural rights accorded employees under merit systems and strong collective bargaining agreements frequently make it easier either to overlook an employee's marginal performance or to transfer rather than discipline the employee if the performance is affecting the morale of other workers.

Citing these value challenges to the creation of conditions that might further motivate public employees points out the mediating role of the personnel department. Many of these value conflicts are felt at the operational level in an organization, and since they involve compensation systems, selection processes, and employee rights, they frequently require compromises that bring the personnel officer's central dilemmas—discussed throughout this book—to the forefront: Who does the personnel officer serve? Is the personnel professional's role that of compliance officer or facilitator?

SUMMARY

This chapter discussed ways that equity and expectancy theories explain employee satisfaction and motivation. It also developed the formula that employee performance depends on ability, motivation, opportunity, and clarity regarding work expectations. The motivating potential of work was linked to job design, then several newer developments of human resource management were briefly described, including quality circles, compressed work schedules, and flextime. Conflicting values that hinder the implementation of productivity programs place the personnel officer in the role of mediator.

KEY TERMS

job satisfaction
motivation
equity theory
expectancy theory
effort-performance probability

performance-outcome probability
outcome valence
Maslow's hierarchy of needs
motivators and hygiene factors
core-job characteristics
opportunity to perform
goal clarity
quality circles
compressed work schedules
flextime

DISCUSSION QUESTIONS

1. Frequently, managers will say that satisfied employees are productive employees. Is this necessarily true? Under what conditions would you find this statement to be accurate?

2. If an employee complains of unfair treatment how might you begin analyzing the complaint using your knowledge of equity theory?

3. Many people believe that it is impossible to motivate public employees because money is not a central feature of governmental reward systems. Based on your understanding of equity theory, expectancy theory, and other relevant variables, what would it take to motivate public employees with money? What might be the costs and drawbacks? The advantages or benefits?

4. Explain the Hackman and Oldham model of job design and contrast it with the scientific management orientation. Is this new approach to job design compatible or does it challenge traditional methods of job analysis, evaluation, and classification?

5. Explain how personnel tasks like job analysis, job design, and performance appraisal affect an employee's opportunity to work and perception of performance objectives.

6. How might the role of personnel professional as a facilitator differ from the role as technician or compliance officer?

CASE STUDY

Requiem for a Good Soldier

"How about Rachel Fowlkes?" Gordon asked. "She's certainly in line for the job. Rachel has had all the requisite training and experience to become an Assistant Director."

Harold Nash, manager of the Department of Health and Welfare, rolled a ballpoint pen between his fingers and rocked slowly in his executive desk chair. "I don't know," he said softly, "I really don't know. Give me another rundown on her experience."

Clifton Gordon opened the manila personnel folder and laid it on Nash's desk. "Six years with this Bureau, but she'd been with the old Vocational Rehabilitation Department for almost nine years before the reorganization. She started as a clerk, was in line for assistant director at the time we reorganized."

"We had too many chiefs as a result of that merger," Nash said. "As I recall, a few people were bumped."

Gordon smiled. "I remember that, all right. She was one that was bumped and I was the one who took over as assistant director."

"How did she take it?" Nash asked.

"No problem," Gordon said. "She was a good soldier."

"A good soldier," Nash echoed.

"She was very capable and versatile," Gordon said. "In fact I relied on her heavily for new personnel training. Many of those green young men she trained are now directors and assistant directors." Gordon pointed to the personnel folder. "Rachel was made acting assistant director of the information and public assistance section four years ago and apparently was seriously considered for the position of assistant director when Tom Walters retired.

Nash shook his head. "Regrettably, I had a difficult choice then as well. I had to choose between a capable career woman and an equally talented young man. Both were on the cert as best qualified. In the end I felt Manpower Research was not the right place in which to place our first female assistant director."

"Now would be a perfect time," Gordon said, "especially in view of the Governor's recent order on the EEO Act and the stress on the utilization of minorities and women. I think that's what all this talk of affirmative action is all about. Wouldn't promoting Rachel be an affirmative action?"

Nash winced. "Don't remind me. That report to the Governor is due shortly! But back to Rachel, promotions must ultimately be based on merit and not on sex or color of skin."

"I agree completely," Gordon replied quickly, "but with all other things being equal, why not select a woman?"

"If that were true, I just might. But all other things are not equal. Not only do I again have several capable candidates along with Rachel on the cert, but there have been problems with Rachel lately."

"I wasn't aware of that. What's happened to Rachel, the good soldier? I can't imagine her causing problems for anybody."

"That's what I'd like to know," Nash said, "For the past six months I've given her several responsibilities and she just hasn't responded the way she used to. Her work output is definitely deteriorating and her attitude is, too."

"What's her complaint?"

"No one seems to be able to put his finger on the problem: I even had her in the office once for a casual chat, but she claimed there was nothing causing her any concern. I mentioned her slipping work performance and she promised to improve."

"And?"

"Oh, she's improved. I guess her work is O.K., but that old spark is gone."

"That's a shame," Gordon said. "Rachel has done so well . . . for a woman."

Nash nodded, "Yes, it is a shame. I'm afraid we'll have to look elsewhere to fill that assistant director position."

Source: U. S. Civil Service Commission Bureau of Training, *The Equal Employment Opportunity Act: Implications for Public Employers.* U. S. Government Printing Office, Washington, D.C., 1973.

DISCUSSION QUESTIONS

1. Using equity theory, analyze how and why Rachel's behavior has changed during the time period of the case.

2. What are the important inputs and outcomes from Rachel's point of view? Who is the focus of her social comparison?

3. What factor(s) has Harold Nash given input credit for that Rachel may have overlooked?

4. Utilizing expectancy theory, analyze how Rachel's behavior has changed during the time period in the case.

5. How has Rachel's estimation of her ability to perform as Assistant Director changed? Has the value she places on different outcomes associated with being Assistant Director changed? Has her expectation changed that good performance in her current job will lead to a promotion?

6. How would you define "old spark" in terms of a performance goal or job standard? How would you feel as an employee if someone failed to promote you justifying it, in part, by your loss of the "old spark"?

7. How do you think Rachel feels at this point in her job? How do you think you might feel? How common do you think the case of Rachel is in modern organizations?

8. Who is responsible for the changes in Rachel's behavior in this case? Who is accountable for them? What is the difference?

9. If you were Harold Nash would you promote Rachel, given the deterioration of her morale and her apparent competent but lackluster performance?

NOTES

[1] Abraham H. Maslow, "A Theory of Human Motivation," *Psychological Review,* 50 (1943), 370–96.

[2]Frederick Herzberg, Bernard Mausner, and Barbara B. Snyderman, *The Motivation to Work* (New York: Wiley and Sons, 1959).

[3]Warren G. Bennis and Edgar H. Schein, with Caroline McGregor, eds., *Leadership and Motivation: Essays of Douglas McGregor*, (Cambridge, Mass.: MIT Press, 1966), pp. 9–10.

[4]Abraham Maslow, *Motivation and Personality* (New York: Harper & Row, 1954), p. 91.

[5]Mahmoud A. Wahba and Lawrence G. Bridwell, "Maslow Reconsidered: A Review of Research on the Need Hierarchy Theory," in *Motivation and Work Behavior*, 3rd ed., Richard M. Steers and Lyman W. Porter (New York: McGraw-Hill, 1983), Chap. 2.

[6]Richard M. Steers and Lyman W. Porter, *Motivation and Work Behavior*, pp. 484–87. Also see Donald P. Schwab and Larry L. Cummings, "Theories of Performance and Satisfaction: A Review," *Industrial Relations*, 9 (1970), 408–30.

[7]Robert B. Ewen and others, "An Empirical Test of the Herzberg Two-Factor Theory," *Journal of Applied Psychology*, 50 (1966), 544–50. Also see Robert Bloom and John Barry, "Determinants of Work Attitudes amongNegroes," *Journal of Applied Psychology*, 51 (1967), 291–94.

[8]J. Richard Hackman and Greg R. Oldham, *Work Redesign* (Reading, Mass.: Addison-Wesley, 1980).

[9]Russ Smith, "Job Design in the Public Sector: The Track Record," *Review of Public Personnel Administration*, 2 (1981), 63–83.

[10]Melvin Blumberg and Charles D. Pringle, "The Missing Opportunity in Organizational Research: Some Implications for a Theory of Work Performance," *Academy of Management Review*, 7 (1982), 560–69.

[11]Edwin A. Locke, "The Ubiquity of the Technique of Goal Setting in Theories and Approaches to Employee Motivation," *Academy of Management Review*, 3 (1978), 594–601.

[12]Stephen Bryant and Joseph Kearns, "Workers' Brains as Well as Their Bodies: Quality Circles in a Federal Facility," *Public Administration Review*, 42 (1982), 144–50. See also George Munchus, "Employer-Employee Based Quality Circles in Japan: Human Resource Policy Implications for American Firms," *Academy of Management Review*, 8 (1983), 255–61.

[13]Simcha Ronen and Sophia B. Primps, "The Compressed Work Week as Organizational Change: Behavioral and Attitudinal Outcomes," *Academy of Management Review*, 6 (1981), 61–74. See also J. Barton Cunningham, "Compressed Shift Schedules: Altering the Relationship Between Work and Non-Work," *Public Administration Review*, 42 (1982), 438–47.

[14]Robert T. Golembiewski and Carl W. Proehl, Jr., "Public Sector Applications of Flexible Workhours: A Review of Available Experience," *Public Administration Review*, 40 (1980), 72–85. See also Glenn W. Rainey, Jr. and Lawrence Wolf, "Flex-time: Short-Term Benefits; Long Term. . . ?" *Public Administration Review*, 41 (1981), 52–62; Simcha Ronen and Sophia B. Primps, "The Impact of Flexitime on Performance and Attitudes in 25 Public Agencies," *Public Personnel Management*, 9 (1980), 201–207.

[15]*New York Times*, May 11, 1983, p. 8.

13

Training and Development

Training is often considered the most visible and popular of all personnel activities. Managers endorse training because it promises to make employees more skilled, and hence more productive, even though these benefits must be weighed against the loss of work time while the employee is being trained. Employees like training because it offers a break from their jobs (if they don't like them) or increased skills, which they can use to master a current or prospective position.

Yet training is only beneficial in those situations where employees have a skill deficiency. It will not replace inadequate selection criteria, improper job design, or inadequate organizational rewards. To illustrate these points, two authors relate an incident that took place in a factory.[1] Periodically, top management required that foremen attend training courses on the collective bargaining contract so as to avoid inadvertent grievances. These courses were expensive (particularly in terms of the foremen's time away from work) and relatively ineffective. So the company did away with the training lessons and, in their place, management instituted a contest. The foremen were divided into groups, and it was announced that the company would buy a steak dinner for the team that compiled the most correct answers to a list of situations covered by the collective bargaining contract. For weeks excitement was high as each group completed its research. When the results were tabulated, *all* teams performed excellently. Not only was the increase in knowledge greater than would have occurred through a formal training session, but the cost was less. Everyone got the steak dinner.

By the end of this chapter you will be able to:

1. Differentiate those situations for which training is appropriate from those for which it is not
2. Discuss the objectives and techniques of new employee orientation
3. Describe methods for assessing training needs among existing employees
4. Describe the steps used in designing a training program
5. Discuss the criteria for training program evaluation, including cost-effectiveness
6. Discuss the objectives and techniques of career development
7. Discuss supervisory training, team-building, and organization development
8. Relate training and development to values such as social equity and productivity

WHEN IS TRAINING APPROPRIATE?

The example at the beginning of the chapter illustrated that training is frequently used as a solution to an organizational performance problem without considering the alternatives. Table 13–1 summarizes the causes of performance problems, the preferred organizational responses to them, and the personnel activity involved.

Many organizations ignore the performance problem if it is insignificant or if there is no readily apparent solution. The second response to a performance problem involves examining the selection criteria to determine if they really reflect the SKAs needed to perform the job; and if not, raising the standards or reexamining the criteria themselves. This involves a trade-off between the higher salaries that must be paid to attract more

TABLE 13–1. Organizational Responses to Performance Problems

	SITUATION	ORGANIZATIONAL RESPONSE	PERSONNEL ACTIVITY
1.	Problem is insignificant	Ignore it	None
2.	Selection criteria are inadequate	Increase attention to selection criteria	Job analysis
3.	Employees are unaware of performance standards	Provide feedback	Orientation, Performance evaluation
4.	Employees have inadequate skills	*Provide training*	Training
5.	Good performance is not rewarded Poor performance is not punished	Provide rewards or punishments, and connect them to performance	Performance evaluation, Disciplinary action

qualified people, and the higher cost of on-the-job training after they are hired, plus the greater risk of losing them to a competitor once they are trained. The third response is the easiest to implement, for it involves merely clarifying performance standards by providing orientation or feedback to employees. This assumes, of course, that performance standards have already been established for the job. The fourth possible solution is to train employees by giving them the job-related skills needed to meet current performance standards. Finally, supervisors may offer greater rewards to employees who meet performance standards, or initiate disciplinary action against those who do not.

Analysis of the above options leads to the conclusion that some are more difficult to implement than others. Changing selection criteria or rewards and punishments may be difficult since these involve changes in job evaluation and flexible compensation plans. Because training is one of the easiest options to implement, the chance is relatively great that it will be used regardless of its appropriateness to the situation.[2] In sum, you can train people and increase their *ability* to perform their work, but generally you are in for a disappointment if you think you can train people to expend more energy on their job.[3]

NEW EMPLOYEE ORIENTATION

Employees' initial response to training should come early in their job tenure, through orientation. Orientation is the process by which new employees and the organization clarify their respective perceptions and expectations. Since the clarity of the relationship between employees and organizational managers is the basis for productivity, client service, and retention of employees, proper attention to new employee orientation should reinforce a pattern—established during a realistic job interview—for successful future work relationships.

The traditional approach to personnel management frequently involves the disjointed application of separate techniques without much recognition of the cumulative impact of personnel practices on employees. From the employee's point of view, orientation provides a chance to discover the organization's work expectations, and to learn about the work setting as a coherent whole. From the manager's point of view, it provides the opportunity to clarify the organization's structure, functions, and work relationships and expectations.

The orientation process begins with the first messages a prospective applicant receives about the organization and the vacant position. Either the agency personnel office or the central agency staff communicates basic information about the position through the job announcement. If this information is complete and accurate, it can aid the applicant in deciding whether the job is attractive, and help dispel false expectations that might result in quick turnover after hiring.

The responsibility for providing new employees with clear and accurate information about benefits, policies, and services falls upon either the central personnel agency and/or the agency personnel office. Relevant information such as the following should be included in an orientation handbook for new employees. For the legal protection of both parties, employees should be asked to sign a form attesting that they have read and understood the organization's personnel policies and procedures:

EEO/AA	Employee handbooks should contain a statement attesting to the organization's compliance with relevant law and regulations, including those on sexual harassment.
Wages	How often do employees get paid? What is the time lag between the end of the pay period and the paycheck?
Hours of Work	What are the normal hours and days of work? Are employees eligible for overtime? Is it required? Are they compensated for overtime through overtime pay or compensatory time ("comp time")?
Leave	At what rate do employees accrue annual leave, sick leave, etc? From whom must they obtain approval to take leave?
Benefits	What health and life insurance benefits are subsidized by and/or available through the employer? In each case, clarify employer/employee contributions, application procedures, and eligibility requirements.
Performance Evaluation	What type of probationary period evaluation determines whether the employee stays or is discharged? Specify the criteria, methods, raters, and time frame used in the organization's performance evaluation system.
Disciplinary Action	What work rules apply to employees, and what are the penalties for violating them?
Grievances	What should an employee do who feels unfairly treated?
Promotion and Reassignment	How are employees notified of available vacancies for which they are eligible to apply?
Union	Are employees represented by a union? If so, what are the responsibilities and benefits of membership?

It is the responsibility of either the personnel office or the supervisor to communicate organizational objectives, structure, and setting to employees. Because supervisors and coworkers are often totally immersed in their organization, it may require some extra effort to take the time to orient new employees. However, the advantages of formal orientation are compelling. It allows employees to visualize their jobs in the context of the larger organization, and it contributes to the development of more accurate and positive information about the formal organization than can usually be gained through on-the-job orientation by other employees, who will orient the new employee to the informal organization. An understanding of both formal and informal organizations is important. The former is the established structure, functions, and policies; the latter is the impact of operational realities and personalities on them.

The employee's immediate supervisor is responsible for orientation toward the specific job. For this purpose it is extremely helpful that the job description be accurate and complete, for this can be used as the basis of the discussion. If the description contains performance standards, such as is the case with a results-oriented job description (ROD), it can even be used to set the original performance expectations, which will form the basis for subsequent performance evaluation. Failure of the supervisor to provide this information to the employee results in increased job stress, for it is unrealistic to expect employees to perform well when they have to first guess what is expected of them.

In sum, then, new employees must be oriented to four different things: (1) general position description data, (2) organizational benefits, policies, and services, (3) organizational objectives, structure, and setting, and (4) position tasks, conditions, and performance standards. Each of these should be presented in ways appropriate to its importance. For example, information about the position must be clear and accurate to comply with affirmative action laws, and to ensure a supply of qualified applicants. Written job announcements, supplemented by current listings of available vacancies, are the best methods of communicating this information. Organizational rules and regulations are best communicated through a handbook, supplemented by whatever clarification is necessary by supervisors or agency personnel staff. Organizational objectives, structure, and setting are best communicated by films, slides, or written public relations material, supplemented by short presentations by agency supervisors to new employees. In selecting supervisors to orient new employees, the personnel managers should take care to select those whose presentation of the organization is likely to be stimulating, organized, and factual. These first impressions will, of course, strongly affect an applicant's views about a given organizational unit. The employee's position orientation should be conducted by his or her direct supervisor, and the same guidelines apply here as to any counseling situation. Table 13–2 summarizes the relationships among orientation subjects, methods, and organizational units.

In addition to this formal orientation process, the new employee's coworkers will continue to provide an informal orientation that either reinforces or contradicts—but always enlarges!—his or her knowledge of the

TABLE 13–2. Orienting the New Employee

SUBJECTS	METHODS	RESPONSIBLE PARTY
1. General position description data	Job description, job vacancy announcement	Central personnel agency or agency personnel office
2. Organizational benefits, policies, and procedures	Handbook of personnel rules and regulations or oral presentation	Central personnel agency or agency personnel office
3. Organizational objectives, structure, and setting	Oral presentations, films, and slides, and public relations handouts	Personnel manager, immediate supervisor, and agency executives
4. Position tasks, conditions, and performance standards	Job description, MBO conference, and informal counseling	Supervisor
5. All of the above	Nonverbal behavior, informal conversations, and work relationships	Coworkers and clients

agency and the people in it. Initially, this informal orientation may be completely nonverbal; new employees will learn about the agency by watching their more experienced coworkers interact with clients, with each other, and with supervisors. Is the work climate friendly or hostile? Are supervisors democratic, autocratic, or free-rein? Are clients treated with concern or with boredom and disdain?

These initial reactions are soon augmented by on-the-job training by coworkers concerning organizational history, structure, work relationships, and production norms. How much work is expected? What quality is acceptable? What kinds of clothing, mannerisms, and behavior are desirable here? What rewards and punishments are used by management to provide feedback or to motivate employee performance? This informal orientation process is a valuable and necessary supplement to formal orientation.

ASSESSING TRAINING NEEDS

It is more difficult to assess the training needs of existing employees than it is to orient new employees. In one respect, however, they are similar. Management may require training for all employees in a job classification without regard for data concerning a particular employee's performance. For example, all newly appointed supervisors may be required to take training in supervisory methods and delegation; or employees whose jobs require extensive public contact may be required to take communications training. This first type of training-needs assessment may be termed a *general treatment need.*

The second type of training-needs assessment is based on *observable performance discrepancies.* These are indicated by problems such as standards of work performance not being met, accidents, frequent need for equipment repair, several low ratings on employee evaluation reports, high rate of turnover, the use of many methods to do the same job, and deadlines not being met. In this case, management's job is to observe the jobs and workers in question and uncover the difficulties. This may be done through observing problems, interviewing, questionnaires, and performance appraisal, and by requiring employees to keep track of their own work output.

A third type of training-needs assessment is related not to present performance discrepancies, but to *future human resource needs.* For example, an organization contemplating the purchase of microcomputers will need to either hire people skilled in their use, or train existing employees to use them. This type of training-needs assessment is not based on a present performance discrepancy, but on the anticipation of a future discrepancy caused by technological advances or changes in mission, which must be anticipated by training.

DESIGNING A TRAINING PROGRAM

Once the training manager, or supervisor, has noted that a problem exists, this individual must first decide if it is a training problem. As was noted above, it is possible to resolve performance problems through changes in feedback, selection, or reward systems as well as through training. Or it may simply be easier to discharge the employee if this can be done during the employee's probationary period.

If training is an appropriate solution, the training manager or supervisor must decide on the proper training program. The appropriateness of a particular training method depends upon the objective—identification of what you want employees to know or to be able to do is mandatory. Usually, knowledge-centered objectives require the acquisition of knowledge or the changing of attitudes. Performance-centered objectives include specific terms such as "to calculate," "to repair," etc.

The appropriateness of a training method depends upon the objective. Some different training methods, and the situations for which they are appropriate, are shown in Table 13–3.

Most supervisors will conduct the training themselves, since training is a basic supervisory function. Other possible choices are other supervisors, qualified coworkers, training specialists within the agency, or out-

TABLE 13–3.   Training Objectives and Methods

PURPOSE OF TRAINING	PREFERRED TRAINING METHOD
Work orientation	Lecture, films, handouts
Job skills	Demonstrations
Human skills	Group discussion and role play
Management skills	Group discussion and case studies
General education	Lecture, work books, home study

side consultants. On-the-job training is preferred by employees and supervisors because it offers tangible skills without much reduction in productivity and any administrative costs.[4] Since the work unit must continue normal operations while training takes place, short (1- to 4-hour) sessions conducted frequently are most practical, though longer sessions may be advisable if skill deficiencies are greater or if replacement employees are available. Traditional training is directive and teacher-oriented. Newer techniques are more facilitative and trainee-centered.[5] For example, group discussions, case studies, and role play are techniques commonly used to involve trainees and thus internalize the learning process. By encouraging the trainee to integrate material presented with his or her own knowledge, and by reinforcing that integration through performance at the training session, the likelihood is increased that training will result in the learning of new behaviors.

EVALUATING TRAINING PROGRAM EFFECTIVENESS

To be effective, training must be an appropriate solution to an organizational problem; that is, it must be intended to correct a skill deficiency. For optimum learning, the employee must recognize the need for acquiring new information or learning new skills, and a desire to learn must be maintained. Whatever performance standards are set, the employee should not be frustrated by the trainer who requires too much or too little.

Many learning theories revolve around the idea of reinforcement. If certain behavior is rewarded positively, then this is classified as positive reinforcement. If negative rewards are provided, this is termed negative reinforcement. It is natural that people tend to repeat response patterns that give them positive rewards, and avoid repeating actions associated with negative rewards. If employees in a training situation are given no feedback, there is no opportunity to receive positive reinforcement.

This is why it is extremely important that supervisors understand training, for they are the ones who have the best opportunity to observe performance problems, show employees the correct work method, provide feedback, and connect subsequent rewards or punishments to performance through the performance appraisal and compensation process. Most organizational training is informal and occurs on the job, through precisely this process.

To be justified, training must demonstrate an impact on the performance of the employees trained. By determining how well employees have learned, management can make decisions about the training and its effectiveness. The mere existence of a training staff, an array of courses, and trainees does not ensure that learning is taking place. Because training is both time-consuming and costly, evaluation of training should be built into any program.

Training can be evaluated at five levels: reaction, learning, behavior, results, and cost-effectiveness.

Reaction	How well did the trainees like the training?
Learning	To what extent did the trainees learn the facts, principles, and approaches that were included in the training?
Behavior	To what extent did their job behavior change because of the program?
Results	What increases in productivity or decreases in cost were achieved?
Cost-effectiveness	Assuming that training is effective, is it the least expensive method of solving the problem?

The first two measures of effectiveness can be demonstrated by interviews or questionnaires administered to trainees at the training site. Changes in job-related behavior or results are best measured by comparing employees' responses with data gathered from supervisors concerning employee behavior or productivity. There is no doubt that this criterion of effectiveness is important. George Odiorne observes:

> . . . the systems approach to evaluation of training starts with a definition of behavior change objectives sought through a conscious development effort. This definition then remains a yardstick for measurement throughout the course and achievement against the stated goals is the measure of success. All other forms of evaluation measure the internal character of the activity itself, not the effectiveness of training.[6]

However, several factors contribute to the difficulty of establishing or measuring training effectiveness criteria. First, the effectiveness of training depends upon how relevant the chosen criteria of effectiveness are to employee productivity. Measures of workload and employee or supervisory attitudes toward training must be supported by changes in employee behavior along dimensions specified in the training-needs assessment and training program design.

Training itself is often considered an organizational reward, a status symbol, or a vacation from regular work duties. Some commentators emphasize the ceremonial significance of training, pointing out that individuals receive prestige and other intangible rewards from training. While merely being selected for training does not significantly affect one's job attitudes or satisfaction, satisfactory completion of the training program can result in improved job satisfaction, with improved attitudes in the area of promotional chances and supervision.[7]

The evaluation process itself may induce employees to improve their productivity.[8] A. C. Hamblin comments on this "Hawthorne Effect" by noting that:

> . . . by studying [the employee's] job behavior after training, one may cause him to behave differently; his behavior will be shaped by the evaluation as well as by the training.[9]

Most important, typical training evaluation models are not sufficiently controlled to discount the influence of other variables on subsequent employee performance. The most common training validation model is the uncontrolled pretraining and posttraining test design, in which performance of trainees is measured prior to training and again following training. Such a design ignores the impact of other variables besides training on behavior—trainee maturation, other organizational activities, and rewards. An alternative method, one that involves similar pretests and posttests for a matched control group, controls for these or other variables that might affect test results. However, it is usually difficult to explain to management why some employees must *not* undergo training for the effectiveness of the program to be demonstrated. Figure 13–1 summarizes the differences in procedures between controlled and uncontrolled pretests and posttests.

FIGURE 13–1. Training Effectiveness Validation Models

Uncontrolled

Pre–test ⟶ Training ⟶ Post–test

Controlled

Pre–test (Group 1) ⟶ Training ⟶ Post–test (Group 1)

Pre–test (Group 2) ⟶ No Training ⟶ Post–test (Group 2)

While relatively few studies use the dual-group control method, at least one research team reports validation of training effectiveness through its use.[10]

Cost-effectiveness is the final evaluative criterion. While training may be an appropriate solution to an organizational performance problem, and while it may be effective in changing employee behavior, it is not cost-effective unless the cost of the training program is less than the cost of the problem, and less than the cost of other available solutions. The cost-effectiveness of a training program is determined by subtracting the cost of the program from the cost of the problem. *Problem costs* are the tangible, economic losses an agency suffers as a result of using untrained personnel. These include:

Equipment breakdown: cost of downtime and repair
Salaries and benefits: wasted compensation for unproductive employees
Monitoring and quality control: cost of some employees inspecting work completed by others
Personnel costs: increased recruitment, selection, or sick leave abuse costs

Training program costs are the expenses incurred in developing, implementing, and evaluating the training program:

Program development: salary and fringe benefits for the training specialists' time spent in assessing needs, setting training objectives, and selecting training methods
Program presentation: costs of room rental, supplies, equipment, marketing, handouts, refreshments, and trainers' salaries
Trainee expenses: trainees' salaries and fringe benefits during training, travel, lodging, and per diem (if applicable)

After totals have been obtained for both categories, subtract program costs from problem costs. If the training program will cost less than the projected cost of the problem for a six-month period, it is cost efficient. The more the problem cost exceeds the program cost, the greater the chance that training will be cost-effective. For example, a program that will reduce costs by $10,000 over six months, at a cost of $1,000, should be easy to sell to a supervisor or a training manager.

In addition, training-program proposals should also consider intangible problem costs such as reduced employee morale, client complaints, or loss of legislative support. Although dollar figures cannot realistically be assigned to these costs, they are often influential in the decision about whether to hold a training program. For example, in the case study at the end of this chapter, the Mayor's anger at poor park maintenance is an intangible cost, yet it is the critical factor in getting the department to develop a preventative vehicle-maintenance program.

CAREER DEVELOPMENT

Career development is the combination of future training needs and human resource planning. From the employee's viewpoint, it provides some predictability in future career paths in the organization and signifies the organization's long-term interest in its employees. For the organization, it provides some assurance that employees will be available to fill positions that will be vacant in the future.

In cutback management situations, most agencies do not do a good job of career development. For one thing, their human resource forecasting tends to be reduced in time to one annual budget cycle, so that they become less interested in developing proactive responses to future program priorities. For another, employees tend to be more concerned with keeping their jobs rather than advancing to new ones.

Yet all agencies must engage in some form of career development. During recruitment, personnel managers and supervisors must be able to advise employees of possible career options and the likelihood of their fulfillment given the employee's present education, experience, or other qualifications. Affirmative action compliance requires that agencies establish policies and procedures for announcing promotional vacancies, screening applicants, and notifying individuals not selected of the reasons why, so that they can undertake improvement efforts.

However, public personnel managers can do much more than this to help employees advance. They can provide employees with accurate information about available jobs in the organization, and they can candidly discuss the employee's skills and qualifications for the position. By working with the employee's supervisor, they can design developmental assignments for the employee, or assist the employee to "make his or her own job" on the basis of insight into organizational needs.

Personnel managers and supervisors should remain alert for cues that signify an employee feels "stuck" in a dead-end job. Gradual declines in productivity, increased absenteeism or excessive use of alcohol or drugs may be signs of an implicit decision to lessen contributions to the job because the job can no longer provide the rewards the employee desires. It is important for supervisors or personnel managers who counsel employees during these periods to use nondirective techniques, such as those described in Chapter 17. If the employee has been productive in the past, attempts at directive counseling or threats of reduced organizational rewards will only serve to increase alienation and resentment. Instead, the counselor should offer the employee straight information about the satisfactory or unsatisfactory nature of current performance, available career options, and internal upward mobility programs.

The supervisor should also recognize that many career decisions are based on nonwork factors. The career of a spouse, children's education, and the employee's personal lifestyle all influence job decisions. When life decisions and career decisions become entwined—as they most always do—the wise supervisor listens to employees and lets them make their own decisions. After all, each of us faces life with unlimited goals, and sooner or later we find ourselves forced to recognize the reality of limited time and resources. This is as true for personnel managers and supervisors as it is for their employees.

One problem with career development from the supervisor's viewpoint is that success in developing an employee increases the chance that the employee will become more attractive to other employers. Yet training and development are a supervisory responsibility. The supervisor can best deal with this situation by balancing short-term productivity needs with long-term employee development needs, recognizing that both are important. This is sometimes difficult, particularly when one realizes that supervisors are more likely to be rewarded for short-term productivity than for long-term employee development, and developed employees will leave the organization if it cannot adequately compensate them for their contributions.

SUPERVISORY TRAINING, TEAM BUILDING, AND ORGANIZATION DEVELOPMENT

Organizational supervisors and managers are responsible not only for their own work performance, but also for that of their employees. Consequently, the objective of supervisory training is to develop managerial and supervisory skills in order to help management personnel to get work done through others, and to help their employees work "smarter." Some of the typical types of training provided to managers and supervisors are supervisory techniques, delegation, time management, and stress management. Ironically, many supervisors who value training for their subordinates resist it for themselves because they consider skill deficiencies a weakness which they are reluctant to expose to their peers. The smart personnel manager can overcome this by focusing training on general treatment needs rather than observable performance discrepancies. Role play, case studies, and simulations are the preferred training methods.

Managers and supervisors are responsible not only for training individual employees to improve their work skills, but also for helping to improve the quality of those employees' work relationships. This process is called *organization development* (OD), which developed in the 1960s as a combination of *sensitivity training,* which focuses on work relationships in a small group, and *action research,* which is based on gathering data and "feeding it back" to participants to enable them to change their own behavior. OD is similar to training in that both are change-oriented, action-oriented, and aimed at employees throughout the organization.[11] However, OD is participant-oriented rather than trainer-oriented; it seeks to increase productivity by increasing employee identification with the objectives of the organization rather than by increasing employee job skills; and it focuses on the process variables that comprise human interaction rather than the work product itself.[12] A comparison of OD and training is shown in Table 13–4.

One widely used OD technique is *team building,* which assists members of an organization to work more closely together. Typically, team building begins when an OD consultant is called into the organization by top management to diagnose and correct a problem in the relationships within a department, or between one department and another. Rather than define the problem initially, the OD consultant will invite all employees to describe the strengths and weaknesses of the organization. Data are collected anonymously through questionnaires or discussion groups, and shared within the organization. Next, employees are asked to identify specific work problems that reduce organizational effectiveness. Those problems involving relationships among work units are discussed by employees from those groups, with each group being responsible for proposing a solution, defining the specific steps involved, and specifying who is responsible for seeing that they are carried out. Once the solutions are agreed upon by employees, management must also agree to assist in implementing the solutions in order for them to work. Then the employees follow up to make sure that the changes have improved productivity by improving work relationships.[13]

The steps involved in this team-building process illustrate another typical characteristic of OD. It generally moves through a six-step change process.[14] These six steps are:

1. *Problem perception*—sensing that a problem exists because previous work methods or relationships are no longer effective

TABLE 13–4.　OD and Training Compared

ORGANIZATIONAL DEVELOPMENT IS:	TRAINING IS:	BOTH ARE:
1. Participant oriented	1. Trainer oriented	1. Change oriented
2. Process oriented	2. Task oriented	2. Action oriented
3. Focused on relationship between individual and organization	3. Focused on one work area	3. Applicable to employees throughout the organization

2. *Diagnosis*—defining the nature of the problem
3. *"Unfreezing"*—reducing reliance on unsuccessful methods by increasing knowledge about alternatives that may work better
4. *Increased experimentation*—committing time and money to testing these alternatives
5. *"Refreezing"*—integrating these changes into the organization's natural work processes
6. *Limiting change efforts* to those organizational activities or relationships for which they are appropriate

Because OD is intended to change work relationships rather than work skills, it is related both to training and the new methods of designing work that were discussed in Chapter 12. Indeed, it shares several assumptions and methods in common with such productivity improvement techniques as "Theory Z" and "quality circles," which were discussed there.

TRAINING AND OTHER PERSONNEL ACTIVITIES

Training is a developmental personnel activity. That is, it is most closely related to increasing or maintaining the productivity of employees. Yet it is also tied to two other major dimensions—procurement and allocation.

The opportunity for training and development is one inducement for applicants to work for an employer. The skills provided, and the sequencing of career opportunities so as to provide for development, do much to assist an employer in the recruitment process. This is the advantage of having developed "model career patterns" for employees: They serve to link human resource planning with career development. Training is also one device by which organizations may increase the employability of underutilized groups. By providing training through trainee assignments or apprenticeship programs, employers may reduce the negative impact of lack of education, limited experience, or absence of credentials among particular individuals or groups.

Training also affects reward allocation, particularly if it is provided to employees whose performance is substandard. Prior to disciplinary action, employees should be given the opportunity to undergo training, lest the problem be traced to a deficiency of skill rather than inadequate reward or punishment. As the discussion at the beginning of the chapter indicated, it is most important that training be tied to rewards; otherwise, the organization is likely to find that increased skills will not increase the probability of desired performance. Remember, an employee's performance depends upon both ability and motivation.

SUMMARY

Training and development are important because they are the means by which the organization maintains and increases employee skill and, hence, productivity. Training begins with orientation, which is the process by which employees are informed concerning their jobs, the organization, and specific performance expectations.

Of the many methods for assessing training needs, the most commonly used is observable performance discrepancies. These indicate the objective that should be established for the training program, be it knowledge, skills, or performance improvement. The training program should be designed so that the method is appropriate to the objective, the training population, and the circumstances of the organization.

Training is frequently used in situations for which it is not appropriate. To be effective, training must have the objective of providing skills, rather than curing a problem based on improper job design, inadequate selection criteria, improper feedback, or insufficient rewards.

Training for future positions is termed *career development*. It corresponds to the employee's need to have more specific information on career opportunities within the agency. It is important that personnel managers and supervisors provide this information, even in a cutback management situation.

Frequently, poor productivity is caused by poor work relationships rather than inadequate job skills. If work relationships are the culprit, organization development techniques such as team building are often used to alleviate the problem.

DISCUSSION QUESTIONS

1. What are the objectives of training and development?
2. How do you differentiate between those performance problems for which training is appropriate, and those for which it is not?
3. What are the objectives and techniques of employee orientation?
4. What types of observable performance discrepancies can be used to assess training needs?
5. How can training programs be evaluated?
6. What are the objectives and techniques of career development?
7. How is organization development similar to and different from training? What techniques does OD use to diagnose and correct problems in organizational relationships?
8. How does training relate to other dimensions of personnel such as allocation and procurement?

KEY TERMS

training
career development
orientation
performance discrepancy
training-needs assessment
general treatment need
training evaluation
cost-effectiveness
model career pattern
organization development (OD)
sensitivity training
action research
team building

CASE STUDY: VEHICLE MAINTENANCE IN A CITY'S PARKS DEPARTMENT

Prosperity is a pleasant American city with a population of about 750,000. Its citizens are deservedly proud of their parks. Many years ago, far-sighted civic leaders annexed thousands of acres of woodland into the city limits so that today Prosperity has the highest percentage of incorporated land as parks of any American town.

Yet Prosperity's Parks and Recreation Department has problems maintaining these parks and running recreation programs within a limited budget. The director has chosen to deal with resource constraints by concentrating maintenance activities on the busier parks, and deferring purchases and maintenance of equipment.

However, this strategy is no longer working. As the existing equipment gets older, it spends more time in the department's repair facility. The head of the maintenance department is careful to schedule routine preventative maintenance for all equipment, but this schedule is seldom followed. There is such a demand for the equipment during the spring, summer, and fall that the department director is often forced to choose between performing equipment repair or providing needed park maintenance. Park maintenance crews usually wait until heavy summer thunderstorms to bring equipment in for maintenance work. When this happens, the work crews sit idle because there are no extra vehicles, and the vehicle maintenance staff is flooded with more work than it can handle. Employees are often poorly trained in equipment operation, basically because supervisors are generally overburdened with other tasks. As a result, damage to vehicles, trees, and city property is often heavy.

You are the administrative assistant to the department director. He has just received a phone call from the Mayor's office complaining of poor maintenance, idle work crews, and heavy expenses for equipment maintenance. He orders you, "Do something about the problem!"

Divide the class into groups consisting of four or five students in each group. Within each group, read the case study and develop answers to the questions below, using the information provided. If no information is provided, make your own assumptions about the problem. After you are done, compare your answers with those developed by other groups.

1. To what extent is this problem due to inadequate selection criteria, inadequate feedback, a skill deficiency, or inadequate rewards and punishments? In the space supplied, indicate the percentage of the problem that is due to each problem, and what (in general) you would do about it.

Cause	Percentage	Solution
Inadequate Selection Criteria	_____	_____
Inadequate Feedback	_____	_____
Skill Deficiency	_____	_____
Inadequate Reward	_____	_____

2. What are the observable performance discrepancies that are due to a skill deficiency?

Whose Discrepancy?	What Discrepancy?
_____	_____
_____	_____
_____	_____
_____	_____

3. For each group with an observable performance discrepancy, define the training objective.

Group	Training Objective
_____	_____
_____	_____
_____	_____
_____	_____

4. For each group, what training methods are appropriate? Specify type of training, location, format, and trainer.

Group	Method
_____	_____
_____	_____
_____	_____
_____	_____

5. What would the training cost? For each training program, include the cost for trainer's salary, trainees' salaries, training materials, and any other necessary expenses. Use the following information to compute these costs.
   a. Training can be performed by manufacturer's representatives free of charge, by city trainers at $45 per hour on a reimbursable basis, or by department employees and supervisors at the cost of their salary and benefits.
   b. The department employs 40 park maintenance employees at an average hourly salary of $4.25, plus 25 percent for benefits.
   c. The department employs 12 equipment and vehicle maintenance employees at an average cost of $6.50 per hour, plus 25 percent for benefits.

Training Program   Cost

_____   _____

_____   _____

_____   _____

_____   _____

6. Would training be cost-effective? Compare the cost of each of the above training programs with the costs of the problem they are designed to correct. Use the information provided below, and compute costs and benefits over a three-month period.
   On an average work day, 25 percent of the park maintenance equipment is in the shop for repairs. Ten percent is scheduled maintenance; 15 percent is emergency repairs. The maintenance director estimates that the total value of equipment and production lost through down-time is $1000 per day.
   When equipment is in the shop, its crew sits idle. There is enough reserve equipment to employ full crews when maintenance is scheduled, but not to utilize them when repairs must be made on an emergency basis.
   During the winter, as many as half of the vehicle maintenance employees are idle because the equipment is not being used.

Training Program   Savings?   Cost Effective?

_____   _____   _____

_____   _____   _____

_____   _____   _____

_____   _____   _____

7. Given this information, what combination of personnel practices would you recommend to the department director to solve this problem? Consider changes in human resource planning, job analysis, selection, compensation, and training.

_____

_____

_____

_____

NOTES

[1]Paul W. Thayer and William McGehee, "On the Effectiveness of Not Holding a Formal Training Course," *Personnel Psychology*, Vol. 30 (1977), 455–56.

[2]Jay Nisberg, "Performance Improvement Without Training," *Personnel Journal* (December 1976), 613–15.

[3]Paul Mager and Peter Pipe, *Analyzing Performance Problems* (Belmont, Calif.: Wadsworth, 1980).

[4]Martin Broadwell, *The Supervisor and On-the-Job Training* (Reading, Mass.: Addison-Wesley, 1975).

[5]John M. Ivancevich and J. Timothy McMahon, "Group Development, Trainer Style and Carry-over Job Satisfaction and Performance," *Academy of Management Journal* (September 1976), 395–412.

[6]George S. Odiorne, *Training by Objectives* (New York: Macmillan, 1970), p. 181.

[7]Fred P. Adams, "The Ceremonial Side of Training—Of What Value to First-Line Supervisors?," *Training and Development Journal*, Vol. 30 (October 1976), 34–37.

[8]Michael F. Gordon and Stephen L. Cohen, "Training Behavior as a Predictor of Trainability," *Personnel Psychology*, vol. 26 (1973), 261–72.

[9]A. C. Hamblin, *Evaluation and Control of Training* (London: McGraw-Hill, 1974), pp. 67–70.

[10]Herbert H. Hand and John W. Slocum, Jr., "A Longitudinal Study of the Effects of a Human Relations Training Program on Managerial Effectiveness," *Journal of Applied Psychology*, 56 (5), 1972, 412–17.

[11]W. Warner Burke, "A Comparison of Management Development and OD," in W. Clay Hamner and Frank L. Schmidt, *Contemporary Problems in Personnel: Readings for the Seventies* (Chicago, Il.: St. Clair Press, 1974), pp. 224–30.

[12]Mike Sparks, "Organization Development and Training" (unpublished manuscript, University of Southern California, Los Angeles, 1971).

[13]Jack Fordyce and Raymond Weil, *Managing with People* (Reading, Mass.: Addison-Wesley, 1971), pp. 89–184.

[14]Wendell L. French and Cecil H. Bell, Jr., *Organization Development* (Englewood Cliffs, N.J.: Prentice-Hall, Inc., 1973), pp. 45–73.

14

Performance Evaluation

Performance evaluation plays a key role in the development of employees and their productivity. As depicted earlier in Figure 11−1, the appraisal of performance provides employees with feedback, leading to greater clarity regarding organizational expectations and to a more effective channeling of employee ability.

When the formal performance appraisal process leads to organizational decisions regarding promotions and pay it is subject to the same validity and reliability checks applied to methods of selecting employees. Where the results of an unsatisfactory appraisal lead to a disciplinary action it is subject to due-process guarantees ensured both in union contracts and legislation.

Even though the appraisal or evaluation function is related to employee productivity and employees' desire to know how well they are doing, rarely are supervisors or employees satisfied with the appraisal process. On the one hand, in some organizations it is not taken very seriously and is viewed as a waste of time. In other cases it plays a major role in the distribution of organizational rewards and frequently becomes the source of considerable tension in the employee–employer relationship. For example, in 1983 President Reagan placed the quality of public education on the nation's political agenda by calling on school districts to provide incentive pay for the best teachers. Both the National Education Association (NEA) and American Federation of Teachers (AFT) have endorsed compensation schedules based on seniority and educational credits. As a political necessity these unions softened their opposition to incentive pay in 1983, but it is doubtful that individual school teachers will follow suit. The fear that the appraisal process will lead to compensation based on favoritism or subjective evaluation is underscored in a statement the NEA convention drew up following the President's initiative. According to a *New York Times* report, the NEA established the following criteria for a merit pay plan:

1. Administrators who do the evaluating must be trained in assessing effective teaching.
2. All plans must be developed with teacher participation.
3. There must be nothing intrinsically divisive about the plan, pitting teacher against teacher or teacher against administrator.
4. No capricious political whim may be involved in the selection process, and academic freedom must be maintained.
5. Eligibility must not be limited to a predetermined percentage of a teaching force.[1]

One senses an emotional intensity in these statements and can understand that while reward systems based on seniority may not be performance-based, they do protect against the lightly masked fears underscored in this NEA statement. It may also be worthwhile to recollect that some time ago teaching positions in certain municipalities were used as patronage jobs.

By the end of this chapter you will be able to:

1. Describe and distinguish between seven performance evaluation methods (graphic rating scales, ranking, forced-choice, essay, objective, critical incident, and behaviorally anchored rating scales)
2. Discuss the comparative validity, reliability, and cost of various evaluation methods
3. Describe the supervisor's motivation to assess the performance of subordinates

PURPOSES OF PERFORMANCE EVALUATION

There are four major purposes of performance evaluation: (1) to communicate management goals and objectives to employees, (2) to motivate employees to improve their performance, (3) to distribute organizational rewards such as salary increases and promotions equitably, and (4) to conduct personnel management research. First, it is clear that performance evaluation reinforces managerial expectations. After instructing employees what to do, it is management's responsibility to follow through by providing feedback on how performance matches the stated criteria. Second, the purpose of providing feedback, or constructive criticism, to employees is "performance improvement." Evaluation, then, should encourage employees to maintain or improve their job performance. Third, organizational managers can best ensure performance improvement by providing equitable rewards—economic, social, or growth—commensurate with performance. Lastly, performance evaluation can serve as the best means of validating an organization's selection and promotion criteria. If jobs have been evaluated accurately, and if people have been selected for those jobs based on job-related skills, knowledge, and abilities, then their subsequent on-the-job performance should be satisfactory or better. If not, there are defects in the job analysis, selection, or promotion criteria—or in the performance evaluation system itself.

PERFORMANCE EVALUATION AND THE LAW

Title VII of the 1964 Civil Rights Act, as amended (1972), requires employers to validate any personnel technique that affects an employee's chances for promotion. This includes performance evaluation. For this reason it is strongly suggested that personnel managers adopt one of the performance-oriented techniques discussed later in this chapter. Latham and Wexley[2] cite the Civil Service Reform Act of 1978 as providing the model for a sound, straightforward approach to performance appraisal. The Act requires most federal agencies to:

1. Develop an appraisal system that encourages employee participation in establishing performance standards
2. Develop standards based on critical job elements
3. Assess employees against performance standards rather than each other or some statistical guide like a bell curve

It is interesting to note the parallel between these requirements and those applying to techniques for the selection of employees. The common ground is found in the overall mandate that personnel decisions be based on job-related criteria.

EVALUATION CRITERIA

As we saw in the selection and promotion processes, the fundamental question is: "What factors should be evaluated?" There are only two basic criteria, *person-based* and *performance-based*, though some evaluation methods employ a mixture of the two types. Person-based systems assess an employee's personality traits, characteristics, and aptitudes and often lead to very subjective assessments. These systems are being replaced with performance-based systems or a method that merges the two approaches. In the person-based system, the rater compares employees either against other employees or against some absolute standards. Performance-based systems measure each employee's behaviors against previously established behaviors. As can be expected, each criterion has advantages. Person-based systems are, beyond a doubt, the easiest and cheapest to design, administer, and interpret. For example, many organizations evaluate employees on the extent to which they possess desirable personality traits—initiative, dependability, intelligence, or adaptability. Ratings are easily quantified and compared with past evaluations or ratings of other people or units through computerization so that the evaluation process can be completed by frequently overburdened supervisors in a minimum of time. However, person-oriented evaluation systems share the same drawbacks as trait-oriented job-evaluation and classification systems—they have low validity, low reliability, and are of dubious value in improving performance.

First, such systems are invalid to the extent that personality characteristics are unrelated to job performance. For example, organizational and environmental characteristics heavily influence the nature of a given position, and, by implication, the kinds of skills or characteristics needed for successful performance. Thus, it is impossible to specify, for all positions in an organization, a uniform set of desirable personality characteristics that can be demonstrably related to successful job performance. Second, the reliability of trait-rating is frequently marginal at best; for instance, two supervisors may have very different definitions of loyalty, depending on their views of the job or their level of expectation for their employees. Third, comparative trait evaluations are not useful for counseling employees because they neither identify areas of satisfactory or unsatisfactory performance nor suggest areas where improvement is needed. Since an employee's personality characteristics are central to his or her self-concept, it is difficult for supervisors and employees to discuss them without lapsing into amateur psychologizing and defensiveness. As a result of their low validity and reliability, person-oriented systems are not very useful for personnel management research aimed at validating selection or promotion criteria.

For these reasons, most performance specialists advocate the use of performance-based systems, namely, those which evaluate job-related behaviors. In fact, person-based systems rarely can stand the test of legal scrutiny, which examines their reliability and validity in relation to actual job performance. In contrast to person-based systems, performance criteria communicate managerial objectives clearly, are both highly relevant to job performance and highly reliable, and fulfill the purposes of reward allocation, performance improvement, and personnel management research. If objective performance standards are established between employees and supervisors through some process of participative goal setting, the employee becomes clearly aware of the specific behavioral expectations attached to his or her position.

Second, the fact that desired behaviors are specified makes the evaluative criteria highly valid—that is, the job behaviors themselves are evaluated rather than personality characteristics *believed* to be related to performance. Third, evaluation is highly reliable because the use of objective performance standards enables raters, employees, and observers to determine whether or not predetermined performance standards have been met. As a result, changes in salary levels, promotions, or firings can be amply justified by reference to employee productivity. Reward allocation decisions can be explained to employees by discussing their performance objectively rather than by arguing about the desirability of changing certain negative personality traits. Areas where performance improvement is needed can be identified for counseling, training, or job assignment purposes. The performance-based system increases job-related communication between employees and supervisors, primarily because performance standards must be altered periodically to meet changes in organizational objectives, resource allocation, or environmental constraints.

However, performance-based systems are considerably harder to develop than are person-based systems. Because performance standards will vary (depending on the characteristics of the employee, the objectives of the organization, available resources, and external conditions), separate performance standards must be developed for each employee, or for each class of similar positions. Second, the organization may wish to specify desired methods of task performance as well as objectives. Third, the changing nature of organizations and environments means that employee performance standards may also change, and seldom at regularly scheduled or administratively convenient intervals. As a result, supervisors will need to spend more time working with employees to develop performance standards and subsequent evaluation interviews. Since supervisors are rewarded primarily for improving their work unit's short-term productivity, they may view developmental counseling as an inefficient use of their time.

Fourth, it is difficult to develop objective performance standards for many staff people or for positions that are complex or interrelated in a job series. For example, the effectiveness of a personnel department's selection procedures can best be evaluated by examining the subsequent performance of recently hired employees. Yet an employee's performance is also subject to other influences: the quality of the performance standards-setting process, the relationship with others in the work unit, and environmental factors. An example would be when teachers point out that student performance is much more influenced by home environment, peers, level of ability, class size, and other factors that complicate the assessment of teachers based on student performance. Since evaluative standards are individualized, computerized scoring or interpretation of results is difficult.

Lastly, it is difficult to compare the performance of employees with different standards. If each of three employees has met previously established performance standards, how does a supervisor decide which of them should be recommended for a promotion?

EVALUATION METHODS

While the "criterion question" concerns whether personality characteristics or behavior will be the object of evaluation, the "methods question" concerns the format or technique by which the criterion will be evaluated. Seven methods are commonly used:

Graphic rating (or adjectival scaling)
Ranking
Forced-choice
Essay
Objective
Critical incident (or work sampling)
Behaviorally anchored rating scales (BARS)

Some of these techniques, primarily the first three, are more adaptable to person-oriented systems. Others are utilized primarily by performance-based systems.

1. *Graphic-rating scales* are the most easily developed, administered, and scored format. They consist of a listing of desirable or undesirable personality traits in one column and beside each trait a scale (or box) which the rater marks to indicate the extent to which the rated employee demonstrates the trait. An example of graphic rating scale appears in Figure 14–1.

2. *Ranking techniques* are similar to graphic-rating scales in that they are also based on traits. However, they require the rater to rank-order each employee on each of the listed traits. While they overcome one fault of graphic-rating scales, namely, the tendency of raters to rate all employees high on all characteristics, it is difficult for raters to rank more than ten employees against one another.

3. *Forced-choice techniques* are the most valid trait-rating method. Based on a previous analysis of the position, job analysts have determined which traits or behaviors are most related to successful job performance. Several positive traits or behaviors are given in the form of a multiple-choice question, and the rater is asked to indicate the one that corresponds most closely with the ratee's job performance or personality. Because supervisors are

FIGURE 14–1. Graphic Rating Scale

Appraisal of Personnel

Person Evaluated_____ Position_____

Location_____

PERFORMANCE FACTORS	Out-standing	Very Good	Good	Satis-factory	Unsatis-factory	Un-known
1. Effectiveness						
2. Use of time and materials						
3. Prompt completion of work						
4. Thoroughness						
5. Initiative						
6. Perseverance						

ABILITIES, SKILLS, AND FACULTIES

	Out-standing	Very Good	Good	Satis-factory	Unsatis-factory	Un-known
7. Technical skills						
8. Communication skills						
9. Judgment						
10. Analytical ability						
11. Ability to organize						
12. Ability to inspire and influence staff						
13. Ability to inspire and influence others than staff						
14. Flexibility and adaptability						
15. Imaginativeness and creativity						
16. Ability to develop subordinates						
17. Breadth of concepts						

ETHICAL CONSIDERATIONS

	Out-standing	Very Good	Good	Satis-factory	Unsatis-factory	Un-known
18. Loyalty to department						
19. Loyalty to peers						
20. Loyalty to subordinates						

(continued)

FIGURE 14–1. *(Continued)*

	Out-standing	Very Good	Good	Satis-factory	Unsatis-factory	Un-known
21. Sense of ethics						
22. Cooperativeness						
23. Responsibility						
24. Commitment of service						
25. Open-mindedness						

Date Evaluated _____ Evaluator_____

The above appraisal was reviewed with me on _____

_____

(Signature of Person Evaluated)

Comments_____

unsure which item is the "best" response according to the person who designed the test, forced-choice techniques reduce supervisory bias. Naturally, they are disliked by supervisors, who want to know how they are rating their employees. An example of the forced-choice format appears in Figure 14–2.

4. The fourth evaluation technique, the *essay,* is among the oldest and most widely used forms of evaluation. The rater simply makes narrative comments about the employee. Since these may relate to either personality or performance, the essay method is suitable for person- or performance-oriented systems. However, it has the disadvantages of being time-consuming, biased in favor of employees with supervisors who can write well, and it is impossible to standardize. It is frequently used in conjunction with graphic-rating or ranking techniques to clarify extremely low or high ratings. But the burden on supervisors is so great that when essay elaboration is required to justify high or low ratings, supervisors have a tendency to rate employees toward the middle of a normal curve.

5. The *objective method* is a measure of work performance—quality, quantity, or timeliness—against previously established standards. It is used most often in private industry by companies with piece-rate pay plans; however, public sector organizations are adopting a variant of this approach by measuring workload indicators. For example, employment counselors may be evaluated on the number of jobs they fill or on the percentage of placements who remain on the job after three months.

6. The sixth technique has been termed *critical incident* or *work sampling.* It is an objective technique that records representative examples of good (or bad) performance in relation to agreed-upon employee objectives.

It has the same advantages and disadvantages of performance-oriented systems generally. One precautionary note, however: To the extent that the selected incidents are not representative of employee performance over time, the method is open to distortion and bias. Figure 14–3 presents an example of a critical incident evaluation form.

7. *Behaviorally anchored rating scale* (BARS) is a technique that employs objective performance criteria in a standardized evaluation format. The personnel manager who wishes to use BARS develops a range of possible performance standards for each job task and then translates these statements into numerical scores. To be job related, these performance-oriented statements must be validated by job analysis (see Chapter 9, "Job Analysis and Classification").

BARS are handy because they make use of objective evaluation criteria and are easy to employ. But they are time-consuming to develop. Table 14-1 presents an example of a behaviorally anchored rating form for student performance in a classroom setting.

FIGURE 14–2. Forced-Choice Performance Evaluation Format

Person Evaluated_____

Position _____

Organization Unit_____

Date_____

Instructions: Please place a check on the line to the left of the statement that best describes this employee.

1. This employee
   ____ a. always looks presentable
   ____ b. shows initiative and independence
   ____ c. works well with others in groups
   ____ d. produces work of high quality

2. This employee
   ____ a. completes work promptly and on time
   ____ b. pays much attention to detail
   ____ c. works well under pressure
   ____ d. works well without supervisory guidance

3. This employee
   ____ a. is loyal to his or her supervisor
   ____ b. uses imagination and creativity
   ____ c. is thorough and dependable
   ____ d. accepts responsibility willingly

Person Evaluated_____

Position _____

Organizational Unit_____

Time Period _____ to _____

Employee Objectives	*Examples of Successful or Unsuccessful Performance*
1.	a.
	b.
	c.
	d.
2.	a.
	b.
	c.
	d.
3.	a.
	b.
	c.
	d.

FIGURE 14–3.   Critical Incident Performance Evaluation Format

So far our discussion has emphasized that the purpose of an employee evaluation system must be clearly stated and that evaluative methods must be suitable to the evaluative criterion chosen. Table 14–2 summarizes these relationships.

While Table 14–2 points out the uses of each appraisal method, judicial reviews of discrimination cases involving appraisal instruments will be forcing more uniformity in future performance evaluation systems. Feild and Holley[3] report that on the basis of their research examining employment discrimination court decisions involving appraisal systems, the following characteristics clearly contributed to verdicts for the defending organizations: A job analysis was used to develop the appraisal system; a

TABLE 14–1. Behaviorally Anchored Rating Scales (BARS) Evaluation Format

Student Evaluated _____ Course: _____ Dates: ____ to ____

EVALUATIVE CRITERIA	COURSE GRADE			
	A	B	C	D
1. Term paper (75 percent of course grade)	Meet criteria for a grade of "B" and in addition: Develop new insights, theories, or solutions	Meet criteria for a grade of "C" and in addition: Analyze and critically evaluate existing knowledge presented in lectures, discussion, and outside reading	Completed by date scheduled in course outline; repeat existing knowledge from lectures and outside reading. Follow proper style (grammar, organization, footnotes, and bibliography)	Not completed by date scheduled; not meeting minimum criteria for a grade of "C"
2. Class participation (25 percent of course grade)	Meet criteria for a grade of "B" and in addition: 1. Listen to and evaluate the class participation of other students 2. Show ability to analyze and evaluate material presented in lecture and discussion	Meet criteria for a grade of "C" and in addition: 1. Participate in class discussions 2. Demonstrate correct factual knowledge of concepts and theories from lectures and reading	Attend class as scheduled or notify professor in advance of absences	Not meet criteria for a grade of "C"

TABLE 14–2. Performance Evaluation Systems

PURPOSE	CRITERIA	METHODS
Communication of objectives	Performance-oriented	Critical incident (work sampling), objective measures, BARS
Reward allocation	Person- or performance-oriented	Graphic rating, ranking, forced-choice, BARS
Performance improvement	Performance-oriented	Critical incident (work sampling), objective measures, BARS
Personnel research	Performance-oriented	Essay, work sampling (critical incident), objective measures, BARS

behavior-oriented versus person-oriented system was used; evaluators were given specific written instructions on how to use the rating instrument; the appraisal results were reviewed with employees; and the defending organizations tended to be nonindustrial in nature.

RATERS

An employee's performance may be rated by a number of people.[4] The immediate supervisor most commonly assesses the performance of subordinates. This is expected, for it reinforces authority relationships in the organization and frequently is seen as the primary function that distinguishes a superior from subordinate. Because the superior-subordinate relationship is affected by so many factors, supervisory ratings are easily biased. Self-ratings can be employed to promote an honest discussion between superior and subordinate about the subordinate's performance. But self-ratings receive mixed research support; some studies find them inflated; others see them deflated in comparison with supervisory ratings. Peer ratings, while infrequently utilized, have proven acceptable both in terms of reliability and validity. However, peer ratings are difficult to sell to employers. Subordinate ratings are equally rare, and their main function is to provide data to begin discussions of the superior-subordinate relationship in a work group.

CHARACTERISTICS OF AN EFFECTIVE EVALUATION SYSTEM

Given that different evaluation methods are suitable for different evaluative criteria, several guidelines follow for the effective use of evaluation systems by public organizations.

First, it may be wise to utilize separate systems for separate purposes. It seems clear when one looks at the purposes of appraisal systems that two fundamentally different supervisory roles can be detected. If the purpose is allocation of rewards, the supervisor or other rater becomes a judge. On the other hand, if the purpose is to improve employee performance, the supervisor is a counselor, coach, or facilitator. The fact is that supervisors assume both roles in their day-to-day work, but the roles are difficult to sucessfully integrate. It may well be that different appraisal instruments lend themselves to the different functions, just as different times should be set aside to discuss allocation decisions and developmental issues with employees.

Second, raters should have the opportunity, ability, and desire to rate employees accurately. Since employee understanding and acceptance of evaluative criteria are keys to performance improvement, it follows that employees must participate jointly in the determination of goals. The performance evaluation system must be job related, must allow the opportunity for interaction and understanding between evaluator and evaluatee, and must serve the performance improvement needs of both the individual and the organization.

Third, job evaluation and performance evaluation need to be more closely related by developing occupation-specific job descriptions that include performance standards as well as duties, responsibilities, and minimum qualifications. Such job evaluations must specify the conditions under which work is to be performed, including such factors as resources, guidelines, and interrelationships. Necessarily, they will be specific to each occupation and perhaps to each organization as well.

Fourth, evaluation must be tied to long-range employee objectives such as promotion and career planning. It is not an end in itself; neither are its short-term consequences (changes in pay or performance levels). The conflict of this suggestion with the first one is more imagined than real. While performance improvement is administratively separate from promotional assessment and organizational human resource planning, both employees and organizations realize that performance appraisal relates to rewards, promotional consideration, and career planning.

THE HUMAN DYNAMICS OF THE APPRAISAL PROCESS

In a recent review of appraisal methods and processes, Latham and Wexley[5] cite research showing that over half of the 293 firms surveyed had put in place a new appraisal format within the previous three years. Despite the attention appraisal techniques have received in the past decade, however, the authors of this research claim that appraisal systems are "still widely regarded as a nuisance at best and a necessary evil at worst."[6] Considering that feedback is essential to goal accomplishment and productivity occupies the limelight, why have appraisal systems been regarded so lightly prior to their judicial scrutiny?

One reason is that all employees are not interested in productivity. When the case load of an income maintenance worker in a social service agency is increased because of budgetary constraints to the point where the emphasis is on the quantity of cases processed rather than the quality of service rendered, the individual worker begins to value his or her welfare, working conditions, and equity of the work load more than productivity. A second reason is that multiple sources of performance feedback exist in an organization with the formal appraisal system constituting only the most visible and tangible. People in organizations are constantly receiving and interpreting clues about others' opinions of their behavior. A third reason, the one deserving of more detailed attention here, concerns the human dynamics of the appraisal processes as opposed to issues like the reliability and validity of the appraisal instrument itself.

Douglas Cederblom[7] has recently provided a review of literature about the appraisal interview—the formal part of the appraisal process where the rater and the person being rated sit down to talk about the employee's performance. He found three factors contributing to the success of the appraisal interview. First, goal setting during the interview seemed positively associated with employee satisfaction with both the interview and its utility. Underlying the goal-setting process, discussed in Chapter 12, is the employee's confidence in the rater's technical knowledge about the subordinate's work. Second, the encouragement of subordinate participation in the interview—"welcoming participation," "opportunity to present ideas or feelings," and "boss asked my opinion"—seemed to produce positive subordinate assessments of the interview process.

Last, the support of the rater expressed in terms of encouragement, constructive guidance, and sincere, specific praise of the subordinate also results in positive feelings about the interview.

Criticism from superior to subordinate produces mixed results. On the one hand, a certain amount of criticism should lend perceived credibility to the superior's assessment. On the other hand, research rarely shows much lasting change in an employee following a supervisory critique. In part, this is because few raters know how to provide a constructive critique of an employee, and when a trait-rating form is used, employees inevitably interpret criticism in personal rather than behavioral terms. The obvious here warrants mention. Anything in an appraisal interview that produces a defensive employee reaction (regardless of the rater's intent) is likely to detract from the subordinate's satisfaction with the interview and is unlikely to have much success in altering an employee's behavior at work.

In looking for reasons why appraisal systems seem to have little real effect as a managerial tool despite their theoretical promise, Nalbandian[8] has turned for an explanation to the performance formula introduced in

Chapter 12, Performance = f(motivation × ability). He argues that the appraisal tool an organization uses may increase a supervisor's ability to assess employees, but many factors affecting the willingness of supervisors to evaluate employees seem easily overlooked. From an expectancy theory perspective, raters anticipate few positive outcomes from an honest attempt to rate subordinates. Most supervisors generally believe they know who their effective and ineffective employees are even if they cannot articulate their reasoning to someone else's satisfaction. From the supervisor's perspective, then, the formal appraisal process duplicates an assessment the supervisor has already made. Thus, when the supervisor conducts an appraisal it is frequently seen as benefiting someone else.

In addition, many authors and practitioners have pointed to the emotionally discomforting outcomes, the ones with negative valences, that the rater associates with the appraisal interview. This is where the supervisor's assessment of the employee must be communicated face to face.

Even though most employees want to know how their supervisor regards their performance, supervisors commonly associate negative outcomes for them as personally resulting from appraisal interviews. When employees argue; sulk; look distraught, bewildered, or disappointed; or threaten to file a grievance because they disagree with the supervisor's assessment, most supervisors will exper:ence such behavior in negative terms. The supervisor is likely, then, to find ways of behaving in the future that will not stimulate these kinds of employee responses. Is it any wonder that supervisors are prone to assess employees very similarly, with most employees rated at least satisfactory? In fact, in many organizations a satisfactory rating is a sign of disapproval.

Behaviorally-oriented rating systems are designed to make assessments more objective and, thus, more acceptable to employees. Unfortunately, bad news is bad news regardless of whether it results from an objective or subjective assessment. As long as appraisals affect promotional opportunities and compensation, the appraisal process will produce a certain amount of anxiety for both rater and subordinate.

SUMMARY

This chapter has identified the purposes and methods of assessing employees as well as the legal framework affecting the appraisal process. The benefits and costs of each method were described, and the human dynamics of the appraisal process were discussed briefly.

Ultimately, in order to produce an effective appraisal system several ingredients are necessary. These include:

1. Promoting to supervisory positions people who, among their other qualifications, want to supervise and will not look upon the appraisal of employees as a necessary evil

2. A reliable and valid appraisal tool that has been developed with employee participation and which focuses on performance rather than personal traits
3. Training programs directed at supervisory use of the appraisal instrument, and understanding of the human dynamics surrounding the appraisal process
4. Rewards for supervisors who competently and seriously approach the appraisal function
5. An open discussion and understanding of the superior-subordinate relationship at work

KEY TERMS

person-based rating system
performance-based rating system
graphic-rating scale
employee-ranking scale
forced-choice techniques
essay format
objective
critical incident
BARS

DISCUSSION QUESTIONS

1. Describe the four major purposes of performance evaluation. Do you think all four can be accomplished with one appraisal method? Are the four purposes complementary?
2. Draw up a list of pros and cons for person-based and performance-based rating systems.
3. Identify four characteristics of an effective rating system. Why are the four so difficult to implement?
4. Utilize an expectancy theory perspective (Chapter 12) to analyze the effort supervisors can be expected to put forth to assess employees honestly and accurately.

EXERCISE 1

Write a critical incident describing the behavior of an aggressive employee. Compare your critical incident with those written by others in a small group. How do you account for the divergence of incidents with regard to the term *aggressiveness,* which is so commonly used at work? Is aggressiveness a positive or negative term?

1. Discuss the utility of a term like *aggressiveness* as a rating criterion.
2. Discuss the importance of inter-rater reliability with regard to a term like *aggressiveness*.
3. In a group, pool your critical incidents and see if you can develop a rating scale with behavioral anchors for employee aggressiveness.

EXERCISE 2

The accompanying exhibits display the appraisal instruments used in two organizations. Review the exhibits and respond to the questions.

1. Which of the two forms is more job related? Note how the form evaluating the head nurse is part of a job description—similar to the results-oriented job description in Chapter 9.
2. Discuss the two forms with regard to the following criteria:
   a. Job relatedness
   b. Cost in developing
   c. Ease of completing
   d. Use in counseling and developing employees
   e. Use in promotion, pay, or other personnel decisions
   f. Rater bias
   g. Use in providing specific feedback
   h. Accuracy in measuring employee performance

NOTES

[1]*New York Times,* June 30, 1983, p. 8.

[2]Gary P. Latham and Kenneth N. Wexley, *Increasing Productivity Through Performance Appraisal* (Reading, Mass.: Addison-Wesley, 1981), pp. 28–30.

[3]Hubert S. Feild and William H. Holley, "The Relationship of Performance Appraisal System Characteristics to Verdicts in Selected Employment Discrimination Cases," *Academy of Management Journal,* 25 (1982), p. 397.

[4]Richard J. Klimoski and Manuel London, "Role of the Rater in Performance Appraisal," *Journal of Applied Psychology,* 59 (1974), 445–51. See also Allen I. Kraut, "Prediction of Managerial Success by Peer and Training-Staff Ratings," *Journal of Applied Psychology,* 60 (1975), 14–19.

[5]Latham and Wexley, p. 2.

[6]R. I. Lazer and W. S. Wikstrom, *Appraising Managerial Performance: Current Practices and Future Directions* (New York: The Conference Board, 1977).

[7]Douglas Cederblom, "The Performance Appraisal Interview: A Review, Implications, and Suggestions," *Academy of Management Review,* 7 (1982), 219–27.

[8]John Nalbandian, "Performance Appraisal: If Only People Were Not Involved," *Public Administration Review,* 41 (1981), 392–96.

EXHIBIT 1.   EMPLOYEE RATING

Date of Rating _____

White—Personnel; Canary—Dept/Div.; Pink—Employee

Rating Period: From _____   To _____

___ Probationary
___ Annual
___ Special
___ Final

Soc. Sec. No.	Activity	Class	Obj.	Employee Name

INSTRUCTIONS

Evaluate employee's performance and behavior to the degree he or she meets job requirements, taking into consideration all factors in the employee's performance. Individual factors under each trait should be designated, where applicable, as (+) high; (✔) average; (−) low. The overall mark for each trait should be indicated by placing an (x) in the applicable columns labeled Outstanding, Above Average, Average, Below Average, and Unsatisfactory. BEFORE RATING EMPLOYEE, PLEASE REVIEW YOUR RATING MANUAL.

TRAIT	Outstdg.	Above Average	Average	Below Average	Unsat.
Quality of Work — Accuracy — Completeness — Oral expression — Written expression — Soundness of judgment in decisions — Reliability of work results					
Work Output — Amount of work performed — Completion of work on schedule — Physical fitness — Learning ability					

Work Habits	Organization and planning of assignments	Compliance with work instructions				
	__ Job interest	__ Observance of work hours				
	__ Attendance	__ Conscientious use of work time				
Safety	Care of equipment, property and materials	Personal safety habits				
Personal Relations	Cooperation with fellow employees	Dealing with the public				
	__ Personal appearance and habits	__ Ability to get along with others				
Adaptability	Performance in emergencies	Performance under changing conditions				
	__ Performance with minimum of instruction	__ Self-reliance, initiative & problem solving				

FOR USE IN RATING SUPERVISORS ONLY:

Supervisory Skills	Leadership	Fairness & impartiality				
	__ Acceptance by others	__ Communicating problems to others				
	__ Decision making	__ Training-Safety				
	__ Effectiveness and skill in planning and laying out work					

(continued)

EXHIBIT 1. (continued)

TRAIT	Outstdg.	Above Average	Average	Below Average	Unsat.
General Evaluation Indicate by an (x) in the appropriate column your own general evaluation of the employee's rating, taking all the above and other pertinent factors into consideration. A written statement must be made on the reverse side of this form if the rating is OUTSTANDING or UNSATISFACTORY on this item.				*	*#

Signature of
Rater's Supervisor: _____

Signature of
Rater: _____

Title: _____   Title: _____

*An (x) here indicates loss of annual salary increase
#An (x) here indicates employee must be rated again in 90 days
TO EMPLOYEE: Your signature is required; however, it does not imply that you agree with the rating.

_____   _____
Date   Employee Signature

EXHIBIT 2.

JOB DESCRIPTION

PERFORMANCE
EVALUATION

Probationary Review [ ]
Merit Review [ ] Special [ ]
Present Grade ___ Step ___
Name _____
Date of Hire _____
Evaluation Due Date _____

JOB
TITLE ___Head Nurse—___
Primary Nursing Unit

Department Nursing   Date December 1983

Job Code No.___   Date ___

Job Title of Person Supervisor/Primary

To Whom Reporting Nursing Coordinator   Pay Grade ___   Revised June 27, 1984

Job Summary: Supervises, educates, role models, manages a professional and non-professional staff responsible for comprehensive, continuous, coordinated, and individualized patient care.

RESPONSIBILITIES	PERFORMANCE STANDARDS	Attained? Yes/No	IF NO, HOW CAN SUCH BE ATTAINED?
ASSESSMENT:			
1. Assesses knowledge and skills of unit professional and non-professional staff members.	Makes observations of nursing skills practiced. Judges staff members' individual levels of performance. Enters assessment notes into employee progress file every six months.		
2. Assesses nurses' capability to perform primary nurse functions.	Observes performance.		
3. Assists staff with assessment phase of nursing process in nursing care of patients.	Counsels staff members when necessary to assure best assessment of patient needs.		
4. Assesses staff needs for education.	Communicates needs to education and training department.		
5. Assesses patients for best room and primary nurse assignment.	Makes assignments accordingly.		

15

Employee Safety and Health

The health and safety of public employees are important to public agency personnel managers for two reasons. First, health and safety are a *sanctions*-related issue. The regulations of the Occupational Safety and Health Act (OSHA), which protect employees against agency violations of health or safety standards, apply to both public agencies and private companies. Second, this topic is a *development*-related issue because there is increasing evidence that healthy employees are happier and more productive than unhealthy ones. Also, the high cost of employee illness and premature death makes it imperative that human resources be maintained and rehabilitated.

Some illustrations will provide evidence of the impact of employee health and safety on personnel expenses. An economist at the National Institute of Health estimates that a white collar company would save about $466,000 in medical costs for every 1000 employees by helping them reduce disease factors in their lives. The results of a ten-month study by the Canada Life Assurance Company in Toronto show an employee turnover rate of 1.5 percent for a group that exercises compared to a rate of 15 percent for nonexercising workers. Given an estimated average cost of $6250 for hiring and training each new management and clerical employee, the annual savings on nine health-promotion programs would be $510,000 annually for each of the nine groups. At a cost of $2.8 million for conducting the programs, the company comes out ahead by about $1.8 million. George Pfiffer, president of the American Association of Fitness Directors in Business and Industry, reports that ". . . [health care benefits] is the highest-escalating cost in the benefit package, [rising] at [a rate of] 20 percent per year. Companies are trying to find cost-effective ways to contain health benefits."[1]

By the end of this chapter you will be able to:

1. Discuss the sanctions applied to public employers through the Occupational Safety and Health Act (OSHA)
2. Discuss the relationship between employee health and productivity
3. Describe the effects of alcoholism, drug abuse, and job stress on employee productivity
4. Discuss the role of the personnel manager in promoting employee health and safety

OCCUPATIONAL SAFETY AND HEALTH ACT (OSHA)

The prevention of work-related accidents is of primary concern to public personnel managers. Estimates of the number of job-related injuries range from 2.5 million to 8.5 million annually.[2]

In addition to the personal pain and suffering caused by these incidents, they are also significant because of the associated organizational costs. These include not only the direct cost of reduced productivity, but other hidden costs of sick leave, employer insurance payments (for disability and worker's compensation policies), and the cost of processing injury-related grievances or lawsuits. These costs represent billions of dollars annually. Moreover, government employees (particularly those in public safety positions) receive occupational injuries at more than three times the rate of employees in other jobs.[3] Given the high costs of disability retirement, this is a startling figure.

The cost of work-related injuries, and their social consequences, led the federal government to pass legislation regulating private and public employers. The Occupational Safety and Health Act (OSHA) was passed in 1970 to ensure that working conditions for all Americans meet minimum health and safety standards. Under the provisions of this Act, the Occupational Safety and Health Administration (OSHA) in the Department of Labor was charged with setting health and safety standards, inspecting public agencies, and levying citations and penalties to enforce compliance.

While most of the OSHA regulations apply to industrial plants and private industry, many regulations pertain to government agencies as well. Typical regulations for office buildings include standards for number and size of entrances, lighting, ventilation, fire protection, and first-aid facilities. OSHA field office employees inspect agencies routinely, and act upon reported violations or injuries. If the work place does not meet standards, inspectors report violations and the field office director may impose financial penalties. While public agencies are generally not subject to monetary fines, they are subject to administrative sanctions like letters of reprimand.[4]

Particularly for public agencies, OSHA compliance is also accomplished through the contract administration process. Unions will identify unsafe working conditions, bring them to the attention of state or federal OSHA officials, and monitor agency compliance. A lack of compliance will cause union officials to file grievances, or to apply direct political pressure on agency managers through elected officials. The most recent examples of this were the pressures exerted by postal workers' unions to have management remove asbestos insulation used in many older buildings, or move post offices to safer facilities.

The Occupational Safety and Health Act does *not* establish federal standards with which state and municipal agencies must comply. While states may choose to comply with the federal criteria, most states have chosen the option of designating a state agency to administer the plan. If this second option is chosen, the state must then develop standards at least as effective as those promulgated by the Occupational Health and Safety Administration under federal regulations; must staff the agency with qualified employees, and must submit required reports on agency compliance to the Department of Labor.[5]

Both employers and employees have rights and responsibilities under OSHA. These are summarized in Table 15–1.

Table 15–1 indicates the effect of OSHA in sanctioning employers for unsafe working conditions, and providing for employee rights in correcting these conditions. Both employer and employee responsibilities relate to the sanctions process. That is, they prescribe behavior and outline sanctions for noncompliance. Employer and employee rights relate to due process concerns for both parties. For example, the employee has the right not to be harassed for reporting a violation; the employer has the right to contest a violation notice. Both rights and responsibilities are a part of the sanctions process.

As a public personnel manager, you can exert an influence on several aspects of the organization that affect occupational health and safety. These include workplace conditions, selection criteria, employee orientation procedures, reward systems, training, and job design.

You can improve workplace conditions by aiding facilities managers and safety engineers in correcting unsafe working conditions reported by employees or supervisors. If other managers object to the cost and inconvenience of safety regulations, you can provide them with information on the costs of noncompliance in terms of job-related injuries, workers' compensation insurance rates, disability retirement, and grievances.[6]

You can investigate jobs that have a high rate of job-related injuries to

TABLE 15–1. Employer and Employee Rights and Responsibilities Under OSHA

EMPLOYER RESPONSIBILITIES

1. Provide a hazard-free workplace and comply with OSHA rules, regulations, and standards
2. Inform all employees about OSHA and make copies of standards available for them to review upon request
3. Furnish employees with safe tools and equipment
4. Establish, update, and communicate operating procedures to promote health and safety
5. Report fatal accidents to the nearest OSHA office within 48 hours
6. Keep OSHA-required records of work-related injuries and illnesses, and post summary figures each February
7. Cooperate with the OSHA compliance officer by providing names of authorized employee representatives for inspectors to accompany or consult with during inspections
8. Not discriminate against employees who properly exercise their rights under OSHA
9. Post OSHA citations of apparent violations and abate cited violations within the prescribed time period

EMPLOYEE RESPONSIBILITIES

1. Read the OSHA poster at the job site
2. Comply with all applicable OSHA standards
3. Follow all employer safety and health rules and regulations, and wear or use prescribed protective equipment while working
4. Report hazardous conditions to the supervisor
5. Report any job-related injury or illness to the employer and seek treatment promptly
6. Cooperate with the OSHA compliance officer conducting an inspection if he or she inquires about safety and health conditions in your work place
7. Exercise your rights under the Act in a responsible manner

EMPLOYER RIGHTS

1. Seek advice and off-site consultation by writing, calling, or visiting the nearest OSHA office (OSHA will not inspect merely because an employer requests help)
2. Be advised by an OSHA compliance officer of the reasons for an inspection
3. Have an opening and a closing conference with the inspection officer
4. File a Notice of Contest with the nearest OSHA area director within 15 working days of receipt of a notice of citation and proposed penalty

EMPLOYEE RIGHTS

1. Review copies of any of the OSHA standards, rules, regulations, and requirements that the employer should have available at the work place
2. Request information from your employer on safety and health hazards, precautions that may be taken and procedures to be followed if involved in an accident
3. Request (in writing) an OSHA inspection if you believe hazardous conditions exist
4. Have your name withheld from your

(*continued*)

TABLE 15–1.   *(Continued)*

EMPLOYER RIGHTS	EMPLOYEE RIGHTS
5. Apply to OSHA for a temporary variance from a standard if you can furnish proof that chosen facilities or method of operation provide employee protection that is at least as effective as that required by the standard	employer, upon request to OSHA, if you file a written and signed complaint
6. Influence the development of job safety and health standards through participation in OSHA Standards Advisory Committees	5. Be advised of OSHA actions regarding your complaint and have informal review, if requested, of any decision not to make an inspection or not to issue a citation
	6. File a complaint to OSHA within 30 days if you believe you have been discriminated against because of asserting a right under the act, and be notified by OSHA of its determination within 90 days of filing
	7. Have an authorized employee representative accompany the OSHA compliance officer during the inspection tour
	8. Respond to questions from the OSHA compliance officer, particularly if there is no authorized employee representative accompanying the compliance officer
	9. Observe any monitoring or measuring of hazardous materials, and have the right of access to records on those materials
	10. Submit a written request to the National Institute for Occupational Safety and Health for information on whether any substance in your work place has potential toxic effects in the concentrations being used, and have your name withheld from your employer if you so wish
	11. Object to the abatement period set in the citation issued to your employer
	12. Be notified by your employer if he or she applies for a variance from an OSHA standard, testify at a variance hearing, and appeal the final decision if you disagree with it
	13. Submit information or comment to OSHA on the issuance, modification, or revocation of OSHA standards, and request a public hearing

Source: U.S. Department of Labor, *All About OSHA* (Washington, D.C.: U.S. Government Printing Office, April 1976).

determine if the incidence of accidents or injuries is less among certain groups of employees than others. For instance, you may find that older employees are less likely to be injured in a certain job than younger ones. Or vision, hand-eye coordination, and physical strength or ability may be related to employees' ability to perform a job safely. If these are related to performance on the job, they can validly be included as selection criteria when screening applicants for the position. This is not only important for preventing accidents, but also for reducing the financial costs of disability retirements. It may also minimize employer liability.

Employee orientation programs should contain information on work safety, potentially hazardous conditions that may be encountered on the job, emergency evacuation procedures, the location of fire extinguishers and alarms, and procedures for reporting job-related injuries or illnesses. This will increase employee concern for health and safety, and it will also emphasize the importance of health and safety regulations to supervisors.

The reduction of injuries and accidents can be one objective of training programs sponsored by the personnel department. Safety and health problems do represent a tangible cost to the agency, and cost-benefit models can be applied to evaluate the efficiency and effectiveness of proposed training programs in these areas.[7]

However, neither feedback nor training will be effective at inducing compliance unless employees and supervisors are rewarded for safety. Since most local governments are self-insured, it makes sense to pass on some of the savings from safety to responsible employees in the form of incentive programs. For example, some cities award savings bonds to employees whose job duties require the use of a city car, and who drive for a year or more without any chargeable accidents. In the case study at the end of Chapter 13, one answer to equipment breakdown is to reward employees with bonuses or time off when they bring equipment in for scheduled maintenance and avoid unscheduled repairs through careful operation. Many European and Japanese factories show great concern about safety, and they post the number of hours worked by all personnel since the last "time lost" accident. These types of rewards not only encourage employees to be conscious of safety, but also emphasize to managers the relationship between safety and productivity. Needless to say, it is important not only to reward employees for safe work habits, but also to reward their supervisors for recognizing, evaluating, and controlling occupational health and safety hazards.[8]

In many cases, high accident rates are caused by faulty job design. A job that is alternately boring and stressful, or a job that requires the use of dangerous equipment, increases the risk to the employee. Perhaps the personnel department can redesign the work procedure so as to reduce these factors.[9] For example, many nurses are physically unable to lift and move heavy patients, so hospitals have assigned this duty to male nurses' aides. Yet hospitals are frequently understaffed, particularly on the night shift, so that nurses often end up doing this themselves. Often, the result is a disabling back injury. This situation could be prevented by greater recognition of the costs of *not* filling nurses' aide positions, or by redesigning the nurse's job to avoid lifting heavy patients.

EMPLOYEE HEALTH AND PRODUCTIVITY

Healthy employees are more productive in that they are likely to live longer, work harder, and enjoy their work more.

Heart disease is the leading cause today of death in the United States. Over 175,000 people under age 65 die each year from heart disease; and for each fatal heart attack, between one and two nonfatal ones occur.[10] Although the rate of heart disease has recently declined, it was estimated in 1962 that the annual cost of heart disease was $3 billion in direct medical costs and $29 billion in lost productivity from disability and death. A more current estimate is $50 billion annually.[11] Additional costs are generated by disease and death due to strokes and high blood pressure.

Today's personnel managers are coming to recognize that by encouraging exercise, proper diet, nonsmoking, and effective methods of reducing job stress, they can reduce the cost of premature death or disability to the agency and its employees. Dr. Richard Keelor, director of program development for the President's Council of Physical Fitness and Sports, stated:

> Business spends $19.4 billion per year due to premature deaths of employees. Heart attacks alone cost private industry about 132 million workdays per year, or 4 percent of the gross national product. All of these health problems can be greatly alleviated by regular exercise for sedentary office workers.[12]

Evidence also supports the notion that healthy employees are happier and better workers. Surveys at several private companies indicate that employees who exercise regularly are absent less often than nonexercisers.[13] While it is hard to attribute objective productivity increases to a single cause, most employees who feel physically fit agree that they think and function better in the office. This feeling of physical well-being carries over into the decisions that they make at work, and into their relationships with colleagues.

After looking at some specific employee health problems, we will return to a discussion of the things that a personnel manager can do to improve employees' physical health and productivity.

ALCOHOLISM, DRUG ABUSE, AND STRESS

A good deal of recent management literature has focused on job stress as a cause of heart attacks, stroke, and high blood pressure. Although the relationship between these diseases and improper diet, smoking, and lack of exercise is relatively well established in the medical literature,[14] the effects of job stress on employees are more complex. First, it is frequently difficult to determine whether job stress is generated by the job or by the individual's response to it.[15] On the one hand, jobs differ in the level of stress they place on employees. Some jobs, such as air traffic controller, are considered highly stressful because they require employees to make high-risk decisions quickly, constantly, and with a minimum of information. Others are considered less stressful. Table 15–2 lists some high- and low-stress jobs.

But stress is caused not only by the job, but by the employee's reaction to job pressure. Many observers believe that some employees react to job situations in ways that increase pressure rather than alleviate it. They divide employees into two groups: *Type A* (those who are impatient, aggressive, and achievement-oriented), and *Type B* (those who are relaxed, passive, and accepting). According to this theory, stress is caused by the employee's reaction to a situation rather than by the situation itself.

An additional complicating factor is that stress is both desirable and undesirable. Stress can be a constructive force that impels employees to seek new answers to problems. It can generate creative and adaptive responses to organizational demands. Most reward systems depend upon the stress created by unmet employee needs to motivate performance beneficial to the employee and the organization.

But stress can be debilitating if the employee perceives pressure as being too great, or the situation as being "out of control." Employees who

TABLE 15–2. Stress and Occupations

LEVEL OF STRESS	OCCUPATION
High	Firefighter
	Police officer
	Air traffic controller
	Secretary
	Nurse
	Manager
	Librarian
Low	College professor

constantly perceive themselves as being caught between internal demands for perfection, and external pressures which they cannot handle, will derive harmful effects to themselves and to those around them. They may become depressed and withdrawn psychologically; they may withdraw physically through sick leaves or disability retirement; or they may seek self-destructive methods of avoiding stress such as alcohol or drug abuse.

Alcohol and drug abuse, and their effects on employee performance, are among the most widespread and perplexing problems with which personnel managers must deal. Because the use of legal and illegal drugs is so widespread in today's society, and because drugs and alcohol are accepted means for employees to cope with job stress, abuse of these substances is common. It is estimated that over 60 million Americans consume alcohol, up to 20 million use marijuana, 8 million use cocaine, and millions of others use tranquilizers, barbiturates, and amphetamines.[16] Federal studies suggest that one working American in ten has a drinking problem, and that untreated alcoholism costs American businesses $19 billion annually in lost production alone.[17] A 1970 survey of industrial firms by the American Association of Manufacturers reported that 40 percent of the managers who responded felt they had drug problems in their companies, up 13 percent in two years.[18] While data do not support the assumption that minority group members are more heavily involved with drug abuse than other employees, the increased hiring of disadvantaged job applicants under minority hiring programs has tended to increase personnel managers' perceptions of drug problems.[19]

Alcohol and drug abuse are important because they decrease productivity, increase absenteeism, and heighten job-related injuries.[20] Table 15–3 summarizes these effects.

Most public agencies are ill-equipped to deal with alcohol and drug abuse because they do not understand the problem and have not developed systematic personnel regulations, programs, and procedures to resolve it.

It is difficult to determine the nature and extent of the problem. Employees are aware of the employer-imposed penalties for use of drugs and alcohol on the job, and of the legal penalties for use of illicit drugs. In most cases, these laws and regulations serve to make employees more careful to hide the signs of alcohol or drug abuse from their employer.

TABLE 15–3.   Effects of Alcohol and Drug Abuse on Employees

Productivity	decrease
Absenteeism	increase
Sick leave abuse	increase
Tardiness	increase
Job-related injuries	increase

Several solutions are appropriate. First, personnel managers should develop policies regarding alcohol and drug abuse. A dual policy toward employees whose abuse of drugs or alcohol affects workplace safety and productivity seems most appropriate. On the one hand, personnel directors should take steps to protect and rehabilitate employees who are substance abusers by referring employees to outside agencies qualified to deal with the problems. Because employees fear reprisal or being stigmatized, these referrals should be kept confidential. Moreover, an employee's health insurance should include treatment of alcohol- and drug-related problems.

On the other hand, the personnel manager must take steps to protect the organization and its clients against low productivity and poor client service by documenting inadequate performance and following disciplinary action procedures specified in the agency's personnel manual or collective bargaining agreement. Supervisors and personnel managers should be diligent in following proper disciplinary action and grievance procedures to provide employees with proper counseling about their inadequate performance, and to discuss the situation with the affirmative action officer and union steward. At the same time, the interests of the agency must be protected by keeping accurate and confidential records of critical incidents reflecting objective and measurable decreases in an employee's productivity. This prepares the personnel manager for counseling, disciplinary action, or discharge proceedings against the employee.

While both of these alternatives may be appropriate responses to the problem, the experience of many companies indicates that it is more cost-efficient to rehabilitate employees than to fire or retire them for substance-abuse infractions.[21]

Furthermore, selection interviewers should screen job applicants for signs of alcohol or drug abuse. Applicants whose reliance upon alcohol or drugs may interfere with the productivity, health, and safety of employees may be disqualified for selection on these grounds. Finally, the personnel department should train supervisors to recognize employee behavior patterns that may be related to alcohol or drug abuse, namely, frequent absences, poor or fluctuating performance, or increased accidents.

PROMOTING EMPLOYEE HEALTH AND SAFETY

Human resources are the most important assets of any organization. As various commentators have reminded us, the cost to an organization by employees' premature death, disability retirement, illness, and sick leave abuse is tremendous. Given that healthy employees are more satisfied and more productive than others, what can the personnel manager do to improve employee health?

Initially, it is important that personnel directors collect accurate information on the costs of poor health within their own agency. Some examples:

> What are the dollar costs for lost time due to sick leave in general and to heart disease, strokes, or high blood pressure in particular?
>
> How many employees are alcohol or drug abusers, and what is the cost of this in lost time or accidents?
>
> What does the agency pay in worker's compensation insurance?
>
> What is the employer's contribution to health or hospitalization insurance?
>
> What are the costs of recruiting, selecting, and training replacement employees?

Personnel managers can focus on those positions that have a high rate of accident, illness, or substance abuse, and consider using medical criteria as selection standards. Job analyses should include descriptions of the minimum physical qualifications required for satisfactory task performance. While problems with validating certain selection criteria (such as minimum height and weight standards for law-enforcement officers) and increased concern with expanding employment opportunities for the physically handicapped have made public personnel managers reluctant to impose physical standards for selection, many such standards are obviously related to performance. For example, visual acuity can be required of pilots and police officers; x-rays of the back can be required of laborers whose jobs require lifting. In a recent case, the Richmond, Virginia fire department required that new firefighters be nonsmokers, because of the enormously increased risk of disability retirement due to lung damage among firefighters who smoke.

It is also important that organizations establish clear performance expectations, provide frequent feedback on performance to employees, and offer training and counseling to those employees whose performance is substandard. The organization's personnel practices may contribute to job stress by heightening employee uncertainty over the inducements-contributions contract. The organization can minimize this by proper orientation, the use of results-oriented job descriptions (RODs), informal supervisory feedback and "coaching," and nondirective counseling. These techniques will help the employee feel that the organization is seeking to reduce unnecessary job stress, rather than contributing to it.

Stress may also be caused by problems relating to organizational authority patterns, conflict resolution methods, and work relationships. Unfortunately, most organizations encourage people to "bottle up" job stress by discouraging open conflict, by requiring obedience to authority, and by limiting the degree to which employees may respond to problems or situations on their own initiative. Such methods of job design or decision making force employees to internalize stress or take it out on each other through informal feuds and petty bickering. To minimize these tendencies, personnel managers should interest other managers in experimenting with more facilitative organizational styles, such as "Theory Z," quality circles, and other techniques described in Chapter 12.

Lastly, employees should be encouraged to maintain or improve their own capacity to deal with stress by emphasizing proper diet, exercise, and nonsmoking. If funds are available, agency management may wish to construct health facilities on the premises, as many law-enforcement agencies have done. If less money is available, memberships in conveniently located health clubs may be partially subsidized by the agency, or offered as an option in a flexible compensation program. If no funds are available, the agency can still encourage employees to swim, jog, or bicycle as part of a personal fitness program. The agency can encourage bicycling by providing locked and covered parking for employees who pedal to and from work. It can encourage proper nonsmoking by removing cigarette machines from the premises; it can encourage proper diet by influencing the food provided at agency cafeterias and vending machines.

Under the provisions of the Health Maintenance Organization Act of 1973, employers who offer health benefit plans to employees must give them the option of membership in a health maintenance organization (HMO) as an alternative to traditional health care coverage, such as that offered by Blue Cross/Blue Shield. These plans provide for prepaid health care, and they thereby reduce the cost of care and the incentive for health care providers to inflate this cost. However, it should be noted that HMOs are not without problems. One technique by which they reduce the cost of health care is by using paraprofessionals to screen healthy employees, which can result in lower-quality health care.

The personnel manager should actively engage in career development planning with employees. By counseling employees as to their career opportunities, supervisors and personnel managers can prevent many health problems that manifest themselves in alcoholism, drug abuse, "burnout," and heart disease.

SUMMARY

Personnel managers should safeguard employees by being concerned about organizational conditions that generate accidents, and the medical problems caused by job stress: heart disease, strokes, high blood pressure, and alcohol and drug abuse.

Police officers, firefighters, and sanitation workers are particularly prone to job-related injuries. The personnel manager should know and follow the provisions of the Occupational Safety and Health Act (OSHA), which provides for federal or state regulation of working conditions.

Personnel managers can contribute to employee well-being by providing information to other managers on the link between health and productivity. They can also use medical standards as selection qualifications where appropriate; reduce job stress through better orientation, feedback, and training; seek to change organizational conditions that generate dysfunctional job stress; and provide employees with career development counseling.

Problems of alcohol and drug abuse by employees should be dealt with through counseling and medical referral and by collecting information on performance problems that can be used to institute disciplinary action, should this become necessary.

DISCUSSION QUESTIONS

1. What is the Occupational Safety and Health Act (OSHA), and why is it important to public personnel managers?
2. What is the relationship between employee health and productivity?
3. What are the effects of alcoholism, drug abuse, and job stress on the employee's productivity?
4. What should be the policy of the public personnel manager in dealing with problems of alcohol and drug abuse?
5. What can the public personnel manager do to promote increased employee health and safety?

KEY TERMS

Occupational Safety and Health Act
Worker's compensation
disability retirement
medical selection criteria
job stress
alcohol and drug abuse
organizational climate
health maintenance organization (HMO)

CASE STUDY: THE ALCOHOLIC EMPLOYEE

Robert Meyers was recently promoted to supervisor of the Operations Control Section, one of the branches of a large federal agency. After a few days on the job, he realized that he had an employee with a drinking problem.

Paul Watson was black, a Vietnam veteran, and was employed as a messenger. His job, which was the lowest paid in the organization, involved pushing a cart filled with computer printouts from one office to another. Paul was never sober at work, but he controlled his drinking so that he was never drunk either. His speech was slurred, his eyes were bloodshot, and his clothes were unkempt. He drank on the job, and he hid his bottle—Richard's Wild Irish Rose was his favorite—in a utility closet near his messenger station.

One day Robert Meyers decided he had had enough. He confronted Paul with the wine bottle that he had found in the utility room, and he asked Paul into his office for a conference.

ROBERT MEYERS   Paul, I'm tired of your damned drinking! You're always drunk, your clothes smell, and you fall asleep at your desk. I want it to stop!

PAUL WATSON   Mr. Meyers, I know I got a drinkin' problem, but I do my job—just ask anybody!

ROBERT MEYERS   Why don't you do something about it? Don't you realize you're killing yourself?

PAUL WATSON   Mr. Meyers, I know I get sick from drinkin' so much. But I can't help it. I hurt my eyes in the war—back in 'Nam when a camp stove exploded—that's why they're so bloodshot.

ROBERT MEYERS   Don't rationalize! You're a drunk, and I want you to get help or get out of here!

Paul Watson did not show up for work the next day. His wife called in sick for him.

After this unsatisfactory series of events, Robert Meyers confronted the personnel director.

ROBERT MEYERS   I'm having a problem with one of my employees, Paul Watson. He's an alcoholic. What can we do to get him help or get him out of here?

PERSONNEL DIRECTOR   Paul's a real problem. You want to see his file? He's been written up for drunkenness and time and leave violations by every supervisor he's had for the past ten years.

ROBERT MEYERS   But that's incredible!

PERSONNEL DIRECTOR   I know. But who wants to take the responsibility for firing a black disabled veteran? The affirmative action people and the DAV would be on our case. The agency director would never back us up.

ROBERT MEYERS   But how am I supposed to run an office with him stumbling around talking to himself? Can't we force him to get help?

PERSONNEL DIRECTOR   I've tried. The VA hospital would take him, but he

	doesn't want to go there—says the VA treats him like an animal.
ROBERT MEYERS	So this will just keep on 'til he can't come to work any more, and then we'll be able to fire him for abandoning his position.
PERSONNEL DIRECTOR	I'm afraid so. When he's absent without leave for three days running, and when his wife forgets to call in for him, then we'll be able to nail him—not before.
ROBERT MEYERS	The poor bastard!
PERSONNEL DIRECTOR	I know. But maybe he'll get a disability retirement out of it. When you count his military service, he's got over fifteen years seniority. Maybe he'll take the money and check himself into the VA and get dried out.

Six months later, Paul Watson was discharged for abandoning his position. The agency agreed to give him a disability retirement if he would agree to undergo treatment for alcoholism. He checked into a VA hospital, stayed there for a few weeks, and then disappeared.

Discussion

After reading this case study, then pick three students to play the roles of Robert Meyers, Paul Watson, and the Personnel Director. Read the case study as a role play. Afterwards, discuss the following questions:

1. What mistakes did Robert Meyers make in his conversation with Paul Watson? What suggestions would you offer him as improvements?
2. What is the agency's policy toward alcohol abuse? What suggestions would you offer the Personnel Director as an improvement?
3. Is this situation typical? If not, describe your experience with agencies that do things better. If so, what suggestions can you offer to keep this unfortunate situation from repeating itself?

NOTES

[1] Calvin Lawrence, Jr., "Shaping Up the Bottom Line," *The Miami Herald* (March 28, 1983), Bus. Sec. pp. 1, 8.

[2] Willie Hammer, *Occupational Safety Management* (Englewood Cliffs, N.J.: Prentice-Hall, Inc., 1976), p. 6.

[3] Midwest Center for Public Sector Labor Relations, "OSHA in the Public Sector," *Midwest Monitor* (Jan.–Feb. 1976), 1.

[4] John F. Yarbrough, "When a Municipality Faces the OSHA Act," *National Safety News* (May 1975), 102–103.

[5] *Occupational Safety and Health Act of 1970*, P.L. 91-596, 84 Stat. 1590, 29 U.S.C. s. 651 [1976].

[6] John L. Pickens, "Effective Loss-Control Management," *Management Review* (December 1977), 40–43.

[7]Robert Kreitner, "Employee Physical Fitness: Protecting an Investment in Human Resources," *Personnel Journal* (July 1976), 340–44.

[8]Henry M. Taylor, "Occupational Health Management by Objectives," *Personnel*, Vol. 57, No. 1 (Jan.–Feb. 1980), 58–60.

[9]Roger L. M. Dunbar, "Manager's Influence on Subordinates' Thinking About Safety," *Academy of Management Journal* (June 1975), 364–69.

[10]J. Stamler, "Primary Prevention in Mass Community Efforts to Control the Major Coronary Risk Factors," *Journal of Occupational Medicine*, Vol. 15, No. 1 (January 1973), 54–59.

[11]Stamler, *ibid.*

[12]Richard Keelor, "Physical Fitness Pays Off in Productivity," *Personnel Journal* (December 1976), 600.

[13]Jack Martin, "The New Business Boom—Employee Fitness," *Nation's Business* (February 1978), 68–73.

[14]A.M. Gotto, L. Scott, and E. Manis, "Prudent Eating After 40: Relationship of Diet to Blood Lipids and Coronary Heart Disease," *Geriatrics*, Vol. 29, No. 5 (May 1974), 109–118.

[15]Alan A. McLean, "Job Stress and the Psychological Pressures of Change," *Personnel* (Jan.–Feb. 1976), 41–49.

[16]Richard Bauman, "'High' Employees," *Supervision* (October 1977), 3–4.

[17]Brian Dickerson, "Ignoring Alcoholic Employees is Norm, Health Officials Say," *The Miami Herald* (May 31, 1981), pp. 1F, 5F.

[18]Vernon Louviere, "Drug Sickness; No Company Immune," *Nation's Business*, Vol. 60 (November 1972), 20.

[19]Susan Halpern, *Drug Abuse and Your Company* (New York: American Management Association, 1972), p. 13.

[20]Rolf E. Rogers and John T.C. Colbert, "Drug Abuse and Organizational Response: A Review and Evaluation," *Personnel Journal* (May 1975), 267–69.

[21]"Troubled Employees' Rehabilitation Seen Profitable to Business," *The National Underwriter: Health and Life Insurance Edition* (November 12, 1977), p. 17.

16

Labor–Management Relations

The *sanctions* process represents the authoritative control, by interest groups inside and outside the organization, of the relationship between employees and management. These can be organized employees, interest groups, or elected officials. In Chapter 15 we discussed the sanctions function briefly by concluding that employee health and safety was both a developmental activity—because it improved employee productivity—and a sanctions activity—because it represented the interjection of outside OSHA agencies into agency policies and practices. Several other personnel activities are also involved with sanctions. They are: collective bargaining, grievances and disciplinary action, and the constitutional rights of employees.

No other area of public personnel management represents as dramatic a shift in control of discipline as does the evolution of labor-management relations. It has gone from unilateral management control of personnel policies in the 1950s to shared control by management, unions, and the legislature today. In the 1960s, when most public employee associations and unions were insignificant in size, people asked, "Should public employees have the right to join unions and bargain collectively?" In the 1970s they asked, "Should public employees have the right to strike?" Today, the question is more likely to be, "How can the objectives of labor be balanced against the interests of management and the public so that strikes are no longer necessary?"

The change in attitudes shows how laws, power, and labor relations practices have evolved over the past 20 years. Just as affirmative action represents the response of administrators toward demands for social equity by disadvantaged groups, so collective bargaining represents the response of administrators toward employee demands for increased control of wages, benefits, and working conditions. Today, over half the nation's public employees are union members, and two of the three fastest growing unions in the United States—the American Federation of Teachers (AFT) and the American Federation of State, County and Municipal Employees (AFSCME)—are public employee unions.

The sanctions process is organized to protect the fundamental value of employee rights. This places it in greatest conflict with those personnel activities that support the other three values underlying public personnel management: social equity, political responsiveness, and administrative efficiency. We would therefore expect that collective bargaining would seek to negate or "capture" the personnel activities regulated by these opposing values. Some illustrative examples will show how this occurs.

Collective bargaining conflicts with affirmative action in that unions generally oppose attempts to replace the seniority system with minority promotion quotas or voluntary affirmative action. This is because unions generally consider affirmative action as opposed to their members' rights. Unions oppose political efforts to remove positions from either the classified service or the bargaining unit, because this reduces union strength and union members' rights. Lastly, unions are likely to oppose management efforts to "streamline" work rules (such as those forbidding employees from working outside their job classification) on the grounds that these rules prevent managerial abuses against employees.

By the end of this chapter you will be able to:

1. Differentiate between private and public sector labor-management relations laws and practices
2. Describe the history of labor-management relations at the federal, state, and local level
3. Describe the primary practices involved in collective bargaining: unit determination, recognition and certification, contract negotiation, and contract administration
4. Discuss the relationship between labor-management relations and other personnel activities
5. Compete an exercise ("Costing a Contract"), which shows the relationship between budgeting, personnel management, and labor-management relations in local government

PUBLIC VERSUS PRIVATE SECTOR LABOR-MANAGEMENT RELATIONS

Although many of the practices involved with public and private sector labor-management relations (LMR) are identical, their underlying legal framework (and the agencies that ensure compliance with that framework) is completely different. A brief look at the legislative history of private and public sector LMR, and the practices of collective bargaining by public and private agencies, will clarify these differences.

In the private sector, collective bargaining began in the late-1800s with the rise of industrial unions (The Congress of Industrial Organization) and craft unions (The American Federation of Labor). In the face of bitter opposition by management, aided in many cases by the federal court system, these unions gained political power and legal protection. The New Deal brought about the passage of the Wagner Act (1935), which union leaders hailed as the "Magna Carta of organized labor." This law recognized the right of all private employees to join unions for the purpose of collective bargaining, and it required that management recognize and bargain collectively with these unions. It prohibited the use of many previously common labor practices by management: "blacklisting" union members, signing "sweetheart contracts" with company unions, etc. It established a federal agency—the National Labor Relations Board (NLRB)—with the responsibility of certifying unions as appropriate bargaining representatives, supervising negotiations to ensure "good faith" bargaining, and adjudicating deadlocks (impasses) that might arise during contract negotiation. This law was counterbalanced (from management's point of view, at least) by the Taft-Hartley Act (1947), which prohibited labor unions from engaging in unfair labor practices and which allowed states to pass "right to work" laws (statutes forbidding unions from requiring that employees be union members in order to apply for employment).

Yet with the exception of a minor provision of the Taft-Hartley Act prohibiting strikes by public employees, and the provisions of the Postal Service Reorganization Act (1970) which provide for supervision of U.S. Postal Service collective bargaining by the NLRB, neither the Wagner Act, the Taft-Hartley Act, nor the NLRB is involved at all in public sector labor management relations. Rather, LMR in the public sector is regulated by a complex set of laws that apply differentially to federal, state, and local governments.

HISTORY OF PUBLIC SECTOR LABOR RELATIONS

Federal

The process of collective bargaining, as usually understood, cannot be transplanted into the public service. It has its distinct and insurmountable limitations when applied to public personnel management. The very nature and purpose of Government makes it impossible for administrative officials to represent fully or bind the employer in mutual discussions. The employer is the whole people who speak by means of laws enacted by their representatives in Congress. Accordingly, administrative officials and employees alike are governed and guided, and in many instances restricted, by laws which establish policies, procedures or rules in personnel matters. Particularly, I want to emphasize my conviction that militant tactics have no place in the function of any organization of Government employees.[1]

This opinion, expressed by President Roosevelt in a 1937 letter to the head of the National Federation of Federal Employees, echoes two assertions that have influenced LMR in the public service until the present time. The first assertion is that public employees have no right to withhold services from their fellow citizens. This is the basis for the "no strike" clause in federal and most state collective bargaining laws. The second is that their salaries and working conditions should be established by the people, acting through their legislative representatives, rather than through collective bargaining. This is shown by the difference between the definition of "management" in the private and public sectors. In the private sector, management is defined as the owners or corporate board of directors. In public agencies, management is not only agency executives, but also the elected officials who must ratify a negotiated contract to make it binding.

Within this philosophical framework, the legislative history of federal LMR begins with the passage of the Pendleton Act in 1883. Prior to that date, government employment was appointive and subject to the spoils system. With the passage of the Pendleton Act, workers who had gotten their jobs through the merit system of competitive examinations began to realize that they had a stake in these jobs; simultaneously, politicians began to lose interest in protecting government employees because their jobs were no longer subject to political favoritism.[2]

This combination of events led to the establishment of employee organizations whose purpose was to improve pay and working conditions, by direct lobbying of Congress and by collective bargaining. The Lloyd-LaFollette Act (1912) granted federal employees the right to organize and petition Congress.[3] However, this Act was unsuccessful for several reasons: the prohibition of strikes by federal employees; the inability of public employee unions to convince a hostile court system that government agencies were, in fact, conducting reprisals against employees active in the unions; and widespread use of the Sherman Anti-Trust Act and the Interstate Commerce Act against federal unions.[4]

As was mentioned in the introduction, the passage of labor reform legislation during the New Deal era effectively and intentionally bypassed federal employees. The Wagner Act (1935) encouraged collective bargaining, defined employee rights, and prohibited unfair labor practices by employers, but it excluded federal employees and employers from these provisions.[5]

Given the advances made by private sector unions, it was evident by the 1960s that the federal government needed a more contemporary and comprehensive labor relations policy. The result was the issuance of a series of executive orders between 1961 and 1975 that gradually granted federal employees the right to join unions and to bargain collectively. Public employees' unions were recognized as legitimate bargaining agents in 1961. Binding grievance arbitration with management was permitted (though not required) in 1969, and the scope of bargaining was broadened in 1975.

In 1978, Congress passed the Civil Service Reform Act, Title VII of which incorporated these executive orders into legislation, and it created an agency (the Federal Labor Relations Authority) formally authorized to mediate disputes between unions and agency managers. Though this law has clarified such issues as unit determination, scope of bargaining, and impasse resolution procedures, national agency employees still may not strike or bargain collectively over wages and benefits, both of which are set by Congress. The most significant variation from this practice is the U.S. Postal Service. Collective bargaining for this agency, an independent government corporation, is supervised by the NLRB rather than the FLRA.

The limitations imposed on the collective bargaining rights of federal employees make their extent of unionization somewhat surprising. In the decade from 1963 to 1973 alone, the percentage of federal employees who were union members increased from 8 percent to 57 percent, and it has continued to increase more gradually since then.[6] This is no doubt due to the unions' effectiveness at bargaining over working conditions, and of their direct lobbying activities with Congress.

State and Local

It is much more difficult to comprehend the status of state and local government collective bargaining. With the exception of federal affirmative action laws (such as the Equal Pay Act of 1963) and court cases (such as *National League of Cities* v. *Usery*), each state is responsible for developing its own laws which regulate collective bargaining for state agencies, and for all local governments within the state as well.

State governments have often gone beyond the federal government in enacting laws to clarify LMR for their employees and for employees of local governments within their jurisdictions. Forty-three states presently have enacted laws affording at least some public employees the right to "meet and confer" or negotiate on wages and working conditions. Public employees in six states are not covered by any labor relations laws, with the possible exception of no-strike provisions applicable to public employees.

Most states with collective bargaining laws have designated boards or agencies like a public employee relations board to administer these laws. This includes the functions of unit determination, unit recognition and certification, resolution of impasses during contract negotiations, and resolution of grievances arising under contract administration procedures.

Over one quarter (26.7 percent) of all state employees are members of collective bargaining units. In 1980, the latest year for which data are available, there were 22 work stoppages in state government, involving 16,019 employees.[7]

In our federal system of government, both the federal and state governments have sovereign powers. Local governments, however, are created and regulated by state governments, so they have no sovereignty. With respect to collective bargaining, this has meant that they cannot enter into collective bargaining agreements with employee organizations unless the state has passed legislation authorizing them to do so.

In the forty-three states allowing some form of collective bargaining, over 14,000 governments were conferring or negotiating with over 33,000 bargaining units by 1980. Since 1956, the two fastest growing unions in the country have been the American Federation of State, County and Municipal Employees (AFSCME) (whose membership rose by 166 percent), and the American Federation of Teachers (AFT) with a startling 257 percent increase.[8] Of greatest significance is the fact that both these unions organize state and local government employees exclusively.

Today over 4,113,000 local government employees (43 percent of the total) are in bargaining units. About half of these are working in education as teachers (1,740,000), administrators (306,000), or paraprofessionals (120,000). The remainder are concentrated in such fields as office workers (323,000), custodial and service employees (338,000), police and fire (408,000), transit (115,000), highway maintenance (103,000), and health and social services (127,000).[9]

Table 16–1 is a summary of LMR data for all state and local governments, as of 1980. It provides useful information on the types of dispute resolution, number of employees included in bargaining units, the number of work stoppages, and the number of employees involved in them. Table 16–2 provides more detailed information on these same issues for each state, and for local governments within each state.[10]

COLLECTIVE BARGAINING PRACTICES

Thus far in this chapter we have had occasion to use a number of technical terms to describe the collective bargaining process. This section will discuss both the meaning and the general application to public sector collective bargaining of the following terms: scope of bargaining, unit determination, recognition and certification, contract negotiation, impasse resolution, ratification, contract administration, and unfair labor practices.

Scope of Bargaining

Applicable federal or state laws will generally specify which items may be negotiated between management and unions. If these laws specify which

TABLE 16–1. Policies, Bargaining Units, and Represented Employees

ITEM	STATE & LOCAL GOV'T	STATE GOV'T	LOCAL GOVERNMENT					
			Total	County	Municipal	Township	Special District	School District
No. of Gov'ts	79 928	50	79 878	3 040	18 878	16 827	26 010	15 123
Gov'ts with Labor Relations Policies, Total	14 302	43	14 259	755	2 624	1 088	913	8 879
Type of Policies: Collective Neg. Only	6 511	4	6 507	338	1 093	513	362	4 201
Meet & Confer Discus. Only	2 050	8	2 042	84	403	47	206	1 302
Collective Neg. & Meet & Confer Discussions	5 741	31	5 710	333	1 128	528	345	3 376
No. Employees in Bargaining Units	5 115 166	1 001 842	4 113 324	581 076	1 180 592	145 030	148 264	2 058 362
In Gov'ts with Collective Negotiations Only	1 864 473	59 479	1 804 994	201 737	327 088	71 309	74 031	1 130 829
In Gov'ts with Meet & Confer Only	266 636	59 780	206 856	32 848	43 970	229	20 260	109 549
In Gov'ts with Collective Bargain. & Meet & Confer	2 984 057	882 583	2 101 474	346 491	809 534	73 492	53 973	817 984

Percent of Employees in Bar. Units	38.4	26.7	43.0	31.4	46.1	36.8	30.6	48.2
In Gov'ts with Collective Negotiations Only	14.0	1.6	18.9	10.9	12.8	18.1	15.3	26.5
In Gov'ts with Meet & Confer Only	2.0	1.6	2.2	1.8	1.7	0.1	4.2	2.6
In Gov'ts with Collective Bargain. & Meet & Confer	22.4	23.5	22.0	18.7	31.6	18.6	11.1	19.2
No. of Work Stoppages	480	22	502	63	125	17	23	252
No. of Employees Involved	217 076	16 019	233 095	15 708	70 924	1 695	17 366	111 383
Final Method of Resolution: Agreement of Parties	94	4		14	32	4	6	38
Mediation	176	6		11	31	3	5	126
Fact Finding	30	1		4	3	2	2	21
Injunction	69	4		16	23	2	6	22
Other	95	7		12	33	7	4	39

U.S. Bureau of the Census, *Labor Management Relations in State and Local Governments: 1980, Series GSS No. 102* (Washington, D.C.: U.S. Government Printing Office, 1980), p. 23.

TABLE 16–2.   State and Local Government Labor Relations Policies, Bargaining Units, and Represented Employees, by State and Type of Government: October 1980

ITEM	NO. OF STATE AND LOCAL GOVERNMENTS	NO. OF STATE GOVERNMENTS	NO. OF GOVERNMENTS (TOTAL)	NO. OF EMPLOYEES ORGANIZED	PERCENT OF FULL-TIME EMPLOYEES ORGANIZED
Alabama					
Number of Governments, 1977	953	1	952		
Governments with Labor Relations Policies, Total	37	2	35	State Government 14 405 Local Governments 41 767	State Government 24.4 Local Governments 33.1
By Type of Policy:					
Collective Negotiations Only	3	—	3		
Meet and Confer Discussions Only	22	1	21		
Both Collective Negotiations and Meet and Confer Discussions	12	1	11		
Meet and Confer Discussions					
Alaska					
Number of Governments, 1977	151	1	150		
Governments with Labor Relations Policies, Total	30	1	29	State Government 10 837 Local Governments 10 329	State Government 67.9 Local Governments 70.3
By Type of Policy:					
Collective Negotiations Only	16	—	16		
Meet and Confer Discussions Only	1	—	1		

(continued)

	State Government / Local Governments		
State Government	6 323		18.1
Local Governments	35 489		37.6

Both Collective Negotiations and Meet and Confer Discussions — 13 | 1 | 12

Arizona

	Total	State Government	Local Governments
Number of Governments, 1977	420	1	419
Governments with Labor Relations Policies, Total	103	1	102
By Type of Policy:			
Collective Negotiations Only	13	—	13
Meet and Confer Discussions Only	68	1	67
Both Collective Negotiations and Meet and Confer Discussions	22	—	22

Arkansas

	Total	State Government	Local Governments
Number of Governments, 1977	1 347	1	1 346
Governments with Labor Relations Policies, Total	66	—	66
By Type of Policy:			
Collective Negotiations Only	5	—	5
Meet and Confer Discussions Only	55	—	55
Both Collective			

TABLE 16–2. *(Continued)*

ITEM	NO. OF STATE AND LOCAL GOVERNMENTS	NO. OF STATE GOVERNMENTS	NO. OF GOVERNMENTS (TOTAL)	NO. OF EMPLOYEES ORGANIZED	PERCENT OF FULL-TIME EMPLOYEES ORGANIZED
Negotiations and Meet and Confer Discussions	6	—	6		
California					
Number of Governments, 1977	3 807	1	3 806	State Government 105 146 / Local Governments 515 743	State Government 48.1 / Local Governments 65.6
Governments with Labor Relations Policies, Total	1 485	1	1 484		
By Type of Policy: Collective Negotiations Only	510	—	510		
Meet and Confer Discussions Only	386	—	386		
Both Collective Negotiations and Meet and Confer Discussions	589	1	588		
Colorado					
Number of Governments, 1977	1 465	1	1 464	State Government 13 742 / Local Governments 40 113	State Government 37.8 / Local Governments 41.0
Governments with Labor Relations Policies, Total	132	1	131		
By Type of Policy: Collective Negotiations Only	32	—	32		

Meet and Confer Discussions Only	60	—		
Both Collective Negotiations and Meet and Confer Discussions	40	1		
Connecticut Number of Governments, 1977	435	1	State Government 37 961	State Government 78.5
Governments with Labor Relations Policies, Total	187	1	Local Governments 63 682	Local Governments 73.9
By Type of Policy: Collective Negotiations Only	98	—		
Meet and Confer Discussions Only	3	—		
Both Collective Negotiations and Meet and Confer Discussions	86	1		
Delaware Number of Governments, 1977	211	1	State Government 5 978	State Government 40.0
Governments with Labor Relations Policies, Total	22	1	Local Governments 10 948	Local Governments 73.6
By Type of Policy: Collective Negotiations Only	15	—		
Meet and Confer Discussions Only	—	—		

(continued)

TABLE 16-2. *(Continued)*

ITEM	NO. OF STATE AND LOCAL GOVERNMENTS	NO. OF STATE GOVERNMENTS	NO. OF GOVERNMENTS (TOTAL)	NO. OF EMPLOYEES ORGANIZED	PERCENT OF FULL-TIME EMPLOYEES ORGANIZED
Both Collective Negotiations and Meet and Confer Discussions	7	1	6		
District of Columbia Number of Governments, 1977	2	—	2	Local Governments 33 202	Local Governments 72.1
Governments with Labor Relations Policies, Total	2	—	2		
By Type of Policy: Collective Negotiations Only	1	—	1		
Meet and Confer Discussions Only	—	—	—		
Both Collective Negotiations and Meet and Confer Discussions	1	—	1		
Florida Number of Governments, 1977	912	1	911	State Government 82 969 / Local Governments 129 690	State Government 84.5 / Local Governments 38.6
Governments with Labor Relations Policies, Total	212	1	211		
By Type of Policy: Collective Negotia-					

tions Only	146	—	146			
Meet and Confer Discussions Only	9	—	9			
Both Collective Negotiations and Meet and Confer Discussions	57	1	56			
Georgia				State Government	13 409	17.0
				Local Governments	39 261	18.4
Number of Governments, 1977	1 267	1	1 266			
Governments with Labor Relations Policies, Total	16	—	16			
By Type of Policy: Collective Negotiations Only	4	—	4			
Meet and Confer Discussions Only	9	—	9			
Both Collective Negotiations and Meet and Confer Discussions	3	—	3			
Hawaii				State Government	30 226	88.5
				Local Governments	8 867	74.7
Number of Governments, 1977	20	1	19			
Governments with Labor Relations Policies, Total	5	1	4			
By Type of Policy: Collective Negotiations Only	2	—	2			
Meet and Confer						

(continued)

303

TABLE 16–2. *(Continued)*

ITEM	NO. OF STATE AND LOCAL GOVERNMENTS	NO. OF STATE GOVERNMENTS	NO. OF GOVERNMENTS (TOTAL)	NO. OF EMPLOYEES ORGANIZED		PERCENT OF FULL-TIME EMPLOYEES ORGANIZED	
Discussions Only	—	—	—				
Both Collective Negotiations and Meet and Confer Discussions	3	1	2				
Idaho Number of Governments, 1977	973	1	972	State Government	3 512	State Government	25.4
				Local Governments	10 881	Local Governments	38.2
Governments with Labor Relations Policies, Total	114	—	114				
By Type of Policy: Collective Negotiations Only	45	—	45				
Meet and Confer Discussions Only	30	—	30				
Both Collective Negotiations and Meet and Confer Discussions	39	—	39				
Illinois Number of Governments, 1977	6 619	1	6 618	State Government	50 529	State Government	44.3
				Local Governments	176 247	Local Governments	49.1
Governments with Labor Relations Policies, Total	869	1	868				
By Type of Policy:							

	Total	State	Local		State Government	Local Governments
Collective Negotiations Only	338	—	338			
Meet and Confer Discussions Only	216	—	216			
Both Collective Negotiations and Meet and Confer Discussions	315	1	314			
Indiana						
Number of Governments, 1977	2 867	1	2 866		State Government 10 881	Local Governments 65 743
Governments with Labor Relations Policies, Total	351	1	350		State Government 18.7	Local Governments 39.0
By Type of Policy:						
Collective Negotiations Only	149	—	149			
Meet and Confer Discussions Only	25	—	25			
Both Collective Negotiations and Meet and Confer Discussions	177	1	176			
Iowa						
Number of Governments, 1977	1 851	1	1 850		State Government 6 999	Local Governments 46 506
Governments with Labor Relations Policies, Total	491	1	490		State Government 18.2	Local Governments 48.5
By Type of Policy:						
Collective Negotiations Only	286	1	285			

(continued)

TABLE 16-2. *(Continued)*

ITEM	NO. OF STATE AND LOCAL GOVERNMENTS	NO. OF STATE GOVERNMENTS	NO. OF GOVERNMENTS (TOTAL)	NO. OF EMPLOYEES ORGANIZED	PERCENT OF FULL-TIME EMPLOYEES ORGANIZED
Meet and Confer Discussions Only	50	—	50		
Both Collective Negotiations and Meet and Confer Discussions	155	—	155		
Kansas					
Number of Governments, 1977	3 726	1	3 725	State Government 5 949 / Local Governments 24 355	State Government 17.3 / Local Governments 29.4
Governments with Labor Relations Policies, Total	296	1	295		
By Type of Policy:					
Collective Negotiations Only	102	—	102		
Meet and Confer Discussions Only	57	1	56		
Both Collective Negotiations and Meet and Confer Discussions	137	—	137		
Kentucky					
Number of Governments, 1977	1 185	1	1 184	State Government 1 680 / Local Governments 31 007	State Government 2.9 / Local Governments 34.3
Governments with Labor Relations Policies, Total	45	—	45		

Item					
By Type of Policy:					
Collective Negotiations Only	9	—			9
Meet and Confer Discussions Only	24	—			24
Both Collective Negotiations and Meet and Confer Discussions	12	—			12
Louisiana Number of Governments, 1977	459	1	State Government 12 336 Local Governments 36 278	State Government 15.7 Local Governments 26.2	458
Governments with Labor Relations Policies, Total	24	1			23
By Type of Policy:					
Collective Negotiations Only	7	—			7
Meet and Confer Discussions Only	9	—			9
Both Collective Negotiations and Meet and Confer Discussions	8	1			7
Maine Number of Governments, 1977	782	1	State Government 11 794 Local Governments 16 272	State Government 69.4 Local Governments 52.3	781
Governments with Labor Relations Policies, Total	189	1			188
By Type of Policy:					

(continued)

TABLE 16–2. *(Continued)*

ITEM	NO. OF STATE AND LOCAL GOVERNMENTS	NO. OF STATE GOVERNMENTS	NO. OF GOVERNMENTS (TOTAL)	NO. OF EMPLOYEES ORGANIZED		PERCENT OF FULL-TIME EMPLOYEES ORGANIZED	
Collective Negotiations Only	98	—	98				
Meet and Confer Discussions Only	5	—	5				
Both Collective Negotiations and Meet and Confer Discussions	86	1	85				
Maryland				State Government	31 942	State Government	41.3
				Local Governments	87 337	Local Governments	63.8
Number of Governments, 1977	427	1	426				
Governments with Labor Relations Policies, Total	38	1	37				
By Type of Policy:							
Collective Negotiations Only	14	—	14				
Meet and Confer Discussions Only	6	—	6				
Both Collective Negotiations and Meet and Confer Discussions	18	1	·17				
Massachusetts				State Government	50 212	State Government	67.4
Number of Governments, 1977	768	1	767	Local Governments	145 183	Local Governments	73.8
Governments with							

Labor Relations Policies, Total	402	1	401
By Type of Policy:			
Collective Negotiations Only	218	—	218
Meet and Confer Discussions Only	10	—	10
Both Collective Negotiations and Meet and Confer Discussions	174	1	173
	State Government	56 155	54.0
	Local Governments	220 977	76.5
Michigan Number of Governments, 1977	2 627	1	2 626
Governments with Labor Relations Policies, Total	907	1	906
By Type of Policy:			
Collective Negotiations Only	495	—	495
Meet and Confer Discussions Only	9	—	9
Both Collective Negotiations and Meet and Confer Discussions	403	1	402
	State Government	26 281	54.3
	Local Governments	96 159	71.0
Minnesota Number of Governments, 1977	3 439	1	3 438
Governments with Labor Relations Policies, Total	654	1	653

(continued)

TABLE 16–2. *(Continued)*

ITEM	NO. OF STATE AND LOCAL GOVERNMENTS	NO. OF STATE GOVERNMENTS	NO. OF GOVERNMENTS (TOTAL)	NO. OF EMPLOYEES ORGANIZED	PERCENT OF FULL-TIME EMPLOYEES ORGANIZED
By Type of Policy:					
Collective Negotiations Only	311	—	311		
Meet and Confer Discussions Only	26	—	26		
Both Collective Negotiations and Meet and Confer Discussions	317	1	316		
Mississippi				State Government 4 440	State Government 12.1
				Local Governments 9 445	Local Governments 11.3
Number of Governments, 1977	836	1	835		
Governments with Labor Relations Policies, Total	14	1	13		
By Type of Policy:					
Collective Negotiations Only	5	—	5		
Meet and Confer Discussions Only	6	—	6		
Both Collective Negotiations and Meet and Confer Discussions	3	1	2		
Missouri				State Government 16 181	State Government 27.3
				Local Governments 59 016	Local Governments 38.5
Number of Governments, 1977	2 938	1	2 937		

Item	Total	State Government	Local Governments	Employment	Percent
Governments with Labor Relations Policies, Total	249	1	248		
By Type of Policy:					
Collective Negotiations Only	—	—	—		
Meet and Confer Discussions Only	249	1	248		
Both Collective Negotiations and Meet and Confer Discussions	—	—	—		
Montana					
Number of Governments, 1977	950	1	949		
State Government				7 583	53.7
Local Governments				12 407	47.2
Governments with Labor Relations Policies, Total	217	1	216		
By Type of Policy:					
Collective Negotiations Only	102	1	101		
Meet and Confer Discussions Only	28	—	28		
Both Collective Negotiations and Meet and Confer Discussions	87	—	87		
Nebraska					
Number of Governments, 1977	3 425	1	3 424		
State Government				4 415	17.9
Local Governments				26 204	43.8
Governments with					

(continued)

TABLE 16–2. *(Continued)*

ITEM	NO. OF STATE AND LOCAL GOVERNMENTS	NO. OF STATE GOVERNMENTS	NO. OF GOVERNMENTS (TOTAL)	NO. OF EMPLOYEES ORGANIZED	PERCENT OF FULL-TIME EMPLOYEES ORGANIZED
Labor Relations Policies, Total	382	1	381		
By Type of Policy: Collective Negotiations Only	132	—	132		
Meet and Confer Discussions Only	100	—	100		
Both Collective Negotiations and Meet and Confer Discussions	150	1	149		
Nevada Number of Governments, 1977	183	1	182	State Government 4 012 Local Governments 13 774	State Government 36.4 Local Governments 51.3
Governments with Labor Relations Policies, Total	39	1	38		
By Type of Policy: Collective Negotiations Only	22	—	22		
Meet and Confer Discussions Only	6	1	5		
Both Collective Negotiations and Meet and Confer Discussions	11	—	11		
New Hampshire					

Number of Governments, 1977	507	1	506	State Government	5 334	State Government	41.5
				Local Governments	11 659	Local Governments	46.4
Governments with Labor Relations Policies, Total	116	1	115				
By Type of Policy:							
Collective Negotiations Only	64	—	64				
Meet and Confer Discussions Only	11	—	11				
Both Collective Negotiations and Meet and Confer Discussions	41	1	40				
New Jersey							
Number of Governments, 1977	1 516	1	1 515	State Government	36 986	State Government	45.2
				Local Governments	179 240	Local Governments	66.7
Governments with Labor Relations Policies, Total	882	1	881				
By Type of Policy:							
Collective Negotiations Only	454	—	454				
Meet and Confer Discussions Only	19	—	19				
Both Collective Negotiations and Meet and Confer Discussions	409	1	408				
New Mexico							
Number of Governments, 1977	315	1	314	State Government	4 590	State Government	14.7
				Local Governments	17 218	Local Governments	41.7

(continued)

TABLE 16–2: *(Continued)*

ITEM	NO. OF STATE AND LOCAL GOVERNMENTS	NO. OF STATE GOVERNMENTS	NO. OF GOVERNMENTS (TOTAL)	NO. OF EMPLOYEES ORGANIZED	PERCENT OF FULL-TIME EMPLOYEES ORGANIZED
Governments with Labor Relations Policies, Total	41	1	40		
By Type of Policy: Collective Negotiations Only	5	—	5		
Meet and Confer Discussions Only	29	—	29		
Both Collective Negotiations and Meet and Confer Discussions	7	1	6		
New York Number of Governments, 1977	3 307	1	3 306	State Government 173 271 Local Governments 560 878	State Government 82.6 Local Governments 81.7
Governments with Labor Relations Policies, Total	1 124	1	1 123		
By Type of Policy: Collective Negotiations Only	625	—	625		
Meet and Confer Discussions Only	21	—	21		
Both Collective Negotiations and Meet and Confer Discussions	478	1	477		

North Carolina						
Number of Governments, 1977	875	1	874	State Government	31 164	38.1
				Local Governments	40 072	19.9
Governments with Labor Relations Policies, Total	—	—	—			
By Type of Policy:						
Collective Negotiations Only	—	—	—			
Meet and Confer Discussions Only	—	—	—			
Both Collective Negotiations and Meet and Confer Discussions	—	—	—			
North Dakota						
Number of Governments, 1977	2 706	1	2 705	State Government	3 540	30.9
				Local Governments	7 537	40.9
Governments with Labor Relations Policies, Total	193	1	192			
By Type of Policy:						
Collective Negotiations Only	70	—	70			
Meet and Confer Discussions Only	40	—	40			
Both Collective Negotiations and Meet and Confer Discussions	83	1	82			
Ohio						
Number of Governments				State Government	29 060	27.5

(continued)

TABLE 16–2. *(Continued)*

ITEM	NO. OF STATE AND LOCAL GOVERNMENTS	NO. OF STATE GOVERNMENTS	NO. OF GOVERNMENTS (TOTAL)	NO. OF EMPLOYEES ORGANIZED	PERCENT OF FULL-TIME EMPLOYEES ORGANIZED
...ments, 1977	3 333	1	3 332	Local Governments 170 169	Local Governments 50.8
Governments with Labor Relations Policies, Total	778	1	777		
By Type of Policy:					
Collective Negotiations Only	398	—	398		
Meet and Confer Discussions Only	94	—	94		
Both Collective Negotiations and Meet and Confer Discussions	286	1	285		
Oklahoma Number of Governments, 1977	1 695	1	1 694	State Government 2 101 / Local Governments 35 306	State Government 4.2 / Local Governments 36.6
Governments with Labor Relations Policies, Total	198	1	197		
By Type of Policy:					
Collective Negotiations Only	56	—	56		
Meet and Confer Discussions Only	72	—	72		
Both Collective Negotiations and Meet and Confer Discussions	70	1	69		

Oregon							
Number of Governments, 1977	1 449	1	1 448	State Government	18 976	State Government	48.3
				Local Governments	57 088	Local Governments	67.5
Governments with Labor Relations Policies, Total	392	1	391				
By Type of Policy:							
Collective Negotiations Only	206	—	206				
Meet and Confer Discussions Only	23	—	23				
Both Collective Negotiations and Meet and Confer Discussions	163	1	162				
Pennsylvania							
Number of Governments, 1977	5 239	1	5 238	State Government	73 208	State Government	60.3
				Local Governments	218 727	Local Governments	66.8
Governments with Labor Relations Policies, Total	1 182	1	1 181				
By Type of Policy:							
Collective Negotiations Only	579	—	579				
Meet and Confer Discussions Only	28	—	28				
Both Collective Negotiations and Meet and Confer Discussions	575	1	574				

(continued)

TABLE 16-2. (*Continued*)

ITEM	NO. OF STATE AND LOCAL GOVERNMENTS	NO. OF STATE GOVERNMENTS	NO. OF GOVERNMENTS (TOTAL)	NO. OF EMPLOYEES ORGANIZED		PERCENT OF FULL-TIME EMPLOYEES ORGANIZED	
Rhode Island							
Number of Governments, 1977	120	1	119	State Government	16 817	State Government	88.3
				Local Governments	20 506	Local Governments	85.9
Governments with Labor Relations Policies, Total	48	1	47				
By Type of Policy:							
Collective Negotiations Only	21	—	21				
Meet and Confer Discussions Only	2	—	2				
Both Collective Negotiations and Meet and Confer Discussions	25	1	24				
South Carolina							
Number of Governments, 1977	585	1	584	State Government	7 669	State Government	13.2
				Local Governments	17 402	Local Governments	18.4
Governments with Labor Relations Policies, Total	9	—	9				
By Type of Policy:							
Collective Negotiations Only	1	—	1				
Meet and Confer Discussions Only	6	—	6				
Both Collective Negotiations and							

Meet and Confer Discussions	2	—	2			
South Dakota Number of Governments, 1977	1 729	1	1 728	State Government Local Governments	1 554 8 329	State Government Local Governments	13.7 41.0
Governments with Labor Relations Policies, Total	196	1	195			
By Type of Policy: Collective Negotiations Only	61	—	61			
Meet and Confer Discussions Only	39	—	39			
Both Collective Negotiations and Meet and Confer Discussions	96	1	95			
Tennessee Number of Governments, 1977	907	1	906	State Government Local Governments	13 995 59 835	State Government Local Governments	23.7 38.7
Governments with Labor Relations Policies, Total	71	1	70			
By Type of Policy: Collective Negotiations Only	38	—	38			
Meet and Confer Discussions Only	8	1	7			
Both Collective Negotiations and Meet and Confer Discussions	25	—	25			

(continued)

TABLE 16-2. (Continued)

ITEM	NO. OF STATE AND LOCAL GOVERNMENTS	NO. OF STATE GOVERNMENTS	NO. OF GOVERNMENTS (TOTAL)	NO. OF EMPLOYEES ORGANIZED		PERCENT OF FULL-TIME EMPLOYEES ORGANIZED	
Texas							
Number of Governments, 1977	3 897	1	3 896	State Government	21 658	State Government	14.0
				Local Governments	148 042	Local Governments	29.7
Governments with Labor Relations Policies, Total	118	1	117				
By Type of Policy:							
Collective Negotiations Only	13	—	13				
Meet and Confer Discussions Only	95	—	95				
Both Collective Negotiations and Meet and Confer Discussions	10	1	9				
Utah							
Number of Governments, 1977	490	1	489	State Government	8 578	State Government	35.8
				Local Governments	23 168	Local Governments	60.6
Governments with Labor Relations Policies, Total	55	1	54				
By Type of Policy:							
Collective Negotiations Only	11	—	11				
Meet and Confer Discussions Only	26	1	25				
Both Collective							

Item					
Negotiations and Meet and Confer Discussions	18	—	18	State Government	6 824 · 65.5
				Local Governments	6 143 · 48.7
Vermont					
Number of Governments, 1977	548	1	547		
Governments with Labor Relations Policies, Total	158	1	157		
By Type of Policy:					
Collective Negotiations Only	102	1	101		
Meet and Confer Discussions Only	11	—	11		
Both Collective Negotiations and Meet and Confer Discussions	45	—	45		
Virginia				State Government	18 908 · 21.8
				Local Governments	44 098 · 27.0
Number of Governments, 1977	460	1	459		
Governments with Labor Relations Policies, Total	—	—	—		
By Type of Policy:					
Collective Negotiations Only	—	—	—		
Meet and Confer Discussions Only	—	—	—		
Both Collective Negotiations and Meet and Confer Discussions	—	—	—		

(continued)

TABLE 16–2. *(Continued)*

ITEM	NO. OF STATE AND LOCAL GOVERNMENTS	NO. OF STATE GOVERNMENTS	NO. OF GOVERNMENTS (TOTAL)	NO. OF EMPLOYEES ORGANIZED	PERCENT OF FULL-TIME EMPLOYEES ORGANIZED
Washington					
Number of Governments, 1977	1 669	1	1 668	State Government 23 293 Local Governments 83 055	State Government 36.2 Local Governments 66.7
Governments with Labor Relations Policies, Total	476	1	475		
By Type of Policy:					
Collective Negotiations Only	284	—	284		
Meet and Confer Discussions Only	11	—	11		
Both Collective Negotiations and Meet and Confer Discussions	181	1	180		
West Virginia					
Number of Governments, 1977	597	1	596	State Government 3 301 Local Governments 24 728	State Government 8.8 Local Governments 42.6
Governments with Labor Relations Policies, Total	32	1	31		
By Type of Policy:					
Collective Negotiations Only	7	—	7		
Meet and Confer Discussions Only	15	1	14		
Both Collective Negotiations and					

Meet and Confer Discussions	10	—	10				
Wisconsin							
Number of Governments, 1977	2 519	1	2 518	State Government 28 223	Local Governments 105 957	State Government 53.9	Local Governments 68.7
Governments with Labor Relations Policies, Total	601	1	600				
By Type of Policy:							
Collective Negotiations Only	324	1	323				
Meet and Confer Discussions Only	10	—	10				
Both Collective Negotiations and Meet and Confer Discussions	267	—	267				
Wyoming							
Number of Governments, 1977	387	1	386	State Government 3 039	Local Governments 6 980	State Government 36.5	Local Governments 35.7
Governments with Labor Relations Policies, Total	44	—	44				
By Type of Policy:							
Collective Negotiations Only	14	—	14				
Meet and Confer Discussions Only	21	—	21				
Both Collective Negotiations and Meet and Confer Discussions	9	—	9				

U.S. Bureau of the Census, *Labor-Management Relations in State and Local Governments: 1980, Series GSS No. 102* (Washington, D.C.: U.S. Government Printing Office, 1980), p. 9.

issues are bargainable, the scope of bargaining is considered limited or *closed*. However, if no restrictions are placed upon bargainable issues, the scope of bargaining is *open*.

Nonetheless, certain issues are usually excluded from the scope of bargaining because they are management prerogatives. Among these are agency objectives, agency structure, and work methods or procedures. The Civil Service Reform Act (Title VII) prohibits federal employees from bargaining over wages and other economic issues such as retirement and health benefits, which are established by Congress. Most state collective bargaining laws allow or require bargaining over wages, benefits, and working conditions.

Yet the distinction between issues included in bargaining—or excluded from it—is not always clear. Issues that management considers excluded as "work methods or procedures" are often held by the union to reflect member rights or important public policy issues. For example, class size (for teachers) and two-officer patrols (for police) fall into this category. Their bargainability must be clarified by the state labor relations agency.

Unit Determination

Before collective bargaining can occur, a primary responsibility of the federal or state collective bargaining agency is to determine appropriate criteria for the formation of unions. The two most commonly utilized criteria are to divide employees by agency or by occupation. Agency bargaining units establish each state or local government agency as a separate bargaining unit. While this offers the advantages of working within existing agency management structure, it can cause a proliferation of bargaining units and inequities among agency contracts.

An alternative is to group employees into general occupational classes, usually on the basis of the state of local government's job classification system. This will result in the establishment of bargaining units such as health, public safety, teachers, general civil service employees, state university system employees, and so on. This method has the advantage of limiting the number of collective bargaining units and automatically including employees of new agencies in preestablished units. It also clarifies, on a system-wide basis, which employees are excluded from participation in bargaining units because their jobs are managerial or of a policy-making nature.

Both agency-based and occupation-based methods of unit determination require the creation of coordinating mechanisms to ensure that negotiated contracts treat employees in different agencies or occupations equitably. Some public organizations—New York City, for example—have opted to establish a multilevel system of bargaining. Agency-based units bargain over salaries and benefits, while department- and occupation-based units bargain over work rules and grievance adjudication procedures.

Both management and labor tend to prefer a relatively small number of bargaining units. From management's viewpoint, it avoids the problems of bargaining with multiple unions and having one union "whipsaw" you against the others (by demanding that any changes in pay, benefits, or working conditions recently negotiated for one union apply to all other unions with which management is negotiating). Established unions also prefer fewer bargaining units because they reduce the pressure on union leaders, and increase the power and responsiveness of the union.[11] Small and growing unions are more likely to favor proliferation, because it increases the chance that they can gain "a piece of the action" from their larger competitors.

Recognition and Certification

Once appropriate bargaining units have been established by the federal or state labor relations agency, unions are free to organize employees for the purpose of bargaining collectively. While no uniformity among state laws exists, recognition and certification procedures are generally similar in all states, because New York State's Taylor Law was used as a model by many of them.

An employer may voluntarily recognize a union as the exclusive bargaining agent for employees in that bargaining unit without a recognition election *if* the union can demonstrate that a majority of the employees in the bargaining unit want to be represented by that union. This is done by showing signed authorization cards from the employees. A sample authorization card is shown in Figure 16–1.

If voluntary recognition does not occur, the union can win recognition through an election. Here, employees are offered the option of either supporting any union that has been able to show support (through signed authorization cards) from 10 percent of the eligible employees), or for declining union representation. Depending on state law, winning the recognition election requires that the union win either a majority of the votes cast, or a majority of the votes from the eligible members of the bargaining unit, regardless of the actual number of votes cast.

Once a union has been voluntarily recognized or has won a representation election, it is formally certified as the exclusive bargaining agent for that unit by the federal or state labor relations agency. Certification requires that management recognize this union as the legitimate representative of employees, and that it engage in collective bargaining with it over all items required or permitted by applicable collective bargaining law.

AFSCME AUTHORIZATION FOR REPRESENTATION

I, the undersigned, hereby designate the American Federation of State, County and Municipal Employees, AFL-CIO (AFSCME) as my collective bargaining representative, authorizing AFSCME or its agents or representatives to act for me as collective bargaining agent in all matters pertaining to rates of pay, hours, and other terms and conditions of employment.

Last Name	First Name	Middle Initial

Street	City	State	Zip

Classification – Department	S.S. Number	Phone

Job Title _____   Signed _____

Date Signed _____

FIGURE 16–1. Sample Authorization Card.

Contract Negotiation

Contract negotiation usually begins immediately following recognition and certification. The union may be represented by a professional negotiator who has negotiated similar contracts with other state or local governments. Management should be represented by an experienced negotiator supported by a team of experts—the personnel manager, the budget officer, a lawyer, and some managers who understand the agency.

In most states, negotiation occurs "in the sunshine." That is, negotiations are conducted in public because states have an "open meetings law" that prohibits government officials from determining public policy in secret. Prior to the negotiations, it is important that management's negotiator reach a clear understanding with elected officials concerning their preferred contract provisions (particularly with respect to economic issues) and their minimally acceptable contract provisions. Prior to negotiations, it is also necessary that the management team marshal personnel and budgetary data to support their positions. Good negotiation is impossible without good research.

Negotiation itself is concerned with both task- and process-oriented issues. Both sides see it as the opportunity to shape organizational policy. As in any strategic contest, each side attempts to discover the other's strengths and priorities, while keeping its own hidden until the opposition appears most willing to concede on an issue. Good negotiation depends on the negotiator's ability to marshal facts, sense the opposition's strong and weak points, and judge the influence of outside events (such as job actions or media coverage) on the negotiations. "Good faith" bargaining requires negotiators to work for the best deal their side can get, while still remaining receptive to the preferences of the other party.

Impasse Resolution During Contract Negotiations

Two types of impasses may occur during collective bargaining. The first are disagreements over the substance of negotiations (such factors as pay or benefits). The second are disagreements over the interpretation of a contract that has been negotiated and approved. The first of these will be discussed below, and the second in the section on contract administration.

If management and labor are unable to resolve differences through two-party contract negotiations, there remain three procedures involving intervention by a third party: mediation, fact-finding, and arbitration.[12] The order in which these are employed, and whether they are used at all, will depend upon the provisions of the state's collective bargaining law (or federal law, if the negotiation involves a federal agency).

Mediation is the intervention of a neutral third party in an attempt to persuade the bargaining parties to reach an agreement. This may be an independent individual, or a designated agency such as the Federal Mediation and Conciliation Service (FMCS). It is in the interest of both parties to attempt to reach a voluntary mediated settlement, since this is the last stage at which they will have full control over contract provisions.

If mediation is not successful, negotiations may progress to the second step—fact-finding.[13] A fact-finder appointed by the federal or state collective bargaining agency will conduct a hearing at which both sides present data in support of their positions. After these hearings, the fact-finder releases a report to both parties, and to the public, that outlines what he or she considers a reasonable settlement. Although this advisory opinion is not binding, the threat of unfavorable publicity may make either side more willing to reach a negotiated settlement.

If fact-finding is unsuccessful, the final stage may be arbitration. Essentially the same procedures are followed as in fact-finding; however, the arbitrator's formal report contains contract provisions that are binding upon both parties.

None of these impasse resolution procedures are recommended unless it is evident that neither party believes it can compromise any further. All are costly, time-consuming, and introduce a third party into the conflict.[14] A contract arrived at through arbitration can also be difficult for labor and management to understand and work with. Remember that the arbitrator's primary objective is to reach agreement; it becomes the responsibility of management and employees to implement a contract that may conflict with their established procedures, program priorities, or budgets.

If the cost of the negotiator is shared by labor and management rather than being paid by the state labor relations agency, then both parties have an interest in reaching a quick settlement.

Ratification

Once a contract has been negotiated by representatives of labor and management, it must be ratified by both the legislature and the union's membership before becoming law. For the union, ratification requires support of the negotiated contract by a majority of those voting. For management, it requires that the appropriate legislative body (state legislature for a state bargaining unit, city commission or county commission for a local bargaining unit, or school board for a school district) appropriate the funds required to fund the contract. Because most states have laws or constitutional provisions prohibiting deficit financing of operating expenses, revenue estimates impose an absolute ceiling on the pay and benefits that may be awarded to a union through the contract negotiation process. Nor is it considered "bad faith" bargaining for a legislature to refuse to ratify a negotiated contract on the grounds that projected revenues will not meet projected expenses.

The requirement that a negotiated contract be ratified by the legislature is a key difference between negotiations in the public and private sector. The private sector obviously has no such restriction. This has also limited the application of binding arbitration to public sector contract negotiations, in that courts have frequently held that the legislature cannot delegate its responsibility for keeping expenditures within revenues. Although union advocates frequently protest that the legislature is biased toward management, state laws require that the state or local legislature take all interests into account—including those of the union and its members—in deciding whether to ratify a negotiated contract.

Contract Administration

Once a contract has been negotiated, both the union and management are responsible for administering its provisions. Key actors in implementation include the union steward, a union member who will interpret the contract for the employees and serve as their advocate and representative to management; the organization's supervisors, who will be implementing contract provisions relating to day-to-day employee-employer relations; and the personnel manager, who is management's expert in what the contract actually covers.

Conflicts are bound to arise during contract administration because reaching compromises during negotiations often requires agreement on what will later turn out to be ambiguous contract language. For example, if negotiations are stuck with regard to the amount of working time the shop steward may spend on union business, the parties may agree on the following language: "a reasonable amount of time not to exceed two hours per week." Once the contract is ratified, the steward may begin taking the two hours (which is consistent with the contract). However, the supervisor may claim that he or she has management's right to approve when this time will be taken. When the shop steward takes time off without supervisory approval, the supervisor will probably initiate disciplinary action, which the shop steward will grieve. Negotiations will then be needed to determine whether either the shop steward or the supervisor's actions constitute a violation of the contract's provisions.

Part of the contract will therefore outline the process for resolving grievances that occur during contract implementation. The process may begin very informally with discussion between the union and management representatives. If the grievance is not satisfactorily resolved at this level, it may be appealed through more formal channels up to a neutral third party. Binding grievance arbitration is the norm (in contrast to the lack of binding *interest* arbitration over contract negotiation impasses).

Management should view the grievance process as a potentially beneficial effort by employees to correct unjust or inadequate personnel management practices. It can serve as an internal evaluation device, a means of instituting planned change, and as a method of redressing inequitable organizational practices. It is recommended that supervisors and public personnel managers know the contract, maintain open lines of communication with employees, meet and deal informally with union representatives over potential grievances, exhibit uniform and adequate documentation for all personnel actions, and keep the record open to unions and employees.[15]

Unfair Labor Practices

Federal and state collective bargaining laws all include lists of personnel practices regarding bargaining process that are forbidden to labor and management. In this regard, it is most important that management remember that employees have an *absolute* right to organize and bargain collectively (in federal agencies, and in those states where enabling collective bargaining legislation exists). Management has no corresponding right to prevent employees from doing so. This means that management cannot seek to influence the outcome of a representation election by coercing, threatening, or intimidating employees. It can present information on the comparative advantages and disadvantages of union membership; it can restrict union organizing to public locations (lunchrooms, bulletin boards) that do not interfere with the work of the organization or do not occur on company time.

During negotiations, each party is bound to "bargain in good faith." This means that each party will listen to the other side and will negotiate. A "take-it-or-leave-it" attitude can lead to a formal charge of failing to bargain in good faith. The charge would be filed with the relevant labor relations authority (like the Public Employee Relations Board) established by the state's collective bargaining law, and would result in an investigation and possible sanctions against one of the parties.

Whether or not public employees should have the right to strike is a hotly contested issue in public agencies because it pits fundamental rights against each other. On the one hand, public employees are guaranteed constitutional protections of association and expression. In addition, there is strong justification for extending to employees the same right to withhold their services as a bargaining weapon that private employees enjoy. On the other hand, the importance of public services to the public, and the monopolistic nature of most public agencies, strengthens the argument that public sector strikes are less tolerable than those in the private sector.

How has the legal system reacted to this conflict in values? Federal and most state laws prohibit employees from striking in order to increase their ability to win a negotiated settlement from management. Under these laws, striking employees are to be dismissed and striking unions fined or decertified (forbidden to engage in further collective bargaining). Yet public employees continue to strike despite these laws. In some cases, like the 1970 federal postal workers' strike, legislators have forgiven the strikers. In others, like the air traffic controllers' strike of 1981, striking employees have been fired and the union decertified.

How public sector strikes are handled seems to depend partly on applicable laws, partly on the relative power of the union, and partly on the ability of the government to find replacement employees. Varied treatment can be seen by comparing the postal workers' strike with the air traffic controllers' strike. In 1970 the federal government had no other method of delivering mail, and postal unions were relatively strong, so the workers were rehired with a substantial pay increase. In 1981, however, an economic recession had reduced the number of commercial flights, supervisory and military personnel provided ready replacements for strikers, and the 10,000-member Professional Air Traffic Controllers Organization (PATCO) was relatively insignificant in size and power, compared with the 600,000 postal workers who struck a decade before.

LABOR-MANAGEMENT RELATIONS AND OTHER PUBLIC PERSONNEL MANAGEMENT ACTIVITIES

At the beginning of this chapter it was noted that labor-management relations symbolize the impact of employees and employee organizations on the terms and conditions of employment. In sum, the method of determining these items has shifted from unilateral control by management (with legislative approval) to bilateral control by labor and management (with legislative adjudication). This has meant a basic change in the relationship between the public personnel manager and agency employees. Where the personnel manager is formally considered a member of management, and where he or she sits "across the table" from the employee representatives, it is no longer possible for personnel to claim the role of impartial balancer of the interests of employees and management.

Collective bargaining has been a key influence on public personnel management because it defines the relationship between the employee and the organization, and it symbolizes the conflict between employee rights and the other three dominant values (political responsiveness, administrative efficiency, and social equity). Because the sanctioning activity of unions means that they can influence the outcome of all other personnel activities (including those related to allocation, procurement, and development), this influence has been considerable. What exactly have been the consequences of this change for various public personnel management activities?

Collective bargaining agreements have generally not restricted management's right to plan human resource needs within budget restrictions and agency objectives. They have, however, considerably restricted management's ability to establish and utilize criteria other than seniority as the basis for employee retention during a reduction-in-force. The issue here is whether other values (such as management's desire to retain productive employees, or an affirmative action advocate's desire to keep employees from underutilized groups) can influence the RIF process. Given management difficulties with objective productivity measurement, and the Supreme Court's reluctance to tamper with "bona fide" seniority systems, it is likely that employees in positions affected by an RIF will continue to be discharged on the basis of seniority.

Both agency managers and unions are required to comply with affirmative action laws. In this sense, collective bargaining has not influenced procurement as much as both unions and management have been affected by affirmative action. Although "bona fide" seniority systems are protected, systems developed after 1964 which discriminate against particular groups are illegal. Redress may require that particular applicants or employees be given "fictional seniority" to enable them to compete fairly for promotions or reassignments.

The compensation and benefits granted to public employees have been particularly affected by collective bargaining. Control over these activities has passed from management to the legislature, which now has three roles in the process: to pass enabling legislation governing contract negotiations, to pass appropriations bills funding negotiated collective bargaining agreements, and to pass substantive legislation incorporating noneconomic issues into the jurisdiction's personnel laws and regulations. It is interesting, however, to assess the effect of collective bargaining on salaries. The Bureau of Labor Statistics indicates that concern over wages was the major issue in 70 percent of the strikes occurring between 1978 and 1980. Yet the average rate of increase in teachers' salaries during this period was *less* for the 30 states with collective bargaining than for the 20 without it. From these data it appears that factors other than whether states had passed collective bargaining legislation—factors like urbanization, the local economic climate, and the relative demand for teachers—may have been more significant determinants of teacher salaries.[16]

The particular effect of unions on dismissal and disciplinary action against public employees will be discussed in greater detail in Chapter 18.

In sum, because of its mediating and sanctioning responsibilities, no area of public personnel management relates to as many personnel activites as does labor-management relations. It is the responsibility of the public personnel manager to help reconcile these diverse interests for the sake of organizational effectiveness.[17]

SUMMARY

Collective bargaining in the public sector is a relatively recent development; most of its growth has occurred only in the past 20 years. Its legal basis is somewhat confusing because federal, state, and local collective bargaining practices are regulated by separate laws (rather than uniformly through the National Labor Relations Board, as is the case with the private sector). Yet despite the difficulties of reaching agreement on wages and benefits (because agency management must share bargaining power with Congress, a state legislature, or local commission), public sector unions have grown at a phenomenal rate.

Despite the differences in enabling legislation, collective bargaining practices are similar to those in the private sector. There are some major exceptions, however, namely, shared control with the legislature makes binding arbitration on wages and benefits constitutionally difficult to achieve, and the unique nature of public services makes strikes less tolerable.

DISCUSSION QUESTIONS

1. What are some major differences between private- and public-sector collective bargaining laws and practices in the United States?
2. Describe the legislative history of federal collective bargaining.
3. Describe the legal status of collective bargaining in state and local governments.

4. Define each of the following terms:
   a. unit determination
   b. recognition
   c. certification
   d. scope of bargaining
   e. contract negotiation
   f. impasse resolution
   g. ratification
   h. unfair labor practice
   i. contract administration
   j. binding arbitration
5. How has collective bargaining affected the role of the public personnel manager?
6. How has collective bargaining affected each of the following public personnel activities: compensation, reduction-in-force, promotion, disciplinary action, and grievances?

KEY TERMS

Wagner Act
National Labor Relations Board (NLRB)
Taft-Hartley Act
Civil Service Reform Act (Title VII)
Federal Labor Relations Authority
state labor relations agency
scope of bargaining
unit determination
recognition
certification
contract negotiation
impasse resolution
mediation
fact-finding
(binding) arbitration
interest arbitration
ratification
contract administration
grievance
unfair labor practice

EXERCISE: COSTING-OUT A PUBLIC SECTOR CONTRACT

The Town of Mangrove Junction, located in southeast Florida, has a population of about 22,000. Its city government employs about 120 people, including 16 public works department employees responsible for operating the town's three garbage trucks.

The public works employees are represented by Local 330 of the American Federation of State, County and Municipal Employees (AFSCME). The composition of the bargaining unit and the salaries of the positions are shown in Table 16–3.

Every spring, the Mangrove Junction city manager and public works director sit down and negotiate a contract with AFSCME Local 330. Economic issues are addressed every year; noneconomic issues every three years, unless both labor and management agree to discuss them more frequently. Only economic issues are being negotiated this year.

The union demands are:

A $1.00 per hour increase in the salary of trash truck operators
A $.50 per hour increase in the salary of trash assistants
An increase in paid holidays from ten to 12 annually

As the management negotiating team, your first task is to compute the present cost of salaries for these 16 employees. Do so in the space below, using the following formulae:

   a. *trash truck operators*
      2080 hrs./yr. × $13.00/hr. × 3 emp. = $ _____
   b. *trash assistants, step 1*
      2080 hrs./yr. × $7.50/hr. × 6 emp. = $ _____
   c. *trash assistants, step 2*
      2080 hrs./yr. × $8.50/hr. × 7 emp. = $ _____
                          Total salaries = $ _____

Second, compute the total cost of ten paid holidays per year for each of these groups:

   a. *trash truck operators*
      80 hrs. × $13.00/hr. × 3 emp. = $ _____
   b. *trash assistants, step 1*
      80 hrs. × $7.50/hr. × 6 emp. = $ _____
   c. *trash assistants, step 2*
      80 hrs. × $8.50/hr. × 7 emp. = $ _____
                       Total vacations = $ _____

Third, compute the additional salary costs involved in paying the salaries requested by the union, and add them to the current salary total:

   a. *trash truck operators*
      2080 hrs. × $14.00/hr. × 3 emp. = $ _____

**TABLE 16–3. Mangrove Junction Public Works Department
Sanitation Section Bargaining Unit 1983–1984**

CLASSIFICATION	NUMBER OF EMPLOYEES	SALARY
Trash truck operator	3	$13.00/hour
Trash assistants		
step 1	6	7.50/hour
step 2	7	8.50/hour
Total	16	

    b.   *trash assistants, step 1*
        2080 hrs. × $8.00/hr. × 6 emp. = $ _____
    c.   *trash assistants, step 2*
        2080 hrs. × $9.00/hr. × 7 emp. = $ _____
                  Total projected salary = $ _____

Fourth, compute the additional holiday costs involved in increasing the number of paid holidays from ten to 12, under the new projected salary rate. This increase in vacations combines the increase in vacation benefits (ten days to 12) plus the "roll-up"—the increased value of those vacation days caused by the increase in salary.

    a.   *trash truck operators*
        96 hrs. × $14.00/hr. × 3 emp. = $ _____
    b.   *trash assistants, step 1*
        96 hrs. × $8.50/hr. × 6 emp. = $ _____
    c.   *trash assistants, step 2*
        96 hrs. × $9.00/hr. × 7 emp. = $ _____
        Total projected vacation cost = $ _____

Finally, give the total increase in salary and vacation benefits requested by the union, as both a dollar figure and a percentage of the current benefits. (It should be noted here that other monetary items such as Workers' Compensation, pension contributions, and sick leave pay will also be affected by changes in pay and benefits.)

$$\frac{\text{New projected salary}}{\text{Current salary}} = \text{projected increase} \_\_\_\_\%$$

$$\frac{\text{New projected vacations}}{\text{Current vacations}} = \text{projected increase} \_\_\_\_\%$$

$$\frac{\text{Total projected salary} + \text{vacations}}{\text{Current salary} + \text{vacations}} = \text{projected increase } \underline{\hspace{2em}}\%$$

Based on these figures, what economic and other considerations would you advise the Mangrove Junction City Manager to study before negotiating a compromise with the union? Consider the rate of inflation, the tax base of the city, the productivity of the trash crews, and any other variables you consider relevant.

NOTES

[1] Wilson R. Hart, *Collective Bargaining in the Federal Civil Service* (New York: Harper & Row, 1961), p. 85.

[2] Sterling D. Spero, *Government as Employer* (New York: Remsen Press, 1948), p. 107.

[3] Robert M. Godine, *The Labor Problem in the Public Service* (Cambridge, Mass.: Harvard University Press, 1951), p. 65. The Lloyd-LaFollette Act in U.S. Code, 37 Stat. 579.

[4] Kurt L. Hanslowe, *The Emerging Law of Labor Relations in Public Employment* (Ithaca, N.Y.: New York State School of Industrial and Labor Relations, Cornell University, 1967), pp. 35–37.

[5] Felix Nigro, *Management-Employee Relations in the Public Service* (Chicago: Public Personnel Association, 1969), p. 25.

[6] *AFL-CIO Manual for Federal Employees*, No. 138 (Washington, D.C.: AFL-CIO, December 1973), p. 10.

[7] U.S. Bureau of the Census, *Labor-Management Relations in State and Local Governments: 1980, Series GSS No. 102* (Washington, D.C.: Government Printing Office, 1980), p. 23.

[8] Bureau of National Affairs, "Enactment of Public Employee Labor Relations Laws Seen to Cause Strikes," *Arbitrations in Brief*, 759 (May 15, 1978), 25–27.

[9] U.S. Bureau of the Census, p. 9.

[10] U.S. Bureau of the Census, pp. 23–48.

[11] Chester A. Newland, "Collective Bargaining and Public Administration," in Gilbert Siegel (ed.), *Human Resource Management* (Los Angeles: University Publishers, 1973), pp. 384–92.

[12] Karl A. vanAsselt, "Impasse Resolution," *Public Administration Review* (March–April 1972), 114–19.

[13] Midwest Center for Public Sector Labor Relations, *Questions and Answers on Fact-Finding: A Practitioner's Guide* (Bloomington, Ind.: School of Public and Environmental Affairs, Indiana University, 1978), pp. 1–22.

[14] William R. Word, "Toward More Negotiations in the Public Sector," *Public Personnel Management* (September–October 1973), 345–51.

[15] A. K. Wnorowski, "Once You Have an Agreement: How to Avoid Grievances," *Personnel Journal* (October 1970), 843–46.

[16] *The Effect of Collective Bargaining on Teacher Salaries* (Vienna, Va.: Public Service Research Council, 1981).

[17] David Lewin, "Collective Bargaining Impacts on Personnel Administration in the American Public Sector," *Labor Law Journal* (July 1976), 426–36.

17

Disciplinary Action and Grievances

The relationship between employees and their work organizations is a dynamic one; it changes constantly as each party readjusts both its expectations of the other, and the contributions it is willing to give in return. All of this happens informally. At a formal level, two processes have been established for use by the organization and the employee when either one feels that its expectations of the other have been grossly violated. These two processes are disciplinary action and grievances. The former is used by the organization to sanction employees for violations of work rules or expectations; the latter is used by employees who feel their rights have been violated by the organization. Thus, it is helpful to see these processes as opposite sides of a coin.

In 1974, a black man was hired as a cook by a major Midwestern hospital. The hospital had a four-month probationary period for all new employees. At the end of that period, he was discharged for poor attendance. He immediately filed an unemployment compensation claim with the state Employment Security Division. Because unemployment cannot be awarded if the employee is discharged for cause, the agency first had to make a determination on this issue. It decided that the firing had not been justified; the hospital appealed, but it lost the appeal.

The discharged employee filed formal charges of racial discrimination with the state Civil Rights Commission and the EEOC. The investigations conducted by these agencies indicated that although the former employee had been absent from work a good deal, the hospital's personnel policies contained no clear standards as to what was "acceptable" or "unacceptable" absenteeism during the probationary period. Furthermore, the hospital could not provide data on the absenteeism records of *white* employees retained or discharged at the end of *their* probationary periods.

Because no clear standard existed, and because the hospital could not document that the attendance record of this employee was worse than that of other employees who were retained, the EEOC ordered the hospital to rehire him, or face charges against it in federal court. The hospital rehired the employee and paid him the back pay and benefits he would have earned had he remained in the hospital's employ (less unemployment compensation received).

Within two months, the employee had received several reprimands for poor attendance. Yet it remained extremely unlikely that the hospital would be able to discipline him for these, since the EEOC had previously criticized the agency for discriminating against him. The hospital personnel director resigned to take another position (it was not clear whether his resignation was related to the outcome of this case).

There are no winners in this case study, except perhaps the employee. Certainly not the employee's supervisor, the hospital's clients, or the personnel director. Why did it turn out this way, and what can be done to prevent it?

By the end of this chapter you will be able to:

1. Define disciplinary action and grievances, and discuss their objectives
2. Discuss applicable laws
3. Describe employee counseling techniques
4. Describe the criteria for effective disciplinary action, and discuss how to establish and operate disciplinary action and internal grievance systems
5. Describe the internal and external channels through which public employees can seek redress of grievances

OBJECTIVES AND DEFINITION

A disciplinary action is an employer-imposed reduction in organizational rewards *for cause*. Disciplinary actions include written reprimands, suspensions, reductions in rank or pay, and firing. They do not include temporary layoffs or work force reductions that arise from budget cuts or lack of work. Rather, they are caused by specific behavioral incidents by the employee that result in low productivity or violations of agency rules and regulations.

Grievances are complaints by employees concerning unfair treatment in the distribution of organizational rewards or punishments. Employees may allege that they are not being treated equitably with respect to their contributions to the organization, or with respect to other employees. They may also use the grievance system to appeal what they consider unfair disciplinary action instituted by the organization.

Disciplinary action and grievance systems constitute the mechanism by which the organization and the employee seek to achieve equity in their relationship. This equity is of two forms: substantive and procedural. Substantive equity concerns the justice of organizational rewards or sanctions in comparison with employee contributions, or with other employees. Procedural equity refers to the existence of adequate impartial mechanisms (grievance and appeal systems) for ensuring substantive equity. Both of these will be discussed in greater detail under "due process" in Chapter 18.

THE LEGAL ENVIRONMENT OF DISCIPLINARY ACTION AND GRIEVANCES

Substantive equity in the recruitment, selection, compensation, evaluation, and discipline of employees is required by the affirmative actions laws described in Chapter 5.

> Title VII of the 1964 Civil Rights Act, as amended (1972) by the Equal Employment Opportunity Act, explicitly prohibits public agencies from discriminating in employment practices (hiring, firing, compensation, or the terms, conditions, or privileges of employment) on the basis of nonmerit factors.
>
> The Equal Pay Act of 1963 requires employers to compensate men and women equally for work requiring equivalent skill, effort, and qualifications.
>
> The Age Discrimination in Employment Act (1967, as amended, 1976) prohibits employers from discriminating on the basis of age.
>
> Section 504 of the Vocational Rehabilitation Act of 1973 prohibits employers from discriminating against handicapped people in employment situations where, with "reasonable" modifications, they can perform the major functions of the position.

From these laws, it can be seen that affirmative action has an important effect on public employee *sanctions* as well as *procurement*. That is, the same laws that prohibit employment discrimination have also set up compliance agencies and enforcement mechanisms through which employees and applicants can protest alleged violations of their employment rights. Thus, these laws, agencies, and procedures have a judicial impact on the agency in that they are an outside "check" on the legitimacy of disciplinary action.

COUNSELING THE UNPRODUCTIVE EMPLOYEE

Disciplinary action is the last step—never the first—in dealing with an employee whose performance is substandard. It assumes that a number of other questions have already been asked regarding job design, selection, orientation, performance appraisal, training, and compensation:

Job design	Are the tasks, conditions, and performance standards of the position reasonable and equitable?
Selection	Does the employee meet the minimum qualifications established for the position?
Orientation	Were organizational rules and regulations, and position requirements clearly communicated to the new employee?
Performance appraisal	Was the employee's performance adequately documented, and was the employee provided with informal and formal feedback on the quality of his or her performance?
Training	Does the employee have adequate skills to perform the required tasks at the expected level of competence?
Compensation	Is good performance rewarded, or are there factors in the work environment that make it impossible or punishing to perform well?

Disciplinary action therefore represents the *last* step in supervising employees because it symbolizes a failure to adjust the inducements-contributions contract by other, less formal, means. It is primarily a supervisory responsibility, since most performance problems are handled informally within the work unit with minimal involvement by the personnel department.

If the performance problem cannot be resolved informally by the supervisor and other employees within the work unit, the supervisor may request that formal disciplinary action be taken by the personnel department. If this occurs, it is the personnel manager's responsibility to ensure that all other possible causes of the performance problem have been considered. Figure 17–1 shows the sequential process of personnel activities that occur prior to disciplinary action. It is the primary responsibility of the employee's immediate supervisor to ensure that each of these steps is followed. Together they represent the counseling and disciplinary action process. They involve all the skills that a supervisor is expected to possess.

Yet the public personnel manager has three important responsibilities with respect to disciplinary action. Initially, the personnel department is responsible for establishing the process. Once it has been established as part of the agency's personnel rules and regulations, the personnel director is frequently responsible for counseling unproductive employees and for assisting the supervisor in implementing evaluation and training procedures to improve performance or institute disciplinary action. Lastly, the personnel director is responsible for making sure that the system is applied equitably.[1] Again, we can see that the personnel manager has both a facilitating and a policing role.

It is often necessary to confront an unproductive employee in order to bring the person's poor job performance out into the open. This is done

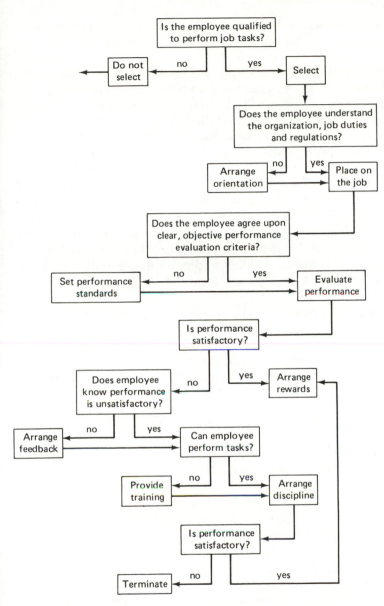

FIGURE 17–1. Disciplinary Action and Other Personnel Activities

through a counseling session. The personnel manager should prepare for this session by reviewing its objectives, namely, behavioral change in the direction of increased productivity. Its purpose is not to attack the employee's personality, habits, or attitudes; nor is it intended to intimidate the employee or to drive him or her out of the organization. Here are some guidelines to follow in preparing for a counseling session.

Separate your needs and feelings from the needs of the organization and the employee. As an organizational employee and representative of management, it is your responsibility to weigh the needs of both the employee and management. You may be called upon to counsel employees whose attitudes, language, or personal habits bother you. These are not your concern. Their productivity is.

Focus on unacceptable performance. The purpose of counseling is to identify and remedy areas in which an employee's work performance is unsatisfactory. In order to keep the discussion focused and to document claims of low productivity, you will need to have valid, reliable written records concerning employee performances relative to both absolute standards and to the performance of other employees doing similar work under similar conditions.

Have backup help available. If you suspect that the employee's low productivity is related to personal problems, be prepared to refer the employee for medical or psychological help. Do not attempt personal counseling. Not only are you unqualified for this, but this investment of your time will not necessarily result in productivity increases, which is, after all, your major objective.

Clarify policies, rules, and procedures. Make sure that your rules, regulations, and policies are clear to the employee, either through discussion or by evidence that the employee has acknowledged receipt and understanding of them during the orientation process.

Pick the right time. Counsel employees only when you are sure that they and their supervisor cannot correct the problem without loss of productivity. Do not counsel when you cannot spend the time to do it right, or when the employee is not likely to be receptive (for example, Monday mornings or Friday afternoons).

Pick the right place. Counsel employees in a private setting. Make the location as comfortable as possible and arrange seating so that you sit next to the employee, rather than on the other side of the desk. Do not engage in other activities (phone calls, visitors, or signing memos) while counseling takes place.

Know the supervisor's expectations. In advance of the counseling interview, know what job performance is minimally acceptable to the supervisor (if the problem involves job performance rather than compliance with organizational rules and regulations).

Decide on a directive or nondirective approach.   In a *directive* interview, the personnel manager does most of the talking. While his or her approach is calm and relaxed, the employee should sense that directions are being given rather than feelings solicited. Directive counseling is considered appropriate in situations involving violations of agency regulations, or where the employee has been previously counseled concerning performance deficiencies. *Nondirective* counseling requires that the supervisor or personnel director listen as well as talk. The objective here is to "draw the employee out" so that he or she can discuss performance problems without fear of reprisal. It is appropriate where a performance problem has not previously been discussed with the employee, or where the employee evidences a gradual deterioration in productivity or work habits. Since nondirective counseling will presumably have been performed by the supervisor prior to the involvement of the personnel director in the process, this chapter will focus on directive counseling techniques.

With the preparation for a successful counseling interview completed, you are now ready to begin the interview. Here are some suggestions.

Greet the employee warmly and honestly.   Make him or her feel as comfortable as possible under the circumstances. However, avoid the use of humor. Counseling is serious business, and humor can cause substantive remarks to be misconstrued.

Observe the employee's body language.   Be alert for signs of hostility or defensiveness, and gauge your interview style accordingly.

Move quickly to a discussion of performance.   Begin to discuss the employee's performance problem as quickly as possible. Preliminaries are necessary, but performance is the subject of the interview.

Use documentation.   At all times, refer to documented facts concerning the employee's poor performance. Avoid generalities, and at the same time keep from making the interview a litany of poor performance incidents unless it is apparent that the employee does not agree that performance is a problem.

Use praise cautiously.   The employee will be more likely to respond to criticism if it is "sandwiched" between praise. Employees should be made aware that you recognize their good points, and that these are the reasons why you're offering counseling and assistance now. However, some employees' performance is so poor that praise is a falsehood. Be blunt in such cases.

Do not label or categorize. Labeling, name-calling, or other forms of stereotyping are not productive. They distract attention from performance, and they provide evidence of agency discrimination.

Be clear and consistent about the sanctions you are prepared to invoke. Be as clear and consistent as possible about your performance expectations of the employee, and about the organizational punishments you will apply if those are not met. Do not set performance expectations unless you can defend them with reference to absolute standards or the productivity of other employees. Do not threaten the employee with punishments you are legally unable or personally unwilling to invoke.

Make a plan with the employee. Based on your expectations, make a plan with the employee that establishes performance expectations, sets a time limit for their accomplishment, and sets forth the consequences of lack of improvement.

Offer help. Offer whatever help you and the employee consider appropriate. This could include feedback, training, job counseling, or referral to outside community resources for psychological or medical problems. Get a commitment from the employee to either accept or not accept this help.

Write up the counseling session. Retain records in case future misunderstandings arise concerning the nature of the employee's performance problem, the alternatives presented by the personnel manager, or the employee's reaction to these alternatives. You may request that the employee sign a copy of this written record to acknowledge that counseling has occurred; but you cannot require this.

The relationship between the agency and the employee will take one of two courses after the directive counseling interview. If the employee has refused help, then it is the supervisor's responsibility to monitor the employee's performance during the preestablished time period and to inform the employee of his or her performance. If performance remains unsatisfactory, it is the supervisor who recommends disciplinary action, and it is the personnel director who follows through with it. If job performance improves, the supervisor should inform the employee and the personnel manager of this and reward the employee accordingly. If the employee requests help, it is the supervisor's responsibility to continue to monitor performance, and the personnel manager's responsibility to provide help through the organization or through referral to community resources.

Thus, it can be seen that the supervisor and the personnel manager need to play mutually supportive roles for the disciplinary action system to work effectively. The personnel manager must establish a clear and equitable system; the supervisor must provide adequate supervision of employees and enforce work rules fairly. If discipline is required, it cannot be done except by the personnel department on the basis of information provided by the supervisor.

Establishing Disciplinary Action and Grievance Systems

It is important that disciplinary action systems and procedures provide for protection of the employee's substantive and procedural rights. Documentation that shows that the employee's performance is contrary to expectations of other employees must be provided. The employee must be given ample opportunity to respond to these charges. Figure 17–2 provides a diagram of typical disciplinary action and grievance procedures.

FIGURE 17–2. Disciplinary Action Procedures

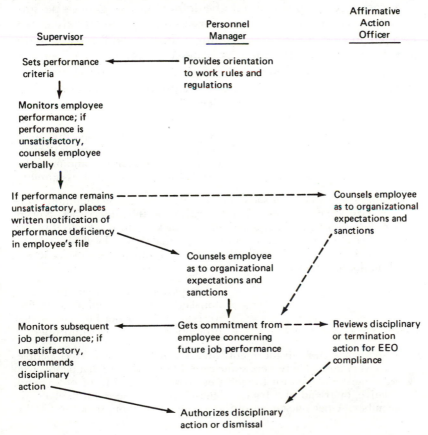

Note that if the employee is a member of a minority group, the affirmative action officer should have prior knowledge of disciplinary action.

The purpose of disciplinary action is to protect the organization against unproductive employees. Grievance procedures, on the other hand, are developed to protect employees against the inequitable allocation of organizational rewards and sanctions.

There has been comparatively little research into the background characteristics of employees who file grievances. While many personnel managers regard these people as "bad apples" in the agency employee barrel, some studies indicate that grievances may be a normal response of articulate and aggressive employees to what they perceive as poor management practices.[2] As is the case with disciplinary actions, grievances represent the last resort in a sequence of efforts to communicate with management.

Management should establish internal grievance policies that clearly establish the right of employees to file written complaints concerning alleged unfair management practices, and procedures for hearing these complaints in the agency. The specific items that may arise and be the subject of a grievance complaint should be defined in the agency's personnel rules and regulations. If a collective bargaining agreement exists, they will be defined in the collective bargaining contract. Topics such as the following will probably be included as issues contained in a negotiated contract or in personnel rules enforced by a civil service board. Under each possible area of grievance is an example of organizational behavior related to it; the material is from the exit interview files of a state agency.

Work assignments

Employees may feel that they have been assigned a job for which they are under- or overqualified, and may protest this as an invalid work assignment.

I don't know how other sections are, but in our section conditions were very bad. There is too much favoritism by the supervisors. Not all employees are treated equal; some are picked on. Blacks are favored only because they are afraid of them, and that they will yell "discrimination" when whites are really the ones discriminated against. There is also a lot of unfairness as to who does what work.

Promotion

An employee may feel that the promotional criteria established for a position were not valid or not utilized, or that promotional procedures improper.

The chances for advancement, unless you knew the correct people, were very poor. There were some cases I knew for sure that people who were most qualified for the job were passed over in favor of a friend, relative, or friend of a friend. There was one case in particular I remember. A person started out at a Clerk I position, took the test for

Clerk-Typist I, failed the test, but still secured a Clerk-Typist II position elsewhere in the department.

Poor supervision

Employees may feel that supervision is inadequate, and that supervisors are biased or incompetent.

The people I worked beside were nice, for the most part. There was a supervisor in the position above me who was only 19 years old and lacked the knowledge of how to handle the situation. I brought this up to her supervisor and was told that it could be made very hard for me if I "caused waves," so I gave up my job.

Political interference

Conflict arises between elected and appointed officials, or among supervisors.

Also, the department should back up their own policies. I found several cases during my five years of employment when I received a memo dictating what my actions should be in certain circumstances, which I followed to the letter. However, if someone complained to the department heads stationed in the capital, they changed the rules on the spot and left me looking like I didn't know my own job. In general, I feel that the state should quit playing politics with civil service employment. Then they could get a little efficiency back into the system.

Racial or sexual discrimination

It is a little unfortunate that the chiefs are allowed to carry on, then customers make comments to the effect "Are he and missy still playing doctor or hanky panky in the halls or in the observation booth?" The same chief allows some of his girls to do whatever they want and only a few have to toe the line anytime the others crack the whip. It's also a shame the same man is capable of destroying your future.

In any of these instances, it is important the agency establish informal and formal internal grievance procedures. The following steps are recommended:

Informal counseling.   The aggrieved employee should meet and discuss the situation with his or her supervisor.

Formal grievance.   If informal counseling is unsuccessful, the aggrieved employee should be urged to file a formal grievance. The purpose of this is to initiate a permanent record to protect the employee against loss of appeal rights, and to provide a formal basis for response by the supervisor and the agency.

Consultation between the supervisor and the personnel director. After the grievance is filed, the personnel director should consult with the employee's supervisor to verify facts presented in the grievance. If the personnel manager and the supervisor are unable to agree on a solution that meets the employee's needs, adjudication occurs.

Adjudication.   An agency supervisor, or panel of supervisors, is appointed by the chief executive to review the facts of the case. This person or panel may call the employee, the personnel director, and the supervisor as witnesses. Although the adjudication hearing is an administrative rather than a judicial proceeding, employees should be allowed to have a lawyer present if they so desire. At this hearing, it is the responsibility of the personnel director to make sure that the agency's internal disciplinary action procedures have been followed.

Appeal.   Following the outcome of the adjudication hearing, either side may appeal to the agency head for a reevaluation of the decision.

EXTERNAL GRIEVANCE CHANNELS

The foregoing discussion indicated that employees can seek redress of grievances by following procedures established by management. While these procedures should be available, most employees do not consider them to be impartial. Nor do the various interest groups that represent employee interests.

As a result, public personnel managers should recognize that other grievance channels exist: civil service boards, union grievances, affirmative action complaints, direct legislative action, and civil court proceedings.

In most public agencies, the power of managers and the personnel department to make and enforce personnel regulations is limited by either a personnel or a civil service review board. This can be the Merit Systems Protection Board (MSPB) for federal career service employees, or civil service boards or personnel boards found in most state and local governments. Remember, the original intent of civil service systems was to remove political influence from the hiring and the *firing* of public employees. Consequently, the disciplinary actions of management and the personnel manager are traditionally subject to review by an outside group. These boards or commissions are usually appointed by the legislature; they are usually required to comprise employees, the personnel director, and citizens.

Relationships between the personnel manager and the civil service review board can range from agreeable to hostile. In the best of circumstances, the review board acts as a check upon the imposition of ill-advised discipline by supervisors who have learned to depend on an in-house grievance system to invariably back them up. In other cases, however, the board can frustrate managers by subverting the agency's personnel regulations or disciplinary procedures.

If the agency's employees are covered by a collective bargaining agreement, then this contract will restrict the management's ability to apply disciplinary action unilaterally. In fact, management may be unable to discipline employees *at all,* unless the contract specifically includes the agency's personnel rules and regulations, and specifies the disciplinary action that management may initiate for alleged infractions of those rules and regulations. Assuming that these items have been included in the collective bargaining agreement, the process of *contract administration* is the branch of labor relations that deals with the enforcement of these contract provisions. While this topic was discussed in greater detail in Chapter 16, some discussion at this point is appropriate because of its relationship to disciplinary action and grievances.

Under the terms of most collective bargaining agreements, either labor or management may file a grievance against the other. In this sense, a grievance is a formal, written complaint alleging that a violation of a previously negotiated contract has occurred. The contract will provide for specific procedures for resolving grievances, usually culminating in binding arbitration by a neutral third party.

If the employee alleges that substantive violations of equity have been caused by nonmerit discrimination, this type of charge can be investigated by an affirmative action compliance agency. This would include discrimination in selection, promotion, training, compensation, or disciplinary action, on the basis of age, sex, race, religion, physical handicap, or national origin. The discussion of affirmative action laws, compliance agencies, and compliance procedures is given in Chapter 5.

Particularly in smaller local governments, employees who consider themselves discriminated against will seek redress of grievances through indirect or direct legislative action—an appeal to the city commission, for example. The employee can go directly to an elected official, or can go to an influential friend in the community who then informally raises questions with a friend on the city council. This is particularly likely to occur if no appointed civil service review board exists. By ordering a solution to the problem, the legislature, if it so chooses, can countermand the disciplinary action instituted by the personnel director or the city manager. This may also result in indirect changes in personnel rules and regulations, since commission action may also have an effect on general municipal ordinances.

Lastly, employees may file a direct civil suit in federal court. For reasons that will be made clearer in Chapter 18 (Employee Rights), public employers have responsibilities to treat employees equitably that extend far beyond those recognized as applying to private businesses. The court system, as always, is the avenue of redress for those who believe their rights have been violated, in particular their Fourteenth Amendment rights to the equal protection of the laws, and to due process in the deprivation of property. It should be realized that the courts have viewed tenure of office as property.

Many public personnel managers feel unfairly burdened by the multiple grievance and appeal channels available to their employees. They feel that these make disciplinary action unlikely, since a decision favorable to the employee in any one of these arenas will prevent its application. They may also feel that some systems—particularly civil service review boards, affirmative action compliance agencies, and union contract administration hearings—are biased in favor of the employee.

What can they do about it? In one respect, little. The multiplicity of appeal channels is deliberately designed to inhibit unilateral decision making by management. But the personnel director can restrict the number of channels by requiring that employees covered by a collective bargaining agreement choose, in advance, whether they want to appeal through the civil service review board or the union grievance process. If all positions are either exempt from civil service and union coverage, or included in the bargaining unit, the municipality can even eliminate the duplicative civil service grievance process and rely entirely upon union grievances or direct political appeals. The personnel director can also suggest that the city commission avoid direct involvement in personnel actions and delegate these matters to an appointed civil service review board.

SUMMARY

Disciplinary action and grievance systems are the methods by which both employees and the agency seek redress of alleged inequities in their relationship. These inequities can be either substantive or procedural.

It is important that the personnel manager view disciplinary action as the last step in this process, rather than the first. It should be invoked only when other causes of poor performance have been eliminated, such as improper job design, inadequate selection criteria, lack of performance standards, insufficient training, absence of feedback, or lack of adequate compensation. Nondirective counseling should be attempted before directive counseling is used.

Public employers should institute internal grievance systems to resolve disputes equitably over the imposition of disciplinary action. They must recognize, however, that employees and interest groups are not likely to regard these systems as impartial. Because of this, other external grievance avenues have been established, namely, civil service review boards, affirmative action compliance agencies, union contract administration procedures, direct legislative action, and civil suits.

DISCUSSION QUESTIONS

1. What are the objectives of disciplinary action and grievances?
2. What federal laws govern the disciplinary action process for public agencies?
3. What techniques should public personnel managers use in counseling unproductive employees?
4. What criteria and procedures should public personnel managers use in establishing internal grievance systems?
5. What are the objectives of external grievance systems, and how do they affect the role of the public personnel manager?

KEY TERMS

disciplinary action
grievance
substantive equity
procedural equity
directive counseling
nondirective counseling
documentation
grievance procedures
civil service review board
civil suit
contract administration

CASE STUDY: JUAN HERNANDEZ V. LOS ANGELES COUNTY

Introduction

Metropolitan Los Angeles County is the largest local government in California. County government is divided into about 50 operating departments and employs about 20,000 people. Among the departments is the Office of Data Processing Center (DPC).

Juan Hernandez, a Hispanic male, was employed by the DPC on July 15, 1972 as a data processing trainee. On May 10, 1973 he was promoted to the position of Computer Operator I and attained permanent status in that position six months later. He remained in that position until his termination on March 9, 1982.

This case study will examine the circumstances leading to his dismissal, his role as a union steward for Local 121 of the American Federation of State, County and Municipal Employees (AFSCME), and the various steps involved in his termination. It will reach conclusions relating to the disciplinary action and grievance process in public agencies in general.

Juan Hernandez' Employment History

From his initial employment until April 1977, Juan Hernandez' record reflected satisfactory and dependable service. On April 25, 1977, however, he received a written reprimand for loading 25,000 United Fund cards into a computer punch backwards, thus rendering them useless (Exhibit A).

Mr. Hernandez reacted to the reprimand by a letter of rebuttal which indicated that he disagreed sharply with management's allegations of his lack of general competence (Exhibit B).

In October 1977, he received an evaluation summarizing his performance as "in need of attention." His scheduled merit increase was deferred for three months. Although the overall tone of the evaluation was encouraging, it implied an incompetence in his ability to grasp the concepts of a large computer system. Mr. Hernandez appealed the evaluation, but withdrew the appeal when he received a satisfactory evaluation along with his merit increase three months later.

In January 1978, the Director of Operations for the DPC brought about a reorganization that resulted in Mr. Hernandez being switched from the day to night shift. Despite his objections to this change, Mr. Hernandez' employment continued satisfactorily for the next 18 months until he suffered a severe on-the-job injury on July 26, 1979. A portion of the raised computer floor collapsed while he was on it carrying a box of computer paper. His resultant knee and leg injuries caused Mr. Hernandez to be absent from work for 425 hours.

Upon his return to work on October 27, 1979, he was presented with a formal record of counseling dated July 29, 1979, just three days after his injury had occurred. This record, which was prepared by his supervisor as a summary of the informal counseling that had occurred with him, cited a number of infractions (Exhibit C).

On June 29, 1981, Mr. Hernandez was given a formal record of counseling citing his involvement in a technical failure that occurred in the computer room at the main console (Exhibit D).

Shop Steward

On July 27, 1981, Mr. Hernandez was elected to the position of shop steward representing the DPC employees with AFSCME Local 121. During his term as shop steward, he aided several employees who were contemplating filing grievances against the DPC on the grounds that the agency was illegally testing computer operators prior to giving them permanent appointments.

Termination

On January 9, 1982, Juan Hernandez was himself given an "unsatisfactory" performance evaluation based on his failure to complete certain training courses. He refused to sign this evaluation (Exhibit E).

On January 23, 1982, he was charged one day without pay for calling in sick the day before the start of his scheduled one-week vacation. Upon returning to work, he submitted a doctor's statement excusing him for the absence. This doctor's statement, coupled with other evidence, would later prove the grounds for his termination.

Mr. Robert Hess, an administrative officer for the DPC, began to compile evidence that Mr. Hernandez had falsified doctors' statements that excused several of his absences. He had observed that the handwriting of doctors' excuses dated June 15, 1981 and January 23, 1982 did not match the handwriting of other excuses obtained from the same doctor for the injuries suffered in his 1979 accident. In addition, the excuses in question were written on Pacific Hospital of Los Angeles forms, while the others were not.

Interviews were conducted with the physician, Dr. Herman Wilbanks, and with Mr. Vincent Pico, administrative resident at Pacific Hospital. Dr. Wilbanks denied writing the excuses; and Mr. Pico confirmed that Mr. Hernandez had not been a patient at the hospital on the dates in question.

Mr. Hernandez then altered his story by stating that the excuse that he had submitted for the January 23 absence was a copy of the original. He claimed that his daughter, a pre-med student at Long Beach State University, had copied the original one "as practice for her classes," and he had mistakenly submitted the copy. However, the Los Angeles County Crime Laboratory Bureau confirmed that the handwriting was the same on both forms (Exhibit F).

On March 10, 1982, Mr. Hernandez attended a scheduled disciplinary action meeting in the office of the Deputy Director of the DPC. He was represented by the union. At this meeting, he was given a termination letter and a disciplinary action report effecting his dismissal. He signed the form at the union representative's advice.

Appeal Hearing

An appeal hearing was held on May 10, 1982. Mr. Hernandez was represented by AFSCME Local 121; Los Angeles County was represented by the County Attorney's Office.

The impartial hearing examiner concluded that violations 1 through 4 were not substantiated, but that the charge of a false claim of leave was substantiated. Mr. Hernandez' termination was sustained (Exhibit G).

Conclusion

Both collective bargaining agreements and disciplinary action procedures provide for progressive discipline of employees for poor performance, and they protect employees against unfair harassment or unsubstantiated allegations.

In the case of Juan Hernandez, the pattern and timing of management's disciplinary action against him are both suspect. A casual review of his record of disciplinary action indicates that it followed on-the-job injuries and his election as shop steward.

On the other hand, it is also clear that Mr. Hernandez' work performance was frequently careless or incompetent. Moreover, his falsification of medical excuses was flagrantly dishonest. Management's efforts to substantiate this required the spending of much time, money, and effort. It was also aided by the fact that the DPC, as a computer-oriented agency, was able to establish objective performance standards (in terms of quantity, quality, and timeliness of production). By monitoring these incidents, it was able to document irregular performance incidents.

Yet despite management's advantages, the only incident of willful misconduct that was upheld was the falsification of medical statements, an infraction relating to personnel rules rather than productivity. The lesson to be learned from this is that management, in the final analysis, when attempting to terminate an employee who is backed by union and legal representation in front of an impartial examiner, must have documentation that unquestionably proves guilt on the part of the employee charged with the violation of a concise, tangible regulation.

DISCUSSION QUESTIONS

After finishing the case study and studying the Exhibits carefully, be prepared to discuss the following questions in a small group, and to defend your answers in subsequent class discussion.

1. Did the employer (the Data Processing Center) provide Mr. Hernandez with clear performance standards from the time of his employment to the time of his termination?
2. Did the DPC provide Mr. Hernandez with adequate informal counseling concerning his performance discrepancies prior to initiating formal counseling and disciplinary action?
3. Did the employer adequately document Mr. Hernandez' alleged violation of clear performance standards?
4. Who, if anyone, benefited from the outcome of this case study?

EXHIBIT A. REPRIMAND RE UNITED FUND CARDS (APRIL 25, 1977)

April 25, 1977

To: Juan Hernandez
From: Richard White
      Computer Supervisor I
Subj: Reprimand

On April 13, 1977 you were assigned to read United Fund Cards into the card punch. The next day it was found that all 25,000 cards were punched incorrectly because they were fed into the machine backwards. Because United Fund had no more cards on hand, this required that new cards be printed at considerable cost and waste of time.

This situation caused a great deal of consternation on the part of top officials in DPC. As a senior computer operator, you should know enough to feed cards into the card punch correctly, or to ask for instructions if you are unsure of what you are doing.

Unless your performance improves, an unsatisfactory performance evaluation may result, or other forms of disciplinary action may occur. As always, I stand ready to help you with any advice and assistance you consider necessary.

I have read this letter and have been given a copy. My signature hereupon does not signify agreement or disagreement with its contents

———————————————— Juan Hernandez

EXHIBIT B. REBUTTAL FROM MR. HERNANDEZ (APRIL 25, 1977)

April 30, 1977

To: Mr. Otto Gesellschaft, Director, DPC
    Mr. Richard White, Supervisor
From: Juan Hernandez
      Computer Operator I
Subj: Answer to Reprimand

Mr. Richard White has forced me to sign a letter of reprimand which I totally disagree with. The purpose of this letter is to demand that you review the facts of the case and vindicate my reputation.

While it is true that the punch cards were fed into the machine backwards, two other operators as well as myself were assigned to this job. Yet none of these people received reprimands. Mr. White said that the United Fund people had to have someone to blame, and that because the other two employees were trainees they were not responsible, but I don't think this is fair.

There have been other incidents where employees have improperly set up machines and never received reprimands. For example, Stephen Hays caused improper printing of over 200 time sheets last year.

This reprimand is injurious to my character, my reputation, and my future. I demand that it be withdrawn as prejudicial.

EXHIBIT C. RECORD OF COUNSELING (JULY 29, 1979)

Record of Counseling

Employee Name: Juan Hernandez
Classification: Computer Operator I
Department: DPC
Date: July 29, 1979
Date of Hire: July 5, 1972
Employee Status: Permanent

Several incidents underscore a pattern of behavior that is of concern to me. You show increasing disregard to operational and personal conduct and have failed to take responsibility for your actions. I am bringing these items to your attention in an attempt to make you realize that your attitude is detrimental to your performance.

On Tuesday, May 20, 1979, at approximately 0900 hours, you approached Mr. White to ask to be allowed to leave at 1500 hours to go to the Credit Union. You stated that you would make up the time by not taking your lunch hour. Mr. White told you not to do that; to take the usual lunch hour, then to write a leave slip for one hour. You agreed and Mr. White had the impression that it was settled.

When you were asked by the time clerk to produce a leave slip for your absence, you presented a 15-minute leave-without-pay slip and indicated that Mr. Manny Ramirez had asked you to watch a job until it was finished and that this prevented you from having your lunch hour at the usual time; and that you had taken lunch and break at 1500 hours, thus the remaining 15 minutes represented your actual absence. I have checked with Mr. Ramirez and all members of his group and have found that neither he nor his staff had asked you for any special assistance.

On a previous occasion, a similar event took place and you were absent from the Computer Room without authorization.

The incident involving a box of forms improperly mounted was also brought to your attention; you denied having done it although a number of people actually saw you putting the forms on the printer.

I expect that you will give this matter prompt attention and proper consideration and will make every effort to avoid creating similar situations. I consider this very important and feel that counseling you at this time may help us avoid having to resort to stronger disciplinary action. I am also offering you an opportunity to discuss with me your plans to improve your attitude and your overall performance. I am willing to help you.

EXHIBIT D. RECORD OF COUNSELING (JUNE 29, 1981)

Record of Counseling

Employee Name:　Juan Hernandez
Classification:　Computer Operator
Department:　DPC, Computer Room
Date:　June 29, 1981
Date of Hire:　July 15, 1972
Employee Status:　Permanent

This formal counseling is a result of an incident which occurred on 6/9/81 involving potential damage to the System 3000 data base. This incident was witnessed by the following people: Mr. Ronald White, EDP Operations Supervisor; Mr. John Pardo, DPC Assistant Director; Mr. Donald Jenkins, Systems Programmer; and Ms. Maria Melendez, Teleprocessing Coordinator.

When program CICS (S337) would not run, the need to reload System 3000 Data Base became evident. Mr. Hernandez was the senior person on the console at this time. This process should require about ten minutes system outage if procedures are exercised normally. In this case, the total outage was in excess of 35 minutes because:

1.　Mr. Hernandez failed to assume senior operator responsibility when the problem became evident. It was necessary for Mr. Pardo and Mr. White to intervene and demand Mr. Hernandez to assume responsibility.
2.　Mr. Hernandez was unfamiliar with procedures required to terminate and restart System 3000. These procedures should be familiar to a Senior Computer Operator I since they have remained unchanged for over three months.
3.　Mr. Hernandez responded "GO" to a CICS startup message he was instructed not to respond to, resulting in a requirement to cancel CICS again and reload to avoid data base damage.

The essence of this counseling is to inform Mr. Hernandez that he must be more willing to assume responsibility in the absence of a Computer Operator II. Also, he must familiarize himself with existing procedures within the computer room.

These errors must be corrected immediately. Additional errors regarding these or other operational procedures may result in progressive discipline to include formal reprimand, suspension and/or termination.

Supervisor/Date　　　　　　　　　　　　　　　　　Employee/Date

EXHIBIT E. EMPLOYEE EVALUATION (JANUARY 9, 1982)

Interim Performance Evaluation

This interim performance evaluation on Mr. Juan Hernandez is brought about by Data Processing's concern for Mr. Hernandez' technical abilities and our continued desire to assist him to further his own knowledge and skills.

Since the relocation of this Computer Center to the Regional Data Processing Center facility, massive hardware and software changes have occurred. Coupled with these changes, Data Processing has also offered to all of its employees a massive educational and training program. In an environment such as ours, changes mandate a continual update to each employee's knowledges and skills. Nowhere is this more essential than to those actually involved in the understanding, manipulation, and daily operation of the computer itself. It is necessary that each Computer Operator understand his duties and responsibilities to the Center, the Community, and fellow Computer Operators.

It is for this reason that you are receiving this Performance Evaluation.

1. In June 1981, you received a formal written counseling pertaining to your inability to function while at the console.
2. In October 1981, your Performance Evaluation indicates a "needs improvement" in the achievement of objectives and use of tools and equipment. A recommended action is clearly outlined to assist furthering your technical expertise by attending courses offered within the Center.
3. During the months of October and November 1981, two classes on the Payroll System and the operation of the OMICROM system were offered. You were the only operator to fail both courses.
4. You are currently enrolled in the OPS-JES2 course. This course takes an average of 6 to 10 hours to complete. You started on November 1, 1981, and the last computer "logon" for you was December 12, 1981, which reflects only 3.5 hours.
5. You still have not signed up to take required training courses in BFD or MVS.

We recognize that it is sometimes difficult to leave your work station to attend classes; however, this has not been the problem. In the schedule listed below, we will allow you as much time from now until January 23, 1982 to complete or retake the following courses:

1. Complete OPS-JES2, approximately 6.5 hours remaining.
2. Initiate and complete the OMEGAMON course, approximately 5 hours.
3. Initiate and complete the MVS course, approximately 15 hours.
4. Retake the examinations on the Payroll system and OMICROM courses, approximately 2 hours.

It is expected that you, as a senior Computer Operator I with over 10 years experience in Computer Operations, will sustain a passing grade in all of the above mentioned courses. You must be prepared to respond to either a written or oral quiz upon completion of each course.

If you cannot elicit a passing grade for each of the above courses, the Data Processing Center has no recourse but to consider demotion and/or suspension. This Department will offer you as much assistance as is possible to help you attain the knowledge and skills necessary to function in your position.

EXHIBIT F. CRIME LABORATORY BUREAU REPORT

County of Los Angeles
Public Safety Department
Crime Laboratory Bureau

LABORATORY ANALYSIS REPORT

DATE: March 5, 1982
LACPSD Case #101374
Victim:
Defendant: Juan Hernandez

To: Robert Hess
Administrative Officer
Data Processing Center
County of Los Angeles

The evidence listed below was submitted to this laboratory on March 5, 1982 by Robert Hess:

— Exhibit A: Questioned Pacific Hospital Prescription Form dated 6/15/81
— Exhibit B: Questioned Pacific Hospital Prescription From dated 1/23/82

Findings, Opinions: The two questioned hospital prescription forms were written by the same author. The author's handwriting is identical to that of the defendant.

Respectfully submitted,

Silas Smith

Silas Smith, Criminalist
Questioned Documents Examiner
Crime Laboratory Bureau

EXHIBIT G. HEARING EXAMINER'S REPORT

Monk, Murphy, Tannenbaum, and Endicott
Attorneys at Law

Hearing Examiner's Report

Date: June 20, 1982
To: The Honorable Samuel Shapiro
County Attorney
County of Los Angeles

The Honorable Jeremy Irving
Attorney at Law
AFSCME Local 121

On May 10, 1982, the Hearing Examiner heard testimony and considered evidence relative to the termination of Mr. Juan Hernandez from the County of Los Angeles, Data Processing Center.

The following charges were advanced to support termination:

1. alleged violation of time and leave regulations, as described in the formal record of counseling that Mr. Hernandez received on July 29, 1979
2. alleged willful negligence in the performance of Mr. Hernandez' job duties in the improper printing of forms, as described in the formal record of counseling which he received on July 29, 1979
3. alleged willful negligence in the performance of Mr. Hernandez' job duties in the failure to properly load programs CICS (S337) so as to prevent damage to the System 3000 Data Base on June 9, 1981, as described in the formal record of counseling which he received on June 29, 1981
4. alleged failure to complete required training courses (MVS, Payroll system, OMICROM, OMEGAMON, and OPS-JES2) by January 23, 1982, as required by his performance evaluation of January 9, 1982
5. alleged falsification of physician's excuses for sick leave for June 15, 1981 and January 23, 1982, as described in the Laboratory Analysis Report dated March 5, 1982, LACPSD Case #101374)

Having evaluated all evidence and testimony presented relative to these charges, the Hearing Examiner finds that insufficient evidence exists to document discharge on grounds 1, 2, 3, or 4. However, under the terms of the collective bargaining agreement between AFSCME Local 121 and the Board of Supervisors of the County of Los Angeles, dated October 27, 1981, sufficient evidence has been presented to document discharge on ground 5.

Discharge is hereby affirmed.

NOTES

[1]Lewis R. Amis, "Due Process in Disciplinary Procedures," *Labor Law Journal* (February 1976), 94–98.

[2]John Price, *et al.,* "Three Studies of Grievances," *Personnel Journal* (January 1976), 33–37.

18

Employee Rights

In 1980, the U.S. Air Force discharged Sergeant Leonard Matlovich for homosexuality. Using arguments that had traditionally proven successful, the Air Force contended that Sergeant Matlovich's homosexuality made him a security risk—his job required that he have access to top secret data, and his sexual preferences made him subject to blackmail to avoid exposure.

Rather than accept these arguments, or his discharge, Sergeant Matlovich sued the Air Force for reinstatement. He argued that he had compiled an outstanding performance record during his 12 years in the service. He had been awarded the Bronze Star during the Vietnam War. Moreover, he insisted that he had never kept his homosexuality a secret; indeed, the Air Force had known about it when it twice allowed him to reenlist, granted him his top secret security clearance, and favorably evaluated his performance. He concluded that he had been punished solely because he openly admitted his homosexuality, not because the Air Force had shown that his sexual preferences had in any way interfered with the performance of his duties.

Sergeant Matlovich and the Air Force settled out of court. In return for $98,000 in compensation and $62,000 in back pay, he dropped his suit for reinstatement. Legal critics viewed the case in both positive and negative terms. It was a victory for employee rights over what many felt was blatant and arbitrary treatment of homosexuals; but it failed to answer the fundamental question of whether the military has the right to exclude individuals solely on the basis of their sexual preference.

The issue here is not whether homosexuals should be allowed into the military, though the case seems to revolve around that point. The issue is one of rights. What particular rights do public employees have, by virtue of their government employment, that are denied to private sector employees? In investigating this question, we will begin with an examination of the values that underlie public employment. That is, some values—primarily those underlying constitutional protections and merit system regulations—offer strong support to the concept of employee rights, while others (such as administrative efficiency or political responsiveness) are more apt to force employees to conform to a more narrow range of behavioral or attitudinal expectations. Next, we will examine the critical difference between public and private employers. In brief, this discussion will conclude that government as *employer* has some of the same obligations to protect employees' rights as does government as *government* to protect the rights of citizens. This right extends not only to the rights of equal protection and due process, but also to specific constitutional protections of expression and association.

Recently, much concern has been voiced about problems of sexual harassment of employees. This section will describe the problem, trace the case law and legislation related to it, and suggest appropriate measures for public personnel managers to deal with the issue.

The conflict between an employee's right to privacy and the public's right of access to personnel records is also a sensitive topic.

Concern has increased in recent years because public employers are liable, both individually and organizationally, for damages caused by their violation of the constitutional rights of employees or other citizens. How can public administrators work effectively toward political and managerial objectives, while at the same time safeguarding the rights of employees to the extent required by constitutional and civil service protections?

Lastly, increased concern for employee rights, and for the legal safeguards established to protect these rights, should not blind us to the fact that this value often conflicts with those of political responsiveness and administrative efficiency. These conflicts will be discussed in the last section.

By the end of this chapter you will be able to:

1. Discuss the values (political, merit system, constitutional, and managerial) that affect public employment in the United States
2. Discuss the impact of constitutional protection of due process on disciplinary action and discharge of public employees
3. Discuss the impact of constitutional rights of equal protection on sexual harassment
4. Discuss the impact of constitutional protection of First Amendment freedoms (political expression, and diversity of ideology, morals, and appearance) on public employees
5. Discuss the conflict between freedom of information and employee privacy

6. Discuss the liability of public employees for violating the constitutional rights of employees or other citizens
7. Discuss the conflict between "due process" and organizational effectiveness

PUBLIC EMPLOYMENT VALUES

The extent to which employees have rights depends upon the predominant value that underlies the public employment system. Therefore, the effect of different sets of values on the concept of employee rights needs to be examined.

Under a patronage system, the dominant value enforced by the personnel system is *political responsiveness.* That is, the purpose of the personnel system is to maintain bureaucratic responsiveness through limited tenure in office. Just as an individual's hiring is based on his or her political or psychological ties to an elected official, so is the person's discharge the moment the elected official feels these ties no longer exist, or the elected patron is thrown out of office.

Civil service systems were created to reduce the impact of "politics" on administrative agencies. Consequently, civil service reformers supported selection and retention on the basis of merit. In other words, the health of the political and administrative system was tied to the protection of employment rights for civil service employees.

As Chapter 3 indicated, the strength of the civil service reform movement was considerably augmented by its ties with administrative science; the apoliticization of government went hand in hand with increased administrative efficiency. Yet it must be remembered that the primary value of administrative science is increased administrative efficiency, which assumes a different conception of employee rights than that posited by the civil service reformers. For administrative science, administrative efficiency is accomplished by developing and elaborating bureaucratic principles of organization, namely, hierarchical authority, division of labor through a system of position classification and evaluation, and reliance on standard operating procedures as decision rules. In many cases, these principles have resulted in the development of rules of employee behavior that tend to restrict the rights of employees in ways not contemplated by civil service reformers. For example, police officers are frequently prohibited from wearing beards, just as military personnel are prohibited from having long hair (or being homosexuals). The organization's concern here is to increase efficiency by enforcing standardized forms of behavior or dress.

The primary concern of the constitutional perspective is the *protection of individual rights.* The Constitution reserves all rights not specifically granted the national government, or the states, to the people. It guarantees to all citizens equal protection under the law, and it prohibits the government from depriving anyone of the right of life, liberty, or property without due process of law. The federal government, in its dealings with employees, must be scrupulously careful of employees' rights as citizens. The Matlovich case, for example, pits a fundamental constitutional right of employees (freedom of association) against the value of managerial efficiency (although this value must be stretched considerably to apply restrictions against homosexuality).

It can be seen that one's conception of employee rights will differ according to which of these values is considered predominant. The predominant value will in turn be determined by the pattern of social, political, and legal changes that occur over time. For example, the era of patronage was followed by the civil service reform movement, which was reinforced and reinterpreted by administrative science, which was in turn succeeded by increased concern for constitutional rights.

THE RIGHT TO DUE PROCESS IN DISCIPLINARY ACTION

It has become popular to assert that civil service rules "hamstring" management by making it impossible to discharge or discipline employees protected by civil service systems. In one respect, this statement is correct. As we shall see, public employees, unprotected by affirmative action laws or union contracts, have rights to their jobs that far exceed those of their private sector counterparts. Yet this statement is also incorrect, for these rights are ultimately derived from constitutional rights of due process, rather than to the civil service regulations that may spell out these protections. Constitutional protections accorded public employees are an extension of governmental responsibility to protect employees rights as citizens.

Similarly, it has become popular, usually around election time, to accuse the "bloated bureaucracy" of being unresponsive to the wishes of taxpayers or elected officials. In particular, civil service rules and regulations are blamed for this condition. Yet the landmark case involving this conflict was decided on the basis of the employee's constitutional right to freedom of political association.[1] In this case, a political appointee of the Cook County (Illinois) Sheriff's Department protested his routine discharge when the incumbent political party was thrown out of office. In deciding the case, the Supreme Court was faced with a conflict between the historical practice of patronage dismissals to ensure political responsiveness, and the individual employee's right not to be discharged from a public job, without due process, solely on the basis of political affiliation. Although historically the Court had supported political patronage as necessary for political responsiveness, in this case it resolved the question in favor of the individual, except for policy-making positions, and those where a confidential relationship existed between the employee and a political appointee (such as between a boss and a secretary). Although questions still abound concerning the nature of a policy-making or confidential position, this case establishes a clear protection for the due process rights of public employees in general. Thus, it may be expected that subsequent court cases will increasingly limit the dismissal of employees for reasons of political patronage.

Due process, in this instance, is simply the right of an employee to a full and impartial opportunity to appeal disciplinary action (including discharge) by management. It includes the right to be informed of the reasons for disciplinary action, to respond to those reasons by presenting other information, and to have that response impartially considered and reviewed in the organization before a final decision is made. It is based on the Fourteenth Amendment to the Constitution, which prohibits the government from depriving a person of "life, liberty, or property . . . without due process of law." Central to this right is the assumption that an employee who has passed a probationary period, and whose performance has been rated as satisfactory, has the expectation of continued employment as long as the job exists. The job is thus the "property" of the employee, and government cannot act to deprive the individual of it in an arbitrary or capricious fashion.

It is important to note that this property interest in a job makes government agencies entirely different from their private sector counterparts. In private businesses not covered by union contracts, management can discipline or discharge employees arbitrarily, at its own discretion. Employees are protected only to the extent that management is prohibited, by affirmative action laws, from discharging or otherwise disciplining employees on the basis of nonmerit factors (that is, age, sex, race, religion, handicap, or national origin). For example, the owner of a chain of athletic shoe stores can discharge the manager of a store on the spot because of differences of opinion over how the store should be run. This could never happen in a public agency where such a charge would be analogous to dismissal for "political reasons."

Yet the public employee's rights to a property interest in his or her job is not absolute. Indeed, the case law on this issue is somewhat confusing. In *Bishop* v. *Wood,* the Supreme Court ruled that a North Carolina police officer could be dismissed without a hearing.[2] Bishop (the officer) claimed that as a permanent employee who had passed the six-month probationary period, he had an expectation of continued employment, thus creating a due process right to notice and a hearing; and that the false reasons for his dismissal violated his right to liberty. The Court ruled *against* Bishop, holding that "the due process clause . . . is not a guarantee against incorrect and ill-advised personnel decisions." However, the minority Justices in the 5–4 decision disagreed strongly. Based on a prior case, *Arnett* v. *Kennedy,* they claimed that Bishop had a property right to his job unless there was cause to fire him, and thus that dismissal could only occur upon prior written notification of inadequate performance.[3]

The dismissal of public employees, even those with no "property" interests, may also involve the infringement of "liberty" interests that are also protected by the due process clauses of the Fifth and Fourteenth Amendments.[4] In a general sense, the Supreme Court has defined "liberty" as the right of an individual to enjoy "those privileges long recognized as essential to the orderly pursuit of happiness by free men."[5] More specifically, with respect to public employees, liberty is not offended by dismissal itself, but rather by the reasons for dismissal which either (1) damage the employee's good name, reputation, honor, or integrity, or (2) sufficiently stigmatize the employee so as to foreclose other employment opportunities.

When a liberty interest is in fact implicated by termination, the Constitution mandates that certain procedural protections be afforded. In such instances, due process requires that the employee be notified of the reasons for dismissal, and that he or she be provided a hearing which constitutes the opportunity to clear his or her name.[6] The specific form and timing of these procedures depend largely on an appropriate accommodation of the competing interests of government and employee.

It also appears that the impartiality of the hearing process need not be absolute. In *Hortonville Joint School District* v. *Hortonville Educational Association*, the High Court ruled that the Fourteenth Amendment's due process clause did not give the striking teachers the right to have their discharges reviewed by a body other than the local school board that dismissed them. The Court said that there was no constitutional basis for depriving the school board of its statutory right to discipline employees, even if the board was a party to the dispute.[7]

Therefore, the legality of firing public employees appears controversial, given three issues: employee property rights to a job, the right of due process prior to discharge for cause, and employees' liberty interest in their jobs. Together, depending on one's viewpoint, these three issues constitute either valuable protections to public employee rights, or "red tape" that limits governmental responsiveness and efficiency.

SEXUAL HARASSMENT

As the proportion of working women in the job market has increased, and as their concern with sexual harassment has turned more vocal, this issue has become increasingly important to public personnel managers. This section will describe the incidence of sexual harassment, cite the legal protections employees have against it, and discuss policies and practices that agencies should consider adopting to minimize the problem.

Although most research on sexual harassment has been conducted since 1979, available data indicate that it is quite widespread. For example, the Merit Systems Protection Board reported that 42 percent of female and 15 percent of male federal employees had been sexually harassed during a two-year period.[8] Similar figures have been reported by state employees in Illinois and Florida.[9]

Although sexual harassment was not originally considered a violation of civil rights laws, recent court cases have ruled that Title VII of the 1964 Civil Rights Act prohibits it. In *Bundy* v. *Jackson,* a federal district court ruled that an employer "which created or condoned a discriminatory work environment was in violation of Title VII.[10]

The EEOC adopted guidelines interpreting sexual harassment in September 1980.[11] These guidelines define sexual harassment as discrimination on the basis of sex when submission is a condition of employment, submission or rejection is the basis for employment decisions, the behavior interferes with work performance, or it creates an intimidating, hostile, or offensive work environment. Favoritism resulting from submission to requests for sexual favors can be considered sex discrimination against other employees.

The development of case law and regulations protecting employees from sexual harassment has clearly presented public agency managers with a legal liability issue. Under the EEOC guidelines, employers are liable for the actions of their employees, and this liability can result in the award of substantial damages or out-of-court settlements.[12] Public agencies should respond to this situation by:

Developing policies

Designating an official responsible for policy development and compliance

Providing an appeal and grievance procedure for cases of alleged sexual harassment

Communicating to all employees what the policy is, officials responsible for its implementation, and their rights to appeal or grieve

Providing training to sensitize supervisors and employees to the issue of sexual harassment

THE FIRST AMENDMENT RIGHTS OF PUBLIC EMPLOYEES

Similar conflicts between administrative efficiency and public employee's rights have occurred with respect to the First Amendment freedoms (rights to politics, ideology, morals, and appearance). As Rosenbloom indicates,[13] conflict has existed between these constitutional values and the value of administrative efficiency because political neutrality and uniformity of ideology, morality, and appearance are characteristics of bureaucratic organizations organized to promote administrative efficiency.

The Right to Political Expression and Association

Initially, political neutrality was promoted as a value by civil service reformers because it was a reaction against the patronage politics of the "spoils system." If the process of administration was politically neutral, and conducted according to managerial standards of efficiency, then the intrusion of politics tended to undermine this objective—or so the logic went. Early Supreme Court decisions supported the concept of political neutrality by separating the employee's constitutional right to freedom of political expression and association from his or her right to a public job. It held that since holding a government job was voluntary rather than compulsory, government could impose restrictions on political activity without interfering with the employee's First Amendment rights. In *McAuliffe* v. *New Bedford,* Justice Holmes upheld the constitutionality of state and local political neutrality regulations by concluding that "the petitioner may have a constitutional right to talk politics, but he has no constitutional right to be a policeman."[14]

In subsequent cases, this conclusion has continuously been upheld: The dangers of a politicized bureaucracy have been considered more urgent than the individual employee's right to political participation. Today, employees in the federal government and most state and local governments cannot hold civil service jobs while running for office, cannot campaign (or be forced to campaign) for political candidates on their own time, and cannot be involved as officers in the political campaigns of elected officials. Federal prohibitions against political activity are embodied in the Hatch Act; similar prohibitions for state and local government employees are termed "little Hatch Acts."

The Right to Ideological Diversity

During the 1950s, the desire for managerial efficiency and the cold war hysteria of the McCarthy era combined to force public employees into greater ideological uniformity. Employees were denied jobs, or fired from jobs, on the basis of their political and social beliefs. Thus, dismissals for political disloyalty (for such reasons as support of pacifism, racial integration, or socialism) could be justified not only as supporting the United States ideologically, but as promoting the increased efficiency of the bureaucracy.

However, these abuses of constitutional rights did not last beyond the cold war. The Supreme Court found that diversity of thought or expression did not mean disloyalty. In addition, the public employee's right to due process in disciplinary action or discharge proceedings increased opportunities for such violations of rights to be detected.

The Right to Moral Diversity

Public personnel administrative regulations have also sought to control the "moral" behavior, especially in a sexual sense, of public employees. . . . [A] major reason for imposing uniformity seems to be the elimination from the public sector workforce of human characteristics that could cause friction between workers or opposition among the public and thereby reduce efficiency.[15]

To some extent, the federal courts have dismissed such regulations on the grounds that personal moral preferences, in and of themselves, do not constitute a threat to the security or efficient functioning of the agency. However, as we have seen from the case of Sergeant Matlovich, no clear precedent has been established that would protect the absolute right of employees to moral preferences—particularly sexual ones—in the absence of data indicating that their performance was unsatisfactory.

Appearance

If uniformity of ideology and morals is characteristic of the bureaucratic ideal, it is not surprising that uniformity of appearance is too. Traditionally, federal courts have upheld standards of dress and personal grooming of public employees, particularly military and law-enforcement personnel. In *Kelley* v. *Johnson,* for example, the Supreme Court held that grooming regulations that restrict hair length for police officers are permissible. It concluded that the Constitution does not guarantee the personal liberty of police officers to choose a style of personal appearance when the code is justified in the interest of "esprit de corps."[16]

EMPLOYEE PRIVACY AND FREEDOM OF INFORMATION

Two principles govern the ways in which public agencies get and use information. The first is privacy: the right of each individual to control personal information by restricting access to it by public agencies or employers.[17] Questions of the right to privacy most often arise when outside organizations or supervisors seek access to personnel files that agency employees consider private. For example, creditors may seek information about an employee's salary so that they can go to court to collect debts. Or information about an employee's race or sex is often required to determine whether an agency is complying with affirmative action laws.

One of the best responses to the question of maintaining employee privacy comes from the International Business Machines Corporation (IBM), which, ironically, has also done much to raise the issue of employee privacy through its development of automated data systems. The president of IBM recommends that:

> Employees have the right to routinely review and correct misinformation in their own files.
>
> Supervisors' access be limited to job-related information, such as performance appraisal and previous work assignments.
>
> Public access be limited to general information, such as the fact that employees work for the agency, their current jobs, and the dates when they were first employed. Creditors, attorneys, or private employment agencies may not have access to data unless authorized by the employee or required by law.[18]

However, rights to employee privacy are also restricted by a second principle governing the collection and use of public information—*freedom of information.* That is, the public is entitled to see all information that does not violate employees' right to privacy, or that does not drastically hamper the agency's ability to function. In addition, many states have "sunshine" laws that guarantee public access to public records, including employees' personnel files.

Public agencies themselves frequently use information to increase their own reputation or political "clout." For example, the collective bargaining negotiator for one city sought to increase public opposition to wage increases for police officers by publishing their salaries, by name. Or agencies may withhold information they consider damaging to agency efficiency or employee rights. For instance, school districts may refuse to release data on disciplinary actions or hearings involving teachers, on the grounds that such disclosure would increase parent complaints or demands for transfer, or violate the rights of teachers in pending cases.

The understandable tendency of public agencies and administrators to use or withhold information for their own benefit has led to efforts to define the public's right of access to information. At the federal level, Congress passed the Freedom of Information (FOI) Act in 1966 and amended it in 1974. This Act gives all persons the judicially enforceable right to see the records of federal government agencies. There are some major exceptions: classified national defense and foreign relations secrets, purely internal management matters, confidential information protected by other laws such as the Privacy Act, investigative files of law-enforcement agencies, and trade secrets. Many states have passed similar laws for state and local agencies within their jurisdictions.

Naturally, disputes arise between requesters and agencies concerning whether requested items fall within the exempted categories just mentioned. In general, agencies still tend to withhold information that may be exempt on the grounds that, once released, it can never be recalled. Moreover, though the reasonable costs of processing information searches are paid by the requester, lack of internal agency guidelines and of sufficient personnel to process requests have led to some administrative problems. Nonetheless, the FOI Act continues to be an important policy statement protecting the public's right of access to public information.

DISSENT AND WHISTLEBLOWING

The understandable tendency of public organizations and administrators to withhold self-incriminating information from the public is counterbalanced by *whistleblowing*. This is a form of dissent that focuses public attention on behavior that the "whistleblower" considered illegal or unethical.[19] It is the moral imperative behind the whistleblower's desire to change agency policy that distinguishes uses of organizational information.

Whistleblowing is a well-publicized phenomenon because it plays upon the public's desire to expose corruption and increase responsiveness or efficiency in government agencies. In the past decade there have been several well-publicized examples of whistleblowing: Watergate, the Pentagon Papers exposé of the Vietnam War by Daniel Ellsberg, and the revealing of C-5A transport planes' cost overruns by U.S. Air Force auditor Ernest Fitzgerald.

Yet despite its popularity with the press and the public, whistleblowing does not occur frequently. Employees usually blow the whistle only as a last resort, when the conflict between their ethical standards and their perception of their agency's behavior is so great as to leave them no choice. In such cases, they have exhausted all possibilities for internal dissent through the policy-making process, and they are willing to endure the social isolation and organizational punishment that normally accompany being labeled a traitor by other administrators.

How should whistleblowing be evaluated? On the one hand, it divides the agency and undercuts its management. On the other hand, it prevents managers from hiding information harmful to the agency or its managers, using specious reasons such as security and efficiency. Whistleblowing therefore represents a classic conflict between the constitutional right of free expression and the desire of managers to restrict the flow of damaging information out of the agency in order to preserve managerial efficiency or maintain political support.

Given that whistleblowing is valuable because it helps ensure the accountability of agencies and is a constitutionally protected right, how can it be encouraged without undermining the hierarchical structure of authority on which bureaucratic organizations are based? Internally, it is suggested that agencies establish ethical standards during employee orientation as a part of job expectations; assign to the planning administrator the responsibility of exploring any negative ethical implications of proposed policies; evaluate present or past programs according to ethical standards. Externally, the most widely adopted solution is the passage of laws that protect whistleblowers from reprisal by their public employers. For example, the Civil Service Reform Act of 1978 empowers the Merit Systems Protection Board (MSPB) to investigate reprisals against whistleblowers, and it prohibits certain punitive personnel practices.

Yet these laws and internal procedures do not resolve the conflict between administrative efficiency (hierarchical control and uniformity of ideology) and political responsiveness and individual rights. At best, they represent procedures for resolving this dilemma on a case-by-case basis.

PUBLIC EMPLOYEE LIABILITY

The introduction to this chapter indicated that the question of employee rights frequently represented a conflict among the values underlying the public personnel system, be they political responsiveness, administrative efficiency, or the constitutional rights of employees. In the section on First Amendment rights, it also concluded that the Supreme Court had in recent years tended to support the rights of public employees to differences in ideology, morality, and appearance.

Underlying these issues was a general realization that the growth of bureaucratic power was potentially hazardous not only to the rights of employees, but also to the rights of other citizens. The Supreme Court has confronted this threat by expanding the interpretation of the FOI Act, and by affording individuals greater opportunity to oppose individual administrators in court. This latter change has meant alteration of the previous doctrine of personal immunity of officials (an extension of the traditional common law doctrine of *sovereign immunity*) in favor of increased recognition of citizens' rights to sue administrators for abuses of authority, and to collect compensatory and punitive damages for harm resulting from these abuses.

Traditionally, administrators came to share the same immunity from civil suits arising out of actions connected with their official functions, as had formerly belonged only to legislators and judges. Until the 1970s, the Supreme Court had held, particularly in the cases of *Spalding* v. *Vilas* and *Barr* v. *Matteo,* that:

Under the Spalding-Barr line of reasoning, then, many of the actions of the agents of the administrative state are cloaked in immunity. The citizen who suffers wrongful action has no recourse in court; there is no effort made to render the administrator directly accountable to the citizen even in extreme instances of negligent or purposeful harm. The needs of the administrative state for smooth operation are placed above protections for the citizenry.[20]

Given the inevitability of administrative abuses of citizens' rights, and the willingness of the Supreme Court to consider means of curbing the power of the administrative state in favor of the constitutional rights of employees and other citizens, this doctrine of sovereign immunity began to change in the 1970s. In the cases of *Scheuer* v. *Rhodes* (1974) and *Wood* v. *Strickland,* the High Court altered the doctrine of sovereign immunity to one of *limited immunity.* This revised doctrine held that administrators were not immune from liability of damages if they knew or reasonably should have known that the actions they took within the sphere of their official responsibilities would violate the constitutional rights of employees or citizens. In brief, administrators have no immunity if they act with malice or knowing disregard of established constitutional rights. Because the determination of "reasonable knowledge" is looser than "knowing disregard," the revised immunity doctrine enunciated by these two court cases places public administrators in much greater risk of liability than before. The doctrine of sovereign immunity has effectively been discarded, except that it still applies to the actions of administrative officials who act as adjudicators.

Administrators who are found, through federal court decisions, to have maliciously or knowingly violated others' constitutional rights are liable for compensatory and punitive damages. In some cases these judgments have had little effect because of administrators' inability to pay. Yet law-enforcement and health care agencies have generally adopted professional liability insurance that insures them, up to stated policy limits, against claims for damages arising out of their performance of job duties—except for punitive damages. It is therefore difficult to oppose implementation of the concept of limited sovereignty on this basis. Instead, one must conclude that it offers admirable protection for the constitutional rights of citizens and employees, and for the legitimate exercise of authority by public administrators.

DUE PROCESS AND ORGANIZATIONAL EFFECTIVENESS

Throughout this book we have seen that heightened concern with one value system—and with those personnel activities that relate most closely to that value—will result in unforeseen negative consequences for opposing values and declining interest in the activities typifying those values. In this case, increased concern for employee rights has had a negative effect on both political responsiveness and administrative efficiency. A closer look at organizational responses to the demand for increased due process will clarify these relationships.

First, it is clear that the case of *Elrod* v. *Burns* has resulted in diminished political responsiveness through the patronage system. The Supreme Court's ruling in this case has been criticized because it (1) downplays the state's right to restrict freedom of association in favor of the values of political responsiveness and managerial efficiency, (2) it does not define the relationship between partisan values and effective performance, and (3) it ignores the positive contributions that political parties can make to government.[21]

In addition, concern for protection of employee rights through due process causes organizations to resort to legal decision-making processes. These processes increase the time and cost involved in conflict resolution by introducing a third party, and they increase the likelihood that managers will seek to maintain their flexibility by "netherworld behavior"—carefully documenting personnel practices to avoid liability, yet acting clandestinely so as to preserve their own flexibility and authority. It remains to be seen what the effect of this value conflict will be on the larger issue of organizational effectiveness.

SUMMARY

A continual conflict exists among political responsiveness, managerial efficiency, and the constitutional rights of employees, that is reflected in the issue of employee rights. Although traditionally the courts have supported managerial efficiency, this is now counterbalanced by increased concern for employees' constitutional rights to due process, ideology, appearance, and morality; and whistleblowing; and against sexual harassment.

DISCUSSION QUESTIONS

1. What opposing values have affected public employment in the United States, and what has been their effect on employee rights?
2. What is "due process," and how does it affect disciplinary action and discharge of public employees?
3. What is sexual harassment, and what steps should public agencies take to prevent it?
4. What is the current status of the law concerning political expression and diversity of ideology, morals, and appearance for public employees?

5. How have governments chosen to resolve the conflict between freedom of information, administrative efficiency, and employee privacy?

6. Under what conditions are administrators liable for damages resulting from their official actions?

7. What are the consequences for organizational effectiveness of concern for employee rights to due process?

KEY TERMS

political responsiveness
managerial efficiency
employee rights
due process
property interest
liberty interest
sexual harassment
First Amendment rights
Hatch Act
employee privacy
freedom of information
Freedom of Information (FOI) Act
whistleblowing
sovereign immunity
limited immunity

CASE STUDY: BLOWING THE WHISTLE ON METRORAIL[22]

In 1978, Metropolitan Dade County (Florida) began construction of a 20-mile elevated transit system linking city suburbs with the downtown area. The project was controversial when approved by county voters; it remained controversial throughout the construction process, with many critics accusing the county of slipshod management that resulted in delays, cost overruns, and inferior quality construction.

In 1983, serious allegations of poor construction became the subject of public hearings before the County Commission. These allegations were raised by Sarosh Dhondy, a Metrorail design engineer who had been fired from his position as vice-president for mass transit after publicly criticizing Metrorail construction.

At the hearings, Dhondy showed blueprints indicating that steel reinforcing rods in the pillars supporting the elevated Metrorail track had either been misplaced or left out; that the concrete used in these pillars was structurally defective because of honeycombing; and that the pillars themselves had been misaligned. He said, "This is going to cause failure. Trains are going to be on the ground because of this! It's against my design. The design cannot function. There will be total failure."

In response, Metrorail managers and their hired consultants questioned Sarosh Dhondy's motives and credentials. Warren Higgins, Metrorail manager, observed, "Mr. Dhondy does have difficulty working with a team." Charles Schimpeler, project chief for Metrorail's consultants, noted: "As a structural analyst, [Mr. Dhondy] made substantial contribution to the design of the [support pillars]. . . . [He] has never had over-all design responsibility because he is not a licensed professional engineer." He added that the design defects Mr. Dhondy pointed out were either nonexistent or had been corrected.

The commissioners' reaction to the hearing was mostly negative. One charged that Dhondy had "threatened the integrity of this system." Others demanded that he turn his information over to the federal inspectors already sent by the U.S. Urban Mass Transit Administration to evaluate Metrorail construction.

Dhondy promised to "cooperate." But he had a counterproposal of his own: The Commissioners should provide him with a top-notch technical review team and a budget of $2.5 million to personally review the flaws. This the commissioners refused to do. Failing that, he would try to get enough petition signatures in Dade County to get a referendum blocking the system. Shouted Dhondy, "The issue has got to be settled, and you all are going to stop pussyfooting. Until you stop pussyfooting, I hold the upper hand over you all!"

Case Discussion Questions

After reading the case study, break into discussion groups of four or five students each. As a group, develop answers to the following questions. Then defend your answers in general class discussion.

1. To what extent does this case study represent conflict among political responsiveness, administrative efficiency, and employee rights?
2. Was Mr. Dhondy discharged for whistleblowing? Were his rights violated?
3. In this case, how should the conflict between management's desire to withhold information from the public, and the whistleblower's moral responsibility to make that information public be resolved?

NOTES

[1]*Elrod v. Burns,* 427 U.S. 347 [1976].
[2]*Bishop v. Wood,* 96th S. Ct. 2076 [1976].
[3]*Arnett v. Kennedy,* 94 S. Ct. 1633 [1974].

[4]*Wisconsin v. Constantineau,* 400 U.S. 433, 437 [1971].

[5]*Arnett v. Kennedy,* 416 U.S. 134, 157 [1974].

[6]*Hortonville Joint School District v. Hortonville Educational Association,* 96 S. Ct. 2308 [1976].

[7]U.S. Merit Systems Protection Board, *Sexual Harassment in the Federal Workplace—Is It a Problem?* (Washington, D.C.: U.S. Government Printing Office, 1981).

[8]Douglas I. McIntyre and James C. Renick, "Protecting Public Employees and Employers from Sexual Harassment," *Public Personnel Management,* Vol. 11, No. 3 (Fall 1982), 282–92.

[9]McIntyre and Renick, p. 286.

[10]U.S. EEOC, "Discrimination Because of Sex under Title VII of the Civil Rights Act of 1964, As Amended: Adoption of Final Interpretive Guidelines," *Federal Register,* November 10, 1980.

[11]McIntyre and Renick, pp. 289–91.

[12]David H. Rosenbloom, "The Sources of Continuing Conflict Between the Constitution and Public Personnel Management," *Review of Public Personnel Administration,* Vol. 2, No. 1 (Fall 1981), 3–18.

[13]Rosenbloom, p. 13.

[14]Rosenbloom, p. 9.

[15]*Kelley v. Johnson,* 96 S. Ct. 1440 [1976].

[16]Daniel M. O'Brien, *Law and Public Policy* (New York: Praeger, 1979).

[17]Frank T. Cary, "IBM's Guidelines on Employee Privacy," *Harvard Business Review,* Vol. 54 (September–October 1976), 80–90.

[18]Alan F. Westin, *Whistleblowing, Loyalty and Dissent in the Corporation* (New York: McGraw-Hill, 1981).

[19]David H. Rosenbloom, "Public Administrators' Official Immunity and the Supreme Court: Developments During the 1970s," *Public Administration Review,* Vol. 40, No. 2 (March–April 1980), 169.

[20]Kenneth J. Meier, "Ode to Patronage: A Critical Analysis of Two Recent Supreme Court Decisions," *Public Administrators Review,* Vol. 41, No. 5 (September–October 1981), 558–63.

[21]Donald E. Klingner and John Nalbandian, "Due Process and Organizational Effectiveness," unpublished manuscript, 1983.

[22]The following material is drawn from two articles that appeared in *The Miami Herald,* April 6, 1983, p. D1: Charles Whited, "Rail Designer: Whistleblower or Pesky Scold?", and Rick Hirsch, "Metrorail Says Supports Sound."

19

Human Resource Management Evaluation

Previous chapters have described public human resource management as the performance of systemic functions (allocation, procurement, development, and sanctions), the objectives of which differ due to the continual tension among the values that influence outcomes for these activities (political responsiveness, individual employee rights, social equity, and administrative efficiency). The control and adaptation function enables human resource management, as an organizational activity, to remain responsive to the objectives of organizational managers and to adapt to changes in environmental conditions.

Given that it involves a range of activities and a diversity of values, the control and adaptation function is complex. An investigation of it requires exploration of a number of issues. First, the nature and purposes of program evaluation must be discussed in order to clarify who evaluates human resource management programs, and why. All evaluation is political in that it reflects the conflicting values of administrators, elected officials, researchers, and interest groups. What criteria do they use?

Second, the role of management information systems in collecting and disseminating the information used to evaluate human resource management programs is critical, for the human resource management information system (HRMIS) functions as the "driver" that provides both the rationale for evaluation and the capability for carrying out quantitative evaluation techniques. What are the objectives of management information systems, and what role should the public personnel manager play in designing them? Third, human resource evaluation enables the public personnel manager to assess the health of specific personnel activities in order to respond to questions frequently asked concerning their effectiveness. What are these questions, and how does the human resource evaluation system enable the public personnel manager to respond to them? Lastly, the role of values in human resource program evaluation is critical, for the way in which a program is evaluated influences the relative strength of values such as political responsiveness, employee rights, administrative efficiency, and social equity.

By the end of this chapter you will be able to:

1. Discuss the objectives of program evaluation, describe the different groups that evaluate programs, and identify the criteria they use
2. Discuss the relationship between a management information and human resource program evaluation, and the role of the public personnel manager in designing and using a human resource management evaluation system
3. Describe how evaluation can help the human resource manager assess the effectiveness of specific personnel activities
4. Discuss the relationship among core public personnel values, ethics, and human resource program evaluation

PROGRAM EVALUATION: WHO, WHY, AND HOW

Chapter 11 discussed productivity by defining the differences between efficiency, effectiveness, and responsiveness. An *efficient* program is one that accomplishes its objective more cheaply (on a unit cost basis) than other programs or that same program at a previous time. An *effective* program is one that accomplishes its objective regardless of cost or relative cost efficiency. A *responsive* program is one that meets the political needs of the legislature regardless of whether it accomplishes the specific objectives intended in the enabling legislation.

The distinctions among these three evaluative criteria can be clarified by an example. In the late 1960s, federal government employment expanded greatly as the Johnson Administration became heavily involved in both the Vietnam War and Great Society domestic programs. Consequently, the federal personnel agency (the U.S. Civil Service Commission—now the U.S. Office of Personnel Management) conducted much centralized testing and recruitment for federal agencies. In 1969, for example, over 150,000 applicants were tested for postal and civil service positions using machine-scored, multiple-choice examinations. The Civil Service Commission had pioneered in the development of large-scale computerized testing systems during the 1960s, and the system worked with incredible efficiency. People all over the country would take tests on a Saturday, and their application forms and answer sheets would be sent directly from the 2000 nationwide test centers to Washington for computer scoring. By the beginning of the next week, Washington would mail out, to each of the 65 area offices around the country, completed records for each applicant. These included a notice of rating, an examination record card, and a computer printout of eligible applicants in order of their score. The average cost of scoring and processing an applicant's test papers was about ten cents by computer, as opposed to about $3.00 by hand. This system was quite efficient.

With the reduction of federal employment in the 1970s, far fewer employees were hired through these large-scale computerized examinations. Agencies began to demand more authority to hire applicants flexibly at the local level, rather than relying on the Civil Service Commission to provide centralized testing and recruitment. Agency personnel managers felt they could better ensure the quality of employees placed through their own efforts—particularly through the "name-request" system described in Chapter 6—than through the Civil Service Commission. Thus, the centralized computer system, though it continued to be an *efficient* method of testing large numbers of people, came under increasing pressure as agency personnel managers (and applicants) considered it less *effective* under cutback management conditions.

One of the most popular of the examinations given by the Civil Service Commission—for applicants if not for Commission employees—was the Summer Employment Examination. Every winter, about 30,000 college students nationwide took one of three scheduled examinations to determine whether they would be selected for the 1000 summer jobs that federal agencies advertised during June, July, and August. Was this test efficient? Yes, because computerized processing made it possible to test and score large numbers of applicants cheaply. Was this test effective at meeting agency staffing needs? No, because the use of a single mathematical and verbal aptitude test to select employees for a variety of positions (ranging from surveyor to personnel technician) meant that the test was not an effective means of selecting the most qualified person for a position. No, because the limited length of summer employment positions meant that employees' training period and term of employment ended at about the same time, and federal agency workloads were usually lighter in the summer than in the winter.

Yet the summer employment examination was retained because it was extremely *responsive* to political need. To be blunt, it gave hundreds of Representatives and Senators an easy answer when constituents asked them to "Help find my son or daughter a job for the summer so they can afford to stay in school." Rather than using agency contacts to compete with each other for scarce jobs, Representatives could now refer all such requests to the Commission for handling. Once the successful applicants had been selected, the Commission notified not only the new employees, but also the Representative in their district so that he or she could claim credit for the appointment. Consequently, the examination continued to be funded until the reduction in federal employment of the 1970s resulted in the abolishment of so many of the summer positions that the examination had become more of a lottery than a test. Only when there were over 100 eligible applicants for every available job, and when applicants with scores of 97 out of 100 were not selected, did the Summer Employment Examination's low effectiveness begin to outweigh its high efficiency and high responsiveness.

It should be apparent from this example that program evaluation is difficult in that different people will apply different evaluative criteria. In actuality, several types of individuals and groups evaluate public personnel management programs: researchers, planners, managers, executives, interest groups, and legislators.

Researchers are responsible for the initial development of most programs. Typically, researchers design a program in order to test a scientific hypothesis that has not yet been proven valid or invalid.[1] For example, the job satisfaction studies conducted by Frederick Herzberg were initially intended to validate or invalidate his hypothesis about job satisfiers and dissatisfiers, rather than to help organizations increase employee productivity.

Because their primary concern is the relationship among concepts and the validity of theories, researchers are rarely concerned directly with the evaluation of programs from the viewpoint of efficiency or responsiveness. If the hypothesis relates to organizational effectiveness, then this criterion becomes of concern to them.

If a program proves successful in one area, *consultants* and *planners* in other agencies will learn about it. Their interest in evaluation is somewhat different from that of researchers. Planners want to know if a program can be successfully transplanted to their own agency. This type of "technology transfer" is frequently performed by public agencies with the help of consultants. For example, the Intergovernmental Personnel Act (IPA) of 1970 was a federal grant program aimed at increasing the quality of human resource management in state and local governments. University consultants joined forces with state and local personnel directors to apply for federal funding for projects in such areas as training needs assessment, selection, performance evaluation, and human resource planning. In most cases the programs were designed not as original research, but to apply a proven solution to a setting diagnosed as having the same problem. For example, in 1973 the State of Indiana hired several consultants to help it develop a point-factor ranking system of job evaluation. This system was not new; indeed, the project would not have been funded unless the method had proven itself successful over time with other public agencies.

Once a program has been developed and tested, it is given to a *pro-*

gram manager for implementation. Program managers are most directly concerned with program evaluation because they direct the program in question. As leaders, they are responsible for developing information and control systems to ensure that programs can accomplish planned objectives, and will continue to do so over time. Their own performance evaluation and future program budgets may well depend on how successful their programs are.

Program managers are likely to evaluate their programs by using those criteria for which data can be easily collected: inputs, activities, outputs, and cost-efficiency. Input measures include the amount of money or the number of employees allocated to a project. The manager asks, "Did I receive the resources needed to run this program?" The manager's interest in the answer to this question stems not only from the viewpoint of program evaluation, but also from that of personal status.

Activity measures include the functions performed by employees working in the program. The manager asks, "Are my employees working on the activities that are part of this program?" Time cards and workload reporting systems are sometimes not accurate, but their use reflects managerial interest in how employees are spending their time.

Output measures assess the quality, quantity, and timeliness of goods produced or services rendered. Of these, quantity is most easily measured by counting the number of tests scored, number of applicants interviewed, etc. Data on output measures can be easily gathered and compared with other work units or time periods. Output data can be divided by costs to produce unit cost measures of efficiency, referred to previously in the computerized test scoring example at the beginning of this section.

Public agency executives evaluate programs to determine the rewards allocated to their managers and to plan future budget proposals. Evaluation results are used to support requests for continued or increased funding for a program. Unfavorable results are a signal to find a new program manager or to reduce the amount of resources (money and employees) allocated for that particular program.

Interest groups evaluate programs to see if they are getting the benefits promised or anticipated by agency executives. If their members respond favorably to an agency's program, lobbyists will pass this on to the executives and legislators so that the program will be included in future agency planning and be funded by appropriations committees. If constituents respond negatively to a program, lobbyists voice their displeasure to these same individuals, this time with the expectation that the program will be modified or that funding will be reduced.

Legislators, executives, and interest groups are likely to use efficiency, effectiveness, and responsiveness as criteria for program evaluation. If the program is cheap, cost-efficiency will be emphasized (such as the low unit cost figure for computerized test scoring). If the program is the cheapest method of reaching a desired objective, cost-effectiveness will be used. For example, assessment centers are not cheap; it can cost several thousand dollars to test a police recruit for the many physical, emotional, and intellectual qualifications required of a successful police officer. But although this system is *not* cost-efficient, it is cheaper than the alternative of "washing out" unqualified applicants during police academy training, at an average training cost of $15,000 per recruit. If a program cannot be justified on the grounds of efficiency or effectiveness, its moral or political necessity can still be defended on grounds of political responsiveness. Likewise, opponents of an efficient or effective program will concentrate on the reasons why it is not the best political response to an issue.

To repeat, the choice of evaluation criteria depends partly on the nature of the evaluator, and partly on the objectives of the evaluation process.[2] Table 19–1 summarizes the criteria that different types of program evaluators are most likely to use.

HUMAN RESOURCE MANAGEMENT INFORMATION SYSTEMS

The collection and use of information for program planning, control, and evaluation purposes is essential to public administration. Yet it can be deduced from the foregoing discussion that the collection and use of this information need not be systematic. That is, data can be collected and used on an *ad hoc* and piecemeal basis, rather than through a management

TABLE 19–1. Evaluators and Evaluation Criteria

EVALUATORS	EVALUATION CRITERIA
Researchers	Does this program produce the hypothesized results, or not?
Program planners and consultants	Was this program successful when tried before? Cost efficient? Cost-effective?
Program managers	Were adequate *inputs* allocated to the program? Were planned *activities* completed? Were planned *outputs* produced? Was the program successful *here*? Cost-efficient? Cost-effective?
Executives, interest groups, and legislators	Is the program politically defensible? Cost-efficient? Cost-effective? Politically responsive?

information system whose pieces are related to each other and to the objectives of the organization.

For example, a manager can be concerned (as was the director of the municipal parks and recreation department in the exercise at the end of Chapter 13) about a particular problem, such as equipment "down time" and low employee productivity. In the absence of a management information system, a manager will probably collect data on this problem by conferring with supervisors and examining existing records (such as equipment repair costs) to determine the extent of the problem. This will result in the development of a solution that seems correct on an intuitive or judgmental basis. For instance, the manager might propose a training program to increase employees' *ability* to use equipment correctly, or develop an incentive system to increase their *desire* to use it correctly.

Yet it is also possible to design a management information system that routinely collects information on various factors related to organizational effectiveness, and to present this information to managers in the form of reports that they can use to make necessary changes in organizational policies or procedures. In the example of the municipal parks and recreation department, it might routinely produce information on equipment costs, personnel costs, overtime, and productivity. If the method of collecting and compiling information into reports is systematically designed to answer the needs of planners, managers, and other evaluators, it is called a *management information system.*

The way public agencies gather and report data "drives" their planning, control, and evaluation activities. Such information might answer questions like: What does the public want? How much will this program cost? How successful are existing programs?

Let's look at a typical city and see how its human resource management information system (HRMIS) might relate to other governmental activities, from procurement through sanctions. As Chapter 5 indicated, affirmative action is the personnel activity that dominates recruitment, selection, and promotion. The extent to which social equity considerations will influence selection is determined by the extent to which particular groups are underutilized, and the validity of the selection criteria. Both utilization analysis and empirical validation techniques are heavily dependent upon computerized applicant data such as race, sex, age, test scores, and performance evaluations. Thus, a HRMIS is indispensable to the procurement function.

As Chapter 8 demonstrated, the relationship between human resource planning and the politics of public administration occurs during the budget preparation and approval process. The municipal budget phase begins when revenue estimates are matched against program proposals. The cost of proposed programs depends upon such factors as the number and type of employees, their pay and benefits, and the training they will need. All of these data are collected and stored as part of the budget and payroll system.

Employee *development* involves the comparison of employee performance and productivity data against organizational objectives. Performance appraisal systems and organizational productivity data are routinely computerized. Training-needs assessment can be based on computerized skill inventories, and the need for organization development can be highlighted by employee job satisfaction or organizational climate surveys.

The *sanctions* process concerns the involvement of outside organizations such as unions in organizational personnel management. The success of a municipal negotiator, for example, will depend upon how well documented the city's wage position is. An outside arbitrator will accept the position as reasonable only if comparative wage data show that the salaries proposed by the city are comparable with those of employees in similar jobs in similar communities; or that the existing tax structure will not support increased personnel expenses. Both of these require access to a HRMIS, one compatible with the systems in neighboring communities.

Despite this widespread recognition of the importance of HRMIS to public personnel management, some confusion exists concerning both the criteria that should be used to select such a system and the problems associated with its use. First off, public personnel managers need to specify the data elements that they need to provide the information required to answer questions such as those raised above. Data are the facts on employees and positions needed to assess organizational programs. For example, *position data* might include the salary range, occupational code, and organizational location of each position. *Employee data* might include each employee's age, sex, classification, duty location, seniority, pay, benefits, and affirmative action status.

These data elements are summarized to form reports. This is the function most often associated with a human resource management information system. Report generation requires that personnel managers ask, "What reports do we need, and how often do we need them, in order to control agency inputs, activities, or outputs?" Some typical reports produced periodically by public personnel agencies are:

Payroll: total personnel expenditures, by employee, during a pay period

Human resource planning: number and classification of all filled or vacant organizational positions; turnover rate for selected organizational units or occupations

Affirmative action compliance: race and sex of applicants and selections, by organizational unit or type of position

Collective bargaining: total payroll cost at current pay rate and personnel ceiling

Lastly, program planners use current reports as a means of predicting and controlling the future. For example, if personnel costs have increased 10 percent per year for each of the past five years, it would be reasonable to assume that they will increase 10 percent again this year. This forecasting combines the use of current or past data with modeling (the development of assumptions about the future) to help predict the probable outcome of alternative policy decisions. This is the same forecasting method discussed in Chapter 8 as *simulation.*

To sum up, a HRMIS is used to collect and store data, to produce reports used to control and evaluate current programs, and to develop simulations to support policy decisions. Therefore, a good HRMIS is one that provides the kind of information needed to the people who need it when they need it. The personnel manager must decide what the system is to do before computer specialists decide *how* to do it; the HRMIS must be designed to be compatible with the larger organizational MIS; and computerization should be recognized as a change in work technology that also involves such problems as employee insecurity, job redesign, and training needs.[3] Because the costs of some applications are high, HRMIS systems designers need to balance them against user expectations and capabilities.

In addition, the ease with which a HRMIS can collect and disseminate employee data creates potential dilemmas. The first is the conflict between employees' rights to privacy and the public's right to freedom of information. The second is the conflict between the organization's need for hierarchical control and the need for social responsibility as expressed by employees who engage in whistleblowing. The nature of these dilemmas, and some strategies for successfully living with them, were discussed in Chapter 17.

EVALUATING SPECIFIC HUMAN RESOURCE ACTIVITIES

A human resource management information system, when combined with some of the evaluative criteria discussed in the first section of this chapter, can provide essential assistance to the public personnel manager in evaluating organizational performance with respect to specific personnel activities. Some of these applications are shown in Table 19–2.

The control and adaptation function is the means by which public personnel managers remain responsive to changes in environmental conditions that affect the outcome of the conflict among dominant values and the core functions which represent them. In these cases, data supportive or critical of an organization's performance relative to one of the four values would be compiled into reports that managers, executives, interest groups,

TABLE 19–2. HRMIS Applications to Program Evaluation

ACTIVITY	HRMIS APPLICATIONS
Procurement	
Affirmative Action	Compare actual utilization of particular groups with their representation in the labor market; assess organizational affirmative action plan compliance
Recruitment	Compile new hire estimates based on anticipated staffing needs; are current recruitment efforts sufficient to meet them?
Selection	Do an applicant's qualifications meet minimum standards for a given position? Do selected applicants meet performance standards for their positions?
Allocation	
Human Resource Planning	Compile inventory of current employees skills; determine whether these meet forecast future needs
Job Analysis and Classification	How many employees are in different occupations?
Compensation	Determine current pay and benefit costs for all employees; project the cost of alternative proposed pay and benefit packages
Development	
Productivity	Record performance of organizational units; compare to other units or previous time periods
Performance Appraisal	Record employee performance; compare to other employees, performance standards, or previous time periods

(continued)

or legislators would then use to induce changes in organizational policies or procedures (or to compel those changes, if legal sanctions were involved). For example:

> Interest groups or compliance agencies supporting the value of social equity would use utilization data (such as that provided in the example in Chapter 5) to reinforce their contention that the organization should increase affirmative action efforts.
>
> Legislators seeking to control or direct the activities of a bureaucratic organization would use resource allocation data (size of budgets, number of positions) to do so. For example, a city commission seeking to restrict the power of an independent police department would do so by limiting the size of its budget, or by refusing to authorize new positions in that agency.
>
> Managers seeking to increase administrative efficiency would use productivity-related data to recommend changes in work methods. For instance, a city manager concerned about personnel costs in a solid waste department might restrict the use of overtime, investigate possible abuse of sick leave by em-

TABLE 19–2. *(Continued)*

ACTIVITY	HRMIS APPLICATIONS
Training and Development	Summarize training activities and costs; assess training needs by comparing skills; assess OD needs by measuring organizational climate
Employee Motivation and Job Design	Measure employee productivity, turnover, absenteeism, and internal motivation; assess effect of changes in job design on productivity and motivation
Safety	Record injuries, accidents, and illnesses; use these data to change safety regulations, selection criteria, or employee orientation
Sanctions	
Labor-Management Relations	Collect and compare salary and benefit data against that of other positions or jurisdictions; compute the cost of proposed changes in pay and benefits
Discipline and Grievances	Compile reports on the number and type of grievances and disciplinary actions; use these data to recommend changes in work rules, employee orientation, or supervisory training
Constitutional Rights of Employees	Record cases of sexual harassment or civil rights violations; use these to improve affirmative action compliance, employee orientation, or supervisory training
Control and Adaptation	
Evaluation	Collect data through HRMIS to evaluate all public personnel management activities

ployees, or study the comparative cost-effectiveness of more efficient trash collection methods (such as curbside rather than backyard pickups).

Unions seeking greater economic benefits for their members would compare wage, benefit, and productivity data for one county's employees with those of comparable employees in other counties.

VALUES AND EVALUATION

Public administrators are usually not comfortable with ethical choices; they are inclined to consider ethics either unnecessary, because administrative decisions are purely technical and rational, or impractical, because ethics is too subjective to justify to others.

Yet it is inevitable that public personnel managers will be confronted by ethical dilemmas. The dominant theme of this book is the relationship between values and public personnel management activities. It asks personnel managers to view conflicts among dominant values—political responsiveness, social equity, individual employee rights, and administrative efficiency—as inevitable. Not only does resource scarcity prohibit maximum achievement of all these values simultaneously, but each of them can only be maximized at the expense of the others. For example, absolute predominance of social equity as the value underlying selection would result in the subordination of political responsiveness, individual employee rights, and administrative efficiency.

In addition, the use of management information for evaluative purposes presupposes some purpose for evaluation. The evaluator collects and interprets information for the purpose of changing organizational behavior. Just as value-free administration is impossible, so value-free evaluation is a contradiction in terms.

The problem of ethical administration, then, is neither illusory nor easily resolved. It arises inevitably out of legitimate but conflicting role expectations. How can ethical dilemmas be resolved? Four steps are worthy of discussion:

1. Assume that administrative acts have ethical content.
2. Determine in advance whom they affect.
3. Visualize the effect of alternative actions on the people or groups involved.
4. Strive to keep your actions consistent with your own moral standards, or those of your profession.

The only conditions under which administrative acts could be assumed to be devoid of ethical content would be if they were purely technical. Yet the fallacy of the Wilsonian dichotomy, which assumes a firm division between value-oriented *political* decisions and value-neutral *administrative* decisions, is that these two categories cannot be easily distinguished. For example, an elected official may value political responsiveness among bureaucrats and may desire to handpick people who share his or her political values. But employees may value expertise or seniority as the criteria for promotion. How does the public personnel manager, charged with the development or implementation of "technical" procedures for selection, develop selection criteria without choosing between these two values?

If we assume that administrative decisions involve ethical conflict, it is important to determine which role expectations are in conflict and what the nature of the conflict is. In addition to the conflicts among the four dominant personnel values, conflicts also occur among employees, clients, and managers.

Ethical personnel administration requires compassion. Public personnel administrators should foresee the impact of their actions on others. Compassion means empathy, or understanding others' feelings. Consistently being able to visualize consequences of actions is a sign that people have accepted responsibility for their own acts.[4] For example, the U.S. Postal Service recently announced that it was accepting applications for substitute letter carriers. Because of uncertain economic conditions and the high pay and job security of these positions, over 140,000 people in one district office alone filled out applications for the 300 positions available there. Had this many applicants been anticipated? If so, were the effects on the 139,700 unsuccessful applicants considered?

Compassion does not necessarily mean that you agree with others' views. It does include the ability and willingness to explain your decision to those affected by it, and to present reasons with which others can agree or disagree. Although administrators must sometimes make decisions in situations where all outcomes appear unfavorable, sometimes their decisions can meet the needs of conflicting groups. For instance, some methods of job design can make both employees and clients pleased with the results (flextime), or satisfy employees and supervisors (quality circles).

Naturally, there are other guidelines for ethical administrators. These have been developed by members of professional organizations who view ethics as a professional, rather than an organizational, responsibility. The Committee on Professional Standards and Ethics of the American Society for Public Administration (ASPA), for instance, provides not only a set of standards but also material designed to help administrators clarify and evaluate their own values.[5]

SUMMARY

Different groups evaluate human resource management programs on the basis of different criteria, and for different purposes. All of these groups use information for planning, managerial control, or evaluation. To the extent that this information is collected and compiled through a system designed explicitly for this purpose, the organization can use a HRMIS (human resource management information system) to collect data on personnel activities, produce reports, and assess the probable consequences of alternative policy decisions.

Values and evaluation are essential to public personnel administration. The public personnel manager must recognize that conflicts inevitably occur among the four dominant values affecting personnel activities: political responsiveness, social equity, individual employee rights, and administrative efficiency. Consequently, managers must develop techniques for clarifying and resolving the ethical dilemmas inherent in administrative decisions.

DISCUSSION QUESTIONS

1. What are the objectives of program evaluation? Which groups evaluate public personnel management programs, and what criteria do each of them use?

What do people mean when they say they want an objective evaluation of a program?

2. What is the relationship between a management information system and human resource program evaluation? What is the role of the public personnel manager in designing and using the HRMIS?

3. Describe how evaluation can help the human resource manager assess the effectiveness of specific personnel activities.

4. How do program evaluation and the HRMIS affect the outcome of the conflict among the four core values comprising public personnel management?

5. Why are ethical dilemmas inevitable for public personnel managers? What are some guidelines they can follow in seeking to resolve these dilemmas?

KEY TERMS

program evaluation
efficiency
effectiveness
responsiveness
cost-efficiency
cost-effectiveness
information
human resource management information system (HRMIS)
data
reports
simulations
ethics
role conflict
empathy

WALK A MILE IN THEIR SHOES: ROLE CONFLICT AND THE STATE PERSONNEL DIRECTOR

Introduction

Juanita Simmons has been director of the State Personnel Division for two years. Her boss is Bill Conley, the Secretary of Administration and the Governor's chief Cabinet officer. Under the Secretary's direction, she is responsible for all personnel functions in state agencies. Her duties include:

Working with department directors to develop and implement staffing plans
Assuring affirmative action compliance
Working with the Secretary in conducting negotiations with five state employee unions

Representing the state in administrative hearings involving employee grievances

In the past two years, Juanita has gained a reputation for fairness and intelligence in balancing the conflicting demands placed upon her. During the past year, however, her job has become increasingly difficult. For one thing, a state revenue shortfall—caused by cutbacks in federal grant programs plus declines in tax revenue due to the recession and taxpayer revolt—has led her boss, the state Secretary of Administration, to impose a "slowdown" on hiring for all vacant positions. This has caused problems.

Don Harris, Director of Health and Human Services

Juanita Simmons picked up her phone. "Line one," the secretary said, "It's Don Harris." Don is director of the Department of Health and Human Services.

DON: Hi Juanita, How's it going?
JUANITA: Oh, the usual—what's up?
DON: I need some help, Juanita. You know that rehabilitation services department director position we have vacant? We've got to fill it now. The whole department is a mess. The position's been vacant for three months. How does the Governor expect us to meet our objectives if we can't fill the positions we need? Can you do anything to get Bill [Conley, Secretary of Administration] to lift the hiring freeze on the position?
JUANITA: I've got a meeting with him this afternoon. I'll mention it to him and see what he says. I know you've got a problem.
DON: Yeah—tell me about it. Let me know how it goes.

Bill Conley, Secretary of Administration

Bill Conley walked into his office. He was half an hour late for his 1:30 appointment with Juanita Simmons. It had not been a pleasant lunch. The chairman of the House Appropriations Committee had told him unofficially that the Governor's proposed budget didn't have a chance of passing the legislature. "Nobody's going to support tax increases this year. I don't care how you do it, but that budget's got to be cut by 15 percent. If you tell us where to cut, we'll try to make it easy on you. But if you try to go against us on this one, we'll cut the Governor's programs to ribbons."

BILL: Hi, Juanita, How are you?
JUANITA: Okay. How'd it go with the Appropriations Committee?
BILL: Fine! Just fine! Oh, the chairman talks tough, but they know the Governor's got things wired this year. We'll have to give up some of the things we proposed, but the big stuff will get through.

JUANITA: That's great! Does that mean lifting the hiring freeze? Some of the departments are really hurting. I just talked. . . .

BILL: I know—it's tough for all of us. But until revenues increase, and we get next year's budget passed, we've got to hold the line.

JUANITA: Come on—level with me! If things are going so great with the legislature, why not lift the freeze? I'm the one that's got to tell these department directors what the score is! If we can't trust each other, what's the point?

BILL: Juanita, it's going to be tough this year. I need your help with the hiring freeze.

Tom Hall, State AFSCME Lobbyist and Negotiator

Juanita walked slowly back to her office on the fifth floor of the Administration Building, wondering what to tell Don Harris. Waiting for her was Tom Hall, chief lobbyist for AFSCME locals in the state. She had known him for three years, and often sat "across the table" from him at contract negotiations and grievance adjudication hearings.

TOM: Hi, Juanita. How was your weekend?

JUANITA: Not bad—it was nice to get away for a while. How about yours?

TOM: Pretty rough, if you want to know the truth. I met with the chief representatives for the four other state employee unions, and they are hot! The Governor's proposed budget calls for only a 2.5 percent pay hike for state employees. The cost of living has increased 7 percent since last year. There's no way my people will settle for a 5 percent pay cut.

JUANITA: Look, Tom, it's tough all over. The Governor's proposal *does* include major changes in the state pension law, which provide for larger benefits, greater disclosure, and better funding. You know what those are worth. We worked together to get them into the contract last year.

TOM: Sure. But those don't have any front-end cost at all, and they make the Governor look good. Do you realize that the state ranks 35th among states in salaries this year, compared with 32nd last year?

JUANITA: At least we haven't had to lay anyone off this year—is that what you want? Where's the money going to come from, anyway? The legislature is not going to raise taxes, our population has increased 30 percent in the last fifteen years, our roads are falling apart, our schools. . . .

TOM: Who do you think makes the roads and schools work? The employees! Look—I'll give it to you straight. There's no way we're going to settle for a 5 percent pay cut. That's what you and Bill negotiated with us, but we both know that the legislature has the final say. If you won't negotiate with us on a decent basis, we'll have to go around you. That's all there is to it.

Jerry Gross, State Attorney General

Jerry Gross had been appointed Attorney General by the incoming Governor two years ago. His responsibility is to act as the chief legal officer for the Administration. As such, he and Juanita have worked closely together preparing the Administration's case for several employee grievances under both the civil service and collective bargaining systems.

Now they have a tougher problem. Two years ago, the Governor had picked a tough State Police Major (Mike Martinez) to head up a special task force on organized crime. One year later, the Attorney General's office had uncovered information indicating that Martinez was himself involved in drug smuggling and illegal sales of munitions to third world countries. Although Martinez was never indicted or charged with these crimes, he was relieved of his duties as head of the task force.

Now he wanted to come back to state government. Through his attorney, he had offered to compromise: If the state would hire him back as a major in the state police, with his former seniority and benefits, he would accept the position. If it did not, he would leak sensitive data to the press from the task force's files about the possible involvement of top state officials in illegal activities. Jerry wanted to talk with her about the situation before acting on the attorney's proposal.

JERRY:	This one's a mess.
JUANITA:	So what's the problem? Why not call this guy's bluff and see what he's got?
JERRY:	Because the Governor appointed him, and the Governor doesn't want to take any heat over this issue.
JUANITA:	How can we possibly hire him back? He resigned his position with the state police to head up the task force. There's a hiring freeze on now.
JERRY:	That's one of the problems. Apparently the state police personnel director can't locate his letter of resignation. So Martinez' position is that he was temporarily detailed from his job with the state police to head up the task force. Now that he's no longer on the task force, he expects to move back into his old job.
JUANITA:	That's incredible! How could they lose that letter?
JERRY:	That's not all. Mike was one of the leaders of the APS [Association of Police Supervisors]. They're apparently ready to back him on this if it goes to arbitration.
JUANITA:	But when he was appointed to the task force, he left the bargaining unit, and therefore is no longer entitled to use their grievance procedure!
JERRY:	Yeah—if we could find the letter of resignation. He probably had it removed from his personnel file—and from the files of the state police superintendent—while he was still on the task force.
JUANITA:	But surely the Governor's office has a copy. Why not use that as a lever against him!

JERRY: We're back to square one, Juanita. The Governor doesn't want to take the heat for this one. And remember, Martinez was never indicted or charged. There's not enough to justify removing him from the task force without bringing his charges out in the open.

JUANITA: But look what this does to me. I just told the director of health and human services that he couldn't fill that department director vacancy he's had for three months, and now you tell me I've got to request an exception to the hiring freeze in order to place Martinez back in his old job.

JERRY: Look at it this way. The state police don't care one way or the other. His performance appraisals and promotions are evidence that he's a good employee. And besides, he constitutes 50 percent of the Hispanic executives in this Administration.

JUANITA: And I'm the other 50 percent! I still don't see why we should be forced to take the guy back just because the Governor's office won't back us up on the resignation question. I don't think the primary issue is his performance. His legal rights are not the same if he resigned as they would be if he were given a leave of absence.

Role Play

Pick five students to play these roles in the case study:

1. Juanita Simmons, state personnel director
2. Don Harris, state director of health and human services
3. Bill Conley, Secretary of Administration
4. Tom Hall, AFSCME lobbyist and negotiator
5. Jerry Gross, state Attorney General

Read the case study in class, with each student playing his or her role. Later, answer the following discussion questions as a class.

DISCUSSION QUESTIONS

1. Each of the incidents described in the case study portrays the impact of one primary value on the role of Juanita Simmons, the state personnel director. Which values are portrayed by each of the following vignettes?
   Don Harris
   Bill Conley
   Tom Hall
   Jerry Gross

2. What ethical dilemma is represented by each of the vignettes in the case study? Remember—an ethical dilemma is a conflict between two or more values.

3. How do you think Juanita Simmons should resolve each of these dilemmas? What problems would she be likely to encounter in seeking to achieve this resolution? How would you suggest that she overcome these?

4. How could a human resource management information system help her solve these problems, or resolve the ethical dilemmas underlying them?

NOTES

[1] R. Clark, "The Proverbs of Evaluation: Perspectives from CSA's Experiences," *Public Administration Review*, Vol. 39, No. 6 (November–December 1979), 31–35.

[2] E. Goldenberg, "Evaluating Municipal Services," *Public Administration Review*, Vol. 39, No. 1 (January–February 1979), 94–98.

[3] William R. King and David I. Clelland, "The Design of Management Information Systems: An Information Analysis Approach," *Management Science*, Vol. 22, No. 3 (November 1975), 286–97.

[4] Stephen K. Bailey, "The Relationship Between Ethics and Public Service," in Roscoe C. Martin (ed.), *Public Administration and Democracy: Essays in Honor of Paul Appleby* (Syracuse, N.Y.: Syracuse University Press, 1965), pp. 217–28; Paul H. Appleby, "Public Administration and Democracy," in the same book, pp. 333–47.

[5] Herman Mertins, Jr. (ed.), *Professional Standards and Ethics: A Workbook for Public Administrators* (Washington, D.C.: The American Society for Public Administration, 1979).

20

Public Personnel Management in the Future

To comfortably speculate on the future requires an awareness of the past. In some ways history does not extend very far in the general field of public administration when one considers that the initial educational entry into the field came around 1930 at the university level. But the actual practice of human resource management in government extends beyond that decade and even past the Pendleton Act of 1883. Probably the most important fact about the history of public personnel management is that merit systems grew out of a response to patronage abuses and government inefficiency. Advocates of merit systems endorsed the notion that politics belonged to the realm of the elected official, with administration developing as a politically neutral science.

In reality, the administrative arm of government could not separate itself from politics, but the facade of neutrality remained in the public personnel field as in few other areas of administration. The idea that the public personnel administrator acts as the "keeper of the morals" is receding, especially with the growth of public sector unions, but it will remain a strong force shaping the near future of the profession.

The public personnel field also finds itself amidst a second broad and historical trend. The diminishing belief in public personnel administration as a value neutral field has produced greater clarity with regard to two central questions that have faced personnel professionals and technicians for years: Who does the personnel office serve? What role does he or she take?

The emergence of public sector labor relations has forced an answer to at least the first question. Unions protect employee rights first and foremost, and to the extent that merit systems do the same, we see double protection. This is especially true in municipal police and fire services. The United States Civil Service League, a professional association, developed a Model Public Personnel Law in 1971 that clearly establishes the personnel department as a staff function serving the executive arm of government rather than as a neutral body serving both administrator and employee.

As this aspect of the personnel officer's role becomes clarified, it should weight the answer to the question regarding role orientation away from the traditional compliance model. The techniques of personnel management, especially those relevant to the selection and allocation of personnel, qualify as managerial tools. When the personnel professional assumes the traditional compliance officer role, these tools turn into control devices limiting the discretion of line managers and supervisors. In the consultative role, the personnel professional looks beyond the techniques to the purposes they serve, and is constantly looking for ways to modernize the tools of selection, promotion, classification, pay, and performance appraisal so that they can facilitate human resource management.

These, then, are two trends that serve as the backdrop to future developments in specific areas of public personnel management. Our view of the upcoming years grows out of the underlying argument in this book. To recapitulate, there are four basic personnel functions that any organization must fulfill. They include the procurement of employees, the allocation or assignment of work to employees, the development of employees, and the sanction function that serves to establish and maintain the terms of the working relationship between labor and management.

While it would seem a relatively simple task to begin designing techniques and methods to carry out these functions, the fact of the matter is that the world of public personnel management extends far beyond the development of techniques and into the world of politics, because jobs are scarce resources. Moreover, since the core functions are central to the distribution of this resource, the ways the functions are satisfied result from compromises between different values. The values identified as particularly relevant to understanding the public personnel world are: social equity, political responsiveness, administrative efficiency, and individual rights.

These values are expressed in legislation, executive orders, and judicial decisions, which in some ways constrain human resource management and in other cases more directly influence fulfillment of the core functions. The contemporary issues in public personnel management and the trends for the future are found in the ways public personnel officers and departments both influence these value expressions and adapt to them. This interplay takes place on metaphorical bridges we have labeled *mediating activities*. There are four of these in the contemporary field of public personnel management: affirmative action, human resource planning and cut-back management, productivity programs, and labor relations and em-ployee rights.

The future of public personnel management hinges on which of these activities command attention, how they are dealt with, and how deeply personnel professionals get involved in them. Of the four areas, affirma-tive action seems the likeliest candidate to decline in importance except with regard to women's rights. While the courts continue to support dis-crimination complaints, the Reagan Administration's support only for those who have actually suffered discrimination represents a move in the opposite direction. The court's past scrutiny of the reliability and validity of all tools utilized in making personnel decisions has had a fundamental impact in the areas of selection, job analysis, and performance appraisal—an influence that will not easily recede. Regardless of the change in empha-sis toward social equity and affirmative action, the role of the personnel professional may decrease. Advocacy of affirmative action places the per-sonnel manager into a compliance officer role, running counter to the current trend bringing personnel administration and line management closer together. In many public agencies the EEO officer is not located in the personnel unit. This ensures its independence, but also may symbolize a type of organizational estrangement.

The area of labor relations and employee rights also seems to have stabilized after considerable growth and emphasis in the 1970s. But again, the influence of this growth will be felt for some time. Increased unioniza-tion of public employees clearly forces the personnel department into man-agement's camp, like it or not. And the emphasis on the legal rights of employees has reinforced merit system protection against arbitrary person-nel actions. The notion of procedural due process in adverse personnel actions has grown despite counter pressures from advocates of productivity programs, which almost always search for ways to streamline disciplinary procedures.

One area that may continue to grow, even if the rights of public employees stabilize, involves the personal liability of government officials for curtailment of employee rights. Getting sued is no pleasant experience, and avoidance of legal involvement has also reinforced due process protec-tions for employees.

The emphasis of the courts in both social equity and employee rights' claims has required much more attention to the law than ever before. A legalistic orientation to personnel administration, which would run into conflict with administrative flexibility sought in some productivity pro-grams and especially so in an era of cutback management, may still be a realistic projection for the future of the personnel field.

The third and fourth areas of emphasis complement each other. Cut-backs in government revenue and spending have required more attention to the productivity of public employees. These complementary forces squarely place the public personnel professional into a consultative role to line management, with demands of special knowledge from the personnel professional if the role is to be carried out successfully. First, we foresee future personnel departments retaining a cost consciousness that economic conditions and political philosophy forced upon all public managers in the late 1970s and early 1980s. We also see more emphasis in the productivity area on questions of job design, employee motivation, job satisfaction, and flexible compensation packages. The logical implication of this complementary thrust is to develop ways to measure the fiscal impact of human resource management decisions informed by sophisticated knowledge of the applied behavior sciences.

As one looks to the future, some questions arise. We have described the personnel professional of the future as a legal expert, fiscal expert, and expert in the applied behavioral sciences. This is quite a composite, and probably an unlikely combination to find in any one person. But this observation should come as no surprise for those who have grasped this book's major theme. Public personnel administration centers on the management of conflicting expectations traceable to different value premises. These interests have governed the development of the personnel field for some 200 years, and it is doubtful whether in the future a single and consistent orientation to the profession is possible.

Index